AMERICAN CITIES

A Working Class View

AMERICAN CITIES

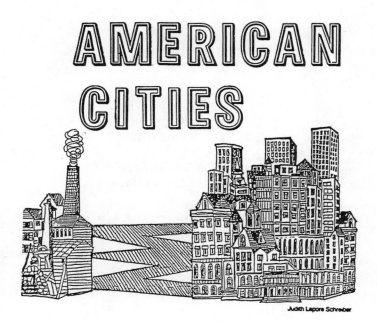

Judith Lepore Schreber

A Working Class View

MORRIS ZEITLIN

INTERNATIONAL PUBLISHERS, New York

To the Memory of
DR. HANS BLUMENFELD

Architect, City Planner, Teacher, Scholar,
Humanitarian and People's Advocate

Copyright ©1990 by International Publishers Co., Inc.
All rights reserved
First edition
Manufactured in the United States of America

Library of Congress Cataloging-in-Publication Data

Zeitlin, Morris
    American cities : a working-class view / Morris Zeitlin.
        p. 224 cm.
    Includes bibliographical references (p.
    ISBN 0-7178-0679-0 : $6.95
        1. Cities and towns—United States—History. 2. Working class-
    -United States—History. I. Title.
    HT123.Z45 1989
    307.76'0973—dc20   89-24542
                                                                CIP

CONTENTS

Illustrations are from

People's Daily World files
New Masses
N.Y. Public Library

Preface

Writers on the cities have largely not addressed the working class cityites who bear the brunt of the seemingly intractable city problems, and who are key to developing the united strength to tackle them. This book begins to fill that role. Moreover, it takes the view that cities are not things in themselves, but artifacts of the class society that has shaped them.

Accordingly, several assumptions guided this work:

First, neither the modern society that develops in cities or the cities that are in turn shaped by society's development can be fully understood without the other.

Second, decay in our cities reflects the political decadence of society's dominant capitalist class.

Third, the declining political and economic competence of the ruling class behooves the working class, the most representative of the multiracial, multinational U.S. people, to move to the center of the political stage and champion the people's interests—and in so doing, save their cities, jobs and homes.

Finally, working class political leadership, too, requires a deeper understanding of the cities and their strategic importance to the class struggle.

I have drawn on the ideas of many whose names are cited throughout the text, both to acknowledge my intellectual debt and to guide readers to further study. I have referred especially, but not exclusively, to the works of radical scholars whose Marxist analyses of urban development have raised the level of knowledge about U.S. cities and urbanization. To additional persons, however, I owe a special gratitude. To architect Isaiah Ehrlich and planning professor Lewis Lubka who, despite very active lives and the many demands on them, gave generously of their time and knowledge to critique the early drafts of this work.

To the late Dr. Hans Blumenfeld, whose seminal essays on the modern metropolis inspired this work and whose wise advice helped steer its course.

I also wish to extend my thanks to that special group of people, the always courteous librarians of the New York and Brooklyn Public Libraries, the Avery Library of Columbia University, the libraries of the University of Pittsburgh, and the Carnegie Library of Pittsburgh, who graciously piloted me through their forests of book stacks.

Portions of this work have appeared in *Political Affairs* and in the *World Magazine* section of the *Daily World*. I am grateful to their editors and staff as well.

But my biggest and most special thanks go to my life mate, Sylvia Goodisman-Zeitlin, whose constant encouragement, geniality, infinite patience, helpful comments, and invaluable technical assistance made this book possible.

AMERICAN CITIES

A Working Class View

INTRODUCTION: Why Study the City?

"To forecast the future," a wise folk saying goes, "you must know the past." Hence, to understand our cities, we need to know how they evolved. To foresee their possible future, we need to understand the societal forces that shape them today.

For most of us—about three-quarters of our people—our lives and making our living depend on the soundness of our cities. As one urban scholar put it, our cities are "The main physical, and more importantly social and political setting in which production, distribution, and the accumulation of wealth take place. Cities mobilize the economy's basic ingredients. They are the places in which basic infrastructural investments (public and private) are located, and in which an organized labor force is concentrated" (Mollenkopf, 1978, 119).

Were it easy to understand the city, it would be easier for local working class politics to be effective. But it isn't easy to understand. We live, work, struggle, learn and organize in a physically, economically, socially and politically bewildering environment. Moving amid its dazzling sights, sounds and smells tries the senses; experiencing its culture, class struggle and politics boggles the mind. The stress inclines many to leave the seemingly inscrutable complexity of the modern city to the experts, "experts" who all too often turn out to be agents and servants of the ruling class.

And that weakens working class politics in the city—and in the nation! For most city political problems—jobs, shelter, energy, education, discrimination, ecology, or health—are national problems. Most of what ails people in New York or Chicago ails people in Seattle, Atlanta or Dallas as well. And while much of the nation lives in small towns and villages, the main economic, social and political forces work and clash in our big, modern cities. How the nation goes is mainly determined in them.

That's true of big cities in other nations as well. Hence, in today's economically and politically interlaced world, what happens in London, Paris or Tokyo affects San Francisco, Pittsburgh or Houston. Indeed, global interaction inevitably increases as science

1

and technology advance, international division of labor expands, and the economies of nations integrate. The industrial revolution which spawned our modern cities now grows cities in all developing countries.

Throughout the world, the modern city has become, or is becoming, the dominant form of human settlement, the center of production and production relations, the arena of class struggle, and the wellhead of the world revolutionary process. Today, growing cities around the globe make front page news in the seats of imperialist power. Humanity develops today mainly through the modern city. Understanding it has become requisite to political intelligence.

How the City Has Been Viewed

Comprehending the city is difficult, in part because modern urbanization is a relatively young historical process; though much studied, it is not yet fully understood. As late as 1900, 60 per cent of the nation engaged mainly in agriculture and lived in the countryside. The life problems of village and town concerned most people and interested most writers and scholars. Only since 1920, when our country engaged equally in industry and turned 51 per cent urban, did cities and city life get equal billing in the nation's attention and literature (Siegel, 3-5).

Constant changes have added to the difficulty. Throughout this century, rapid changes in technology, economics and politics produced equally rapid changes in the city—in its size, physical structure, social composition and weight in the national systems of settlement.

The main difficulty, however, was that most students of the city used poor data and methods in trying to understand it. The studies and the theoretical schemes the social sciences devised since the turn of the century relied mainly on inadequate economic and social statistics. Moreover, they had built-in restrictions. For bourgeois scholars didn't look at the city as a whole or the historic processes that bore upon and developed it, but at its separate elements, and from the limited perspective of traditional academic disciplines.

Demographers, for example, spoke of cities in numerical and census categories. Geographers and regional scientists looked for distance and population relationships between settlements and markets, and for size, function and political influence of cities within the urban system. To economists, cities were what they did. And what they did was develop internal competitive economic activities that competed with those of other cities. Political scientists first saw the city as a juridical entity, then as a managerial service of public enterprise, then as a pluralistic body politic. And sociologists conceived urban development as a series of invasions and successions by different activities and population groups (Rodwin, 69–71). Going their separate ways and often contradicting each other, the bourgeois social sciences produced no overall perspective of the origins, characteristics and growth of the city.

But what precluded clear understanding even more was their philosophical approach—the values implied in what they studied and assumed, how they judged evidence and the way they arrived at conclusions. Most of them saw the city as a chaos of activities among rival individuals—the typical view of positivist-pragmatist philosophy inspiring the bourgeois social sciences. Scholars who held the positivist notions that all knowledge of nature and society is subjective and that, therefore, human experience does not reflect objective reality; who looked at social events in unrelated isolation from each other; who perceived development in society as a repetitive, unchanging, circular movement—such scholars necessarily relied only on empirical data, judged the value of ideas only by their immediate practicality and rejected all theory based on historical analysis as irrelevant abstract speculation.[1]

This social science, molding ideology in capitalist society, pegged people's judgment to surface appearances.[2] Hence the conventional wisdom that "there is nothing new under the sun" because "history only repeats itself." And in that "wisdom" lie the main roots of the difficulty to understand the motive forces in history, human settlement and the modern city.

Urban sociology and other -ologies

Of all bourgeois social sciences, none so much influences how most people conceive the city as urban sociology. Its founder, Robert E. Park, and his followers at the University of Chicago, made empirical studies in the 1920s of how a city's districts and neighborhoods form and change.[3] They soon took a social-Darwinist course depicting the city as a human ecology undergoing processes similar to the natural selection and competitive struggle for survival in the animal world.

The city, according to this fanciful model, is an integrated spatial organization whose inhabitants stay together because they use each other in their struggle to survive. Their mutual dependence enforces an economic order and a way of life, to which they adapt through specialization and accommodation that tends to keep their city environment stable. It also establishes a spatial "pecking order" that gives each part of the city a special function within the overall balance. Thus specialized functions and social groups, using separate zones, serve other parts, functions and groups in a cyclical repetitive process (Ianitskii, 1975, 45–46; Lake, xvi). To illustrate: The city's economy attracts a varied population which distributes itself, through competitive bidding for space, in various sections and neighborhoods. Entrepreneurs, accumulating wealth through the labor of workers, organize production and provide goods, services and jobs. Workers, spending their earnings, provide a market for manufacturing and commerce. Prospering industries, commerce and workers feed tax revenues to finance city government services. Municipal government draws politicians and managers to run the city and reproduce its population. In short: the city attracts and sustains a labor force that enriches entrepreneurs, who create jobs, that generate trade, that feeds city government, that reproduces the labor force, and so on, in an endless circular process. The city's balanced circular movement, however, is not without trouble. Trouble arises, the ecologists explained, when a city's stable functions and zones are disturbed by forcible "invasions" of new and different functions or people, requiring periods of "adaptation" before a new, harmonious cycle begins.

The ecologists' model has had a wide seductive appeal precisely because its simplistic comparison of human society to processes in lower forms of life seemed to explain capitalist society's animalistic behavior. However, equating the evolution and simple order of the animal world with the history and complex social order of human society, the ecologists' model failed to explain why and how human settlements formed and changed over time. Reacting to such criticism, urban sociologists modified the biological model of the Chicago School in the 1940s, but retained its basic ecological concept of balance-producing symbiosis between social groups and zones in the city.[4]

Human communities, they conceded, are more than a natural ecology, for they create a higher independence over their ecological base through economic, cultural, political, and moral ties produced by mutual awareness of common interests and ideals. This awareness leads to a system of symbols, customs and laws allowing a degree of coordination and control (Smith, 3–4). The concession may have propped up the model but did not alter its principal unsound structure.

The almost transparent fallacies of ecologist urban sociology may be traced to its superficial observation of growing U.S. cities in the first third of this century. Focusing on the city in isolation from its historical origins and evolution, it regarded society as having a merely external "cultural regulative" influence on the city. It saw no connection between the social structure in cities and the class structure in society. Indeed, it saw no social classes and class relationships in the city, only many different conflicting groups like landlords and tenants, borrowers and lenders, workers and employers. Nor did it recognize the connection between city formation and capital accumulation, which its research must have shown existed.

Shunning these historical facts led the Chicago School to its topsy-turvy conclusion that cities, formed by some vague independent process, have determined the path of society's development—instead of the other way around. Society's social problems were perceived as "urban problems"; class conflicts, social and racial discrimination and poverty seemed to result from rural migrations to allegedly harmonious urban communities; and heterogeneity seemed responsible for social conflicts in cities. Thus, urban sociology assumed the change from agricultural to industrial production and from rural to urban settlement to have been caused simply by population movements—a view shared by other bourgeois-ologies that saw history as a chaotic movement of unstable masses bearing destruction to stable social orders (Ianitskii, 1975, 9, 42–45).

Other bourgeois social sciences begot similar fallacies. Urban economics and political science, for example, focused on the economic and political life of big cities apart from the economics and politics of their society. Economists pictured cities as spatial concentrations of production, people and markets rivaling other cities. Typically, they focused on a city's "basic economic activities" producing for "export" to other cities to gain the "basic income" upon which it and its economic region depended. Similarly, political scientists assumed the political life within its boundaries to be the basis for understanding the city. City government, they thought, served only to ease the city's economy by providing a municipal infrastructure and services and controlling excesses in private land use and business decisions. The assumption implied that the problems of employment or housing or social welfare are problems the city creates and must deal with alone (Etzkowitz and Mack, 46–50).

Thus none of these theories identifies the social forces causing the political-economic effects in the city, nor the links between them and the political economy in the larger society. Its fallacies aside, however, bourgeois urban sociology greatly advanced empirical methodology in urban studies. It also earned wide praise for its precise focus on life in city ghettos and slums, revealing the social injustice to segregated racial and national minorities. Yet its ecological model lent itself to a vulgarization that offered an alibi for the disclosed oppression. The image of the city as a biological organism soon led to its analogy with the human body and its life stages of youth, maturity and decline—the latter a convenient political apologia for urban decay (Ianitskii, 1975, 45–46).

In conclusion, such an urban sociology reflects positivist philosophy's narrow orientation on single social problems and its denial that cities can be better understood through scientific historical analysis. Perceiving social reality as a series of distinct unrelated events, positivism turned empirical observation and methodology into ends in themselves. It has driven urban sociology and other urban studies into the dead-end street of studying irrelevant trivia, like dating patterns or the popularity of broadcast programs, and mere description of various aspects of urban life (Osipov, 46–47, 50, 65). It can hardly explain, much less cope with, the complexity of tough social problems manifest in our modern cities.

Marxist understanding of cities

Comprehending anything demands, first, an overall view. Once the general is undersood, the relation of its particulars to each other and to the whole becomes clear. This applies to all tasks, be they homemaking, production, office work or scientific analysis. In any task, the worker must first grasp the special universe—the body of things and processes—of the job. A simple universe may be perceived by simply using one's senses. Grasping a more difficult one may call for instruments that expand the range of human eyes or ears. Comprehending a most complex universe requires building a reasoned theory to perceive beyond what the human senses, equipped with even the most ingenious instruments, possibly can. It took Darwin's theory to explain the evolution of life on earth, Einstein's theory to understand space and time and Marx's theory to understand human society.

Investigating bits of urban social reality with purely empirical methods, positivist urban science fails to see that the evidence it observes has been shaped by a historical process. By contrast, Marxism is a holistic science, embracing in its view and analytical method of all society, whose elements—events, artifacts, ideas—make sense only as parts of the evolving whole. It demonstrates that the material world not only exists outside of human ideas, but that human ideas reflect it. Marxism guides analysis of social phenomena from surface appearances to interrelated processes behind them. It finds that, throughout history, changing modes and relations of production have generated social contradictions and formed opposing classes locked in struggle. The struggle between declining conservative and rising progressive classes moves society through evolutionary, or quantitative, changes to revolutionary, or qualitative, leaps from lower to higher social systems.

Marxism examines the development of human settlement in this historical context. Precisely in this overall view of the dialectical interaction between nature, society and human settlement lies the Marxist advantage in understanding the city.

Cities and settlements, it argues, are not self-determinative socioeconomic-political forces. Therefore, cities are best understood by understanding the motive forces in their society and the concrete influences upon them at various points in time. For cities, though factors in their society's processes, chiefly reveal rather than cause them. Bourgeois urban sociology and other -ologies have ignored Marxism, not because Marxism had little to say about the city, but because what it *has* said exposed their own fallacies (Saunders, 11–13).

Bourgeois urban sociologists often reprove Marxism for giving little attention to the city. Compared with the volume of non-Marxist studies of the city and urban life, they say, the Marxist literature on cities falls short. Were that a valid measure of which approach is scientifically the more sound, the non-Marxists would probably win. But the comparison is not relevant or fair. Not fair because much of the non-Marxist output is inspired by little more than academic pressures to "publish or perish." Not relevant because thought in the two camps on the social role of the city springs from diametrically opposite outlooks.

Viewing the city as an autonomous entity and a prime force in social development, bourgeois learned inquiry necessarily focused upon it with high-powered intensity. Marxism, on the other hand, has woven the study of cities and urban affairs into its prodigious analysis of the whole fabric of national and global socioeconomic-political life. In the holistic view of Marxist sociology, the city—isolated from society—is not a valid basis for social theory; and the specialized branches of bourgeois sociology can produce no general theory explaining the evolution of either society or its settlement systems. Moreover, many theoretical problems on which pragmatist urban scholars "stumbled" in their empirical investigations early in the century (social conflict, alienation, ghetto formation, etc.), the founders of Marxism solved long before bourgeois urban sociology was born (Rumiantsev, 13).

Other writers impute to Marxism an ambivalence about the city, for Marx and Engels viewed it as both an embodiment of capitalist evils and a source of potential progress.[5] Were critics of the Marxist classics to read them attentively, they would be spared the confusion they ascribe to these authors. Marx and Engels focused on both opposites in the dialectical unity of the capitalist city. They blamed the poverty and squalor of its working class life not on the city but on the capitalist processes in it.

Engels, in his work on the conditions of the working class in England and his essays on the housing question, made this abundantly clear. He depicted the city as the hothouse of inner capitalist contradictions and explicitly stated that urban poverty can be overcome only through revolutionary social transformation (Saunders, 21–11). He and Marx saw in the cities not only the evils of capitalism but also its nemesis and agent of transition to a socialist society; for in its process of urbanization, capitalism concentrates in its cities the antithetical revolutionary class. Precisely in the cities, where capitalist contradictions most fully develop, the conditions for working class consciousness, organization and struggle most fully mature.

While Marxism points to the progressive potentials in working class concentrations in capitalist cities, it examines urban contradictions and conflicts in the socioeconomic specifics of their time and place. History records examples of urban populaces, as those of some ancient cities, that had little potential for progress and bred many evils. Such examples have moved some writers to despair of all urbanization and cities—a penalty they paid for mechanically applying the specifics of some periods in history to all others. Urbanization, they said, is the source of modern society's social problems. Concentrating populations, it created an alienated working class, displaced established traditions, violated nature, and disrupted stable communities; this was true of cities in the past, is true now, and will always be true.

Such notions, Marxism charges, misread and misinterpret history. They disregard the incongruous facts of cities in history, like those of the medieval artisan guilds and merchants that had no working class; like those of the Mayan civilization, that guarded established traditions; like those of classical Greece that revered nature; and like the caste-based cities of India that cultivated stable communities. More importantly, however, they turn urbanization from an effect of social development into its main moving force. That's false. Urbanization did not create the capitalist mode of production. On the contrary, modern cities issued from capitalist development. Attempts to reduce all social development to urbanization detached from the overall process of history mark the writings of most non-Marxist ideologues. And that's quite understandable. Pinning on urbanization the responsibility for capitalism's evils provides a convenient, even if poorly concealing, ideological whitewash (Smith, 325; Arab-Ogly, 25; Maergoiz and Lappo, 13).

Indeed, such social science seems at odds with itself. On one hand, blaming urbanization for rural displacement, class, racial social conflicts, ghettoes and slums, unemployment and crime, it favors disurbanization. On the other, it acclaims urbanization for stimulating progress in science, technology and the arts, even as it deplores the political growth of the working class in the cities. Thus, some such sociologists look for ways to stabilize and reinforce capitalism by improving urbanization. They propose, for example, to eliminate rural-urban tensions in the world (i.e. conflicts between developing and imperialist countries) through universal industrailization and cultural ties leading toward a single "world city" (imperialist controlled, of course) in order to forestall the world revolutionary process (Ianitskii, 1972, 8–9).

In summary, to set apart the Marxist from other views, Marxism sees urbanization as a facet, not prime cause, of socioeconomic development, one that both results from and affects this development. It neither credits urbanization and cities for creating the modern working class nor blames them for its exploitation. Rather, it sees the working class, cities and their revolutionary potentials as products of capitalist development.

Not only in modern times but throughout history, cities did not simply grow; they have been shaped by, as well as helped shape, succeeding means of production, production relations, social classes and social systems. Modern cities began with the change from mostly rural production in the villages of feudal society to mostly industrial production in urban centers of capitalist society. Precapitalist cities differed from cities today not only in number and size but in economic, social, political and cultural function. In precapitalist societies, cities functioned chiefly as administrative, consumption and religious centers of their farming-based ruling classes. Though they have retained spatial and some cultural continuity across social changes, their internal organization totally changed as modes of production and social systems changed. The Middle Ages, for example, did not simply inherit its cities from preceding eras but redeveloped them to suit the production relations of the then-dominant artisan guilds. In turn, the capitalist mode of production began developing suitable urban forms mainly outside the guild-dominated cities (Arab-Ogly, 25–28; Ianitskii, 1972, 95–97).

Marxism finds modern social evolution proceeding from the contradictions of capitalism and its modern cities as mainly the stages upon which these have been played out in ways specific to each city's concrete conditions (Saunders, 23–24).

While cities in the "old world" have been altered and re-altered since antiquity by successive social orders into colorful patchworks, American cities have been cut out of one cloth, as it were, and fashioned by one tailor. Their history began, along with that of the social order that shaped them, a mere four centuries ago. They bear the imprint of capitalist development through its several periods.

The ruling class in each period pursued profits and accumulated wealth in a variety of ways, but in each stage one or two dominated over the others—agriculture and trade in colonial times, Southern plantations and national trade in the commercial period, commodity production in the industrial stage, and finance capital[6] in the monopoly and present state-monopoly capitalist periods. In each a dominant upperclass has largely determined the course of the nation's economy, politics, culture and the growth of its cities (Hill, 1977, 43).

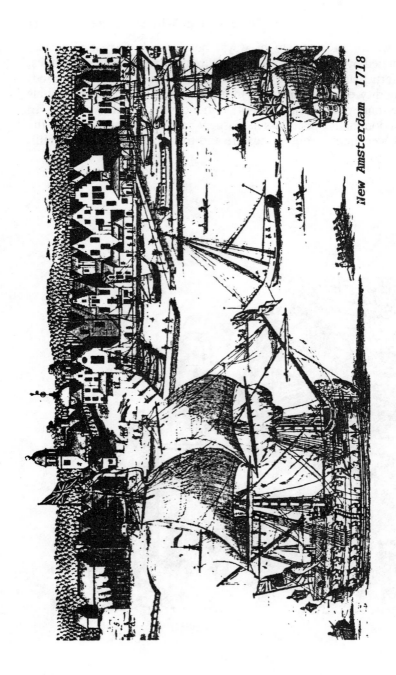

New Amsterdam 1718

PART ONE: *Our Cities Develop under Pre-monopoly Capitalism*

Colonial Boston

I. Colonial Times to the Early 1800s

1. Common Land Use to Private Ownership

When the first colonists set foot on American soil, two incompatible social systems collided. They left the shores of a merchant-capitalist nation and landed on the coast of a tribal society. The gap between the two social systems had its equal in ideology. The native peoples, to whom land was a natural resource like air and water, could not conceive it as private property. They had no idea that the gifts the strangers offered were meant as a price for leaving their tribal grounds.[1]

The colonists, however, came to divide and possess it, cut down its trees, build on it, farm it, trade it, dig up its riches and accumulate private wealth. In the conflicts that followed, the technologically superior invaders inexorably defeated the tribes.

The British had then "vested title" to the seized land in the British Crown; and the Crown divided most of it among favored gentry with a right to hold, use, lease, bequeath or sell their estates. Thus the land along the North American Atlantic seaboard passed from common use to private tenure.

Some 150 years later, the Republic of the United States, heir to the merchant-capitalist society the British brought with them, continued the private land tenure system even as it abolished many of the British land laws and confiscated the huge Tory estates.

The Republic declared its right to eminent domain over all land within its boundaries and its intent to gradually extinguish the Native American Indians' right to what lands they still held in common.

In the Colonial period, most of the merchant-capitalist class, and many of the American revolutionary leaders, speculated in land.

Some even used the power of high office for promotion of land sales. "The very fathers of the Republic, Washington, Franklin, Robert Morris, and Livingston and most of the others," wrote Matthew Josephson in *The Robber Barons*, "were busy buying land at one shilling or less per acre and selling it at $2 in parcels of 10,000 acres or more" (Josephson, 22).

In the 85 years between the Revolutionary and Civil Wars, landowners and speculators in expanding urban areas formed the wealthiest and most influential group in American capitalist society. For most of that era of foot-and-hoof transportation, cities were compact and small, only a mile or two in any dimension. Beyond them stretched fields that could be bought at paltry prices at almost no risk. Given the prospects for economic and urban growth in the expanding Republic, land bought for mere pennies per acre was soon sold and resold for forty times the buying price (Meyers, 89, 158–59; Clawson, 1964, 19). Although the damaging effects of land speculation on the national welfare were evident even then, the prevailing objective circumstances and subjective attitudes forbade its restriction.

Acting upon their own needs and taking a cue from the leading citizens of the Revolutionary period, adventurous settlers often occupied tribal or public lands without legal approval. Land-starved European peasants arrived and struggled for their share of the new lands. The growing Southern planter class added its voracious demands for private land ownership. At first, the Republic's authorities ignored the illegal trespassing, but soon encouraged such acts, especially against the tribal lands, as part of the nation's expansion. To this day, the land grabs and brutal genocide against the Indians in those years have haunted our national conscience.

"In any case," wrote R.W.G. Bryant in *Land: Private Property, Public Control*, "those whose main object was to make a killing for themselves wielded great political power." Ingenious collusions with public officials transferred much of the land from public to private ownership and built private fortunes. For example, in 1810 one John Bingham, a New York City alderman who also chaired the Committee of Finance, caused city-owned land to be sold to a relative and then bought back by the city an an exorbitant price. On other occasions, New York City officials cheaply disposed of city land lying under shallow waters to favored land speculators. The land was later filled in at city expense and resold by the private owners for high profits. Such frauds were common throughout the country (Myers, 114–18) and are not uncommon today.

Thus, right from the start, the private tenure of land determined the course of our urban development. Entrusting control over land use to the "invisible hand" of the market, it ruled out public city planning for the common good. In the fateful years of the 19th century, when rapid economic growth, mass immigration and settlement cast the forms of our cities, land developers "planned" them to suit themselves. Hell-bent for profits and blind to the consequences of their deeds, they laid out new towns and expanded old cities quickly, "packing" their "commodities" in simple gridiron patterns of rectangular blocks and lots to get the most profits.

"The gridiron spread across the country as the natural tool of land speculators," wrote urban historian John Reps in *The Making of Urban America.* "No other plan was so easy to survey, and no other system of planning yielded so many uniform lots, easy to describe in deeds or to sell at auction. The speculators disregarded natural topography, prevailing winds and climatic conditions and reserved little, if any, free land for schools, parks or other public use.

"And so it went across the continent," lamented Reps, "cities for sale through boom and bust . . . an era of wholesale humbuggery and land butchery. The stamp of early speculation remains . . . upon most of our cities. At a pace a hundred times slower than the original development, and at enormous expense, modern city planners are now attempting to erase the worst blotches spilled across the country by the . . . speculative builders of yesterday."

The simplicity of the gridiron plan, it must be said, has some advantages for finding one's way within a strange city; and it works fairly well in a small town or village with an open area in the middle for a common green. But it never suited big cities, either functionally or aesthetically. It never made for good traffic flow, not even in the horsecart days. Its overwhelming dullness and monotony always aroused distaste.

The landowner's ability to augment private profits through the community's boosting the land's market value accelerated land speculation. Having a monopoly over the piece of land lying at the core or in the path of urban growth, the owner may hold it until its inflating market value reaches its seeming peak, or sell it before then to other speculators having similar designs, each successive buyer upping the price of the land. Speculation in privately owned urban land has had disastrous effects on our cities.

With the exception of occasional ostentatious philanthropic bestowals, private land tenure has met social land needs purely on the basis of ability to pay, subject only to minimal regulations when speculators' excesses threatened the conduct of business. When price rather than social need allocated land for urban uses, several unhappy consequences in the formation of cities inevitably followed.

First, choice central spaces have gone to the highest bidder, not the most rational use. High profit corporations squeezed out public and cultural uses equally needing central location. Small businesses and low-rent old housing faced constant pressure from land developers trying to dislodge them for high-rent commercial development. Distribution of land uses by price resulted in a hierarchy of prestigious urban spaces—from high-rent central business districts to a motley of poorer commercial and industrial districts.

A similar hierarchy of residential spaces developed from the richest luxury residential district to progressively poorer and denser housing concentration, down to the most wretched slums. Thus land allocation by price has distorted our cities into patterns of social segregation and a hodgepodge of specialized uses, creating crazy quilts of brocade and burlap patches.

Second, green open spaces, essential for a healthful urban environment, kept shrinking. Having lost their public lands to private ownership, most cities could not afford to buy back the lands they needed for parks and recreation.

Third, building and housing costs kept rising. About one-quarter of the cost, or rent, of new housing in big cities goes to pay the inflated price of the land they stand on.

Fourth, building and population densities kept increasing to compensate for the rising cost of land.

Fifth, cities have tended to sprawl in unplanned ways because builders of new homes and commercial facilities have "leap-frogged" over high-priced city land to cheaper rural and suburban areas. This has wasted urban land, lengthened home-to-job distances, and extended the length and cost of sewer, water, road and transportation lines.

Yet, the contradictions were inescapable, since the capitalist market economy required that privately owned land, like all private assets, be made a commodity convertible into capital before it can be marketed. But being a natural resource, not a product, land does not have the attributes of a commodity. It cannot be reproduced, distributed or refused like other commodities, for each part of it has its own physical properties: it is unique, hence cannot be multiplied; it is stationary, hence cannot be moved; and its use is not optional, for no human can live without it. It is therefore not adaptable to competitive marketing. Indeed, its unique properties endow its owner with monopoly privileges.

Here lies the heart of the paradox. The owner of a piece of land at an advantageous location does not create its advantages. The benefits arise from closeness to centers of economic activity; that is, they stem from community development. Without community life and activity, no market advantages accrue to one piece of land over another. But the private landowner, not society, reaps the socially created advantages of the land's enhanced market value (Blumenfeld, 1970, 83).

Paradoxically, while private land ownership provided one of the main means for capital accumulation in our young capitalist society, it created one of its crippling contradictions, for it restrained the social use of a vital natural resource, the land itself. Private land ownership, developed since the dawn of our urban history within developing capitalism, has left us a legacy of problems that only a socialist USA can someday fully solve.

2. Our First Cities: Crucibles of the American Revolution

Where cities are located materially affects the lives of their people. Climate, topography and soil conditions can make life pleasant in one place and harsh in another. But these factors alone seldom determined the choice of their sites. Most often, social-economic needs decided where a city began. Indeed, most of the world's great cities formed spontaneously; the founders seldom gave thought to their possible future.

Throughout history, when and where farmers produced surpluses, the division of labor began setting apart production of food from production of goods. Exchange of goods arose, market towns formed, technology and goods production improved, and merchants carried the produce and goods along trade routes to profit by trade. As trade widened, the most profitable market towns grew into commercial cities.

Therefore most cities sprang up at trade-route crossings, especially at transfer points from land to water routes, at the confluence of rivers, and where rivers met large inland lakes or the sea. In those commercial cities, the merchants patronized the arts and crafts, promoted ideas and politics useful to advancement of trade, and used artisans and workers to produce, store and transport goods by human and animal muscle, river boats, and sailing ships. In time, ships sailed from commercial cities to the farthest ports of the globe, and the merchant class grew rich and powerful enough to pit its political might and bourgeois-democratic ideas against the trade-restraining rule and dogmas of feudal society's crowns and priests.

The first U.S. cities had similar origins, except that their merchants had to contend with the British Empire, not feudalism.

When the empire rose in 17th century Europe, feudalism was receding before advancing capitalism, and emerging commercial-capitalist states were building empires, raiding other lands for their riches and trade. When it invaded the North American continent, the British Crown was largely a symbol; for all practical purposes, its merchant class was the "king." Over time, the "Crown" set up five trading posts along the Atlantic seaboard—Boston in the North, Charleston in the South, and Philadelphia, New York and Newport in between.

From these posts, it raided and settled the lands of Native tribes, turning them into rural hinterlands where produce, raw materials, furs, gold, silver and gems were moved along waterways to the coast for shipment and sales overseas and to which British-made goods were moved and sold in return. The typical city in the colonial period, was a port—a "trading post"—for raw materials and produce shipped to the "mother" country, goods imported from England and carried to dispersed hinterland markets, and a political seat for regulating the British merchant's conduct of trade.

Colonial merchants and artisans had a hard time trying to profit by local manufacture and trade, for the Crown restrained them to maintain the British merchants' economic-political upper hand. Still, as the port cities grew, multiplied and prospered, local manufacture and commerce developed. In contrast to the isolated hinterland settlements, the port cities gradually formed a close-knit system of markets, trade routes, labor forces, and political ties.

With population and commerce growing throughout the 18th century, the port cities increased in size and complexity. Social diversity grew as the British, to meet growing needs for workers, recruited immigrants from among European landless peasants and oppressed nationalities, and enslaved Africans. The cities' growing populations soon comprised classes and groups of diverse and opposing social interests: merchants and artisans; employers and workers; masters, indentured servants, and slaves. Of these, the merchants—the leading class in the commercial-capitalist society of the colonies—was the smallest. Those who did the work of the colonial cities far outnumbered them.

Reflecting the port cities' main economic activities, dock-workers and seamen formed the largest group. Other worker groups comprised artisans, mechanics and apprentices plying various trades. Free artisans and mechanics included immigrants who had paid their passage to America, and free indentured servants who had served out their time. Many of them were itinerant craftsmen who journeyed from town to town making shoes, clothes, furniture, and did smithing, milling, carpentry and other work. Most artisans, however, owned small workshops and worked either alone or with one or two apprentices, indentured white servants or African slaves. Historians estimate that the latter two made up 80% of all immigrants to the colonies.[2] (Foner, 1947, 19–24; 1976, 3–11).

The merchant's increasing trade and social contact with European capitals had turned the port cities into centers of culture. By 1720, schools, libraries, theaters and newspapers enriched upper-class social life. Merchants, professionals and artisans led in solving the urban problems that began to emerge—building and maintaining public structures, providing in-city transport, street paving, water supply, sanitation, building regulation, fire fighting, and safety. Such typically urban problems appeared in our first cities even when they were quite small by modern standards. On the eve of the American Revolution, Philadelphia had only 40,000 inhabitants; New York, 35,000; Boston, 20,000; and Newport, 12,000. Together they contained less than one-tenth of the colonial population (Foner, 1976, 3; Siegel, 3). Yet this urban minority in a country of farmers stirred the colonies to political action. Sheltering an alliance between their merchants, craftsmen and workers, they provided the stage on which the mass base and leadership for revolutionary anticolonial struggle could form. Thus, typical of the role cities have played in history, our first cities became crucibles for revolutionary political change. By 1760, they grew politically strong enough to challenge the repressive regime of the world's then-mightiest empire (Schlesinger, 1969, 26–29).

The War of Independence from Britain was led by (and for) the numerically small merchant-capitalist class. It could succeed only with the wide support of the exploited colonial working masses who believed that defeat of British rule would improve their lot as well. Bourgeois leadership of mass struggles against feudal and colonial oppression was true of all bourgeois-democratic revolutions of that age; for "side by side with the antagonism between the feudal nobility and the bourgeoisies," explained Frederick Engels, "was the general antagonism between the exploited and the exploiters. . . . And it was precisely this circumstance that enabled the representatives of the bourgeoisie to put themselves forward as the representatives not of a special class but of the whole suffering humanity" (Engels, 1935, 24).

The American Revolution was a momentous historic event that marked a series of historical firsts. It was the first of the bourgeois-democratic revolutions that shook European feudalism to its very foundations. It was the first to oppose colonial power and assert the right of a people to self-determination, setting an example for anti-colonial revolts throughout the world. And it was the first to abolish most feudal laws and customs, improve the position of women in society, and reform the practice of justice. It established a republican form of government, separated church from state, and set a historic precedent in nationalizing the Crown's and Tories' private ownership of land and natural resources (Aptheker 1960, 19, 259–74).

Independence, however, bestowed liberty unevenly. While it released the merchant class from its fetters, it dashed the hopes of many farmers and workers who fought its war. The merchant class soon renounced the revolution's radical social ideas. Enriched and emboldened, it established a constitutional government designed mainly to secure its own economic and political power.

The nation's resources were once more in the hands of merchants, planters and the newly developing capitalist manufacturers.

3. City and Village after the Revolution

Picture our people, country and economy right after the nation gained independence from England. We numbered about four million then, spread out over the eastern one-third of the present United States, and we were a nation of farmers. Mostly farmers, that is.

We also made iron in Pennsylvania, mined and quarried here and there for various stones, minerals and precious metals, did fishing and lumbering in New England and hunting for furs along the wild frontier, produced goods and services, tended ports, sailed ships, and drove wagons and coaches hauling goods and people between the ports and their hinterlands.

But we worked within a commercial-capitalist society which forced us to produce all the surplus we could and sell it to the merchant class for export overseas. We had to export so we could buy the goods we did not produce, which the merchant class brought to our shores for sale.

Commercial capitalism made profit-by-commerce the main incentive for production in the nation's economy. The nation's prosperity depended on the merchants' ability to profitably sell what was produced. The merchant class, therefore, and not the nation's producing classes, organized and dominated the economy and almost all else in the nation.

It had a rough time at first. Right after Independence, the young republic still suffered from the economic effects of colonial rule. For a time, interstate trade wars, underselling by foreign merchants on its home markets, and harassment of its ships by warring European navies interrupted its commerce and slowed down production.

By 1800, however, United States merchants had forged ahead considerably in world trade. They were making such huge profits from trading foreign-made goods, that they refrained from investing in manufacturing at home. This slowed development of national industrial production. Commercial capitalism therefore lingered in the United States into the middle of the nineteenth century, long after industrial capitalism had taken hold in England (Foner, 1947, 48–49).

The War of Independence added new stimuli to economic and urban growth.

First, its demand for war material had raised production and wealth accumulation by war profiteers. This and the cancelling of British debts channeled new private accumulations of capital into manufacture and trade.

Second, lands which had been held by the Crown were released. Forests and mineral deposits opened new opportunities for profits in land speculation, trade and commercial shipping.

Third, independence added new political-administrative functions to the activities of cities, most of which had previously been performed in London.

All this greatly increased the vitality of the ports. Manufacturing gradually rose, attracting more skilled newcomers to settle in towns and cities. The proportion of the urban population over the rural steadily increased. This rapid urban growth within the nation's commercial-capitalist society sharpened the contradictions that had arisen between city-based capitalists and village-based farmers. However, the old settlement pattern and primarily agrarian economy continued to form the economic geography of the United States well into the first third of the 19th century (Glaab, 1).

From the very beginning of this process conflicts emerged, arising from the unequal distribution of the proceeds of trade. The city's merchants manipulated the market to keep prices of home produced goods low and of imported goods high, while its money lenders charged exorbitant interest for farm loans.

The countryside, therefore, was producing most of the goods the merchants traded, but the city retained most of the profits. The cities also exerted inordinate influence in state and federal governments to keep the rural settlements subject to their political will. Thus they kept the countryside impoverished.

The more that commerce expanded and the merchant class

prospered, the more apparent was the disparity in wealth distribution between city and country. The merchants flaunted their luxury and elegant living in the cities, in glaring contrast to the hard labor, isolation and backwardness in the villages and small towns. People in the countryside resented the cities as symbols of deception and greed. The rural hostility erupted in occasional farmer revolts and in the political conflict between the Jeffersonian and Hamiltonian versions of democracy. Jefferson's view advocated an agrarian rather than a commercial-capitalist economy. Having faith in the political wisdom of common people, he favored a decentralized, people-controlled government. Hamilton's philosophy distrusted the people, and wanted a strong central government to control them and to defend a commercial-industrial capitalist economy.

When the U.S. Constitution was framed, the compromise reached between the agrarians and commercial capitalists reflected the economic-political dominance of the latter after Independence, despite the fact that farmers constituted the majority of the nation. Some of Jefferson's principles remain cherished ideals in the nation to this day, but the Hamiltonian political concepts guided, in the main, the governing arm of the ruling class. Having come off second best in the political struggle, the "village" apprehensions increased when farmers began losing their youth to the cities in the years of fast urban growth, from 1820–1860.

Young villagers were drawn to the economic opportunities and social and cultural excitement of the cities—the choice of jobs, the chance of meeting new people, the variety of entertainment and the possibilities for education generated by the cities' economic, physical and cultural growth. The flow of the young and able from villages to cities fed on itself. The more who came and enlarged the cities' work force, market, and social and cultural diversity, the more others were attracted to come to the developing cities.

The increasing market demand and the loss of young labor, in turn, stimulated invention and productivity in the countryside. Agriculture diversified. Farm tools and skills improved. The steel plow and the reaper greatly increased farm output in the North. The South's plantations added rice and sugar to tobacco and cotton growing, and Eli Whitney's invention of the cotton gin in 1793 increased cotton production and sales both at home and abroad. It also stimulated the expansion of Southern slavery until the Civil War.

II. Commercial Capitalism: Intercity Rivalries and Growth

4. City Life Changes in the New Period

In the first decades after Independence, the cities changed little from the way they had functioned on the eve of the Revolution. Production continued in the handicraft mode. Artisans produced either alone or with families and skilled helpers, working and living under their paternalistic care. Production relations between producers and merchants remained essentially the same. As before, artisans and merchants continued to deal amid the usual haggling and cheating.

The dominant merchant class was oriented on commerce and did not intervene in production. The physical form of the cities, therefore, remained nearly as fluid as it had been. It was more like that of pre-capitalist market cities than the rigidly zoned cities we live in today.

Most artisans engaged in their petty commodity production where they lived, on the first floors or rear structures of two- or three-story wooden houses they owned and that were scattered along winding streets about the central market place. Most merchants and store keepers, too, had their offices and stores on the first floors of their homes.

Our early cities thus consisted of mixed, undifferentiated collections of households, workshops and stores. Everyday production, living and trade flowed freely throughout the mixed web of the city. People of different classes, occupations, races, national origins and religious beliefs lived and worked side by side everywhere, with little apparent segregation. Large workshops were rare. The few there were—shipyards, sail and rope shops, printing establishments—usually were located outside the center (Hays, 241–42).

Commercial capitalism did affect, however, the makeup of social groups in the cities. It made room in the center for merchants, professionals, artisans, mechanics, apprentices, servants, seamen, draymen, and others engaged in, or serving, the conduct of commerce. But itinerant workers and the disabled poor, for whom commercial-capitalist society had little or no economic use, had to huddle in ramshackle shanties on the outskirts of cities. Thus by the start of the 19th century, the port cities developed a typical two-part physical form. The main part thrived in the center, the other formed a band of morbid slums around it (Gordon, 25–26).

This urban form extended inland from wharves—the core of the port cities' economic and political life. Throughout the era of commercial capitalism, the wharves continued to attract and condense ever more people and buildings around them, within an ever more crowded limited area, since foot and horse transportation permitted little horizontal expansion.

In the first half of the 19th century, distinct wholesaling, retailing and financial districts began to take shape; distinct places where state and city offices located; and "better" neighborhoods began to appear where the wealthiest merchants and social "elites" built their fine houses. Even they had to stay within easy walking or horse-riding access to their business places in the center, whose relatively small size warranted their owners' daily personal managerial control.

Within the dense central cities, social injustice stood out. The contrast between the comforts and luxuries of the rich and the hard frugal life of the working people aroused bitter resentment that often exploded in protest. But the dominant merchants brazenly flaunted their wealth and threw their weight around in city affairs. They assumed leadership on community problems in ways that would promote their own business interests.

Merchants vied with each other to provide the best possible leadership because their personal prosperity depended on the city's overall welfare. The competitive strength of a city against its rivals to a large measure depended on its inner efficiency and the quality of its leadership. To stay in the race for markets and trade routes, a city had to stay vital, grow in population and skills, and attract and hold people by offering community services that made life easier, cheaper and more pleasant than in its rivals. It had to diligently attack community problems, which always proliferated.

The more the port cities prospered and grew, the more urgent became community measures for public safety and welfare. Individual wells became befouled and needed replacing with public water works. Garbage filled streets made refuse disposal necessary. Increasing traffic required paving the rutted dirt streets and sidewalks. Rising port and market activities demanded new docks and buildings. Street lighting extended the hours of commerce and social activity. The seasonally or cyclically jobless, the disabled, and the poorest newcomers cried out for some means of public relief.

Typically, however, the merchant "city fathers" gave the highest priority to their business projects. They needed no urging to improve street, dock, or market facilities. But they tended to slight or ignore the vital problems of other classes that did not directly affect business profits or the safety of their property. They did nothing, for example, to relieve the plight of the spreading slums.

S. F. Ramsey

5. Strife Among the Cities

After Independence, the merchant class itself plunged into fierce competition. Merchants could not stand still; they had to race against others to stay in business. The object of competition was to maximize trade advantages, to put competitors at a disadvantage or do them in.

Once their countrywide cooperation had defeated the colonial power which denied free trade to them all, commercial capitalists divided into local feuding factions to plot and execute competitive strategies against rival merchants.

Given the poor means of communication and transportation of the time, and the weakness of the still-forming national and state governments, merchant factions could not well maneuver on a national scale. The city, however, was a convenient geographic-political unit for united action against merchants of rival cities.

The rivalry among the port cities for control of markets and trade routes in the vast surrounding rural areas centered on transportation. The city that could first move the most goods most cheaply to and from the largest possible area would come out the winner.

Before Independence and a few decades after, freight was hauled long distances to and from waterways by horse-drawn carts on dirt roads, often too muddy for travel. The need to overcome the friction of distance and the whims of weather pressed everywhere for improvement. Indeed, once improvements began, the constant competition made their continuation essential.

Until about 1810, the rival cities were fairly evenly matched; their economies, populations and trade grew at similar rates. But soon small transportation improvements in the form of turnpikes led to the construction of canals, the use of steamboats, and later, the appearance of railroads.

Spontaneous, uneven development of new means of transport produced winners and losers in the intercity rivalry.[3] The larger a region of influence a city carved out for itself with more efficient and extensive transportation, the stronger its competitive position. Thus the intercity rivalry produced a hierarchy of cities in which the strongest emerged as dominant commercial and production centers, the weaker ones were reduced to subcenters, and the weakest were dwarfed or wiped out (Blumenfeld, 1976, 334).

New York, for example, was able to reach deep inland to the Great Lakes region via the Hudson River and the Erie Canal, and to the European markets by means of its centrally located ice-free port. It became the strongest. It cut transport costs to a fraction of that of hauling by land and captured most of the domestic and foreign trade in the North. This edge, later reinforced by rail lines to the West, established New York's national pre-eminence in trade and production.

Philadelphia and other river or lake port cities like Detroit, Pittsburgh, Cleveland, Cincinnati and Chicago gained a smaller regional reach. They offered lesser opportunities for commerce at the time and were on lower rungs of the city-hierarchy ladder. The narrowly specialized cities which sprang up on the basis of natural resources, such as mining towns, won only minor positions.

Increasing westward migration presented new opportunities for profit. Driven by get-rich-quick fever, land speculators spread out over the western territories luring immigrants, with fantastic notions and baseless promises, to dozens of townsites along main waterways between the coastline and the interior.

Where speculative town building succeeded, surrounding lands were quickly settled, generating production, trade, land sales, and urban growth. Glowing reports of successful new towns muted the stories of failure, and new immigrants kept coming until the War of 1812 checked the tide (Reps, 1965, 360–61).

War production, land sales and new settlement boosted economic and urban growth in the Western lands. By the end of the 1812 War, Pittsburgh, St. Louis, Cincinnati, Louisville and Lexington had grown into sizable towns. New towns, serving at first mainly as the port merchants' distributors of imported goods, soon became thriving market centers in their own right, serving local artisans, nearby farmers, and new immigrants on their way farther west.

Early in the 19th century, capitalists turned from purchase and sale of handicraft commodities to their mass production and sale as a means for capital accumulation. Capitalist society was changing from its commercial to its industrial stage of development.

Historians trace the start of this change to small towns in the countryside which began as collection and distribution points for rural goods destined for port cities, and of imported goods on their way to the villages.

The local farmers' housekeeping and farmstead needs, and the processing and transporting of agricultural products gave rise to local production of tools, earthenware and glass, building materials, paper, salt, soap, cotton bags, wagons, harnesses, crates, barrels, boats and a variety of similar goods. Most inland towns had weaving shops, sawmills, oil mills, iron works, flour mills and brickyards.

Rural areas on both sides of the Appalachian mountains bred many such towns. Before canals and railroads were built, the port cities depended entirely on them for production, processing and shipment of goods to the coast.

Larger inland towns emerged behind every frontier, first from villages in an advantageous location, then as the result of a fusion of neighboring villages. More farmers settled around them, and waves of new settlers passed through them to points farther west, demanding an ever-larger variety and volume of goods and services which the import-export bent coastal merchants did not supply. The towns filled the gap. Pittsburgh, for example, back in 1803, made almost all articles needed to start and maintain life on a new farmstead, from household wares to farm tools (Rubin, 89–93).

The coming of railroads reversed the superiority of water over land transportation. Most water routes were frozen over during a third of the year in the Northeast. Railroads carried the goods the year round, much faster and almost as cheaply. The railroad enabled New York's rivals to capture a greater share of the Western trade.

Baltimore in 1827 built the Baltimore and Ohio Railroad to the Midwest. Philadelphia built the Pennsylvania Railroad across the Appalachian mountains. Many cities at the bottom of the ladder in the intercity rivalry escaped extinction. The great natural wealth of the land, new immigrants, and improving road, rail and river transport offered them a chance to survive and grow.

After 1840, steam generated from coal replaced water power; and railroads began knitting the country together. This enabled factories to locate wherever cheap coal could be had. From then on production throughout the country increasingly centered in factories.

The appearance of factories caused steadily mounting pressures for change within the structure of commercial capitalism. On the one hand, its mode of production fell progressively short of its profit potentials. Growing foreign and home markets demanded volumes of goods far larger than petty handicraft shops could possibly produce.

On the other, wealth amassed in the hands of top capitalists made possible big investments in factories for mass production of many goods.[4]

During the transition from commercial to industrial capitalism, the radical changes in our nation's mode and relations of production altered the social and physical structures of our cities, almost beyond recognition.

While the rural population merely quadrupled between 1800 and 1860, the urban population increased by 24 times. Many towns of 2,500 inhabitants grew to 23,000 and cities of 8,000 or more increased in number from six to 141. New York City grew from a population of 50,000 to 1,175,000; Philadelphia to 565,000; Chicago to 109,000; Baltimore to 212,000; and New Orleans to 168,000. More than half the populations of two states—New York and Rhode Island—moved to cities (Siegel, 4; Foner, 1947, 57).

Within a few decades, the old city forms began to disappear, leaving behind only traces of their former selves: winding streets in old downtowns, historic old buildings and squares, and a few preserved museum towns.

6. The Transition to Industrial Capitalism

Growing inland markets, accumulated capital, and the country's abundant resources and labor skills led to a new mode of production—the industrial factory. Between the 1820s and 1840s, scores of new towns sprang up in the East where textile mills clustered along New England waterfalls, using water power to move large machinery.

Weaving was a widely held skill. Farm women, using muscle-powered looms, wove cloth at home for their own use and for the market.

Water power made it possible to combine power looms and the skill of weavers in a new, more productive organization of labor—groups of weavers working in capitalist factories.

This shift from handicraft to factory production began a transition from the relatively simple commercial stage to the more complex industrial stage of U.S. capitalism. Advancing the mode of production to a higher, more productive level, it started deep changes in the nation's class structure, population distribution, the settlement system, and the social and spatial structure of cities.

The shift steadily concentrated production in the hands of a relatively small class with the capital to own and operate the machines and processes of factories and hire labor. The previously established wide network of artisan home production was unable to compete. Skilled craftsmen and women were gradually forced to join the masses of machine-tending workers in factories.

But the new production methods raised the variety and volume of products, and increased immigration, population movement from village to city, and the size of the working class. Competition among industrial capitalists stimulated a division of labor between cities, towns and regions. Manufacturers tended to specialize in products which local material, labor, transportation and other conditions made producing most profitable. Technology progressed, constantly goaded by competition.[5]

New technology begot new industries, sharpened competition, increased production, and speeded the concentration of factories and people in cities.

Factories tended to cluster in most cities where ship and rail terminals maximized access to both foreign and home markets and minimized transport costs. Population movements followed the factory jobs.

Continuing concentration of factories and people began to radically change the use of space in the cities. The factory system separated production from the home, causing separate residential and industrial districts to form in the centers of cities.

Factory workers employed at subsistence wages, and working from dawn to dark, had to crowd into the center to live within walking distances of their jobs. The horse-drawn omnibus public transportation of those years was too slow and expensive for most.

Urban growth within factory and workers' housing districts therefore filled every possible square foot of space. The crowding created dangerous slums. In New York, for example, population density reached 136 people per acre compared to the 117 people per acre in London's ill-famed slums (Walker 1981, 385–86; Taylor, 138–50).

The slums seethed with anger over the exploitation and degradation, the bad housing and sanitation that working people were forced to endure. But organized resistance had to concentrate its strength to fight the more urgent battles of the day. Militant trade unions and political working-class parties fought in the 1830s for a ten-hour work day, public works to relieve unemployment, and control of speculation.

"Issues such as housing and city services," wrote labor historian Philip Foner, "[were] pushed . . into the background . . . [only] because they seemed frivolous by comparison and would dilute the strength of the struggle on the life-and death issues" (Foner, 1976, 3–19).

It was in the slums of the coastal port cities and in Buffalo, Pittsburgh, Cincinnati and St. Louis of the 1830s that the assertion of working class interests led to the first steps in federating local unions into a national labor movement.

So it was that, only fifty years after liberation from colonial rule, our cities became arenas of struggle against oppression, this time by a homegrown ruling class instead of the British colonial power.

At first many owners built their homes next to their factories because they had to stay close to supervise their operation. In the early years of the transition, therfore, social classes remained spatially close.

But as congestion and horse traffic increased, the center of the city grew ever more noisy, dirty and smelly; and masses of workers, working and living under insufferable conditions, organized, and engaged their employers in militant struggles.

The physical and social environment in the center of the city became repugnant and threatening to the upper and middle classes. Factory owners, merchants, supervisors and better-paid clerks began to leave the center to newly developing peripheral housing and to suburbs promoted by commuter railroad companies, freeing space in the center for industrial and worker-housing occupancy.

The land use pattern of cities began to change from the compact circular shapes of the walking city to starlike forms. Gradually developing urban transportation—first the omnibus, then the horse-drawn streetcar on rails, then the steam engine commuter railroads—began to radiate from the centers of cities to their peripheries.

But most workers—more than half the city population—stayed in the slums, hemmed in between the industrial and business districts on one side and the well-to-do neighborhoods and suburbs on the other.

Our cities had become unstuck. Social and economic stresses generated in the transition from commercial to industrial capitalism was recasting urban space into new molds—from its typically loose center of port, marketplace, home-and-shop houses ringed by slums of the poor to a new form of a dense expanding center divided into port, railroad, business, industrial, and tenement districts ringed by well-to-do neighborhoods and rich suburbs along railroads radiating from the center.

The same requisites for survival that had driven the older Eastern cities into rivalry over trade centers and routes also drove the young Western cities into bitter contests for supremacy and power. Each struggled to control the economic and political life of an extensive dependency in its surrounding countryside. The rivalry bred distrust, jealousy and vindictiveness among the cities, and between cities and the rural dependencies.

It sharpened in the postwar depression, stimulating improvements in water and land transportation as it did in the East. By the mid-1830s, the West sprouted a dozen large towns controlling the economic and social life of smaller towns and villages in large regions of influence. By 1840, cities on Lake Erie and the Ohio River had developed a network of waterways to attract trade away from inland cities.

The railroads dramatically shifted the flow of most trade from the north-south axis of river traffic to an east-west movement by rail. The contest now turned to routing railroad lines to favor one city's merchant-capitalist group over another's and to reach into new areas farther west. Aggressive merchants in Chicago, St. Louis, Memphis and New Orleans framed rival plans for railroads to the Pacific Coast. Chicago, to outwit St. Louis, laid railroads to areas of the Northwest and upper Mississippi and Missouri River Valleys.

Opening new regions for settlement, the railroads set off a new round of booming towns. Indeed, some ostensible railroad companies got into railroad building mainly to obtain government land grants and loans for the purpose of gargantuan trading in land. The lavish federal land grants to induce railroad companies to open the West accomplished their purpose. But they also opened the door to unbridled land speculation and creation of nonviable duplicate towns on competing parallel lines. Inevitably, the collapse of a superfluous railroad also ruined the many towns along its rails (Reps, 1965, 406–12).

In *The Robber Barons*, Matthew Josephson cites many examples of such waste. He tells of one railroad-building company using a grant of public land and funds to lay a line parallel to an existing short railroad. Given the option to buy it, the company chose instead to go around it in a crazy course because it was cheaper to build at government expense than to buy and integrate the existing railroad.

The West was settled and urbanized at a faster rate than the "old" Northeast. Only the South, bogged down in its plantation slave-labor economy, urbanized slowly. Each passing year widened the regional gap (Schlesinger, 1969a, 33). Nevertheless, at the peripheral Southern shipping centers such as Charleston, New Orleans, Louisville, Richmond and Mobile, sizeable cities developed between 1820 and 1860. Along with the systems of transport, local industries and a working class developed. On the eve of the Civil War in 1860, 110,000 workers—one-tenth the national total—worked in its 20,000 manufacturing establishments; 11,000 miles of railroads, one-third the national mileage, crisscrossed the South. Significantly, the larger cities of the South filled a progressive role. With their working-class districts, slums, networks of alleys and abundant jobs, they offered havens to both fugitive slaves and freed workers, providing operational bases for the anti-slavery movement (Aptheker, 1978, 32; Brownell and Goldfield, 16).

Along the rivers, roads and railroads from the Atlantic Coast to the West, commercial capitalism left its mark of rapid growth, ingenuity, technological advance, and social progress. But it also left a trail of waste, dashed hopes, broken lives and a legacy of very difficult problems (McKelvey, 1969, 30–32, 44–45; Schlesinger, 1969a, 30–31; Encyclopedia Americana, 1984 ed., "Railroads" by John N. Stover, v.23, 217–18.)

Comments

Because accessibility has always been an important factor in the location and growth of new cities, most urban scholars have been prone to point to transportation technology, and technology in general, as the determining force in urban development.

However, without competition stimulated by the market economy in commercial-capitalist society, there would have been no compelling reason for intercity rivalry. It was this rivalry that spurred canal, road and railroad building. Capitalist competition (the horse) moved transportation (the cart), not the other way around.

Technology does not develop society apart from its political-economic forces. Society and technological progress interact dialectically, affecting one another, but technology's effects are socially determined, not the free variable that technological determinists claim it is.

This is pertinent to people's politics in the city. Technological determinism leads to the daunting conclusion that the effects of technology, both good and bad, must be resignedly accepted because society is largely helpless before its powers. But historical experience shows that technology and its uses have been determined differently in different social structures. Land speculators plotted new towns in gridiron patterns for convenient sale; rival cities invited each railroad to come through their centers, while the railroads seized as much public land as possible in the process. Inevitably, urban land was misused and a national system of transportation warped by capitalist competition. If there had been public planning for the national good instead of private profits, our transport, settlement and use of resources would have been different and more rational.

III. The Industrial Stage

7. The Civil War: Victory for Industrial Capitalism

Those who live through major political-economic transformations experience the cutting edge of history, for obsolete social orders do not readily yield to the new, and terrible clashes often result.

In U.S. history, the transition from an agrarian to an industrial economy was exacerbated by the uneven development in North and South, the former undergoing rapid growth while in the latter, the older order was still going strong.

Early in its development, the South suffered large-scale, chronic labor shortages. With abundant land available at low cost immigrant white settlers could choose independent farming or handicraft employment. A strong steady world market for agricultural products, especially cotton, sustained extension of the South's slave-based plantation economy through the first half of the 19th century. Outside the plantations, there was also a growth of commercial-capitalist enterprise—railroads, trade, small manufacturing, etc. but at a slow pace relative to the North.

In the North industrial capitalists were expanding production with "free" wage labor, opening markets throughout the country. From the Atlantic coast to the Great Lakes, a huge belt was being settled, urbanized, and industrialized, while the South remained bogged down.

Economic realities were increasingly at odds with the lingering domination, by the South's slaveholder class, over our national government. In the 1830s and 1840s it controlled Congress, the presidency, and the Supreme Court. It aggressively promoted slavery in all the "prevailing and respectable institutions—the press, the churches, the schools, the texts" (Aptheker, 1979, 83).

Such contradictions resulted in inevitable conflict. As an importer of consumer goods, the South objected to the protective tariffs desired by the industrial North, which also pushed for federal financing of canal- and road-building, and the distribution of newly acquired lands in the West into parcels suitable for new factories and farms.

Spokesmen for the South clamored for the spread of slavery throughout the nation. Slavery, however, interfered with industrial capitalism's use of wage laborers, acquisition of western land and formation of a strong national industrial structure.

The South's political hegemony had rested on the weight of its agricultural production and large population. But by the decade 1850–1860, two-thirds of the U.S. population resided in the North, lured largely by apparent opportunities in industry, which, by this time, was producing value roughly equivalent to that of rural production. The shift in power enabled the North to break the South's grip on national government in the 1860 elections. Facing political extinction, the slaveholders rebelled, leading to the 1861–1865 Civil War.

Slavery became the dominant issue in the Civil War, whether owing to simple human revulsion against this human abomination, religious convictions, or, more basically, to the objective political-economic needs of developing industrial capitalism and need to win the war against the South.

In the post-Civil War competition among capitalists, the North had an enormous headstart. During the war, its small industries and relatively short railroad lines had grown rapidly, since the government's expenditure of public funds on war and military requirements gave a huge boost to the store of private capital. Between 1860 and 1870, the value of manufactured goods in the North grew 100%. The number of factory workers went from 1.3 to 2.1 million. Mass produced, relatively inexpensive goods were sent from factories in the North all over the country.

Merchants from the Northeast, with the connivance of bankers, shifted investments from foreign trade to home development in the fields of mining, iron, steel, machine-production and railway technology. Between 1880 and 1890, capital investment in industry tripled, railways stretched from 93,000 to 164,000 miles, and the number of wage workers grew to 5,880,000—moving the United

States from the fourth to the first place in world production (Foner, 1947, 58–59).[6]

Thus the North developed into the country's economically dominant region. Its thriving agriculture,[7] coal and ore deposits, versatile industries, wide transportation network, and big population made it the economic dynamo driving the growth of the rest of the nation.

Rapid Postwar Industrial Growth

Between 1860 and 1910, industrial production increased almost tenfold, a growth rate much higher than that of the urban population (Glaab, 1976, 102).

By 1890, large factories, each employing scores to hundreds of workers, concentrated in sprawling industrial districts in every big city. By 1900, huge one-story industrial complexes, linked by conveyors and railroads and run by thousands of workers, appeared in suburban locations.

A profusion of new tools and products—from home appliances to building construction—made life and work in the cities much easier. The telephone, elevator, electric trolley car, subways, bicycle and automobile began speeding communication and movement, and expanding cities in height and in breadth.

The whole process owed its dynamics to the race for profits. Competition and greed continually goaded industrial capitalists to cut production costs by increasing the productivity of labor with ever more rational industrial machines and methods.

Technological improvements made production more complex, forcing a division of labor in a host of specialized industrial enterprises. These, in turn, improved their own production methods and tools, which extended the division of labor and specialization still further.

This diffusion of production among the many interdependent producers and their suppliers of materials, machines, parts and services required close communication and efficient transportation among myriad establishments. The closer to each other they stayed, the more efficiently they functioned.

Industrial firms therefore tended to concentrate in related clusters. The more specialization branched out, the more such clusters multiplied and grew in size.

The jobs generated by these industrial concentrations drew masses of workers to settle in residential districts at locations reachable by available means of transportation. This created markets that, in turn, attracted more production and service firms and more workers, in a snowballing urban growth.

Thus industrialization and urbanization interacted and augmented one another. While industries built cities, the cities produced, distributed and consumed their goods and services. While industrialization organized and developed the national economy, urbanization kept it going.

The process, although spontaneous, responded to inner laws of its own development. The rational dictates of science and technology, the logical components in the competitive schemes of capitalists and the checks forced on their exploitative aspects by the class struggle combined to produce what social order was possible under the chaos and contradictions of capitalism.

In this process of industrial and urban growth, the cities concentrated most of the nation's production forces: the factories, mills and warehouses; the railroad depots and ports; the masses of workers; the technical and managerial skills; accumulations of capital; the establishments of science, art, education and the rest of the network of the social system's support institutions. The cities became the power centers of the nation's developing industrial economy.

The very building and rebuilding of cities raised production; and increasing production developed and redeveloped cities in continuous interaction. So closely did the two interact that, at times city building primed the pump of the periodically stalled capitalist economy.

During the cyclical crises in the late 19th century, the building of cities—housing, utilities, streets, commercial and public buildings—replaced railroad building earlier in the century as the economy's chief stimulant. The rise in the municipal debt from $200 million in 1860, to $725 million in 1880, and to $1,433 million in 1902—huge sums in 19th century dollars—suggests the degree of economic activity that city building generated in those years (Glaab, 177).

In 1870, the Pacific Coast states of California, Oregon and Washington were stil sparsely populated or unsettled.

But by the end of the century, their linkage by railroads with the Midwest and the Northeast stimulated brisk settlement and trade for their abundant resources, followed by industrial and urban development. In 1910, San Francisco and Los Angeles populations exceeded 250,000; that of Seattle and Portland, over 200,000. More than half of the population of the three Pacific states lived in cities, the biggest of which engaged mostly in manufacturing.

In the Mountain and Plains states, where cattle ranching and grain farming flourished, industries and cities came slowly. Only about a third of their people were urban dwellers. San Francisco, Minneapolis-St. Paul, St. Louis, Kansas City, Denver and Omaha controlled their supply and marketing.

The Southwest, too, lagged far behind. Only 22% of its population was urban. Its chief cities—Dallas, Houston and San Antonio—numbered only about 75,000 (Ward, 44–45).

But in the South, industrialization and urbanization picked up after 1880. The production of pig iron quadrupled between 1880 and 1890; that of timber doubled; the number of textile mills more than tripled; and bituminous coal extraction increased by almost nine times. Auxiliary industries and railroads expanded correspondingly (Aptheker, 1971, 102).

Diversifying their industries and expanding, cities began playing a greater role in the South. Atlanta and Birmingham, especially, had spectacular growth. But the South's continued lag behind the national average showed up in some telling figures. Between 1860 and 1900, its ratio of urban to total population rose from 7.1% to 14.8%, compared with the national average growth from 19.9% to 39%. By 1900, the South had only two of the nation's 27 cities in the over 100,000 class, and none of its 11 cities of 300,000 or more (Rabinowitz, 121).

8. Urbanization

Urbanization—the transformation of national settlement systems from predominantly rural to predominantly urban—is a new historical process. Cities—indeed some large cities—arose even in antiquity. But their share of the world's population was small and their growth was due to causes external to them, such as defense, the administration of a state, or advantageous geographic location.

Modern urbanization is a product of industrialization. The concentration of wealth, complex divisions of labor and the ceaseless search for profits and revolutionary technology required, at every new stage of their development, a wider social and spatial base of operations. Industrial capitalism needed an ever greater concentration of production in ever bigger industrial centers, with ever larger masses of workers. Capitalist production relations gave the cities *internal* causes of growth for the first time in history.

Employing 44% of its labor force in manufacturing by 1890, the Northeast region became known as the American Manufacturing Belt. In 1910, it contained 14 of the nation's 19 cities with populations of over 250,000, and 38 of the 50 cities with more than 100,000.

As early as 1870, the region held over half the nation's urban population. By 1910, about three-quarters of its own population lived in cities. Of its cities, Cleveland, Pittsburgh and Detroit showed extra high rates of growth. Their population surged from less than 100,000 in 1870 to over 450,000 in 1910.

The big industrial cities spun off production to many specialized smaller cities throughout the region. Of the nation's 59 cities in the 50,000-100,000 class engaged chiefly in industry, 42 were located in the Manufacturing Belt (Ward, 39–41).

By both natural increment and immigration, the nation's population almost tripled, soaring from 31,443,000 in 1860 to 91,972,000 in 1910. And, most significantly, its urban population climbed from 28% in 1880 to almost 46% in 1910.

As industries spread to inland cities, and previously dependent areas gained economic strength under local industrial and business leadership, the commercial port cities lost some sway over their surrounding rural areas. They too, however, industrialized and added other economic functions, doubling and tripling their populations.

New York's pre-eminence, for example, weakened with the rise of new factory towns among its old dependents. But the old port city developed a great variety of industries, while new financial, administrative, and cultural functions added to its continued leadership in commerce.

Similarly Boston, Philadelphia and Baltimore developed industries on top of their regional commercial activities. The old ports, in fact, were so advantageous for industrial location that fully 41% of the urban population in the industrial stage concentrated in the biggest 11 cities—all established commercial port centers before 1860 (Glabb and Brown, 102).

The gargantuan growth of the big port cities was one of the remarkable aspects of urbanization in the industrial stage. New York quadrupled its population, reaching 5,000,000 by 1910; Philadelphia tripled its population to 1,500,000, and Chicago reached 2,185,000.

Equally remarkable was the growth in the number of small cities. Between 1860 and 1910, the number of cities in the 10,000-25,000 class rose from 58 to 369; and in the over 100,000 class, from nine to 50 (Glaab, 174).

Thenceforth, new urban growth was to be limited to an occasional city at the site of discovered oil, like Tulsa, Oklahoma, or suburban satellites of older cities. The opportunities for wealth accumulation by founding and booming new towns were gone. Profiting by land speculation was now possible only within the developing cities.

Industrial capitalism profoundly altered the geography of the U.S., changing it from a land predominantly of farms and villages to one of towns and cities. People moved from field to factory, however, more out of necessity than choice. In the post-Civil War years, the rise in the number of farms combined with improved farming methods greatly increased overall agricultural output. Paradoxically, this shrank farm incomes.

Most farmers were farm owners, and the shortage of farm workers stimulated the rapid development of and improvement in labor-saving machinery. Many farmers had to mortgage their farms to pay for the new equipment. By 1890, over 90% of small farms were mortgaged.

Drawing the rural population to the cities speeded the division of labor between city and country. Production of more of the things the villages formerly made—clothing, farm tools, some food processing, and housewares—began to concentrate in the cities.

Industrial capitalism widened the gap between city and country to the utmost, concentrating wealth, industries, cultural opportunities, class interactions and social progress in urban centers.

The urbanization of farmers and penetration of urban relations into the countryside did not proceed evenly everywhere and at all times. It developed spontaneously and varied locally, arising when and where cities boomed, and ebbing when they declined or stood still.

But the urbanization varied everywhere with cyclical fluctuations in the economy. Industrial capitalism experienced two such cycles: one from about 1860 to 1877, the other from 1878 to 1896.

Each cycle began with steadily expanding production, followed by heavy investments in new plants, railroads, building construction and land speculation. They ended in an economic crisis caused by a disparity between an increased capacity to produce and the market's ability to consume.

During the boom years of the cycle, urbanization galloped along with industrialization. City building expanded absorbing waves of new immigrants. At the bust end of the cycle, it slowed along with industrial activity into a general economic and urban decline. Both objective and subjective conditions contributed to the nation's uneven economic and urban development. The anarchic business cycles may be deemed an inevitable objective condition in any capitalist economy.

But the nation also sustained losses from causes of a subjective nature. Uneven development resulted from rivalry between capitalists, some of whom resisted change or were locked into an obsolescing technology (Watkins and Perry, 25–26).

The lack of planning and rivalry of industrial capitalism reduced the function of our interdependent cities to the efficiency of misaligned gear wheels moving a complex machine. U.S. economic and urban progress, great as it was in the industrial-capitalist stage, proceeded at a fraction of what could have been gained with the resources and energy spent.

Within this system, industrial capitalism built cities of great economic and political power, even as its inner contradictions made them highly vulnerable—a fact often missed in the turmoil of national politics.

The industrial-capitalist economy effected dramatic changes in the spatial structures of cities. Its diverse, dynamic activities reshaped the cities of commercial capitalism into large and complex urban areas divided into distinct interrelated districts radiating from the main downtown central business district (CBD).

Formation of separate city districts logically followed from the process of economic specialization. The more that components of mass produced goods were made in big volumes, the less each one cost to produce. Large volume production of parts, in turn, required their production in separate premises, often by specialized contractors. This was true also for wholesalers and retailers who found specialization more profitable. Large offices, also, lowered their costs by breaking down their activities into special divisions or by contracting out some of their functions. The most closely linked firms tended to cluster to specialized subdistricts, and all clusters sought closeness to related clusters within one central area near the piers and railroads, forming the cities' central business districts. Thus, CBDs became the vital production and market cores of the industrial capitalist cities.

Such concentrations, however, could thrive only if their areas had infrastructures that their relatively small specialized firms could not provide for themselves—the huge installations of water supply, drainage and waste disposal, gas, electric, and telephone systems, large rental spaces, streets and public transport, and the labor reproducing institutions of public health, schools, and welfare (Walker, 1978, 187).

At first, private companies provided most of the infrastructure in a redundant confusion of buildings and utilites, turning city growth into a disorderly, slow, helter-skelter process. City officials merely obliged them with piecemeal extension of streets, water, and sewer mains (Peterson, 14). The rising tempo of industrial and urban development, however, demanded a more orderly and rapid expansion of infrastructural facilities.

The decades between 1800 and 1900 witnessed huge public investments in the infrastructures of every big city and their almost total transformation. Durable roads replaced block pavements. Great bridges replaced the slow-moving ferries. Electric street cars and trains replaced the noxious horse-drawn and steam-engine vehicles. New public water and drainage systems were built in 3600 cities. Gas and electricity lines eliminated kerosene lamps. Telephones began replacing hand delivery of messages. Many public buildings were built; universities were founded; museums, schools and libraries were opened. Speculators rushed to profit by erecting marketable floor space next to expanded infrastructures. Applying the inventions of steel frame construction, the elevator and central heating, they filled downtowns with tall buildings, greatly expanding their production and business areas. This enabled ever greater concentration of specialized activities which the continuing division of labor constantly spawned. The capitalist beneficiaries of public largess, however, cunningly evaded bearing its costs. Business-dominated city government financed the construction mostly with taxes levied against the working people.

Entrepreneurs of all kinds flocked to CBDs to benefit from its public facilities. Locating a factory or a business within a CBD had significant advantages. The CBD's rich infrastructure and concentrated variety of specialized production and service establishments combined to give firms located there large *external economies of scale*. Because many specialized firms could share a small part of the great output of other specialized firms and of the city's huge infrastructure, all of them could produce goods and services at the lowest cost and sell them most profitably at competitive prices on the CBD's big market. Like magnets, therefore, their external economies of scale attracted increasing numbers and variety of economic activities to the continually expanding central business districts of big cities.[8]

This, in turn, created rising demands for land and floor space, spiraling land prices and rents. So great were the profits from rents in CBDs that in the last decades of the 19th century, speculators bought up and demolished many homes on large tracts in and around CBDs to erect a variety of industrial and commercial buildings. By 1900, CBDs covered areas larger than the original cities had been at the start of the century.

Toward the end of the 19th century, however, the makeup of CBDs began to change. They began losing factories and gaining managerial, financing, marketing, professional, distributive and other service activities. Introduction of electric power into factories in the 1880s allowed new flexibilities in machinery placement and plant location. Electric motors made linear assembly lines in large one-story plants much more efficient than the old steam-engine system of belts and gears transmitting power in multistory factory buildings built around the power source (Vernon, 51–53).

The high market value of preempted CBD land precluded building the large one-story plants that the new production technology required. At the same time, advances in urban transportation opened new locational possibilties. Railroads readily provided spurs to any large plant locating along city fringes. Within a few years, electric trolley cars and electrified railroads changed the pattern of urban movement and the spatial organization of cities. Free to go fast wherever the rails led them, they broke out of the tight concentric ring growth pattern of the foot-and-hoof cities into a radial burst, changing the limits and directions of urban expansion.[9] Large factories were able to consolidate specialized processes under one roof developing *internal economies of scale* (Ward, 1971, 91). Therefore, they sought locations along railroad sidings on the edges, or outside of, cities. Even for smaller factories, with rising rents and high delivery costs on traffic-clogged streets, CBD location reached a point of diminishing returns. Many moved to peripheral areas.

Most of the industrial exodus from CBDs tended to land in suburbs. The small towns, whose economies and politics factory owners easily controlled, provided hospitable havens for their new factories and an escape from militant labor unions in the cities. After 1900 employment in the suburbs increased twice as fast as in the central cities. The out-movement of industries and of the upper classes to politically independent settlements outside of the big cities began the widespread suburbanization of the 20th century (Ashton, 61–62).

But while factories could locate outside the center, their managements couldn't. Corporate offices needed coordination of their complex business and political ties with the specialized banks, accountants, lawyers, engineers, various consultants, agents and public figures whose dependence on external economies of scale tied them to the center. Corporate managements therefore separated from their factories and located next to their ancillary services in the CBDs. Along with industrial corporate growth, finance capital gained increasing influence over the national and local economies.[10] The head offices of banks and other finance corporations also needed to locate within the business beehive of the CBD. By 1900, banks and other financial offices occupied the most valued central locations, often forcing out established businesses (Ward, 1971, 101).

The CBD became also the center of the city's distribution activities. In the pre-1870 pedestrian cities, retail stores dispersed widely throughout the city to stay within walking distances of their customers. Electric streetcars converging on the CBD, however, now made it easily accessible. Able to draw shoppers from everywhere, the CBDs attracted retail and wholesale stores. Shoppers flocked to the central shops for their wide selection of goods and competitive prices. Toward the end of the nineteenth century, retail establishments and department stores claimed large parts of CBDs.

Other commercial, service, recreational, educational and government functions also tended to locate in the center for its access to the city's work force, audiences, customers and clients. Commercial and service activities outbid small factories for CBD space and pushed them to the outskirts of expanding CBDs to form specialized production subdistricts (Walker, 1981, 387–88).

CBDs therefore provided what coordination was possible in the chaos of many spontaneously forming, competing, and failing private enterprises in the increasingly complex industrial-capitalist cities.

End of Carmine St

Coleman

Drawing by Glenn O. Coleman

9. Division by Social Class

Populations in the industrial capitalist cities were divided into distinct classes. Yet, the decennial censuses taken in the decades of industrial capitalism do not fully reveal the structure of its urban population.

The censuses were designed to inform a capitalist economy, and therefore viewed population mainly as a market resource. They sorted their data in categories useful to business and government, and revealed social-class structure only indirectly and partly.

While industrial-capitalist economics brought the various classes together in the cities, each class had needs unique to its position and role in the society. Each fought for and used urban space in its own interest. The position of class in the nation's economy and its class interests determined its views, organization, politics and effect on the cities.

Three major classes comprised the urban population in the industrial-capitalist age.

The capitalist class included industrial capitalists, financiers, merchants and big landlords—the owners and controllers of the major means of production and wealth accumulation. This class was dominant, though numerically the smallest class.

The middle class, somewhat larger than the capitalist class, was made up of the small owners of means of production, land and buildings, and self- or semi-self employed producers of goods and services—small factory owners, petty landlords, traders, artisans and professionals.

The working class, by far the largest, was composed of the people who, outside of their few personal possessions, owned only their labor power and capacity to produce or serve.

The Capitalist Class

In the post Civil War years, the capitalist class developed several strata of rival capitalists who profited in different sectors of the economy: industry, commerce, banking, real estate and agriculture.

Industrial capitalists, in command of the largest and richest sources of profit, soon led their class in governing the nation and setting national policies against its chief antagonist, the working class.

The wages of labor, they maintained, like the price of commodities, should be governed by the law of supply and demand. Capitalists should be free to do as they please, they argued, regulated only by the hand of the market.

This laissez-faire view justified private accumulation of capital without regard for the national welfare, the merciless ruin of lagging competitors or the cruel exploitation of the working class.

Once this ideology became policy through the entire nation, capitalists were free to develop and legitimize their rapacious, capital-accumulating forms of organization.

The concentration of immense capital within corporations made it possible to increase production in large plants and market more effectively, with greater power to repress labor. The development of large corporations led to the formation of combines, trusts and monopolies controlling whole industries.

Such industrial empires were often reigned over by one powerful capitalist. Thus emerged the notorious "robber barons" and "captains of industry," who were able by their great wealth to manipulate the political life of the nation and do violence to its democratic traditions.

"These barons of coal, iron, or pork," wrote one student of their time. "took possession of the political government . . . of the School, the Press, the Church . . . and through all these channels they labored to advance their politics and principles, sometimes directly, more often with skilled indirection" (Josephson, 316–17).

Entrenched in the nation's economic, political and social institutions, the capitalist class advanced foreign policies, forcing other nations to accept trade on its own terms.

It imposed domestic policies of exploitation and repression of the working class, and urban policies of using city resources to serve its profit interests.

It shared with other classes only what it was compelled to concede. It turned increasingly into a ravaging, repressive, reactionary class, subordinating the other classes into submission through clever cunning or brute force.

The Middle Class

The middle class held an intermediate position in the class structure between the capitalist and working classes.

It consisted of several strata with a wide range of incomes: medium and small owners of production, distribution and service enterprises; professionals; self-employed artisans, brokers and agents; small landlords; and corporate administrators in production, distribution, technology, accounting, construction and other specialized activities which kept sprouting in the diversifying industrial economy.

Most of the upper strata of this class grew in the service of the capitalist class. Dependent on its good fortune and favors, they mostly remained its close ideological and political allies.

The lowest strata of the middle class, however, had close ties with the working class, often sharing its living conditions though not always its class values.

The social position of the middle class was generally uncertain. Economic fluctuations and market competition often pushed its members from one stratum to another, and not infrequently into the ranks of the working class.

But no matter how poor their material conditions, even the self-employed in the lowest strata of the class differed from workers by their private ownership of means of production or services used in earning their living, and by their role in the capitalist market, not as sellers of their labor, but as sellers of goods or services produced.

Its unstable position in society produced in the middle class a corresponding wavering ideology. Nearness to the working class on the social class ladder, especially of its lower strata, generated sympathy, and often solidarity, with its aspirations and struggle for a better life, democracy, justice, and equality.

But as a property-owning, often labor-employing, and competitive seller of goods or services, it developed resourcefulness and aspirations to higher class status, and tendencies to conservatism, individualism, and opportunism.

In major conflicts between the capitalist and working classes and in city politics, the middle class typically avoided involvement to maintain a "middle line," vacillated between the major contending classes and often took a conservative stand.

The Working Class

In the age of industrial capitalism, the nation's workers and their working conditions radically changed. In contrast to the masters of crafts in the days of handicraft production, factory workers became mere adjuncts to mass production machines, ordered about by unscrupulous agents of absentee owners and insolent foremen.

Labor became a mere commodity on the market, bought as needed at the lowest possible price.

Men, women and children labored for poverty wages—twelve hours a day, seven days a week, under the most hazardous conditions. They lived in crowded, foul slums—malnourished and laid low by disease.[11]

Yet, the working class grew steadily, from about 1.3 million in 1860 to 4.25 million in 1890, and over 10 million in 1900. The ratio of employment in manufacturing to that in agriculture changed from one-to-two in 1870 to nine-to-ten in 1910 (Schlesinger, 1951, 93; Foner, 1955, 14).

The working class grew larger with the increase in the number of big factories, favored by growing corporations for their high labor productivity and profits. This growth in numbers, and the concentration of many workers in large plants, helped expand class consciousness. Workers became more aware of their class interests and the power latent in the unity of their large numbers.

The capitalist class, fearful that this growing consciousness would lead the working class to unite and challenge its dominance, schemed to keep it divided. It egged on the cultural, language and race differences between native-born and foreign-born workers to sow distrust and division. Job competition and cultural barriers between workers of different races and nationalities created animosities that made a united struggle to defend their common interest extremely difficult (Field, 35–36).

Workers organized nevertheless. Organization among the mostly white, native-born skilled workers and the mostly foreign-born, or Black, unskilled and semi-skilled industrial workers proceeded separately and took different forms. Skilled workers tended to organize locally by craft. In some cities, craft unions united in city trade councils. Industrial workers tended to form general national unions. Eighteen national unions were formed during the Civil War years.

Attempts were made to federate the national unions and launch a labor party, but the crash of 1873 cut these efforts short. One of the national unions, however—the Knights of Labor—succeeded in organizing skilled and unskilled workers, Black and white, into a single national union. It gained a membership of 700,000—double that of the craft unions—but, losing many of its militant strikes, it dwindled by 1886.

That year, the craft unions federated into the American Federation of Labor—a league of self-governing unions with a combined membership of 550,000. The AFL limited its goals to achieving an eight-hour day, abolishing child labor and improving working conditions.

In 1905, the Industrial Workers of the World (IWW) was organized to champion the cause of the industrial workers. Like its precedessor, the Knights of Labor, it tried to unite the skilled and unskilled, adding to its goals of winning higher wages and shorter hours the eventual appropriation of the means of production and abolition of the "capital and wage system." The IWW waged a militant struggle with a membership of some 60,000 until government persecution for its opposition to U.S. involvement in World War I brought its collapse (Schlesinger, 1951, 93–94, 228–229).

Throughout the post Civil War years of the 19th century, the working class fought exploitation in almost every city from coast to coast. Between 1877 and 1900, there were 24,000 strikes in 128,000 factories involving 6,600,000 workers. In all these struggles, the issues were wages, working hours, the right to organize, and better working conditions.

These seemingly purely economic demands, however, produced political side effects. They forced government to depart from its pretended neutrality in struggles between labor and capital. In the 1880s some safety laws to regulate the use of dangerous machines and sanitary conditions in factories were passed. Winning wage and hour concessions, however, took longer and harder struggles, until the anti-labor employers' associations were finally forced to grant pay raises and the eight-hour day in the skilled trades (Schlesinger, 1951, 100).

The long, bitter, and often bloody struggles for economic improvement stirred political awareness within the working class, especially in the cities hit hardest by years of economic depression. In 1908, the AFL began endorsing political candidates it perceived as "friends of labor."

But trends developed also toward independent labor politics. In many cities, local labor parties formed and ran their own candidates, and the Socialist Party polled 900,000 votes in 1912 (Schlesinger, 1951, 227–228).

Thus within the urban population stood the two opposite classes, locked in production relations and a struggle over the wealth produced. Each acquired unique social and political characteristics from its function and station in society.

The dominant capitalist class, exploiting a land rich in natural and human resources, amassed great wealth and power. In the vigorous decades of the industrial age, it expanded production to unprecedented variety and volumes, and generated great social progress.

But social progress was not its goal. It was the byproduct of its primary motive of capital accumulation. In fact, its self-indulgent life style and blatant show of consumption revealed a callous disregard for the poverty and misery of the nation's working majority. It savagely suppressed democratic efforts by the working class to share in the progress its labor had produced.

The working class, held down at the bottom of the class structure, developed traits all its own. Schooled in the work place, it learned organization and discipline. Finding strength in its numbers, it developed a spirit of cooperation and solidarity. Downtrodden and exploited, it opposed exploitation and social injustice. It was the one class with a vested interest in social progress for all—a fact of great consequence in the further history of the nation and the development of its cities.

10. Urban Housing for the Classes

About the 1830s, leading capitalists began abandoning the centers of cities for new mansions on large landscaped estates in pleasant suburban towns, commuting to their offices in the center by elegant ferries and trains.

Later, prosperous middle-class businessmen began moving to the fringes of cities made reachable by horse-drawn streetcars and omnibuses. Imitating the upperclass suburban style, they built detached private homes in new sections along city outskirts.

This exodus from the cities grew during the 1840s, developed speed during the post-Civil War growth of the upper and middle classes, and reached a high after the 1890s with the rise of corporations and their upper-middle-class strata of managers and professionals (Walker, 1981, 395–96). Of the latter, many bought "town houses" in rowhouse developments on the fringes of cities. The brownstone rows of big Eastern cities are survivors of that period of upper-class outward movements (Ward, 1971, 131).

What prompted the upper and middle classes to move out of the center?

First, the development of hierarchal forms of management in corporations, factories and offices freed their owners from close personal supervision.

Second, they found moving out desirable because of social and environmental problems in the city. The consequences of factory production—smoke from coal-burning steam engines, the ugliness of factory districts, the din and filth of heavy horse traffic—were reason enough for the rich to leave the center of production.

Third, terrible epidemics emanated from overcrowded and unsanitary conditions in the neighboring slums, posing a threat to life and health.

Moreover, the rapid turnover of land ownership in the center of the city by outbidding new buyers left the rich residents guessing who their next neighbors might be. Then there was the nagging problem of rising city taxes to pay for the city's costly new infrastructure, which one could evade with impunity by simply moving one's home out of the city.

But even more, the stress of conflicts with business rivals, the resentment of abused subordinates, and above all, exploitative production relations with their workers made living in the city troubling and dangerous for capitalists. Indeed, the increasing anger of the working class began to worry capitalists early in the century. Militant demonstrations in Boston in the mid 1830s, in Philadelphia in the 1830s and 1840s, and in New York in the 1860s gave ample warning of its lasting antagonism, political challenge and potential revolt (Walker, 1978, 194–96).

This impulse among upperclass circles to flee the troubling center of the city to the comforts of the country probably explains their romantic fascination with the rural ideal of the 19th century romantic writers advocating a return to nature for home life, recreation, and cultivation of cultural pursuits. The stereotyped romantic attacks on the "sinful," "unfeeling" cities by pre-Civil War writers like Henry Adams, Henry James and William Dean Howells, who denounced the "vulgar," "wild" city, drew praise and support from upper- and middle class readers who idealized the myth of the pastoral life (White, 226–227).[12]

Land dealers and builders, seizing the opportunities this presented, embellished the escape to the country with the glitter of "social prestige," accelerating the turn to suburbanization. Toward the end of the century, suburbanization vastly expanded, changing the configuration of almost every big city. New York's suburbs, for example, counted over a million inhabitants; more lived in Boston's suburbs than lived in Boston (Schlesinger, 1969b, 200).

Typically, cities and urban infrastructures expanded in the industrial-capitalist decades at the boom ends of economic cycles, when euphoric expectations of further profits drove capitalists into frenzied investment of accumulated capital and into over-expanding the forces of production.

Often, expansion of urban infrastructures was not a response to market demand but a deliberate speculative promotion to create it. Streetcar companies, for example, built rail lines "to nowhere" and charged low fares to entice an outward movement and stimulate land sales, only to raise fares or "go bankrupt" when their lands were sold.

Commuter-line companies played the same game. They laid out attractively landscaped suburban towns at their railroad stations to lure future commuters to settle in the suburbs (Walker, 1978, 199–200). Land-developing railroad companies were quick to harness new technology to their promotional schemes. Electric trains, able to start and stop more quickly than steam locomotives, made possible closer-spaced stations. This enabled developers to market more urban land, changing suburban growth along railroad tracks from satellite towns to ribbon development.

Cities began extending urban fingers into the countryside. Even rivers and gorges could not stop the expansion when engineers mastered long-span bridge construction. Within the cities, low-fare trolley cars radiated or zigzagged from industrial and business centers to peripheral areas. Homes began to separate, at increasing distances, from work places.

With centrifugal force, the new urban transport flung new residential districts, with their shopping, educational, social and recretional facilities, to the outer edges.

The resourcefulness and shrewdness of capitalists in expanding urban space is undeniable. But the well-propagated belief that the enterprising "elite of society" made all urban progress possible stems from the narrow view of a ruling class struggling to maintain its supremacy.

Where did the trolley and railroad companies, the land developers, and the denizens of chic suburbs obtain the means to create (and abrogate to themselves) the new urban space? Clearly, it came from the social wealth produced by labor—from the surplus value, in fact, produced by the industrial working class. In effect, the working class subsidized the creation of new urban space.

That individual capitalists served as the catalysts in this historically necessary process, and that it took the form of suburbs exclusively for the rich, merely shows how capitalist society misappropriated and misused that social wealth.

The process itself, however, though perverted, was determined by the objective need to resolve the contradiction between the concentration in cities of growing production forces and the social need for living space.

Although the urban expansion drew large numbers of all classes out of the center, the bulk of the urban population continued to live in the central part of the city close to its multiplying shops, businesses, offices and stores.

Working-class districts were built with drab, shabby housing. Crowding the poor in minimal shelters inevitably followed private land ownership and rent profiteering from the housing scarcity landlords maintained. Capitalism thus pegged the quality of housing and its environment to the ability to pay (Engels, 1988).

The land-use map of each city showed small areas of spacious, high-order residential districts for the numerically small upper class; larger, denser, yet neat neighborhoods of the middle class; and the largest and densest areas of the working-class multitudes housed in crowded, unkempt slums and half-slums lacking even the most basic living facilities. Where the working class lived, resided also capitalist society's perpetual "housing problem." Its essence has been that the housing capitalism supplied them was mean and the mean housing it supplied was always kept scarce.

Spatial separation by social class in effect divided the city into hostile territorial enclaves. Although not surrounded by walls or fences, crossing their quite evident boundaries was like an invasion by hostile outsiders. "Whole sections of the city," wrote one student of the age, "were off limits to members of some classes, either informally through fear, or semi-officially, as police picked up and questioned strangers. Notions about class society . . . were concrete and obvious" (Harring, 11).

Working-class districts were not always permanent. Some were rebuilt in whole or in part as the cities changed and expanded. Yet nothing so typified the industrial-capitalist cities as the massive slums, which continue to blot our cityscapes to this day.

Slums formed early in the industrial age. When the upper classes moved to the outskirts, landlords divided the handed-down buildings into tiny apartments and packed their yards with makeshift structures to rent to incoming immigrants and urbanizing country folk. Tenant families were forced to double up in order to pay the high rents.

By the late 19th century, housing shortages, high rents, and overcrowding became chronic in the bulging workclass districts. Landlords crammed families into every conceivable space—in attics, sheds, even in dark, damp and cold cellars. In New York City, for example, cellar occupancy increased between 1840 and 1850 from 7,200 to 29,000 (Ernest, 260–63). The streets of cities, even of small towns, became lined with tenement and row houses in repulsively unsanitary conditions. Wooden privies and a common water pump or well often adjoined each other in backyards. Contamination spread frightful epidemics of cholera, typhoid, smallpox, diptheria and tuberculosis. Life was daily beset with illness and death. Only when the epidemics spread to the districts of the rich did city governments begin to provide piped water supply and sanitation systems[13] (McKelvey, 1968, 26).

As workingclass populations continued to grow, the old handed-down houses gave way to high-rise tenements. In 1880, for example, about 77 percent of city dwellers were renters, reaching 82 to 94 percent in New York City and Boston. The demand for rental housing was high everywhere; so were profits from rent. Annual landlord returns between 10 and 40 percent were quite common (Glaab and Brown, 60). The high rental profits stimulated invention of quick tenement construction techniques and floor plans to crowd the most people into the least space. New York City's speculative builders excelled in this game. In the 1860s and 1870s, they mass built the ill-famed railroad and dumbell apartments. By 1900, sunless and airless tenement buildings housed millions in workingclass districts in New York and other cities (Glaab and Brown, 151–52).

This profitable cheating of the working class on the housing market sent landlords everywhere rushing to line the streets of industrial cities with miles upon miles of wretched tenement buildings. The dreadful congestion this produced has been the talk of the world in newsprint and books. "In 32 acres of New York's 11th Ward," for example, "the density of 986 persons per acre was approached in the world only by sections of Bombay. Portions of Boston, Cincinnati, Cleveland and Chicago were nearly as congested" (Glaab and Brown, 266).

But not until the early 20th century, after many epidemics and fires took their heavy toll of life—and political protests reached a militant pitch—did city governments begin to enforce municipal housing laws requiring light, air, and bathrooms in tenement dwellings (McKelvey 1963, 120; Glaab and Brown, 266; Lubove, 55, 80).

Within their miserable physical environments, however, the slums played an affirmative social role. They provided havens in which newcomers from foreign lands could build bridges between their cultural past and the culture of their new land. The successive waves of poor, often illiterate, village folk arriving between 1880 and 1910 from Southern and Eastern Europe[14] could not integrate as easily within the new nation as earlier English-speaking or urbanized West European immigrants did. They tended to separate into closeknit ethnic communities in their new strange environment, where they clung to their old customs and native language. The countrymen who followed them flocked to the slums as much for available shelter as for the familiar communities they contained (Schlesinger, 1951, 166–67; Ward, 120).

Here the immigrants developed social organizations with a high degree of collective involvement and solidarity, built a network of support functions, and formed defenses against the enmity of authorities, institutions, and upper classes.* For many years after their arrival, hostility without and the solidarity within kept most of them in the slums—the only part of the city most knew. Despite harsh housing conditions, therefore, slum dwellers met efforts to demolish their tenements for CBD expansion with militant resistance (Fried, 1973, 13–14, 39–40, 86). Where resistance failed, they crowded into other slums to reestablish their ethnic communities (McKelvey, 1963, 84–85).

The rural "old home" culture sustained the immigrants in their new homes as they gradually adjusted to city life and industrial production, integrated within the working class, and expanded their views. The city's social and technical environment—its vitality, variety of human contacts and technological change—stimulated their mobility and their liberation from patriarchal dependence and archaic forms of community life (Ianitskii, 1975, 66). Their experiences in the factory system itself constantly suggested the power of collective human achievement and eroded old village outlooks. It weakened the hold of myth and tradition and called up ideas that knowledge, organization, and abundant production could lead the way out of poverty. Such visions raised questions about the justice of

---

*Black and Latino neighborhoods also supply these positive internal functions but as we shall discuss, racial segregation is *imposed*, making the status of racial minorities what has been likened to "permanent immigrants" over several generations.

a social order rife with human misery in the midst of great wealth, and the possibility of a society in which knowledge and social control would offer a more secure life (Turner, 229–230). Growing identification with the values and struggles of the working class integrated the immigrants within their new homeland and city and gradually transformed many ethnic neighborhoods into Americanized workingclass districts.

Toward the end of the 19th century, the pattern of ethnic neighborhoods and workingclass districts began to vary. The change followed technological progress and consequent growth in the size, complexity and mobility of factories. In-factory specialization developed a hierarchy of jobs, skills, and wage scales. Higher-paid workers with steady jobs in outlying big factories began to move outward to the new housing jerrybuilt by profiteering developers. The capitalist establishment egged on the residential dispersion. Landlords, builders and money lenders encourged it for the profits in new urban development, and industrialists hoped it would weaken labor organization and improve reproduction of a skilled and tractable labor force. Wherever the immigrant workers or their descendents ultimately moved, they carried with them the traits of their original ethnic communities. In most subsequent workingclass districts, a high degree of residential stability, attachment to neighborhood, close social organization, solidarity, and mutual aid were dominant features of workingclass community life (Fried, 94, 181).

Most of the low-paid, irregularly employed unskilled and semi-skilled workers, however, stayed in the slum housing near the variety of CBD jobs. As higher-paid workers left, new ethnic immigrant groups took their place to be replaced by still newer immigrants when, in turn, they left. Ethnic neighborhoods formed, therefore, not by a process of constant addition of any one ethnic group but rather by one of a frequent in-and-out movement, and a mixing of different immigrant groups. The slums did not remain permanent neighborhoods of the ethnic groups who had arrived first but served as way stations for succeeding waves of newcomers (Walker, 1978, 200–201; Glaab and Brown, 125–26).

This process excluded, however, the racial minorities, mainly Black, coming to settle in the industrial cities. Employer discrimination restricted most of them to low-skill, low-pay, hard-labor jobs, and landlords segregated them within separate neighborhoods.

Thus, unlike the mostly voluntary settlement of white immigrants within ethnic neighborhoods, settlement within racial neighborhoods was *imposed*. Such neighborhoods were virtual ghettos[15] to which Black, Latin and Native American Indians have been bluntly or subtly restricted.

Racist bias and segregation in the industrial cities had its roots in earlier U.S. history. They went back to "the rape of Africa, the genocidal policy toward the Indian peoples, and the ideological requirements of the slave system" (Aptheker, 1960, 260). Racial segregation had its origins in the alley barrack compounds of antebellum Southern cities where freed and runaway Black slaves were forced to live, shut out from the street by a gate, and in urban segregation of Black residents in the South's post-bellum cities (Spear, 272–75).

The influx of Southern Black migrants to the Northern industrial cities increased the demand for rental housing in the segregated neighborhoods, raising rents and the annual profits of landlords as much as 40 per cent (Glaab and Brown, 60). Landlords were therefore among the fiercest practitioners of racism and promoters of racial ghettos in the most noxious areas of cities (hence cheapest to own and most profitable)—along railroad tracks, near smoky factories, the banks of foul industrial drains, near dumps, junkyards, and similar places.

The system of racial segregation costs the nation dearly. It "has been the greatest single source of human suffering; the greatest single bulwark of political reaction; the greatest single root of spreading moral decay; and the greatest single force producing division and disorganization and ideological weakness in the working class" (Aptheker, 1971, 28).

11. City government, Politics and Class Struggle

The roots of city government go back to the Colonial Period, when the British Crown chartered its colonial towns and appointed administrators to govern them. After the Revolution, the 13 sovereign United States retained the old city charters and assumed the power to charter new cities, towns and villages as subordinate administrative units over explicit territorial areas.

Within our three levels of government—federal, state, and local—cities have had, therefore, no autonomous powers. Legally, they have been "children" of states, with their powers delegated by their respective "parent" state legislatures.

In the class society of industrial capitalism, however, distribution of city services, and benefits, was the subject of struggle between its classes and groups with conflicting interests. City government became not only a branch of the State, with delegated police powers over its defined area, but also an arena of class and group politics in its legislative, judicial and administrative bodies.

Surface appearances therefore led to a common misconception that city government is an independent political entity able to solve social problems by enacting laws, by administrative procedures, or by piecemeal reforms; and that it is an impartial arbiter of class conflict in cities.

Despite their variety in form, our city governments have always been integral parts of the national capitalist State. Like the national State, they performed two basic functions in the interests of the dominant capitalist class. They facilitated the processes of wealth accumulation and they integrated the city's classes and groups into these processes.

67

They have often played the role of arbitrating class conflicts where they surface at the local level, but there is heavy pressure to resolve them in favor of the dominant capitalist class. They were compelled at times to tolerate the participation of the working class in the political process, if only to secure their own legitimacy and maintain the appearance of democracy. They often have settled class conflicts by compromise, but always granting as little as possible to the challenging classes, and keeping the spoils for the wealthy class.

In the course of performing their functions, city governments have gained authority and acceptance primarily because their actions benefiting the capitalist class have had spinoffs that benefited all the people. For example, building and maintaining urban infrastructures to promote profit-making also provided public services. At the same time that public schools and colleges turned out the skilled personnel the industrialists needed, they also opened growth opportunities for the people.

This dual effect of city government provided various benefits and opened doors for the working and middle classes to press for greater material and political gains (Parenti, 1985, 9–11).

The proximity of city governments to large workingclass populations made them necessarily more responsive to people's political pressures than the more remote state and federal levels of government. In fact, many northern industrial cities of the late 19th and early 20th century were ruled by political party machines that wooed urban workingclass masses with material and political favors to assure their electoral support (Markusen, 84).

The political challenge of the working class kept the upperclass in jitters, constantly forcing it to try new ideological arguments and political maneuvers to disrupt and divert its class foe from united opposition to its policies and power grip.

Upperclass governance became increasingly difficult in the cities of the industrial age, in contrast to its unquestioned role in the mercantile period. With even a minimum of democratic rights, the rapidly growing urban working class could outvote the numerically small capitalist class and its allies on crucial issues. Indeed, in many cities the working class was organizing, poised to win electoral power (Harring, 11).

Once this happened, capitalists could no longer head city governments and brazenly impose their will in the cities. Their presence in high city positions drew popular fire. It became a political liability. Besides, they were too busy scrambling for advantage in the expanding industrial economy to risk leaving their businesses for extended leadership in the city government.

Indirect political control through middle-class political brokers seemed more prudent. Withdrawing to its politically safe exclusive suburbs, the upperclass entrusted control of city governments to party-machine politicians who would rule with seeming benevolence toward the people and keep the big-profits game intact.

City government thus became an arena for even more complicated class politics. While it still facilitated production and wealth accumulation, it also could not avoid responding to urgent community demands. The upperclass, however, retained indirect control of the cities by manipulating the politicians through incentives and penalties or, plainly speaking, with blackmailing and bribes (McKelvey, 1963, 86; Harring, 12, 58; Ashton, 58–59; Mollenkopf, 1978,120).

Formation of workingclass neighborhoods in the growing industrial cities of the 1880s and 1890s deeply affected all aspects of urban life, including city government.

In those years, city governments were confederations of city wards, each represented in the city council by an elected councilman.

These councilmen stood up, as a rule, for the economic, housing, educational, health and other concerns of the people in their ward; defended their communities' customs, practices, and institutions; and by political logrolling—that is, trading councilmanic votes—tried to keep city taxes, public works, and city services favorable to their constituents.

With the increasing upperclass movement to the suburbs, and their withdrawal from city leadership, the composition of city councils changed dramatically.

Small businessmen and workers, representing the many poor wards, heavily outnumbered the upperclass representatives from the dwindling rich wards. The majorities of mostly industrial workers and small business people thus exerted considerable leverage in city legislatures (Hays, 1982, 245–46).

The ward-splintered city councils however, coped poorly with promoting the cities' industrial and commercial development. The need for new infrastructures called for more costly public works and administrations than the city councils seemed able to handle.

Upperclass leaders therefore turned to state governments to fund and administer the needed projects. Obliging state governments set up special state boards to develop and administer the facilities and services the cities needed.

This speeded action—but the mix of city and state agencies divided authority, scattered responsibility, and weakened accountability.

Officials of the special state boards, free of democratic controls, soon took to trading with jobs and contracts. Some, who were contractors themselves, awarded contracts to their own or "dummy" firms. Collusion developed among these officials, state legislators and city councilmen to expedite laws and funding for their mutual private benefit (McKelvey, 1963, 88).

The resulting complexity and confusion in city government demanded some new coordinating force. Such a force emerged out of a city's dominant political party.

The party's leadership, set to win elections and keep the party in office, commanded an array of cohesive and disciplined ward organizations. It was familiar with the city's affairs and able to coordinate the city's fragmented administrative structure. Gradually, a city's dominant political party became its unofficial coordinating agency.

Receiving no payment for their voluntary services, party leaders began to fund the party's organization, reward its supporters, and enrich themselves by dispensing city jobs for a price and business contracts and franchises for graft and kickbacks.

The party leaders who managed the patronage and graft most successfully and consistently won elections, became powerful partly bosses whose recognized function was to keep their party in power—but whose objective function was to provide city government with the dependable regularity without which neither the city nor the party machine could function (Glaab and Brown, 168).

Such party organizations were dubbed "political machines" and the political process they managed was known as "machine politics."

Political bosses, most of whom rose from urban ethnic communities, drew their popular support from the solicitude their ward leaders showed to troubled families in their wards. Immigrant families' were helped to find jobs or housing, given help with naturalization procedures, legal aid, food baskets, medical care, or other forms of support in times of stress. They gladly gave their votes to their party benefactors on election days.

They also followed the advice or instructions of the political boss on various social and political matters, either out of obligation or out of awe (Foner, 1980,58).

To the many neighborhood organizations—fraternal orders, clubs, saloons, even organized crime—isolated as they were from the citywide economic, social and political institutions of the capitalist establishment, the poltical boss was a broker and a go-between.

Through the boss and his political machine, ward-based workingclass and middleclass groups had a certain influence on city government (Hays, 1970, 296; Callow, 173).

The real business of political machines, however, was not benevolence to the working and middle classes but to big business—the big capitalists and corporations to whom the party bosses sold franchises and valuable city lands in deals pushed through city and state legislatures with unanimity guaranteed by the political machines (Foner, 1980, 37).

To maintain a political order in which they could prosper, capitalists supported political machines by making both regular and special election campaign contributions. And the political machines responded by selecting candidates approved by capitalists (Newton, 80–81; Foner, 1980, 35–36).

The results of these arrangements were not long in coming. In granting low taxes and long-term franchises to favored utility companies, city councils in effect were conferring monopoly powers. The utility companies, quick to use these monopoly advantages, consolidated into syndicates and holding companies.

The syndicates, which owned utilities in many cities, realized enormous economies of scale and reaped fabulous profits. One such syndicate controlled utilities in 100 cities (Glaab and Brown, 171–72).

Selling favors to big landowners had similar results. Because owners of land in areas where there is high business activity possess the advantages of monopoly, landowners clamored for government investment in various city improvements aimed at boosting the value of their land.

Plots, intrigues and scandals involving windfall profits gained as a result of collusion between big capitalists, politicians and government officials have made headlines throughout our urban history—but they reached the height of corruption under the reign of political machines, then and now.

By the end of the 19th century, landlords turned city halls throughout the nation into virtual marketplaces for the sale of favors in land acquisition and use (Steffens, 3).

The fiscal consequences of this mounting corruption were predictable. Inflated building programs and franchise giveaways plunged cities into heavy debt and escalating interest payments. Both kept rising with the machine-ridden city governments' constant reckless spending and borrowing (Glaab and Brown, 169–70).

William Sanderson

12. The Rise of Urban Reformist Movements

Since the Civil War, almost every big city has been run at one time or another by a political machine. New York had its Tweed Ring, Philadelphia its Gas Ring, St. Louis its Ed Butler Machine, and San Francisco its "Blind Boss" Buckley. Despite their crudeness and corruption, they served the upper class tolerably well in the years of mass immigration and fast urban expansion.

But they were awkward political tools. The anguish of ill-fed, ill-housed and ill-treated workingclass millions roused mounting anger in the factories and slums, an anger the political machines did little to ease.

Some industrial tycoons began to turn to philanthropy, concerned lest open rebellion break out. They donated parts of their accumulated wealth to charitable and educational institutions for public health, education, work safety, housing reforms and public parks. While such programs barely eased the immense urban problems of industrial capitalism, they opened the door to urban reforms.

Around the turn of the century, the upper classes became convinced of the need to resume direct control of city government and end the high costs and favoritism of the political machines.

The machines were losing ground. They had a weak political grip over the immigrants' second generation. They could no longer assure electoral victories through vote buying. Their usefulness to local corporate benefactors had diminished. To boot, they clashed head on with the powerful new national corporations looking for new, sophisticated methods to break the dominance of local monopolies and establish their own political control of the cities (Ashton, 59; Newton, 81).

73

Between 1900 and World War I, widespread opposition to machine politics crystallized into a movement. Its leaders became known as "progressives," their crusade as the "progressive movement," and its period in history as the "Progressive Era."

While this movement was seen as being progressive compared to the political machines, the intent was to reassert the conservative rule of the upper class.

Some of the popular support for the progressive movement grew out of the successes of the "home rule" movement that immediately preceded it. Home-rulers, led by capitalists who had been excluded from state-granted city contracts by the political machines, had won a considerable measure of self-government for the cities.

Some historians also trace the roots of public support for the progressives to the farmer-labor populist struggles waged from 1870 to 1900 against big business influence over the economic and political life of the nation.

Others saw in it a resurgence of progressive traditions that were manifested in earlier workingclass political campaigns; for example, the campaign against slavery, the 1864 campaign against New York State anti-strike laws, the 1866 campaign for a national labor party, the 1869 and 1872 Pennsylvania miners' campaigns to legalize unions and establish state mine-inspection (Foner, 1980, 22–32).

The progressive movement, however, drew its leadership and main support from the upper and middle classes—city business and professional circles. Essentially, it was a disparate coalition of two distinct, though related, movements: the social reformers and civic reformers (Schlesinger, 1951, 201).

The social reformers concerned themselves mainly with the poverty, disease, and demoralization of the working class in the slums. Realizing that masses of people could not extricate themselves from the poverty and squalor that industrial capitalism had thrown them into, social reformers pressed for reforms through government action. They called for public schools, libraries, bathhouses and parks; protection of women's rights; prison and asylum reforms; and a public welfare program.

Social reformers were concerned with the living conditions of the working class because most of them came from the socially and physically adjacent middle class—the ones most exposed to, and shocked by, the misery of the slums.

Standing but one rung higher on the social ladder, many from the middle class shuddered at the possibility of sharing the fate of the working class. With the rise of powerful local corporations, small businesses were losing out and the middle-class's economic position was steadily eroding. Membership in the working class was becoming more of a frightening possibility.

Academics also feared the threat to academic freedom and to their security, faced with the growing influence of corporate trustees in the universities. Lawyers were alarmed over the power of corporations to corrupt the justice system.

By the late 19th century many in the middle class began losing faith in the ability of the "invisible hand" of the market to right the wrongs of capitalism. Most shared the ideal that social progress could be gotten under a few honest, strong leaders who would reform government to assure fair competition and protect the rights of those who work for a living (Schlesinger, 1951, 202; Lubove, 8–9).

Despite their sympathies with the suffering poor, however, middle-class social reformers perceived slums and cities as cesspools of crime, and they feared unions as a potential source of coercion. They feared the working class even more than they feared the monopoly corporations (Foner, 1980, 39–40, 57–59).

By contrast, the civic reformers largely ignored the disastrous social effects of industrial capitalism. They focused on "good government" and on replacing machine politicians with "good men." They pushed legal measures to assure a secret ballot, primary elections for public office candidates, limits on campaign contributions to end support of picked slates, regulation of lobbyists, ending of unlimited franchises to favored corporations, and public ownership of franchised public utilities.

But while the civic reformers attacked corruption in government, they ignored the fact that capitalists like themselves, by pressing for their own profit advantages, were the main source of corruption. Indeed, the "good men," once in office, often engaged in corruption of their own.

Civic reformers did not really aim to abolish corruption. Rather, they rode on the popular disgust with it to accomplish quite another purpose: to end ward representation and the clout it gave to the working and lower-middle classes in city politics (Hays, 1970, 296–97).

That purpose was clearly revealed in their plans for new forms of city government—the Commissioner Plan, the City Manager Plan and the Strong Mayor Plan—all three of which proposed to cut democratic representation and concentrate decision making in a few hands. All proposed to replace ward representation and large city councils with citywide slates for a few councilmen and appointed city managers.

City chambers of commerce, led by industrialists, merchants, financiers and professionals, mounted vigorous crusades to make these plans into law (Glaab and Brown, 181).

Upperclass civic reformers were eager to reform the ward-based councils because in the expanding industrial-capitalist city economy, opportunities for profit clashed with community needs. As industrial capitalism matured, business and social activity integrated on a citywide scale, raising a structure of economic and social organization that bridged over and across those of ward life (Hays, 1970, 295).

The crusade to rout political machines bore mixed results; its success varied with the size of the city. Small cities dominated by upper and middle classes usually adopted one or another of the reform plans.

But most big cities only modified their old form of city government. In some, the power of the mayor was strengthened and some representation was centralized, but the ward systems largely remained.

Why did big cities resist the reformers? Mainly because the working class mounted a defense of hard-won positions in political democracy which proved too strong to crack. Faced with tough resistance, the civic reformers backed off and retreated (Newton, 82–83).

The impulse for reform that moved the upper and middle classes to action in the "Progressive Era" gave birth to various "city betterment" drives, among them campaigns to beautify cities. "City Beautiful" and "Park" movements, led by prominent architects and landscape architects, sought to advance good appearance, amenity and order in cities which had grown ugly and harsh under the anarchy of unbridled industrial capitalism.

Our 19th century cities differed sharply in appearance from their European cousins. The capitalist cities of Europe were not the products of capitalism alone. The traditions of beauty and elegance inherited from a long urban past had conditioned their growth during the industrial era. But our cities were a "profusion of recencies," products "of the speculative urge, of the procession of industrial superventions, of a subordination of natural beauty to utility and profit" (Abrams, 1965, 289).

Laissez-faire capitalism, led by a crude ruling class, dehumanized the cities even as they formed. Except where the rich lived, city streets stretched in monotonous miles of tenements. Networks of railroad tracks and sprawling depot yards penetrated deep into cities and pre-empted the waterfronts, adding soot, grime and noise to the smoke, dirt and din of industrial plants.

Every bit of land that could be built upon and profited from was denuded of trees and vegetation.

Scathing European criticism of the chaos, discomfort and ugliness of United States cities wounded the pride of upperclass elite circles who vied for acceptance in European "society." It moved some to endow city betterment movements. These were not purely altruistic movements, however. Each also had narrow material goals. The City Beautiful, City Planning, Parks, Garden Cities, Conservation and Housing movements all tried to promote the role of their mother professions in the local economy. The ideologies of these movements were laden with self-serving values and concepts reflecting their upper- and middle-class origins and economic self interest.

Leaders of the City Beautiful movement, for example, seized on the common belief that beauty lifts morals to urge large city expenditures on civic projects. The city, they argued, greatly influences social interactions and human behavior with its kinds of land uses and housing. Beauty, achieved even in bits and pieces—a small park here, an improved street there, a dignified city hall or library— would help refine the behavior of slum dwellers and generate civic pride (Lubove, 1–2).

Addressing business circles in a more practical vein, they argued that a beautiful city would promote tourism and trade benefiting the local community (Peterson, 53–54). Leaders of the City Beautiful movement used the 1893 Chicago World's Fair to promote city embellishment on a grand scale.

For decades after the fair, its architectural splendor inspired business leaders and politicians in city after city to build civic centers, improve waterfronts, plant parks, and lay out boulevards in select areas, boosting the market value and tax rates of land and businesses at or near the improved areas. The rest of the cities' vast gray areas, however, remained largely unchanged. Most city dwellers enjoyed such improvements on shopping jaunts downtown or holiday excursions to neighborhoods where the rich lived. But many were uprooted and forced to move when their homes and communities were destroyed to clear the land for the vaunted improvements.

Leaders of the Park Movement came from the upper and middle classes whose values and ideas they shared. They believed, or professed to believe, that the powers of art, nature and beauty could stabilize the strife-torn capitalist society. Its foremost leader, Frederick Law Olmstead, Sr., pushed the idea that parks could mediate class relations by encouraging friendly contacts among people of various classes in pleasantly landscaped surroundings. Moved by his arguments, upper and middle-class leaders who were in a position to carry out the Park movement's proposals, proceeded to create urban parks with the hope of promoting social harmony (Walker, 1978, 196–97).

The Park movement thus left a legacy of municipal park systems and commissions for park development. The commissions, however, could never justify land acquisition for park projects on humanitarian, conservation or aesthetic grounds alone. They had to demonstrate to the cities' upperclass decision makers that, in the long run, the proposed parks would benefit business (Lubove, 39).

The questionable promotional arguments notwithstanding, the City Beautiful and Park movements won wide approval and the works they inspired raised popular expectations. They implanted the thought, unwittingly perhaps, that good architecture and planning should serve all the people; that enjoying urban amenities and good housing was a democratic right; and that providing them in all city districts was a function, if not the duty, of city government.

But city improvement plans throughout the "Progressive Era" bypassed the squalor of factory and workingclass districts. City planning in the industrial capitalist society tilted city plans to serve profit making and to comfort the propertied classes.

World War I ended all city reforms, revived reaction, and

fomented attacks on progressive ideas and actions. President Wood-
row Wilson's "progressive" rhetoric urging the United States to
enter into the war horrified many. With the general disillusionment
in its leaders and programs, "progressive" reformism just wilted and
died.

13. Civic Reforms and the Working Class

Attitudes toward the civic reformers varied. Most of the middle class backed them, but among the working class, feelings were mixed.

On the whole, workers opposed the civic reformers; they felt that ward representation, even with corrupt politicians, had potential to give working people a stronger voice in city councils and a greater share of city benefits. However, they feared and hated the political bosses, who, bribed by employers, used the police and criminals to break strikes.

When in 1902 the Connecticut State Federation of Labor urged trade unions to aid city reform movements against boss rule, the unions responded half-heartedly. They saw little improvement in reform government over boss rule and had good reason to suspect that it might even be worse. The unions feared that the "goo-goos" (as they called the "good government" crusaders) would only replace open graft with more subtle, crafty and pervasive corruption (Foner, 1980, 57).

Workers knew that the reformers cared little about their needs and favored the upper and middle classes; that they never understood the problems of workingclass ethnic or racial minorities whom they thought to be willing tools of political bosses and a cause of corrupt city government. Workers regarded the reformers' passion against saloons as a sign of class contempt. Labor opposed prohibition partly because it would end thousands of jobs, but mainly because the saloon was the poor people's social club where "tired toilers, too poor to pay for any other form of social life . . . [found] relief from the monotony and agony of everyday existence" (Foner, 1980, 59–60). Some civic reformers, in fact, openly showed their class bias. One of their mayors reduced health services, used police to break strikes, and cut tax rates so low that the city lacked funds to pay its school teachers. Most civic reformers postured with greater indignation against saloons than against the lack of schools and parks in workingclass districts (Callow, 177). Workers also distrusted the reformers for excluding unions from their alliances, and for evading charges that they, too, bribed politicians, or maintained foul working and living conditions in the factories and tenements they owned. Some paid working "girls" miserable wages, forcing some of them into the very prostitution they claimed to deplore. Yet, in abhorrence of the anti-union boss rule in city government and lacking another solution, most of organized labor did support many city reform movements—in Detroit, Jersey City, Toledo, Seattle, Buffalo and other cities (Foner, 1980, 61–62).

Labor did score significant gains from its electoral support of civic reformers. It won some new democratic rights like direct primary elections, and direct election of the United States Senate. In some places, labor won the 8-hour day on public works, reduced streetcar fares, better schools, public baths, playgrounds, city hospitals and clinics, free school meals for poor children, evening schools, free libraries and lectures, workmen's compensation laws, protective legislation for women and child workers, and factory inspection laws. Gains significant enough to lend some progressive content to the "progressive" movements. But labor failed to win the legal right to organize and strike or outlawing government by injunction. Nor would the reformers agree to outlaw racist job discrimination or enact laws to improve the poor housing and schools in racial ghettos. The "progressive" reformers had their class limits on social progress (Foner, 1980, 85–86).

Labor also sustained some political losses. The enactment of nonpartisan contests for at-large candidates complicated and raised the cost of election campaigns, sharply reducing the ability of workingclass candidates to win political office. The relatively cheap ward-based elections favored workingclass and lower middle-class candidates known in their communities. Nonpartisan elections shifted voter attention from simply judging a party's program and behavior in office to a confusing appraisal of the positions of many individual candidates. It has discouraged popular interest in city politics and reduced voter turnout.

The upperclass civic reformers thus weakened the political participation of subordinate classes without disfranchising them. They simply upped the cost of raising workingclass issues in the political arena. While seeming to champion democracy, they repressed it for the majority (Newton, 81–82).

With the victory of "progressive" reforms, the working- and middle-class districts lost much of their strength in city politics and government. Their political vigor ebbed the more the upperclass pressed the advantages it won through its civic reforms in city politics (Hays, 1982, 252). This marked the resumption of direct upperclass leadership in urban affairs. Upperclass interests emerged open and clear in the strategy and tactics of city governments. Weakened democracy restrained the growth of new parties, leaving the. cities, and the nation, at the mercy of two, both of which were being turned into parties of big capital (Newton, 77).

Big capital had learned, however, to keep a low profile in public affairs. City executive functions were most often entrusted to members of the middle class who cleared major policy decisions, behind the scenes, with ruling-class leaders. Policy decisions began to flow indirectly from leading capitalists to their trusted agents sitting in state and national cabinets, or as university regents or trustees of cultural institutions, or functioning as governing members of newspapers and churches, collectively forming what sociologists came to recognize as the "power structures" or the "power elite"—acting furtively in a subtle division of rule over national, state, and urban affairs (Josephson, 317).

14. Transition From Industrial to State-Monopoly Capitalism

Toward the end of the 19th century our big cities took on an ever more similar look. Similar industrial, commercial, land and architectural development of our cities in the increasingly integrated economy of the nation tended to produce similarity in their social content and physical form.

In the fateful post-Civil War years of feverish urban growth, land developers, "packaging" their lands in simple, easy to sell rectangular blocks and lots, cast the forms of most cities in uniform gridiron patterns. Speculative builders filled block after block with low-cost look-alike buildings. CBDs were building high-rise office and factory towers; laying pipe and conduit lines in deep trenches snagged traffic at construction sites and along dug up streets. Store-lined streets teemed with shoppers. Every city moved to the beat of a typical rhythm of everyday life. Mornings and evenings, masses of people rushed in clanging trolleycars from their homes to their jobs.

But each passing year, fewer workers rushed to work in big factories and more streamed toward jobs in steel and stone skyscrapers and in glittering stores. The life and form of cities had begun to change as industrial capitalism grew into the monopoly-capitalist era.

The changes emerged out of capitalist competition, which naturally produced an ever greater concentration of capital in the hands of ever fewer victors able to exercise ever wider monopoly controls within the national economy. The major technological advances—improved production of metals, the invention of powerful engines, electrification of factories—speeded the process, for the use of the new technology in production required big plants and greater inputs of capital. At the same time, new technology intensified competition for efficient production and the capture of markets. The high investments in plant and machinery and the greater competitive risks drove groups of capitalists to form cartels, syndicates and trusts—to pool capital and credits and monopolize production, distribution and prices on huge markets (Kozlov, 316–17). The number of such mergers increased from 32 in 1897 to 1200 in 1899, consolidating over 5300 industrial firms into just 218 large corporations (Ashton, 61). At the close of the 19th century, the large corporations, barely a tenth of all capitalist enterprises, controlled 60 percent of the nation's production and dominated its basic metal and machine industries (Callow, 122).

Similar monopolies emerged in other branches of the economy, most notably in financing. To finance big industrial plants, industrialists turned to banks to borrow the large sums of capital needed. The banks, in turn, granted large loans on condition that they sit on the boards of their industrial clients to watch over the use of the borrowed funds. The resulting close association between industries and banks led to cross investments and to combined joint-stock companies. Finance capital gradually gained a monopoly grip on whole branches of industry, the national economy, and national politics. Thus began the new era of finance capital. At the turn of the century, some 500 top monopoly finance capital corporations had a controlling hold on the economic, political, and ideological life of the nation. Their dominance marked the transition from industrial to monopoly capitalism (Kozlov, 328–31).

Comments

Industrial capitalism advanced the nation's economy and technology at a phenomenal pace, establishing the United States as the world's foremost industrial nation, with the most rapidly growing cities. Scholars trying to explain its success offered opinions ranging over the academic ideological spectrum from the pragmatist right to radical left. Most tended to attribute to one factor or another a main causal power. Those on the right generally thought that technology did it; those on the radical left, that the class struggle did.

Those who held that technology had determined the course and nature of urban development argued that technological progress preceded industrial and urban growth—a cause-effect relationship between technology and urbanization. The argument appears plausible when one looks only at the deceptively simple surface. Probing deeper into the social forces that have molded the structure of industrial capitalism, however, reveals a complexity pragmatist eyes have tended to miss.

Technology has affected the process and forms of urbanization not as a primary cause but as an effect of society's productive forces and production relations. Technology has itself been propelled because competitors in the industrial-capitalist market economy had to improve their ability to compete. Viewed thus, one can see economics, technology and urbanization interacting in infinite dialectical cause-effect-cause relationships: intercapitalist competition pushing technology onward to raise productivity, and higher productivity raising competitive pressures for further technological innovations, producing economic and urban growth; urbanization, in turn, expanding markets and greater competition, pushing technology onward, and so on in an endless spiral.

Similarly, the pragmatist view that early city congestion resulted from a lag in urban transportation technology ignores the fact that the subsistence wages then paid to the mass of factory workers forced them to walk to work and crowd close to the factories. Is it not more reasonable to conclude that the extreme exploitation of labor, offering no profitable market to would-be capitalist transport promoters, delayed the development of urban transportation technology? Would not its lag be more reasonably seen as primarily the effect of social production relations?

Pragmatists have also attributed to progress in transportation technology the separation of urban space into special economic and residential districts. Such progress indeed made the separation possible, but did that possibility *cause* the spatial separation? Was not the technological progress, on the contrary, due to increasing specialization caused by competitive pressures to rationalize production and the uses of urban space?

The fallacy of the technological-determinist explanation of urban growth coming from the pragmatist right is fairly evident. The flaw in the one coming from radical left scholars is less apparent. It merits special attention because its premise is based on the class struggle in urban history, which bourgeois urban studies have consistently ignored.

The radical left view suggests that the need of capitalists to control their workers was the main determinant in urbanization. In capitalist society a specific production technology, cities included, is most useful when it helps to maintain capitalist dominance over labor. Capitalists have therefore sought factory locations that would maximize control over workers in the production process and minimize their resistance. In the early industrial years they favored big cities, whose large pools of unemployed outside factory gates helped discipline the workers inside. The big cities also isolated the working class, depriving it of the middle-class support it enjoyed in small towns. The argument concludes, therefore, that industrialists centralized production in big cities in mid-19th century, and decentralized it later because worker militancy made labor difficult to control in big cities (Gordon, 37–42).

The view claims to be Marxist. It merits credit for introducing the class struggle factor. But is isolating the class struggle from its other dialectically interacting economic, political, technological, geographic and cultural factors consistent with Marxist analysis? Indeed, ascribing urban development primarily to production relations contradicts the findings of eminent Marxist urban scholars that "urbanism is more closely related with the development of the forces of production than with production relations" (Blumenfeld, 1978, 60).

Consider this. Would industrial concentration in big cities have taken place had they not attracted capital investment with the profit opportunities that lay in their masses of workers, infrastructures, rail depots and ports, material and machinery stockpiles, specialized services, and markets? Is it not more reasonable to conclude, therefore, that: 1) Industrialists concentrated in big cities for the profit opportunities their external economies of scale and best access to markets offered, and 2) They later decentralized because overconcentrated big cities developed *diseconomies* of scale while big industrial plants developed *internal economies of sale,* and new transport and communication technology enabled easy access to markets from outside the big cities? As to control over labor, access to profitable markets outweighed the advantage of a tractable work force in the industrial-capitalist era. What good could tractable workers have been to industralists if what they produced could not be profitably sold because of poor access to markets?

Owing to the basic contradiction between capital and labor, the class struggle was a significant factor, of course. But it could not be the sole or even main factor in industrial location and urbanization. These were shaped by a complexity of dialectically interacting causes generated by the coercive laws of competition that pushed industrial capitalists to constantly revolutionize the means of production and thus the whole dynamics of industrial-capitalist society.

Among the dialectically interacting causes, city government had been a cardinal force in the growth of cities in the industrial-capitalist age. The then still relatively weak federal and state governments functioning in the laissez-faire climate of the 19th century, and the rise of strong local capitalist elites out of the intercity rivalry, made city government the essential protector of local capitalist growth (Mollenkopf, 1978, 119–20). Although it varied from city to city, its chief role in all cities had been to socialize as many of the costs of wealth accumulation as possible; that is, to provide the most possible city services that aid business, at public expense (Harring, 254).

This needs emphasis to clear up the all too common confusion about the role of government as an impartial guardian of the interests of all the people—that is, of all classes in society. The confusion arises out of the earlier mentioned side benefits to all people of city government functions essential to, hence intended for, promotion of private-enterprise profit making.

The true role of government in capitalist society is more clearly seen in the age of industrial capitalism. Then it was played out more crudely than in later, more sophisticated, periods. But its role remains the same to this day: it is the key to understanding why the provision of city services to the people have been so meager and stingy compared with the generous, even lavish, expenditures on business. The organic ties between government and the ruling class explain the limits on capitalist democracy beyond which politicians, even those "friendly" to labor, dare not, or can not, go. The important lesson is that the defense and extension of democracy depends upon the working class.

This lesson the working class began learning early out of simple class necessity. Even the yet politically green immigrants to the industrial cities resisted the undemocratic upperclass grabs of city resources. Owning nothing and earning little, they wholly depended on city services for health care, sanitation, education, transportation and public safety, which upperclass leaders tried to withhold or curtail (Turner, 231). Their resistance often exploded into bitter conflicts that turned city politics into arenas of class struggle (Mollenkopf, 1978, 119–20).

Even when it lacked organized forms, by its sheer weight of numbers the working class affected the economy, physical make-up, and politics of cities: economically, by mass consumer demand for housing, food, goods, and services shaping real estate, commodity, job, and credit markets; physically, by demands for urban space and facilities; and politically, by generating public issues the cities could not ignore (Blackman, 220).

Through most of the 19th century, the working class influenced city politics mainly by the force of its mass weight. Why did it not evolve organized forms of political struggle to improve its wretched urban living conditions? The answer may lie, in part, in its immigrant origins. Conditioned to bear hardships and tolerate situations they could not readily change, immigrant workers were not yet able to articulate their class interests through city politics. They may have also hoped that the enormous production and building they witnessed all around them would, in time, somehow also benefit them. The chief reason, however, no doubt was that the all-consuming struggle over the crucial issues of wages, hours, working conditions and union rights could not be weakened by concurrent struggles for better living conditions which, labor believed, would automatically follow from union victories. As it turned out, the economic gains the working class won in its hard-fought union battles altered little the class distribution of the fruits of urban progress (Fried, 25). For all these reasons, early working-class action in urban politics took an indirect route. While the maturing European working class began defending its interests by *independent* political action, its American counterpart took the first political steps within non-workingclass, often corrupt, political parties.

The literature on cities has widely discussed corruption in city politics and government. Wittingly or not, it has generally tended to distort the historical evidence. Some historians have hinted that corruption was brought on by "complex social relations" caused by mass urbanization or rural immigrants, obliquely accusing them of innate moral delinquency. Others have explicitly blamed city politicians of working- and middle-class origin, suggesting that corruption and crime were natural products of the "lower classes" and big cities.

Such notions have stemmed as much from an anti-city and anti-working class bias as from a reluctance to acknowledge the true role political party machines have played in our urban history. Bourgeois scholars have been quite disposed to give ideological cover to upperclass failings. They have veiled its resort to surrogate rule through political bosses to mollify angry workers and the lower-middle class when overt upperclass rule of city government became politically risky. They have falsely ascribed political corruption and crime to city life and the working class. On the contrary, sociological studies have shown that crime in cities decreased in the era of boss rule because industrialization and urbanization accommodated immigrants to the socially cooperative life of the cities. Working-class districts, in fact, had become incubators of stable family and community life (Lane, 129–30).

The reasons for urban antisocial behavior under boss political rule lay elsewhere. Some were inherent in the funding methods and structure of boss-ruled organizations. Most are patently traceable to the rivalry between capitalists, their brutal oppression of labor unions, and the deception and fraud normal to the competitive conduct of capitalist business.

Equally reprehensible are the allegations by some historians that the political bosses were 19th-century Robin Hoods—defenders of the working-class poor. All the workers got out of them was menial jobs and petty favors, rarely favorable political decisions. In labor-capital disputes, the political bosses almost always sided with employers (Harring, 11–12). Moreover, putting city politics on an ethnic or neighborhood basis, they fostered parochialism and weakened class consciousness, leaving the working class divided and vulnerable as it moved into the fast changing political life of the 20th century.

The victory of the civic reformers over the party bosses had, therefore, its progressive side even as it served the interests of the reactionary upper class. Along with some gains, however, the working class has ever since faced the problem of altering the reformers' reforms to remove the obstacles they raised to democracy (Walker and Greenberg, 40).

Bourgeois historians have extolled the reformers and, especially, the philanthropists of industrial capitalism. They have been fond of guessing the motive behind their ostentatious generosity:

did they crave fame before their peers or want to appease a guilty conscience? They might better have left such speculation to biographers and considered instead the objective social conditions that produced the phenomena of fanatical social reformers and fabulous philanthropists. Because industrial capitalism lacked the social institutions to manage the consequences of unbridled exploitation of labor or to train a labor force for its technologically developing economy, some of its leaders apparently felt compelled to manage them privately. The slum settlement houses they sponsored, ostensibly to help immigrants to adapt to a new life, also helped to keep potentially "troublesome" unemployed off the streets and to condition working-class young to respect private property and the virtues of hard work. Philanthropically aided education also helped train the many technicians and skilled workers industry needed in a myriad production specialities. Public schools, colleges, universities, libraries, museums and concert halls became essential to reproduction of skilled labor in the industrial age. Hence the philanthropic endowments to some 260 college and universities between 1860 and 1900, and to municipal elementary, intermediate and trade schools (Schlesinger, 1951, 129).

Still, it may be asked, whence came the strong motivation of leading capitalists to give leadership to their cities, whether in philanthropy, reform, or government?

The answer may logically follow from the fact that their fortunes, until well into the industrial-capitalist era, were closely bound up with the fate of their cities. The bigger the fortune, the more this was true. Therefore, they were compelled to give leadership to the affairs of home cities lest city misfortunes rebound to ill effect personal fortunes. That explains why, from the city fathers and boards of trade in the commercial era to the prestigious mayoralities, the civic reformers, power elites, and the philanthropists of the industrial era, leading capitalists kept vigilance over each city's vigor and growth, social problems and conflicts, safety, appearance, and of course, economic and political standing in the region and nation.

The ties of leading capitalists to their home cities loosened toward the end of the era, for the more that individually accumulated wealth merged into rising regional and national corporations, the less personal fortunes depended on any one city. Corporate exploitation of many cities thinned the care of individual capitalists for any one city. Leadership of leading capitalists in their home cities began to weaken, but it did not cease, for their home cities still contained the bulk of their investments and business operations, compelling their continued concern for the local infrastructures, labor force, and markets (McKelvey, 1963, 18). The promise of future higher corporate profits did not yet outdazzle the steady profits their home cities yielded.

Partly because the profit interests of its national corporations drew the upper class to national politics and partly because class strata diversified in the growing cities, the formal leadership in city politics and government moved to a lower strata of the upper class and an upper strata of the middle class—competing for economic and political advantages in the cities. To the working class, it became increasingly apparent that political decisions made at the national level most affected its fate in the cities. Working-class politics therefore increasingly turned toward the national government. Thus, at the turn of the century, our rapidly urbanizing nation divided essentially into two major opposing social forces—the capitalist and working classes—locked in production relations and ceaseless struggle over the wealth they produced. Their stations and functions in society molded each with unique social and political characteristics.

Exploiting a land rich in natural and human resources, the capitalist class amassed great wealth and wielded dominant political power. It expanded production with an unprecedented variety and volume of goods and services and generated much social progress. Social progress, however, was not its goal but a byproduct of its pursuit of capital accumulation. It ran roughshod over the nation's working majority whose wealth-producing labor it arrogated to itself by force and cunning.

The working class developed traits all its own. Schooled in the workplace, it learned organization and discipline. Finding strength in its numbers, it fostered cooperation and solidarity. Oppressed and exploited, it opposed exploitation and social injustice. Of all classes, it alone had a vested interest in social progress—a distinctive quality of vital significance to the future of the nation and its cities.

"Chee, Annie look at de stars—
thick as bed-bugs!"

Art Young

PART TWO: *Cities under Monopoly and State Monopoly Capitalism*

15. The Context of Modern Urban[1] Development

The upperclass emerged from World War I firmly at the driving wheel of the world's richest, most productive country. Its enormous war profits and the access it won to new markets and resources accelerated the concentration of wealth in the largest corporations. Flushed with success and cocksure of their future, rival capitalists recklessly expanded production capacities, rationalized mass production, raised the productivity of labor, and improved transportation and marketing. Riding on high expectations, wild speculation kept inflating the stock market right up to the 1929 crash.

The Great Depression's effect on the welfare of working people was almost immediate. Shrinking production and commerce soon spread unemployment, decreased city revenues, and cut city services. Widespread rent defaults started a wave of evictions. Working-class districts looked sadder than ever, their streets dotted with evicted families huddled on sidewalks around their scanty belongings.

Unemployment, poverty and dislocation aroused the anger of millions and fired up a mass organization of the unemployed. The workers waged a militant struggle against corporate power and the State—for the right to organize, unemployment insurance, jobs on public works, minimum wages and shorter workdays, affordable good housing, health care, and social security . Out of this were born the mass industrial unions and the young CIO.

The militancy and organization of aroused working-class millions shook capitalist society. Frightened of its political implications, the upperclass conceded it could not prevent the wide-ranging reforms of the New Deal. The State enacted public works programs to provide jobs to millions and laws recognizing some of the demands of the expanding, militant labor movement.

The New Deal years erased the last vestiges of laissez-faire capitalism. The State became deeply involved in regulating the national economy and the monopoly corporations were more closely tied to the operation of the State. This began to change the course of society's development.

The New Deal policies blunted the cruel edge of the Depression upon the people but did not bring on an economic recovery. This crisis ended only when the country's productive capacity geared up to feed the maws of World War II.

During and after the war, monopoly capital and the State continued to blend in new ways. Indeed, they shared governing functions. The State no longer merely responded to corporate demands, it initiated economic activities and political deals on behalf of big capital through its fiscal, legislative, and foreign policies. The monopoly corporations aided the State in domestic and foreign affairs with technical knowledge, advice on policy planning and execution, and exchange of top personnel. This close knit concentration of monopoly corporations and the State marked a new stage in capitalist society's development—state monopoly capitalism. It gave the U.S. upperclass preponderant economic and political dominance over the other war-weakened capitalist states for the period of U.S. prosperity and relative stability of the 1950s and '60s.

Integrating the economies of developed capitalist and developing countries in a new international division of labor, monopoly capital exploited huge pools of unorganized cheap labor abroad. Production and jobs began moving not only to low-wage regions of this country, but also to Asian, African and South American countries.[2] Great advances in science and technology speeded the movement.[3] The combined advantage of concentrated huge capital backed by State power, hegemony over a dependent capitalist world, and new advanced technology raised production to new levels yielding enormous corporate profits. Therefore monopoly capital was able for a time to "buy" and maintain relative labor peace and discipline at home. Slightly higher wages and benefits were exchanged for the far higher increases in labor productivity (Edel, 232–33).

By the late 1960s, however, the fortunes of U.S. state-monopoly capital began to change. Its dominance over the capitalist world declined as the other capitalist nations developed competitive muscle and resistance from developing nations had raised the cost of their exploitation. The combined effects of increased competition and rising costs shrank profits, causing the monopolies to curtail traditional production, increase unemployment, attack organized labor, and erode the living standards of the working and middle classes, throwing the nation into yet a new crisis in the 1970s (Edel, 236–37).

Partly in response to the new problems in the capitalist world economy, and partly in attempts to overcome the recession, monopoly capital began to take on new forms, casting the menacing shadows of mammoth transnational corporations over the world, the nation, and the cities.

Vast holdings of the country's industries and resources fell under the control of these transnational corporations in the 1970s and '80s. They grew largely thanks to their great mobility. Operating on a world scale and using flexible production, management, and marketing techniques, they could shift capital from lower- to higher-profit enterprises and to more advantageous geographic locations with relative ease.

They also put more funds into speculative ventures rather than into traditional productive enterprise.

The resulting superprofits gave them competitive advantages. In the dog-eat-dog mergers, buyouts and takeovers of billion-dollar corporations by even mightier ones, they came out on top. The resulting stupendous concentration of capital gave the transnational corporations (TNCs) enormous international economic and political power. In the early 1980s, the 100 largest of them controlled two-thirds of the capitalist world's industrial production. The world's 340 largest enterprises held two-thirds of its assets and reaped two-thirds of its profits. Eighty-five percent of the capitalist world's financial transactions went through the 100 largest transnational banks. Bloated with capital, the footloose TNCs have been investing in profitable ventures abroad and disinvesting in the less profitable industries at home. Often they chose to close, rather than modernize, outmoded plants in unionized industrial cities and shift production to technologically modern plants in geographic locations offering maximum profitability (*Economic Notes*, June 1982, 4).

Thus, in the decades since World War II, the transnationals

have created a new international division of labor and altered the economic relations between countries in the non-socialist part of the world. The old capitalist international division of labor was based mainly on trade between goods-producing developed countries and raw-materials supplying underdeveloped nations. The new one is based mainly on manufacturing extended to newly industrializing countries with trade increasingly conducted between the subsidiaries of transnational corporations producing goods in profitable locations everywhere. For example, the subsidiary companies of an American transnational corporation may make a number of products in France, South Korea, Sweden and Taiwan and sell them through its subsidiary trading companies within those countries and in England, Saudi Arabia, West Germany, Egypt, the United States and Argentina. The transnational thus profits not only from exploiting the labor where its products are made but also from selling them (and other products) on various markets. It therefore takes advantage not only of cheaper labor and production costs wherever in the world it finds them, but also of advantageous marketing conditions. A TNC can grow many such subsidiary tentacles in many parts of the world. Should one or more of them fail in some places, the transnational can absorb their loss and grow new ones elsewhere. This reduces its dependence and accountability to any city or nation. Moreover, commanding economic clout in the countries and cities hosting its subsidiaries, the transnational exercises an inordinate political influence on their governments, in close cooperation with its own national government, to protect and promote its investments and profits. The profitability, adaptability and influence thus gained made the transnationals economically and politically dominant throughout the capitalist world (Cohen, 1981; Hymer, 1979).

In this dominance, we find the roots of the growing plight of our cities. Responding to growing international competition, monopoly corporations have been shifting their manufacturing operations, especially in heavy industries, to new low-wage and least government-regulated centers all over the non-socialist world. This redistribution of industrial production from developed to developing areas both within nations (as from Snowbelt to Sunbelt in the USA), between developed capitalist states where profit-maximizing opportunities appear, and between them and developing nations, has closed "non-competitive" plants in older centers or speeded their rationalization to raise profitability. All this causes major shifts in production and trade with heavy job losses in the long established industrial centers of our big cities.

This explains the increasingly common plant closings in steel, auto, rubber and just about every mass production industry, the rise in permanent unemployment and the spreading decay in the working-class districts of our old cities. But what explains the seeming revival of central business districts and nearby residential areas in some of these cities? And why did this seeming revival stop short of other old cities? The answers lie in other characteristics of transnationals and the way they operate.

The TNCs, other monopolies, and their auxiliary corporations and services have tended to cluster in a few key world cities in which a high order of business infrastructures—stock exchanges, communication hubs, research, engineering, consulting, public relations, design, advertising, and printing companies—have developed. The significance of cities such as London, Paris, Frankfurt, Zurich, Tokyo, Singapore, Hong Kong, Sao Paulo, New York, and San Francisco cannot be measured by mere production, population or areal dimensions. They have become most important as transactional centers, processing information and hosting corporate and related personnel who visit regularly to transact diversified business, collect information, and feast on their amenities and excitements (Gottman, 1977, 23).

In these world capitals of monopoly capitalism, the powerful TNCs locate their main headquarters. From these commanding heights, issue their strategic and tactical economic and political decisions. Free market mechanisms in international trade have thus been gradually replaced by administrative mechanisms within the mammoth monopoly corporations. Spontaneous market activities are increasingly transformed into conscious manipulations under corporate administrative control (Hill, 1984, 133).

In our country, state monopoly capitalism has wrought profound changes in the established settlement system. It has transformed the urban geography of the nation from the historically established distinct cities, towns and villages into a system of integrated metropolises and metropolitan regions. But it had been contorting the process to serve its special interests. As the following pages will try to show, the economic and political fate of whole cities and regions have been arbitrarily determined by the special interests of dominant corporations and the decisions of a few behind-the-scenes men.

16. From Old City to Modern Metropolis

The origins of our modern metropolises go back more than a hundred years to the old commercial cities from which they sprang. In the process of simultaneous concentration of people within cities and decentralization toward the suburbs, the city and its satellites gradually lost their relatively autonomous existence and fused into an interdependent functional whole (Blumenfeld, 1967, 64–65).

The transformation from city to metropolitan forms of urban settlement was caused by changes in the organization of production. It evolved as small industries, thriving on the cities' external economies of scale, began losing ground to big corporations developing more efficient production in big plants outside of cities (Walker, 1981, 399). By 1910, when trolleycars and railroads expanded the cities' boundaries, the unfolding of metropolitan urban forms became quite apparent. The 1910 census identified 44 cities of 100,000 or more as metropolitan centers or emerging metropolises. Even then, the 27.5 million people of these cities and their suburbs made up 30 percent of the nation's population (McKelvey, 1968, 3).

Understandably, recognition of the new urban form lagged behind the fact. Before World War I, what is today the central city was all the city there was. Suburbanite commuters were a relatively few rich who could afford the time and cost of long daily journeys (Vernon, 13).

The trend from city to metropolis became clearly evident after World War I. But, unlike in earlier periods, when expanding industrial production accelerated migration from rural areas to cities, the flow of population was now greatest to city suburbs, both from within cities and the countryside. While new economic activities and jobs sprang up within cities, even more mushroomed outside their borders. Cities burst open and spilled out like ruptured dams. Only about 1920 did its salient features—CBDs and residential suburbs—become prominent and in the 1930s generally recognized in over 100 developing metropolises (Fox, 25–26).

Cities continued to change even during the Depression. Although village-to-city migration slowed, population movement from central cities to suburbs continued. The number of metropolitan areas and their share of the national population kept rising. In 1940, 47.8 percent of the nation lived in 140 metropolises. The metropolis was becoming dominant in our urban settlement system (Fox, 46).

During and after World War II, even more production, commerce, and population moved out of central cities to outer metropolitan areas. In the postwar decades, the increasing number of metropolises and their share of the nation's population proved conclusively that past distinctions between "urban" and "rural" around big cities were fast losing meaning; that urban economic, social, and political life now extended well beyond city limits.

Significantly indicating how general and unrestrainable the process had become, metropolitan development emerged even in the least urbanized regions. The Southeast states—the old South—which was predominantly rural before the WWI—with only 8 percent of its people in 8 metropolitan areas—developed, by 1940, 33 metropolises containing 20 percent of its population. The Southwest also shifted dramatically. Its metropolitan areas increased from 4 in 1910 to 14 in 1940, and its metropolitan population from 7 to 26 percent. Metropolitan development in the Plains and Mountain regions predominated in the 1950s and '60s. By 1970, the Plains had 20 metropolitan areas embracing 49 percent of its population, and the Mountain region had 9 metropolitan areas holding 59 percent of its population. Throughout the country, the function of local economic, social and political integration had shifted from the city to the metropolis (Fox, 34–37).

Indeed, the impact of the science-technology revolution (STR) and growing economic specialization in all industrially developing countries have made metropolitanization a world phenomenon. To the pre-World War II metropolises of the advanced European and North American countries have been added gigantic metropolises like Rio de Janiero, Sao Paulo, Mexico City, Cairo, Bogota, Lima, Beijing, Seoul, Jakarta, Manila, Bangkok, Bombay, Teheran—to name but a few.

Modern metropolises are not merely the old cities "bigger," *they are qualitatively different.* The quantitative socio-economic changes in cities since the mid-19th century have reached a point of qualitative change. "The city which for 6,000 years has existed as one basic form of human settlement together with and opposed to the country is transformed into a completely new form of settlement: the metropolitan area—or 'metropolis' for short—which is neither city nor country, but partakes of the characteristics of both." (Blumenfeld, 1959, 477). In the metropolitan area, city, suburbs, and the countryside around them blend, physically and socially, even across the artificial political boundaries of counties and states, into an interrelated, interdependent whole. "This process, far from destroying the center of the metropolis, has meant an ever growing extension and intensification of its dominance over the periphery. 'Center' and 'periphery' are not mutually exclusive but dialectically united opposites." (Ibid.)

The typical American urban unit in the late 20th century is a metropolis of more than one million people. Almost 75 percent of our people now live within a metropolis and most in the remaining 25 percent live within 25 miles of one (Fox, 24). The metropolis has fully replaced the old city as the principal urban organizing unit and has reached a high level in its own development (Hicks, 125–26). Historically young, however, it is still evolving and changing, but its basic characteristics have unfolded enough to permit a fairly clear, if tentative, definition.

The modern metropolis is a multinucleated territorial system of interdependent urban and rural settlements and land uses functionally dominated by a central city. It is primarily a big production center and labor market. It's chief social advantage is accessibility between a multiskilled work force, a large variety of jobs, and a wide choice of goods and social facilities. Metropolises issue out of their central cities' increasingly specialized division of labor, which tends to separate and decentralize linked economic activities and populations over a network of settlements beyond them, and to centralize management, service and information functions within them. Thus, the metropolis is an expanding system of urban units and open areas spreading outward from a dense and intensive central core in a series of progressively less dense and intensive concentric rings. Because it continually expands from center to periphery, it has no clear border. Its boundaries expand as its transportation and communication systems improve and extend to serve most of its population (Blumenfeld, 1967, 123).[4]

The metropolis may be further defined by noting the main differences between it and its predecessor, the traditional city.

1. Concentrating the nation's present vast and versatile material and non-material productive forces and homes, the metropolis combines the old city's mainly trade, social and governmental functions with the then mainly rural dispersed material production and homes of most of the nation.

2. The population of the metropolis is at least 10 times as large and its area at least 100 times the size of the biggest old city.

3. The metropolis has no fixed physical structure. In contrast to the street pattern and the densely built-up, limited, totally urban space of the old city, the boundless area of the metropolis contains both built-up and open spaces—parks, fields, farms, and forests.

4. In contrast to the city's mixed home and work places, the metropolis' residential, industrial, and business functions are spatially separated.

5. In the city, workshops were small, manned by craftsmen working their crafts throughout their lifetimes. Workplaces in the metropolis are typically large; their workers often change in number, occupation, and jobs.

6. In the old city, shops and worker housing clustered in the center. In the metropolis, they have moved outward, locating freely over its area.

7. Most adults in metropolitan worker households work or seek work, producing a social mobility and fluidity in sharp contrast to the social confinement and traditionalism of the earlier city (Blumenfeld, 1967, 53–54).

Its huge concentration of a wide variety of goods, activities and skills make the metropolis a highly versatile and efficient form of settlement having far greater potentials for production and a full life than its predecessor, the city, has had. Indeed, it is the most adaptable form of settlement in history, most able to sustain and recover from economic adversity, technological obsolescence, or physical disaster (Ibid, 367–68).

The advantages of the metropolis, however, generate some bad side effects. Its enormous concentration of production forces produces huge volumes of waste and traffic, polluting its air, water, and soil. Spontaneous haphazard suburban development results in form-lessness, weakening its urban integrity and spoiling its natural beauty. As distances lengthen between central city and suburbs, class and race segregation increases and living-standard gaps widen.

Most urban planners agree that the technology exists to over-come the physical ill effects (Blumenfeld, 1979, 11). Applying it, however, and overcoming the social inequities, is a political problem amenable only by class politics and struggle. One difficulty is that the socioeconomic unity of the metropolis, in which central city and suburbs are inseparable components, lacks governmental unity. Only a governmentally united metropolis could most fully integrate central-city and suburbs. Instead, the history has been one of discordant integration. Inexorable economic forces have dragged the politically feuding central-city and suburbs kicking and screaming, as it were, into coexistence as conflicting opposites within the objec-tive unity of the metropolis. Thus, we must examine them sepa-rately to perceive their integration within the historically new urban form.

Eastwood

17. The Central City of the Metropolis

Lagging public awareness of urban changes has distorted common perception of today's city. Despite its changed function within the metropolis, the city is commonly viewed as an autonomous geographic-political entity, largely a master of its own fate and responsible for its own growth, stability, or decline.

Urban scholars have repeatedly shown this view to be false. Central cities today are integral parts of the larger economic and political life of their metropolitan regions, within which they play distinct roles. They are the metropolitan centers within which a ruling capitalist class organizes complex production forces for production, reproduction, distribution, and overall development to promote wealth accumulation within regions, the nation, and abroad.

A variety of industrial, commercial and service activities thrive in various parts of the central city, but its most significant central organizing functions concentrate in its core—the CBD. These functions gained in volume and substance as state monopoly capitalism developed, displacing other activities that were historically located at the city's core in the preceding industrial-capitalist age. The displacement has gained momentum since the 1950s and is still going on. Its profound effect on urban development warrants examining it in some detail.

As costs of land, rent and operation rose with crowding in CBDs, the weakest competitors were forced to leave. Big factories and warehouses, needing large floor spaces and quick movement the most, and central location the least, moved out first. The high bidders who had to stay in the center at all costs comprise three groups: those who draw the highest profit from central activities per unit of space, those who depend on close daily communication with linked activities, and those who must be accessible to clients coming from all sides.

Of all economic functions in the metropolis, big corporations and banks draw the highest profits per square foot of space and require central location. Accordingly, the occupancy of CBD space has preponderantly gone to corporate headquarters, central banks, and the high-profit auxiliary corporations serving them (Vernon, 54–55).

Yet, despite the high cost of doing business in CBDs, large numbers of small production, supply, and service firms abound in them. These are firms whose outputs often vary in form and volume. Therefore, they depend daily on direct contact with buyers, sellers, and various specialized services. The fashion sector of the garment industry, or custom-machinery building, for instance, are typical. Their non-standard products demand daily knowledge of new style changes or frequent consultation between customers, contractors, and manufacturers. Many also use non-standard materials requiring frequent negotiation between makers and suppliers. Such companies must stay in the center for two reasons: they must be close to their markets and to each other, and they must hold down the cost of uncertainty due to changing product style and variable production volumes. They survive in their high-cost environment by keeping their operations relatively small and flexible, using subcontractors and suppliers as needed; that is, drawing on the CBDs external economies of scale (Vernon, 31–32).

Finally, functions serving the entire metropolis and beyond— such as government agencies, the mass media, and central political, educational, cultural, health or labor institutions—must obey the law of polarity. They must locate in the center to be accessible to those they must reach out to or who must reach them from many directions. With the main highways and commuter lines converging upon it, the central city's CBD remains the most accessible to all outer parts (Blumenfeld, 1970, 93–94).

Increasingly, however, CBDs have come under the dominance of corporate and bank headquarters. Ever more dependent on a growing complexity of information on financing, production and marketing, they concentrate on CBDs, spawning hosts of auxiliary corporations competing to serve them. With the growing volume of complex corporate operations, the demand for high-rent CBD office space kept increasing. It could be met only by forcibly appropriating land and buildings in the built-up CBDs and dispossessing their users. Profit-eager business interests formed "growth" coalitions with city governments—that ostensibly hoped to make up lost production jobs with new office employment—to legalize clearing large downtown areas of existing uses for new office towers.

Since 1960s, most central cities have been building office towers on a mass scale. Between 1960 and 1970, the 30 biggest added an average of 44 percent in office space, and the 12 biggest doubled it. In 1979 the federal government aided the process by providing a variety of tax incentives and land clearance subsidies to central city developers through some 200 programs. The easy financing let loose a speculative building spree that turned downtowns into depopulated office enclaves, crowded during daylight hours and deserted at night. The rapid rise of new office towers dramatically paraded the dominance of mega-corporate capital along city skylines (Gottdiner, 115–18; Gottman, 1975, 222–23). Redevelopment has considerably renewed downtowns and added vitality to big central cities. Not all central cities, however, have had equal downtown redevelopment and revival. Indeed, it has been quite limited in some.

Why cities share unequally in the downtown bonanza is explained by the ways of the rising TNCs. TNCs plan their global operations in their central headquarters—such as New York, San Francisco, Pittsburgh, Houston or Chicago. Their enormous scope—often exceeding that of a fairly large State—requires obtaining, processing, compiling, and communicating a variety of information on a comparable scale. Far flung production and trade branches correspondingly extend the need for coordination, market promotion, competition control, and political manipulation everywhere they operate. To cope with this managerial complexity, corporations use the services of a great variety of specialized firms and agencies in various fields. Characteristically, such services rely heavily on external economies of scale and on daily close contact with linked activities that the high concentration of diverse office activities in modern CBDs makes possible.

But monopoly corporations make less use of such services in other big cities. Office jobs in Cleveland, St. Louis, or Detroit have grown proportionately less because they are used at a different level in the corporate hierarchy of operations. TNCs and other corporate giants typicaly operate on three levels. The highest level, the seat of top management, determines the corporation's goals, strategy and tactics. The second level translates these decisions into management and programs for the third level of routine day-to-day operations.

The three levels usually separate geographically as corporations expand. Level one functions tend to concentrate mainly in world cities like New York or San Francisco. Level two functions center largely in main national cities like Chicago, Philadelphia or Boston. And level three functions locate mostly in main regional cities like Columbus, Indianapolis, Louisville, St. Louis, or Milwaukee, and comparable cities throughout the capitalist world (Hymer, 1979; Cohen, 1977). Level one, the widest in scope, generates the most CBD activity and office jobs. Level two, smaller in scope and divided among more cities, produces correspondingly smaller CBDs employing fewer workers. Level three, scattered over the widest network of cities, supports relatively small CBDs and generates the least jobs.

Wherever they operate, monopoly corporations have expanded CBDs to suit themselves, intimidating city governments to modernize and maintain them at the city's expense, lest they move their offices, tax money, and jobs elsewhere. City governments have usually complied, believing that an expanding CBD offered the only hope for regaining economic vitality.[5] This belief persists despite data proving it false. Downtown office development may have, in fact, done more economic harm than good.[6] Studies have shown that most of the job growth in central cities has been generated by small city-based manufacturers occupying the old low-rent buildings—the very buildings office expansion has been demolishing, forcing small businesses out of the city. Their leaving has cost cities jobs for mainly city residents. The city loses their buying power and taxes, and has the added costs of unemployment and welfare. Moreover, almost half of the new jobs in expanded CBDs are held by office workers living and spending their paychecks in the suburbs. Their corporate employers think of the city as little more than a place to mine wealth from and leave (Redmond and Goldsmith, 19–21).

Glittering new office towers, eye-catching shopping malls, exotic restaurants, and titillating amusement places have turned modernized CBDs into tourist attractions. A city's visitors, landing in a downtown hotel, taking their pleasure in its new CBD, come away with starry-eyed impressions of a city they have not really seen. The city beyond the CBD has changed too, but in a rather lackluster way. It's been worn down over the decades by population turnovers, economic depression, bank disinvestments, landlord abandonment and official neglect of services.

Population changes in most central cities have complicated their inner development. Because the 1920s' anti-alien laws and the 1930s' Depression slowed immigration to a trickle, city populations grew largely by domestic country-to-city migration, especially from the Black rural South.[7] Southern Black farmers streamed toward East and Midwest industrial cities in large numbers before, during and after World War II; so large, in fact, as to raise their ratio of Black to white population from 17 percent in 1910 to 48 percent in 1950. Comparable ratio changes followed the settlement of rural Mexican Americans in Southwestern cities in the 1960s and '70s and that of idled Puerto Rican farmers in the cities of New York State and the eastern seaboard (Glaub and Brown, 285–86).

The mass influx of racial minorities into a time when entry-level manufacturing jobs were declining sharpened job competition and prejudice against the newcomers. Equally intense was the competition for scarce low-rent housing, exacerbated by the racism inherited from the past. Desperately poor Black and other racial minorities became locked within growing segregated ghettos where growing poverty, hopelessness and resentment inevitably incubated social and physical ills (Glaub and Brown, 287). Continuing arrival of technologically dispossessed rural immigrants seeking city jobs burst the seams of congested ghettos to crowd into housing of adjacent working-class neighborhoods, partly vacated by families who followed suburb-bound industries.

Even by the end of the 1940s, the spreading slums, rising costs of social services, delayed maintenance of the Depression and war years, and the loss of taxpaying industries and populations combined to cause many central cities to decline. To make matters worse, federal policy channeled federal funds away from central cities to finance suburban development. Obliged to quickly provide housing and jobs for millions of returning veterans catching up with delayed family formation, the federal government initiated massive home and highway building programs in suburban areas. Easy mortgage credits and tax incentives lured young central-city families to resettle in new suburbs; local banks and real estate companies, profiting from turnover in housing occupancy, fanned racism in working- and middle-class neighborhoods to goad the hesitant to move. What might have been a rational gradual population expansion toward metropolitan outskirts, the banks and realtors turned into a frantic stampede.

The drain of industries and people left central cities with slowing economies, dwindling revenues, climbing vacancies, crumbling streets and utilities, and rising ratios of unemployed, poor, and aging populations. As monopoly capital denied loans, mortgages and insurance to "poor risk" districts, decline and abandonment of buildings accelerated.

To halt the decline before it engulfed their own heavy investments, corporate leaders prodded city chambers of commerce to form coalitions to push for a federal program of selected urban renewal. The program called upon the federal government to exercize its right of eminent domain to acquire and clear large tracts of high-priced, built-up land and thereby subsidize large-scale private profit-producing redevelopment in central cities with public funds. The federal Urban Renewal Program absorbed the inflated real estate prices of lands taken in selected areas, demolished their old buildings, and sold the cleared land at low prices for high-rent office tower and luxury housing development, upgrading CBD and related areas for corporate use (Smith, 1983, 244).

The Urban Renewal Program carried out its mission at great cost to the working class. During the 1960s and '70s, it tore down low-income housing in large sections of central cities, 80 percent of which was in low-rent residential use. It evicted millions of people and small businesses at the rate of over 250,000 families a year, and destroyed hundreds of working-class neighborhoods, raising rents 50 to 60 percent in the remaining housing stock. The toll was heaviest in the Black ghettos; almost 70 percent of the displaced in the 1960s were Black families (Goldsmith and Jacobs, 61–63; Goering and Lichten, 310; Smith, 1980, 241).

Urban Renewal's attacks on working-class neighborhoods provoked militant community counterattacks. Grassroots neighborhood organizations arose to oppose demolition, often forcing government and developers to the bargaining table. Project officials found targeted neighborhoods ready and waiting for them, "organized to the teeth," often stopping a project "dead in its tracks" (Wilson, 243).

Community organizations demanded compensation and relocation services for the displaced, a maximum share of new low-rent housing in the proposed projects, rehabilitation of remaining old housing in affected communities, better schools, recreation facilities, jobs, and adequate police and fire protection. Some succeeded in forcing a shift from a "slum clearance" approach to one of community preservation, stopping construction of proposed highways through their communities, and building considerable numbers of low-rent dwellings (Cunningham and Auerbach, 223–24).

But by the end of the 1970s, the Urban Renewal Program had accomplished most of its purpose. Federal land subsidies for central-city redevelopment were accordingly reduced. Thenceforth, the huge profits of giant corporations absorbed the high costs of further CBD development, and the high incomes of CBD-oriented households of executives and professionals permitted buying out choice parts of old working-class districts in a new form of displacement—gentrification (Smith, 1983, 295).[8] With the end of the crude and costly methods of Urban Renewal, capital and government attempts to remove working-class populations and small businesses from choice areas of central cities continued by this more cunning and cheaper means. The federal government facilitated gentrification with code enforcement assistance, low-interest rehabilitation loans, neighborhood capital improvement programs, and the like (Mollenkopf, 1981, 17).

Gentrification spread as CBD employment of professionals increased. Many welcomed it as a sign of a back-to-the-city movement of middle-class young repulsed by the suburbs' rising housing and commuting costs and attracted by cheaper renovated housing closer to their CBD jobs. Studies have shown, however, the return-of-sururbanites notion to be a myth. Only 15 to 18 percent of all gentrifiers have come from the suburbs. Most have come from other parts of the same city believing that their gentrified neighborhoods will increase in market value (Lang, 6–7).

Finance capital and State action, however, determined the process more than did the speculative hopes of would-be gentrifiers. Where gentrification took place, it usually began with a developer buying up most properties in a targeted area, rehabilitating a group of demonstration homes, then persuading banks to finance extensive development. But without the aid of the State, much gentrification would be stillborn. The State, at the federal and local levels, has seen in gentrification an opportunity to replace "surplus" working-class populations, soaking up costly city services, with a revenue producing middle class. It has therefore abetted the process by modernizing infrastructures in gentrifying areas, selling public property below cost to gentrifying developers, granting them low interest loans, and paying for all of this by cutting services in working-class districts (Marcuse, 1985, 932).

Capital and city governments also had other reasons for promoting gentrification. When the national economy slipped into doldrums in the late '60s and '70s and profit rates in production diminished, surplus capital tended to flow to real estate and construction, but no longer in the surburbs. Suburban real estate became overpriced while that of cities devalued following the capital flow of the '50s and '60s from cities to suburbs. This real estate landscape of the '70s, coinciding with a rising middle-income housing demand around renewing CBDs, reversed the flow of real estate capital from suburbs to cities and paved the way for gentrification (Smith, Neil, 1983, 293–95).

Gentrification has affected the working class much as urban renewal did, albeit more gradually and on a smaller scale. It, too, has evicted tenants and forced home owners to sell, reducing the housing stock and raising rents and prices of low-income housing. It has similarly driven many to declining inner-ring suburbs, reducing their access to central-city job markets. It brought the same painful loss of community and added hardships and anguish for the elderly. It drove many into debt and forced cutbacks in their standard of living (Clay, 32).

Living standards have been gradually falling in the declining working-class districts in central cities. But the cities themselves have not, on the whole, been declining. Rather, they have been undergoing two simultaneous processes—disinvestment in low-profit working-class districts and investment in their high-profit areas. They have generally shown considerable economic resilience, despite population and manufacturing losses (Hicks, 16–17, 137).

Notwithstanding considerable decay, central cities remain the vital hearts of metropolises. They still are the metropolises' chief source of ideas and skills. They are the metropolitan hubs of transportation, their main markets and stores of goods and materials, the magnets of sellers and buyers and the destination of tourists (Hill,

1978, 230). Finally, the central cities are the metropolises' havens of interest and contrast: of cabarets and discos and sport stadiums; operas, theaters and concert halls; of restaurants, museums, and galleries; of schools, universities and libraries. They welcome the young in search of careers and excitement, shelter the aging whom the suburbs no longer suit well, and accommodate the poor whom the suburbs reject (Abrams, 1965, 13–14).

18. The Suburbs of the Metropolis

Seclusion, rejection, and discrimination marked the formation of suburbs from their beginning. The withdrawal of the upperclass from the city in the 19th century to its exclusive retreats in suburbs, its rejection of the working class, and discrimination since against ethnic and racial minorities have largely dogged their development. Reviling the city and extolling suburban life developed a smug arrogance that has tainted suburbanization with anticity attitudes to this day (Walker, 1981, 396).

Modern suburbs are relatively small, socially homogeneous, politically autonomous municipalities ringing a big central city, forming with it an economically and socially integrated metropolis. Most suburbs specialize as mainly residential, commercial or industrial. They can do this because they can draw on the variety of goods, services and functions available in the other specialized suburbs and the central core of the metropolis.

The upper- and middle-class tendency to suburbanize received a lift, at the turn of the century, from the British utopian reformer Ebenezer Howard's "Garden City" idea. Howard tried to unite what he perceived to be the positive features of city and village into planned, self-sufficient clusters of small settlements surrounded by permanent green belts limited to agricultural and recreational uses. The idea, and its promotion by the British Garden City Movement, aroused longing for orderly, peaceful small-town living in the restless overworked industrial cities, and inspired innovations in city planning worldwide. In the United States, land developers soon debased the idea to the level of ballyhoo for the sale of lots and homes in "garden city" suburbs.

Lest this imply that mainly subjective class preferences motivated suburbanization, let us recall its objective historical causes. The spatially expanding specialization of production within cities has been the root cause of suburbanization. Filling up cities to capacity, expanding production generated the centrifugal force propelling the migration of industries, people, and commerce beyond city limits to satellite suburbs. The early upperclass suburbs may have heralded the decentralization process and colored it with their class ideology and attitudes, but did not cause it. Only the mass location of production beyond city boundaries in the second half of this century made possible, and historically necessary, mass suburbanization and the growth of modern metropolises. Ten cities had sprouted suburbs by 1900, 13 more by 1910, and fully 60 between 1920 and 1940. The mass production of trucks and automobiles[9] gave added impetus to speculative building along the new highways radiating from every big city (Glaab and Brown, 274–78). Industrial growth, however, during World War II and the Korean and Vietnam Wars, and the families formed by returning veterans have turned suburban expansion into a rampant flood. Over 550 suburbs now cluster around New York City, about 1100 around Chicago, nearly 900 around Philadelphia (Herbers, 3).

Some scholars, and conventional wisdom too, have attributed the phenomenon to a general rise in the standard of living and disposable income. Young families with money to spend, they reasoned, wanted out of the impersonal cities with their rising rents, dangers, poor schools, pollution, and noise. They wanted personal ties with their like in close-knit rural communities, thus creating a demand for small suburbs that the normal operations of the market simply stepped in to fill.

Plausible, but only half true. While most new suburbanites sought cheaper dwellings, better schools, open space, and safer living conditions, it is also true that they moved to suburbs because federal urban policy, having chosen to finance radial highways and subsidize suburban mortgages,[10] created these as the sole alternative to the hardships of city life (Ashton, 68; Checkoway, 168; Smith, 1980, 240). Had it also helped central cities to modernize public transit, build affordable quality housing, improve public schools, provide public-works jobs, and generally improve living standards for all city working people, suburbanization would have proceeded at a more deliberate pace (Edel, 233–34).

Instead, suburbs mushroomed at a phenomenal rate. While the flow of people from country to city continued, cities decentralized into suburbs even faster. By 1950 the suburban population was growing ten times as fast as that of the central cities in total population. The suburbs of the 10 largest cities had 70 percent of all new jobs and 95 percent of all new manufacturing. Almost 75 percent of new industrial plants were suburban (Hoch, 46). In the 1970s the suburban population increased by 12 percent while that of central cities decreased by 4.6 percent; over half of the nation's retail dollars and two-thirds of the housing construction dollars were spent in the suburbs (Beusman and Vidich, 42; Ashton, 65). By the late 1970s and 1980s, the suburbs had considerably reduced their dependence on central cities. Of the total commuters in New England, for example, 61.4 percent moved between suburbs and only 3.4 percent between suburbs and CBDs. Even more significant, 85.8 percent of those who lived in the suburbs also worked there. Some suburbs have developed vast auto-oriented commercial-institutional subcenters; some have giant shopping centers, industrial plants, office towers, hospital complexes, colleges and universities, hotels and theaters, rivaling the original CBDs (Conzen, 98; Mills, 7).

Rapid suburban growth has brought enormous profits to monopoly capital via production, real estate, construction, trade, and financing, but its social costs have been appallingly high. Caught up in the town boom fever, developers have indiscriminately destroyed farms and cleared forests. The sprawl of homes has forced high public investments in excessive networks of roads and utility lines; added to travel distances; multiplied crisscross traffic congestion and accidents, and increased air pollution. Long travel time to work has lowered productivity and morale. Each suburb has had to provide its own water supply, waste disposal, safety and school systems—wastefully duplicating each other's efforts. When the cost was too much, a suburb wound up with low sanitary standards and poor public services (Blumenfeld, 1967, 173).

One urban study compared the cost of a typical suburban low-density development with that of a comparable planned high-density development. The study found that the latter saved 44 percent of total development cost, 43 percent of the land cost, 40 percent of street cost, 63 percent of utility costs, 11 percent of operating and maintenance costs, 50 percent of municipal capital cost, 13 percent of municipal operating cost, 50 percent in auto pollution, 44 percent in energy cosumption, and 35 percent in water consumption. "Sprawl," the study concluded, "is the most expensive form of residential development, in terms of economic costs, environmental costs, natural resource consumption, and many types of personal costs."[11] Other studies have shown that as density increases from 3 to 30 dwellings per acre (as in two-family houses on 30×100 foot lots), auto ownership drops by 35 percent, miles driven per auto declines about 45 percent, and the use of public transportation increases fourfold. To boot, total energy consumption for all purposes—including electricity and heating—declines 20 percent. Greater densities further reduce travel demand and energy use without diminishing returns until they exceed 100 dwellings per acre.[12]

The inevitable consequences of wasteful spontaneous private development began to tarnish and fade the suburban romance. Suburbanites who had hoped for easy access to city and country found themselves ever farther from both. The high cost of running public services in small municipalities raised taxes; or, left many suburbs with poor schools, understaffed hospitals, and recurring water, sewer, and sanitation problems. The population pressures from the central cities ultimately broke through racist restrictions at least to the inner ring of suburbs. However this did not solve the social, economic, and community problems of past unemployment and continued poverty. The romantic ideal got its worst lumps, however, from the dominance of the private automobile—a dominance created by suburbia's irrational land use.

Private auto transportation has served suburbs tolerably well where work places are as dispersed as homes or where many suburbanites working in city CBDs parked their cars at commuter trains and bus stations. But as economic activities multiplied and concentrated in large suburban business centers, traffic congestion increasingly slowed movement. The suburbs' low-density traffic origins and high-density destinations are reaching an impasse. The problem defies solution now, even by public transportation, whose economic operation requires high passenger demand at traffic origins as well as at destinations. The private automobile in suburbia has become a problem hard to live with and impossible to live without.

Travel distances and traffic congestion have raised the cost and time of movement to and from work, stores, services, and social facilities for all in the suburbs, but have stressed working-class households the most. The prevalence of two or more workers in suburban families, each going off to a distant job in a different direction, produced many two- and three-car families. Car-pooling has helped in some cases, but has not solved the high costs and the high toll in time and fatigue. These costs have reduced working class participation in educational, cultural and political activities after the day's work. Workers tend to trim their tight money and time budgets by cutting first the expenditures of energy and funds on cultural and civic pursuits outside the home. Such cutbacks by many thousands of working-class households inevitably sap a community's cultural and political life.

The mass media's bent for dwelling on the lifestyles of the rich and famous fosters the notion that the suburbs are peopled mainly by the upper and middle classes. The suburban working class is seldom seen or heard in the mass media—TV, radio and press. The fact is, however, that since the 1960s more and more of the nation's metropolitan working class have made their homes in the suburbs. By 1985, 37.4 million workers lived in suburbs, up from 28.9 million in 1970; 24.7 million lived in central cities in 1985, down from the 33.2 millions in 1970 (Mills, 7).[13]

Segregation of the suburbs by class partly explains the silent treatment the media has meted out to the suburban working class. The upper and middle classes have effectively shut out working class families from settling in their midst by zoning themselves into high-priced, exclusive developments. Most workers therefore followed industries to adjacent jerry-built suburbs that preserved working-class homogeneity (Walker, 1981, 396; Hoch, 47–48).[14] Class segregation is branded upon the suburban landscape. It is manifest in the showy appearance of affluent suburbs sporting manicured lawns immersed in wooded areas, and the modest, plain working-class communities lying, as often as not, near highways, commercial strips, or industrial sites (Levison, 42). Working-class suburbs, with their mass-produced little homes on small lots and their typical bars, bowling alleys, gas stations and stores, look and feel much like the central city's working-class neighborhoods. Most suburban workers are little better off than their central city cousins.

What higher pay they may earn is lost on the higher housing and transportation costs of suburban living (Hamilton, 163–65).

Moving to a suburb saddled most working-class families with new burdens. Buying a home, a car and new furnishings incurred heavy debts and maintenance costs. It often improved their housing conditions at the price of a lower standard of living. Many had to take on second jobs or trim their expenditures on food, clothing, recreation or other essentials. Working-class wives expend much time driving working husbands to and from work, young ones to and from school, and doing the family shopping by auto.

To move has also forced many to make some moral compromises. To protect, or enhance, the market value of their house, homeowners willynilly have tended to take a wary view of neighborhood changes and support exclusionist municipal measures to guard again "invasion" by people or uses that might lower it. However, moving to suburbs did not otherwise significantly alter the class outlook or behavior of working-class families. Their class kinship and life style remained much the same. They did not go "middle class" as the mass media and many scholars would have them believe (Walker, 1981, 394).

Suburbanization has inflicted political losses, however, upon the working class as a whole. Upperclass pundits have acclaimed suburbanization for having relieved pressures on their master's politically most painful spots. Luring millions of working-class families into home ownership in dispersed suburbs, they gloated, muted their cry for public housing, reinforced their trust in the system, dulled their class consciousness, and weakened their ability to organize and fight.

Admittedly, suburbanization gave the ruling class a political break—it made organizing dispersed workers more difficult. Suburban isolation left working-class families physically and spiritually cut off from the solidarity, mass activities, and progressive ideas that high worker concentrations have tended to generate in the central cities. It left them exposed to unchallenged indoctrination by conservative local politicians, institutions, and the commercial media. What unifying influence the compact central city has had on the several working-class strata is dissipated in the sprawl of small suburbs. Social separation by distance has been pried wider by suburbia's divisive political levers. In the balkanized suburbs, different working-class strata have tended to separate into close-knit exclusive communities, obscuring their common interests with their class as a whole. Their local politics have tended to focus on local concerns—property and taxes—breeding apathy toward the greater regional, national, and world issues.

Suburbia's most divisive influence on the working class, however, has come from its racial segregation. Suburbs are typically all-white municipalities fortified with a panoply of zoning and building laws designed to exclude the poor and non-white. The injection of racist ideology has been a factor in their political behavior throughout their development.

In the 1960s and '70s, racist promotion of suburbs had fundamentally affected population distribution in the then rapidly expanding metropolises. It channelled the flight of 2.5 million urban whites into suburbs in a racist reaction to the migration of 3.1 million rural Black people into cities. Joblessness, underemployment, low wages, wretched housing, and lack of public spending rapidly sank the new arrivals into a cycle of poverty and its inevitable byproducts.

Racist prejudice exaggerated the fears of suburbanites over real estate values and community harmony. The politically autonomous suburbs adopted rigorous covenants and zoning laws precluding construction of apartment and low-cost housing, hence settlement by racial minority families (Hock, 47; Blumenfeld, 1967, 172).

Nor was the exclusion of Black families limited to white suburbanizers. The federal government has aided and abetted the practice. The Federal Housing Administration (FHA) had, for a time, enforced a racially restrictive covenant as a condition for obtaining FHA insurance even in areas where racism had little appeal. Suburban developers soon used its racist phrases to promote their "homogenous" suburbs, free from "adverse influence," "inharmonious social groups" and "incompatible social elements" (Abrams, 1955, 234–37). Vigorous public protests eventually eliminated the covenants, but the damage was done. In one suburb after another, 1970 census figures showed only *.01 to .10 of one percent* of non-white inhabitants (*New York Times*, August 15, 1971).

19. Metropolitanization of the South and Southwest

Perhaps the most salient economic and social development of the state-monopoly stage has been the rapid industrial and urban growth of the South and Southwest, the Sunbelt, precipitating great changes in its economic geography. For over half of the 20th century, the bulk of industrial production poured from the Northeast and Midwest, the Snowbelt. On the eve of World War II, nearly 75 percent of the nation's manufacturing jobs were located there. Since the war, the old gaps between regions have considerably narrowed. By 1984 the South led the nation in the share of manufacturing jobs, with 30.9 percent to the Northeast's 24.3 percent, the North Central region's 28.6 percent, and the West's 16.2 percent. Gradually, the economic profiles of all regions have come to resemble each other (Hicks, 120–22). This added enormous productive forces to the nation's economy and huge increases in its gross national product. No less significant, however, have been its socio political effects. It thrust new rural masses into the working class and extended the struggle for political progress to regions of the country long dominated by political reaction.

The South's seemingly meteoric economic growth was, of course, not a sudden phenomenon. Its antecedents go back to the post-Civil War years. The mainly rural postbellum South, dependent on the industrializing North, supplied the latter with raw materials and labor and relied on it for capital, technology and most industrial goods. But at the same time the South's merchant capitalists gradually industrialized and urbanized their region. Almost every important Southern city had been established by 1900. By 1940 each had developed in size and interaction with sister cities enough to assume and profit handsomely from the war tasks assigned to their regions (Brownell and Goldfield, 123–29).

The South's cities burst forth during and after World War II thanks to the massive infusion of federal funds to expand industrial and urban infrastructures. Its temperate climate, vast open spaces, extensive coastline, and abundant cheap labor made the South an ideal location for war production and the staging of military forces. Huge subsidies continued to swell its economic power, hence urban expansion, during the '50s and '60s Korean and Vietnam wars. Its cities grew to five, eight and ten times their prewar sizes—faster than any city ever grew before (Sale, 166,170).

Like bears drawn to honey, monopoly corporations swarmed to feed on the profit bonanza. Capital investment in the South's industries tripled in the '60s; the number of workers increased from 2.4 million in 1950 to 4.4 million in 1972. Service activities also expanded as corporate offices, tourism, and retirement settlements increased urban populations at an annual average of 650,000 newcomers. Within 30 years, the region's population rose from 40 to 80 million (Haas, 174; Sale, 166–67).

While heavy capital investments boomed the Sunbelt economy, heavy disinvestment slowed the Snowbelt. Between 1967 and 1972, the Snowbelt metropolises lost from 14 to 18 percent of their jobs in industry and commerce while the Sunbelt cities had gained 60 to 100 percent. Corresponding population shifts followed. Five of the Sunbelt's metropolises swelled in population to be among the country's top ten (Smith, 1980, 239; Perry and Watkins, 1977, 291–92).

Among the reasons given to explain the seemingly irrepressible southward movement of population and capital, the lure of mild climate and the South's low wage and business costs have been cited the most. These and a complex of other interacting causes have contributed, to be sure, to changing the South from an exporter of people before the 1950s to a powerful population magnet since the 1960s. The underlying cause that set all others in motion, however, has been the shift, since World War II, in the geographic location of maximum profit opportunities. Before World War II, the country's Snowbelt regions with their excellent ports, railroads, inland waterways, and large markets contained the most profitable locations. Since WWII, however, the government has subsidized aerospace and military industries and the rapid application of new technology.

This has fueled a highly profitable economy in the South—luring capital investment from the unionized Snowbelt to the largely unorganized Sunbelt.

The North-to-South capital shift doubled employment in the Sunbelt between 1960 and 1985, and made Miami, Houston, Dallas, Los Angeles, Atlanta and other Sunbelt cities dynamic economic and social centers of national and world fame. The shift of capital investment mainly explains the ups and downs between Sunbelt and Snowbelt cities (Kasarda, 4–5; Hill, 1977, 214,214).

The foremost opportunity the Sunbelt presented to monopoly capital was, of course, the bountiful federal subsidies for building new industrial plants in its regions and the infrastructure of modern utilities and transportation necessary for their operation and access to national and world supplies and markets. The Sunbelt also had large pools of cheap labor reserves available in the moribund countryside around its cities. What's more, its low cost was assured by "right-to-work" state laws banning closed shops. Added to this, tight-fisted municipal budgets in southern states kept Sunbelt local taxes relatively low. To top it all off, open land was abundant and cheap. These advantages presented capitalists with get-richer-quick opportunities they could not resist.

Sunbelt cities had other advantages for investing capitalists. First, having grown late in the automobile age, they avoided the high concentration the Snowbelt cities endured in their early years of poor urban transport. No crowded factory and working-class districts preempted their downtowns. Production and housing were already scattered over their metropolitan areas in a low-density pattern well suited to modern industrial development (Brownell and Goldfield, 134). Secondly, they permitted easier application of modern technology to production and commerce than did the Snowbelt cities. Modern technology moved away from the use of coal, iron and steel to oil, gas, aluminum and titanium—the natural resources of the South.[15] It also reduced reliance on railroads and favored greater use of the air and highway routes better developed in the Sunbelt. In agriculture, too, new technology has favored the large-scale corporate farming that the South's plentiful arable land and long growing season made possible (Sale,166–67). Lastly, city government in the South was simpler and more tractable than in the North. Compared to the complex profusion of governments in Snowbelt metropolises, government in Sunbelt metropolises was much more compliant. Sunbelt metropolises found little resistance to annexation after World War II. San Antonio, Atlanta and Norfolk, for example, greatly increased their areas and population between 1950 and 1960 by annexing neighboring settlements lying in the path of their growth (Abbott, 50–51).

Southern capitalists getting rich in the onrushing tide of capital investment regarded growing metropolises as models of profit-bearing progress. Unlike their northern counterparts who turned their suburbs into inviolable enclaves, southern capitalists looked at suburbs and towns as mere outposts of growing metropolises. They aided metropolitan expansion and government by promoting construction of civic centers, office buildings, highways, hotels, docks, airports and other facilities to strengthen the infrastructure of central cities and their dominance over metropolitan development and politics (Brownell and Goldfield, 143–44; Abbott, 121–22).

All this was true in the initial years of the south's rapid urbanization. As its cities matured, however, they developed the typical contradictions and problems of those in the North. Since 1970, its central cities have steadily lost populations and influence over metropolitan economic and political life. The emergence of politically influential and economically versatile suburbs increased resistance to annexation and to central-city proposals for metropolitan government. Growing poor populations and revenue losses sapped the finances of many central cities. As in the North, decentralization has destabilized not only the central cities but also the inner ring of older suburbs; both have suffered physical and social decay (Abbott, 54, 96–97). The more the Sunbelt's monopoly-capitalist economy resembles the Snowbelt's, the more it develops symptoms of urban decline.

20. Social Classes, and Class Attitudes to Cities

Throughout the 20th century, the nation's urban population grew rapidly. In 1985, its 281 metropolitan areas counted 182.5 million people, or 76 percent of the total—238.7 million—to put the United States among the top urbanized and metropolitanized countries in the world (Statistical Abstracts of the United States).

Changes in production and production relations significantly changed the size and composition of urban social classes. With heightened concentration of capital, the capitalist class grew proportionately smaller and more sophisticated in organization and politics. With improving technology and increasing volume and diversity in production, the working class grew bigger and more versatile in skills and occupations. And the middle class turned into a motley of disparate and unstable middle strata.

These changes in the size and nature of social classes are pertinent to comprehending their present and potential influence on urban political life. Available population statistics, however, obscure them. The U.S. Census population data, in fact, veil the class composition of the population. The Census Bureau lumps all gainfully employed persons under the general category of "labor force," mixing workers with proprietors, janitors with superintendents, farmers with managers and executives. Adding to the difficulty, it does not report variations within occupations. Within the middle class, for example, marginal entrepreneurs differ little in lifestyle from wage workers; some intellectuals belong to the working class, others to the middle class, and some workers are also small entrepreneurs crossing into the middle class. Exact figures, though desirable, are not essential to deriving the relative numerical strength of the social classes; sufficiently instructive rough figures can be extrapolated from official statistics by approximation.

The capitalist class. Concentration of capital had reduced the U.S. capitalist class from 23 percent in 1910 to 16 percent in 1950. By the 1960s, capital concentration reached a new high and the size of the upperclass dropped to a new low—one percent of the country's property owners held 59 percent of its capital.[16] In 1970, the size of the capitalist class stood at about four percent of the population.[17] And in 1986, the Joint Economic Committee of Congress report, *The Concentration of Wealth in the United States*, stated that the top one half-of-one percent (.005) of U.S. families owned over 45 percent of the privately held wealth.

The middle class. The middle class has been shrinking in economic and political importance. Relatively few of its members own sizable means of production or hire large numbers of workers. Concentration of capital in production, commerce, and agriculture has continually narrowed their opportunities and doomed them to an uncertain existence. Yet despite their heavy attrition, small businesses continue to exist in various branches of the urban economy; new thousands appear while other thousands go under. First, urban population growth adds new small stores and service shops because the chain-store corporations find it unprofitable to open branches in all neighborhoods. Second, technological progress opens new opportunities for small auxiliary enterprises in manufacturing, supply, distribution and maintenance because big capital finds it more profitable to use small entrepreneurs than to set up its own auxiliary branches. Third, from the pools of urban unemployed, some turn to eking out a living in petty, precarious, marginal businesses and services.

Perhaps because some of the intelligentsia are independent practitioners who earn medium incomes, the salaried and self-employed professionals as well as the administrative personnel in government and industry have often been called "the new middle class." But only a minority of this group are private employers of labor on any significant scale (Perlo, 1961, 57–64). In the pre-monopoly stage of capitalism, the intelligentsia were mainly members of the professions who sold various services or goods in the form of knowledge, ideas, scientific and technical innovations, books or drawings. In this sense it was a petty capitalist or middle class. In the state-monopoly stage, however, most of the intelligentsia have been transformed into wage or salary workers. They stem from and serve different classes and groups in society, for each social class or group creates its own intelligentsia to articulate its special interests. Most of today's intelligentsia either stand between the two classes, or draw close to or are part of the working class. They constitute a social stratum of whom many are engaged in production, management, and administration. Some serve in positions of command and are close to the capitalist class, but most are merely highly skilled hired wage earners, subject to the same subordination, routine activity and firing as other workers, from whom they differ only in their higher levels of pay (Nadel, 245–87).

Together these widely diverse social groups—the medium, small and marginal entrepreneurs in production, trade, agriculture, and the professions—hardly form a homogeneous social class. Rather, they are a disparate collection of middle strata at intermediate positions between the capitalist and working class. They are the least stable group in the population, tending to sway from one interest to another in economics and politics, and from one inclination to another in religious, artistic and ethical views (Nadel, 225–26). Nadel estimated their total number at about 19 percent of the 1970 labor force, or approximately 23 percent of the 1970 population.[18]

The working class. In a nation thriving mainly on industrial production and living mostly in cities, the working class naturally includes the majority of the population.

How large a majority?

Ironically, our information-glutted society denies this question a plain answer. Bourgeois social scientists have kept it confused in an endless dispute over who does and who does not belong to the working class. Indeed, some have questioned its very existence, using all manner of specious argument to prove that the working class is, in fact, going middle class.

Indisputably, the "blue collar" workers are working class. Bourgeois scholars like to limit its size right there. But even by this narrow definition, blue collars were estimated at 60 percent of the 1970 population (Levison, 26–29). The dispute centers on the "white collar" workers employed in offices and services, many of them in activities not directly related to the production of goods. This mass of workers is often labeled "middle class" and their rising number is cited as proof that the working class is merging into a "middle class society."

Such confusion aside, the classic definition of "working class" is open and clear. The working class embraces all those in society who are compelled to earn their living by selling their labor power (their ability to work) for wages or salaries (Green, 1976, 18–19). Clerks, teachers, or technicians; waiters, sales clerks, or letter carriers—are workers—members of a distinct class of sellers of labor power, manual or mental, and have common class interests arising from that social fact. The different work tasks and work places, or higher or lower pay, do not change the basic class contradiction between them and their employers. Indeed, whether in office or shop, the production relations between workers and employers— exploitation and poorest possible working and living conditions— have changed little over the decades or gotten worse. Furthermore, skill levels of most white collar workers are comparable to those of blue collar workers. Although technological progress has generally upped the level of mental work in both office and shop, most white collar workers perform low- and semi-skilled clerical or technical tasks, and many skilled tasks are soon deskilled through specialization, standardization and mechanization in the office as well as the factory (Green, 1976, 18–21; Walker and Goldberg, 20).

In state monopoly capitalism, the working class has grown larger and more stratified. Heightened labor exploitation, technological progress, and advances in management and marketing techniques have raised labor productivity effecting decreases in manufacturing and increases in clerical and service jobs. In fact, the number of office and service jobs surpassed factory jobs in 1960 and have increased since. For every worker on a factory floor, expanding administration and advancing technology have been putting more workers on office floors to process information, design, coordinate production in related plants, and promote nationwide and worldwide sale and distribution of goods and services. The same processes have been forcing more of the middle class into the working class. Between 1947 and 1974, for example, the number of self-employed in the United States dropped from 19 percent to 9 percent, raising the number of wage and salary employees to about 90 percent of the labor force (Green,1976,17).

Deducting from the census labor-force figures the high-salaried managers, executives and professinals, who properly belong in the capitalist and middle classes, Nadel estimated the working class at 78 percent of the labor force in 1970, or about 73 percent of the nation[19] (Nadel, 94). Perlo thought it reached 85 percent of the labor force in 1986 (Perlo, 1986).

Whatever the exact figures may be, both statistics and pragmatic experience testify that the working class comprises the overwhelming majority of the nation.

Understandably, the attitudes of classes and their members toward cities have differed as their experiences in them have differed. Generally, however, the capitalist and middle classes have had negative views of the city from the outset. Thomas Jefferson, the ideological champion of early agrarian-mercantile capitalism, thought that "cities were ulcers on the body politic" (Schlesinger, 1969, 88).

From its early years on, most of capitalism's ideologues—its novelists, philosophers, journalists, clergymen, social scientists, and politicians—had forebodings about society's development through the city. They conjured up anticity horrors and spun nostalgic images of village and small town life, and advocated abandoning the big city for a life in the countryside lest the "artificial, unnatural" city lead humanity to disaster. This "solution" emerges anew each time capitalism's contradictions sharpen in the cities. Its ideologues rise to "explain" each new crisis as a problem inherent in "urban civilization." Bourgeois urban sociology often led in lamenting the loss of the "natural" small-community life of the village or small town and justifying escape from the "alienating and disorderly" big city to the "friendly community life of human-scale suburbs." Anticity prejudices of the propertied classes were thus widely publicized, creating an ideological atmosphere in which flight from the cities and heavy federal spending in suburban development were generally accepted to be good and wise (Ianitskii, 1975, 227–28, 241–44, 292–93).

In city planning, utopian proposals emerged advocating the ultimate liquidation of big cities by gradual dispersal of their populations into small low-density settlements. Appalled by the squalor and sickliness of England's industrial cities at the turn of the century, Ebenezer Howard proposed a new method of human settlement.[20] Basing his idea on those of the Utopian Socialists and the land-reform and anarchist idealists of his time, he sought to combine the healthfulness of the country with the cultural, technical and political progress of the city.

Howard proposed to "decant" the population of big cities by resettlement in economically, socially and culturally self-sufficient small garden cities of about 30,000. Separated by inviolate agricultural greenbelts, clusters of garden cities would surround a core city, linked with each other by roads and railroads, to form a polynucleated metropolis. The people in these garden cities would live in small buildings, amid parks and gardens, within walking distances of work places and social facilities. Population growth within the garden-city clusters would be "decanted" into new garden cities planned and built on public land. Although he advocated the fusion of rural and urban life, Howard emphasized agriculture. He saw the long-range solution to the ills of industrial capitalism as returning city people to the land.

By 1915, when the British biologist and sociologist Patrick Gedess proposed his Regionalist ideas, the change from city to metropolis was more apparent. Assuming that an "organic" relationship existed between city, country, and industrial areas, Gedess thought that society needed a "civic efficiency" to raise "industrial civilization" to a higher level. He envisioned a technically advanced civilization living in greened cities and suburbs, whose peaceful evolution would be assured through cooperation between cities and countrysides within coordinated regions.[21] Gedess inspired a group of American intellectuals to form a Regionalist movement. Criticizing the decadence of capitalist cities, the Regionalists advocated a sane and noble urban life but had only vague notions on how to achieve it. Like Gedess, they glorified the small town, the neighborhood community, and rural life. Although they actively promoted city reforms, they saw the ultimate solution to the city's problem in its dismemberment and dispersal.

While the Regionalists offered a vague anti-city region, Frank Lloyd Wright's utopia had no territorial limits at all.[22] His Broadacre City would stretch endlessly along great superhighways linking a dispersed society and economy. It would be everywhere and nowhere—the ultimate anticity to end all cities. The eminent architect equated big cities with capitalism and damned both. The big cities, he thought, are the commercial artifacts of capitalist society's dehumanizing sham culture. Capitalism and its cities should be reformed by reviving Jeffersonian democracy and gradually returning city people to the land in a new agrarian civilization. Modern technology, Wright thought, made big cities absolete because it made possible diffusing city functions over the countryside. In his utopian agro-industrial Broadacre City, the people would live noble and creative lives on well designed, private one acre homesteads producing some of their food on small family farms, working at arts and crafts in their own small shops and studios, practicing various professions, or selling their labor to factories and offices scattered among residential and farm areas close to highway intersections.

After World War II, anticity views took on a quasi-rational tone. They moved away from the transparently fallacious utopian proposals to claim attention in social science debates.

Trying to reveal postwar social trends, bourgeois sociologists of the 1960s examined the nation's economic and settlement processes. In accord with technocratic tendencies prevailing at the time, they developed the idea that, in the era of the science-technology revolution (STR), advanced capitalist society stood at the threshold of a "post-urban century"; that urbanization had become a process "beyond the limits of cities"; and that the remaining decades of the twentieth century will see the final phase of urbanization in the United States (Walker and Goldberg, 18).[23] The United States, they thought, was becoming ever less dependent on cities because rapid progress in science and technology and integration of social processes swiftly diminished past restrictions of distance and space. Agriculture and services are industrializing, urban and rural settlements and lifestyles are fusing, and the mass media and modern transportation are reaching out everywhere. Thus, the STR is the absolute shaping force in the "post-industrial society," and its scientific-technical-managerial intelligentsia—the "new middle class"—has become society's leading force (Ianitskii, 1975, 101–14, 116–17).[24] All this led to the conclusion that the social problems of today's cities are not symptoms of social or urban crises but the difficulties attending the transition to an emerging "exterritorial society."

In practice, this theory justified city government "shrinkage" policies against the racially oppressed, the unemployed, the low paid, and the disabled inhabiting city slums. Since the big cities are fated to die, all city government can do is make their declining years as painless as possible on the city budget. Therefore, let the "normal" depopulation of cities be speeded by prodding their "unemployables" to leave. Let schools, health care, security and other social facilities serving the slums be razed. Destroy the infrastructural supports for people's continued residence in the cities or possible return (Delgado, 9).[25] Disinvestment in low-rent housing, plus gentrification, were deemed positive phenomena since the "post-industrial age" needs few unskilled workers. Professionals and technicians can work the "information" economy of the "post-industrial city."

Related in content, if different in method, are the environmentalist reformers' "livable city" ideas aimed to move the city toward its "predestined post-industrial future" through "harmonious" change by means of "enlightened city planning." They urge improved public transportation, parks, street landscaping, pedestrian amenities, pollution and noise controls, improved urban design, and a public policy of stricter controls over corporate and business activity in cities. In practice, however, "livable city"-inspired projects have created gentrified enclaves of daintily landscaped stylish town houses around high-priced "shoppes" and exotic restaurants on chic shopping streets for upper- and middle-class city populations (Walker and Goldberg, 17).

Significantly, the anti-city utopians, sociologists and environmentalists emerged from the middle class and enjoyed wide support and publicity from upperclass controlled universities and media. The collaboration may be explained by two related facts: 1) Anticity ideas promoted the investment and metropolitan political interests of the two suburb-bound classes; 2) for both classes, the city's potential as a center of multiracial working-class political power always evoked apprehension and ill will.

Anticity attitudes have grown also among some strata of the working class. Among some, due to mass media ideological influence; among others, from the village or small town origins of new recruits to their ranks. Rural immigrants bring their small-community cultures with them. Anticity attitudes tend to arise when city environments assault their traditional lifestyles or access to jobs. But there is no evidence whatever that the working-class millions still living in cities harbor anticity attitudes. As a rule, the longer a working class family lives in the city, the more its consciousness is freed from the limits of small town culture and the higher its civic awareness (Ianitskii, 1975, 264–66).

21. City Government and Services

City governments are integral, if indirect, parts of the national State, although they are directly subordinate to the governments of "states" governing its fifty parts. Frederick Engels defined most roundly, perhaps, the function of the State in a class society. He wrote:

> "In order that classes with conflicting interests may not consume themselves and society in sterile struggles, a power apparently standing above society became necessary, whose purpose is to moderate the conflict and keep it within the bounds of 'order'; and this power arising out of society, but placing itself above, and increasingly separating itself from it, is the state" (Engels, 1942, 155).

In our society the State exercizes that power "to organize the various strata of the ruling class and disorganize the working class in order to insure the continuance of the capitalist system by domination of the latter by the former" (Harloe, 7).

In most countries, regional and local governments are directly subordinate to the national State. Its unity is therefore clear. In the USA it is obscured by the historically shaped federal form and the political exigencies that arose in the process of welding separate "states" into one nation. The federal, state and local governments are therefore commonly perceived in their division rather than in their unity (Markusen, 93). But the unity of the State is manifest in the state and local governments' faithful execution of its objectives, namely, aiding private wealth accumulation and using the power of the State against challenges from the exploited class within their jurisdictions (Hill, 1978, 215–16).

Historically, our federal system was limited to the national and state governments. City governments, subordinates in their respective states, had no standing in federal constitutional law and no direct relation with the federal government. They were expected to support themselves with local revenues or, failing that, to seek help from their states. The New Deal policies of the 1930s changed this. Heavy federal aid to cities in crisis established direct relations between the federal and city governments, making the latter, in effect, a third level of government in the federal system (Goodman, 78–79). The ties between city and state governments loosened, especially in the course of rapid metropolitanization since World War II. Laden with outmoded constitutions and conservative anticity legislatures, and lacking funds, the states haven't been willing or able to evolve bold programs to cope with the social and economic problems of metropolitan development.[26]

Federal aid came to the cities through national housing, highway, public works and welfare programs enabling monopoly capital to realize profitable central city land-use changes by speeding the outward movement of industries and razing working-class neighborhoods for high income housing and expanded CBDs. However, these were ad hoc programs. At no time did the federal government adopt an overall urban policy. It sporadically sallied into metropolitan areas to disburse federal funds in the "public interest" leaving the "details" to officials and politicians in and around municipal governments.

Objectively, the shift from state to federal predominance over cities reflected the increasing political power of monopoly capital. The accelerated concentration of capital in the last 40 years has also produced centralized government. As monopoly corporations extended their operations, they shifted their main political weight to higher levels of government. Monopoly capital sought to shorten the administrative distance between nationally concentrated pools of public funds and the metropolises where their investments yielded high profits. Major urban economic initiatives were increasingly taken in Washington and implemented by monopoly-controlled politicians in the metropolis regions.

Thus city governments, still de jure "children" of their states, have become de facto junior partners within the federal system. With all their variety in form, they bear the features of the monopoly capitalist State in their two chief functions: promoting economic processes for wealth accumulations, and integrating the city's people into these processes. They must first provide and regulate the opportunities and infrastructures for profitable activities and then reproduce and control the labor force and its demands. But in big cities, an organized working class and oppressed social groups have often made profit promotion at the expense of the people quite difficult. City governments have therefore come to comprise two kinds of agencies: municipal and supramunicipal.

The municipal agencies (or line departments) have been limited in power and confined to issues steering clear of profit promoting functions. They allow for some democratic participation to appease (or coopt) opposition. But they channel representation, patronage and public services discriminately to neighborhoods and social groups, thus inciting rivalry, dividing and diverting the people from developing a political unity that might threaten the chief function of promoting wealth accumulation (Friedland et al, 1977, 449–62). Here, too, racism is an obvious tool. At times, powerful challenges by the people force city governments to grant reforms. Concessions granted from time to time have produced the untidy layers of seemingly contradictory bureaus within city departments—the fossilized legal remains of past political battles (Fincher,26–30).

The supramunicipal agencies comprise special authorities and quasi-public development corporations, insulated from the political process and democratic intervention, and empowered to autonomously promote and finance profit-generating ventures. Monopoly corporations usually dominate these agencies—the New York Port Authority, for example, or the Bay Area Rapid Transit District in California—staff them with corporate personnel, and control their internal structures, policies, and operations. Through these agencies they acquire land and build public works at costs inflated by subcontract padding, payoffs and kickbacks. Corporate agents also swarm around projects of the municipal line departments, pressing them to favor monopoly interests and slacken control over prices for the products they buy (Friedland et al, 1977, 463–64; O'Connor, 87).

Corporations also bend city governments to their will through their influence in state governments and the network of state and federal regulatory agencies. They surreptitiously intrude into city, state and national politics—causing most high government positions to be filled with officials beholden to them or the kind who respond to bribes and campaign contributions (Etzkowitz and Mack, 48; Sawers, 7). Thus city government has evolved into a political structure of agencies and programs shaped by ruling elites to serve mainly their own interests (Friedland et al, 1977, 461).

Monopoly capital has cast the legal and administrative framework of city government so as to weaken effective democracy and safeguard its rule. It has granted even the smallest concessions to the people only after long struggle and reduced or withdrawn them when opposition abated. The ruling class and the State have dominated by using ideological means via the mass media, the educational system, and pronouncements of influential leaders (Miliband, 266; Harring, 14).

Deluding the people with token democracy and beguiling symbols, monopoly capital has fostered the illusion that elected representatives run city government when, in fact, important proposals affecting the public welfare have generally been drafted in corporate board rooms, negotiated among agents of leading capitalist groups, and brought to city council chambers mainly for formal debate and enactment. Whenever the big corporations, the chambers of commerce and the mass media moguls have agreed, they have normally come to run city government their own way (Adrian and Press, 181).

How well a city government responds to the needs of the ruling and ruled classes within its jurisdiction depends principally on its financial condition and revenue flow. In most capitalist countries, city governments get the bulk of their income automatically from a share of national government revenues and partly from local real estate taxes and some profitable economic enterprises. In the Netherlands, for example, cities routinely draw 89 percent of their income from the national government. In other countries, city governments draw profits from city-owned public utilities and even from industrial and commercial enterprises. Our city governments, however, have to beg the state and national governments, who preempted most avenues of taxation, to help finance almost everything they do (Blumenfeld,1970,96). Our cities collected only three percent of all taxes raised in 1983 while the state governments took 30 percent and the federal government 58 percent.[27] Nor can most cities engage in profit-making enterprises—a source of revenue closed to them by state constitutions.

Yet cities bear the brunt of the national subsidies to corporate profit-making, as well as the task of reproducing the nation's labor force. City fiscal resources have therefore been perpetually strained, especially after the heavy revenue losses suffered in the wake of the outward flight of industries and high-income residents and the federal cutbacks in city aid in the 1980s.

Getting only meager state and federal funding, many city governments have been driven to borrow heavily from banks at high interest rates. Their heavy debts invariably subjected them to their creditors' demands for austerity and fiscal controls that infringed on the rights of the people. Cities were forced to raise taxes and cut back on infrastructure maintenance and vital city services, pitting taxpayers against labor unions, and working-class communities against one another (Hill, 1978, 218–22).

Given the taxation, borrowing, and financial aid limits to which many states subject their cities, gaps develop between a city's revenues intake and expenditures. Since such gaps, or fiscal crises, occur at different times in different cities, our national system of cities usually functions like a sputtering pump.

A city fiscal crisis is a grave matter, for it leads to drastic cuts in services essential to the health and welfare of its people and its economic function. In an advanced industrial society, life and production depend on a complex social organization of specialized labor. Specialized workers and their families depend totally on other workers specialized in providing food, water, energy, sanitation, transportation, education, communication, traffic control, safety, medical and nursing care, recreation, and the myriad other services essential to a modern city's daily life and generation of wealth. To function at its best, a modern city requires, daily, a high level of high-quality public services.

Most of such services are (or should be) provided by the city government. It is responsible for intricate systems of water supply, drainage, sanitation, transportation, energy and communication. It enacts and enforces zoning and building codes, provides industrial parks, and aids urban redevelopment. And it maintains and reproduces the labor force by subsidizing low-income housing, controlling rents, and providing public education, health care, and recreation (Friedland et al, 1977, 451).

City services have expanded along with the growth of the capitalist economy. The more complex and specialized the economy becomes, the more its profitability depends on city services and public regulation of its involved, often conflicting, private activities. The public sector of the economy has become indispensable to the profitable growth of the private sector. Expansion in one has invariably generated expansion in the other (O'Connor, 8–9). Modern technological advances have especially tended to increase the dependence of the private sector on the increasingly complex city infrastructure and services, the cost of which has necessarily risen. The cost of welfare services has increased the most, for as technology raised the productivity of labor, it increased unemployment. Millions of permanently unemployed or underemployed in cities are therefore dependent on public support for survival. City governments have had to provide minimal support to guard the safety of the private sector and the legitimacy of the State (Hill, 1978, 216–17).

Although city services are essential to the life and function of all classes in the city, they are most vital to the working class. Like wages or salaries, they are a form of social wealth distribution. Real family income rises where services are adequate; it drops where they are not. Similarly higher city taxes or service fees reduce family income no less than when the prices of food, clothing or shelter go up. In either case earnings at the point of production are lost at the point of consumption. Reduced city services or cost increases hit low-income families especially hard. Inadequate city services in low-income districts—particularly in health, transportation and education—reduce their residents' access to better jobs, better homes, and a higher standard of life (Miller and Roby, 84–85; Lineabarry, 1977, 4–5).

The distribution of city services has tended to be class and race biased. Upperclass and well-off business and residential districts have gotten the best and the most, those of the working class—the worst and the least. The humdrum appearance of old building fronts where the working class lives is doubly depressing on ill-maintained streets. City Halls regard upperclass districts as important, superior and deserving; and often show contempt for those of the working class as common, inferior and undeserving (Rich, 203).

In recent decades, increased needs, lowered revenues, and federal cutbacks in aid have forced city governments to cut city services and maintenance. Breakdowns in services and infrastructures have become common. That bodes ill for the future, for as the city services and infrastructures deteriorate, so must the profits of capitalist enterprises dependent on them (Friedland, 1981, 370–72).

Conservative city officials—alleging that "free market" competition could provide services cheaper and better—have advocated contracting out city services to private companies. Experience has shown this idea to be unsound. Studies prove that practice varies little between public and private management, and that contracting out does not always lead to competition. It often bogs down in collusion and monopoly practices. Furthermore, contracting out does not save money; indeed, it often costs more. Cost analyses arguing for privatization usually ignore the city costs of monitoring and enforcing private performance and the costs of the back-up capacity a city must maintain should contractors fail to perform, as they often do. The main difference in cost between city departments and private contractors were the lower workers' fringe benefits in private companies—supporting the fear that privatization aims to solve city government fiscal problems by cutting the wages and breaking the unions of city workers (DeLaat, 187–93).

In the suburbs, municipal services vary with the wealth of the suburb. Upperclass suburbs easily manage the cost of good services; middle-income suburbs provide lesser services with some difficulty; and most working-class suburbs can barely pay for the least and the poorest (Woodruff, 45). Most suburbs, in fact, could not afford to provide a public water supply or drainage system within their small areas with their limited funds. Therefore, they have been forced to accept a complex, inefficient network of overlapping ad-hoc district authorities empowered to perform specific trans-suburban functions such as building and operating a water, sewer, or road system. Their governing boards are appointed by state governments or by officials of suburban governments, or may be elected by the local voters. Once empowered, however, they become largely unaccountable to the people. In 1982, almost 28,600 such ad-hoc district governments ruled within the nation's metropolitan areas, considerably reducing the democratic powers of the people within their 38,900 suburbs (Hays, 1982, 254; S.A., 1986, 262).

Fragmented government in metropolitan areas suits the upperclass well, for its loosened democratic controls make corporate manipulation of politicians and officials much easier than in cities (Walker, 1981, 388, 397). Since the 1950s, monopoly capital has gradually pervaded the growing suburban economy. Through a sequence of mergers and takeovers, it managed to absorb the largest land and building corporations to become the dominant force in suburban real estate and construction, as well as industry and commerce (Gertler, 36–39).

Not all upperclass strata, however, benefited from suburban government fragmentation. Some who did not have proposed a metropolitan form of government. The proposals came chiefly from CBD corporate leaders who want to reduce the complexity and cost of doing business across many municipal boundaries within the developing metropolis (Bollens and Schmandt, 1975, 322). But the lure of great profits that the inefficient, fragmented suburban governments presented to monopoly capital in the short run has proved stronger than the prospect of greater profits an efficient metropolitan government might offer in the long run. Although monopoly capital overruled the idea, those who expected to benefit from metropolitan government kept the proposal alive. They even succeeded in centralizing government in some metropolises. In 1959 for example, Miami's Dade County united its 27 municipalities under a single government to which the member municipalities ceded some of their powers. The growing economic and social complexity of suburbia tends to cancel the advantages of fragmented government, even to the strata of monopoly capital whom it profited. The tangled mass of laws, rules, and bureaucracies complicates management in the growing megacorporation for whom even national, let alone suburban, boundaries have become absolute. Metropolitan government that would streamline and maximize profits in the metropolitan market remains an option monopoly capital has by no means ruled out forever.

Should it choose to push the proposal in earnest, it is likely to meet opposition from the suburbs, organized labor, and the Black and Latino communities. Most suburbs have jealously guarded the home rule that enabled escape from the central city's social costs, yet retained access to its economic and cultural benefits. They have consistently opposed metropolitan government for fear of losing this advantage. They could form a formidable bloc and use their preponderant political power in state legislatures to defeat it (Hays,1982,257). Nor is it likely to get support from organized labor because it would tend to restructure labor's hard won political arrangements and coalitions and create serious obstacles to its political action. A metropolitan government would add one more layer of untractable bureaucracy. Finally, the Black community and racial minorities see in metropolitan government proposals attempts to unite the white electorates of the metropolis to thwart their hard-won political gains in the central city (Bollens and Schmaudt, 321; Smith, 1979, 272–73).

Rigorous efficiency is seldom desired in capitalist governments. Indeed, a loose, even if costly, governmental arrangement seems to better suit its warring groups precisely because it is indecisive, inefficient and flexible.

Ruth Gikow

22. City Politics

Throughout the state monopoly capitalist stage, the State has served mainly the interests of the ruling class. That class, however, has not always been of one mind. It has often split into factional divisions over conflicting interests and how to keep contending social forces in line. The State, then, although the domain of the ruling class, has been also an arena of political struggle between class factions and of class politics (Harloe, 7; Parenti, 1984, 14).

At times, politics have led to seemingly strange bedfellows reflecting temporarily coinciding interests peculiar to specific political developments. Politics, then, are specific to a given set of changing class and class-faction relations and must be studied afresh in the context of each time and place. Within this political complexity, however, the class factions have always shared basic economic-political interests expressed in the overall politics of that class.

In our nationally integrated political economy, class interests and conflicts in cities have been at once national and local in scope, calling forth politics both national and local in nature. In the late 1980s, for example, the national issues of peace and international trade have affected the capitalist and working classes differently. The needs and political strategies of one have tended to extend the exploitation of labor, resources and markets within and beyond the nation's borders; that of the other—to preserve peace, provide jobs, and raise living standards everywhere. These opposite national interests have collided in the politics of the respective classes in each city. Conversely, city issues like housing, health, education and jobs, arising in the politics of all cities, have become national political issues. But then there are purely local class issues fought out in only

142

local class politics. The funding or location of schools, hospitals, or other public facilities, for example, affect the lives of local people of different classes and groups differently, leading to corresponding purely local class struggles and politics. This is analogous to national unions leading labor's struggles on national issues, and city or county union councils and locals dealing with issues on the level of city and shop.

American labor's titanic struggles in defense of its economic interests have inevitably drawn the trade unions into national and local politics. But organized labor has marshalled its forces mainly on economic issues, fighting in the political arena haphazardly, with less vigor and insight and less success. Moreover because labor lacks its own political party, monopoly capital can more freely erode at the point of consumption what labor unions have won at the point of production. Raised wages are whittled down by raised prices and taxes and less services.

The political landscape changed radically when strong labor activity in the 1930s, led by the CIO, forced from the ruling class unprecedented concessions. The introduction of social security, unemployment insurance, public housing, public works, and the wage-and-hour law, and the distribution of some of these benefits through city governments, greatly increased the influence of the people in national and city politics. More representatives of the working and lower middle classes sat on city councils expanding city services, taxing corporations and the rich. Cities no longer depended entirely on hidebound state governments for help. The precedent was set for federal intervention in cities with direct aid for employment, housing and public works (Mollenkopf, 1981, 16).

All this began to change by the 1950s. With the nation's economic expansion and the concentration of capital in huge corporations, monopolies and TNCs since World War II, labor's political and economic strength was eroded by anti-labor laws, the phony "red" issue, and the greater strength of U.S. capital from war profits, and rebuilding wartorn Europe. Monopoly capital began disinvesting in central cities and invested in suburban expansion, causing cities rapid losses in economic activities and population. This moved city politics to focus on ways to cope with unemployment and dwindling revenues. The postwar changes crested by the 1960s. By then most surviving New Deal politicians had been replaced by those allied with national and transnational corporations (Smith, 1984, 22). "Pro-growth" coalitions of monopoly corporations, real-estaters, builders, merchants, and their politicians formed to promote national urban renewal, highway, and downtown redevelopment programs. Their "success" exacted heavy costs from city working people. They brought destruction to many stable neighborhoods, higher taxes, longer commuting, greater traffic congestion and pollution (Mollenkopf, 1977, 122–24).

Politicians and the mass media of the pro-growth coalitions were quick to scapegoat the racial minorities for the decline monopoly capital had visited upon the central cities. Racism ran rampant in discrimination against Black and Latino families in housing, employment and city politics. Caught in the vise of economic and political repression, the poverty-stricken ghettos and barrios revolted. The 1965–1967 burning of "ghettos" in 128 cities was the explosion of an enraged people who have finally had enough of the pain, poverty, anguish and insult of ceaseless repression (Perry and Watkins, 1977, 289).

Lest the urban-growth programs be consumed by the fires of mass violence, city government muted the uprisings in cities with city-service reforms and increased political participation of minority neighborhood groups (Friedland et al, 1977, 452–53).

Out of these protests, poor neighborhoods developed a stronger sense of community and neighborhood links leading to mutual aid, communal child care for working mothers, and block associations to deal with landlord neglect, poor city services, and security problems. Such block associations formed building blocks for later neighborhood organization (Mollenkopf, 1981, 34; Susser, 206).

The stormy rebellion of racial minorities, therefore opened new avenues to working-class city politics. This calls for understanding city neighborhoods and the social dynamics of neighborhood organizations.

A *neighborhood* is an informal area of a city containing mostly residential and partly commercial land uses. It has no size definition except that it is subjectively defined by its inhabitants as a familiar territory of the city within walking distance of their homes. Although some of its people form close friendships with neighbors, city neighborhoods are seldom cohesive. Most of their people get to know each other mainly through casual meetings on streets, in stores, schools, churches or other neighborhood facilities. Because a big city's diversity moves neighborhood people to relate and act with people in other parts of the city, neighborhood bonds tend to weaken; few working people take part in their neighborhood's daily life. Yet, even the most aloof neighbors are not indifferent to their neighborhood's living environment. When its integrity is threatened, neighborhood cohesion usually increases, especially where workers own their homes, or in poor working class neighborhoods.

Neighborhoods are often called communities, but the two terms are not synonymous. Unlike a neighborhood, a *community* is not a geographic area. It is an abstract entity; a bond of identity among people based on a kinship of interests, occupation, belief or other common social ties (Mollenkopf, 1981, 320). People may be part of an educational community, for example, or a racial community and live in many different neighborhoods. Community bonds may or may not develop in a neighborhood; hence a neighborhood may or may not form a community.

The close neighborhood ties that ethnic minorities formed in their early years in the city have usually weakened the longer they interacted with people and places outside the neighborhood. Working on distant jobs, visiting scattered family and friends, shopping in central stores, and using central cultural and recreational facilities broadened personal interests, outlooks, and social ties. Although the daily life of mothers and children and some ethnic and religious sects has continued to center in the neighborhood, for most active adults its meaning waned the more they partook in citywide life (Hays, 1982, 252). A strong sense of community has endured the most in racial-minority neighborhoods where poverty and bias has locked people in and driven them closer together for mutual help and common resistance to a hostile environment.

Along with the ebb of community in the wake of "progressive" reforms early in the century, city neighborhoods lost the political strength they enjoyed in the years of party machines. In the 1930s Depression years, however, grassroots resurgence rekindled neighborhood community and political life. Spontaneous neighborhood organization shared food and clothing with distressed families and moved back in the furniture that evicting city marshalls dumped on sidewalks. Throughout the 1930s, working-class neighborhoods seethed with social and political ferment and labor organizing drives. Some cities were even forced to return to the more democratic ward and other systems of representation. The numbers of working class city council members consequently increased (Hays, 1982, 256).

Inspired by the Civil Rights Movement and aroused over the ruin of their neighborhoods by Urban Renewal, the poor formed neighborhood organizations by the thousands (Herbers, 178). By 1970, over 400 battles were fought to stop neighborhood bulldozing. Experience in organization and struggle taught neighborhood people to shed their old inhibitions and develop political savvy. Acting together, formerly submissive people grew articulate in defense of their rights. They developed skilled leaders, gained organizational discipline, and acquired political knowhow the entrenched politicians could no longer ignore (Hays, 1982, 256). Systematically and militantly confronting landlords, developers and officials for redress of grievances, neighborhood organizations steadily gathered political force. They won increasing support in and beyond their neighborhoods and a place of respect in city politics (Lipsky and Levi, 175–76).

Their revolt and organization thrust the working-class neighborhoods into the political arena at the city, state and national levels, forcing the State to offer concessions. Politicians in power hastened to be "good," for their staying in power now depended on millions of new voters newly aware of their own political strength. New federal urban programs were adopted and funded. Some of the funds were channeled through city governments to expand city services in working-class districts; other moneys went directly to newly created neighborhood-controlled economic development agencies (Clawford and Piven, xi–xii).

Neighborhood organizations, however, were not equally farsighted or effective. Some remained weak, acting in defensive isolation against what they perceived to be purely local attacks. They focused on their own neighborhood problems—blurring, even distorting their view of the rest of the city. But neighborhood hardships do not arise in isolation in the complex modern city; hence, fighting them purely locally soon proved a discouraging tilting at windmills. The landlords and developers were not neighborhood based. They had intimate ties within the city's economy and with the State, thus had to be fought on a similarly large political scale if victories were to endure.

In some neighborhoods, utopian ideas emerged advocating carving autonomous neighborhood governments out of the city. The idea gained prominence for a time among Black neighborhood people angry and frustrated over the racism of arrogant city officials. If some city departments, like the police, fire, and education can decentralize, they reasoned, why can't all city functions operate on a neighborhood basis, governed by little city halls? (Bollens and Schmandt, 258–60; Kotler, 31–36). Anger blinded its proponents from seeing that the idea was futile simply because city neighborhoods are integral parts of the larger whole. Their people make their living by drawing on its big pool of jobs and rely on city services made possible by the city's big-scale operations. Advocacy of "little city halls" served only to confuse and divide neighborhood people and, in the end, discredit its proponents.

While some focused on narrow neighborhood problems, most went beyond local concerns to attack the wider city issues of bank redlining, utility rates, and taxes. Many enhanced their political weight in city politics through alliances with ethnic community groups and tenant, home-owner, and labor organizations to win improved city services, rent control, city jobs, and influence in federal neighborhood revitalization programs (Cunningham and Auerbach, 236).

Even as the State conceded to some demands of neighborhood organizations, it conspired, and sometimes succeeded, to weaken them by cunning and deception. When militant neighborhood opposition to evictions and bulldozing grew too strong for repression by police methods, the State tried breaking it by coopting its leaders in city-sponsored "advisory councils," "planning boards," and other "citizen participation" schemes. The schemes trapped neighborhood leaders in long negotiations with officials and developers that flagged rank-and-file spirits and deterred neighborhood action. Neighborhood leaders negotiating endlessly often won only token gains for they lacked the political power that flows from aroused organized numbers, clear goals, and resolute leadership—the kind of power "citizen participation" tended to deny them (Coit, 298–99; Cunningham and Auerbach, 224).

Many neighborhood leaders grew to expect benefits to continue from city halls inclined to appease discontent lest it again get out of hand (Boyle, 12, 32). But when the economy skidded downward in

1974, monopoly capital turned aggressive. Liberalism vanished from corporate rhetoric. Business journals began ranting against the "welfare state," with racist and autocratic overtones. Monopoly capital saw the solution to the economic recession as an upward distribution of the national wealth. Threatening to close plants and withhold capital investment if organized labor did not give up its gains, monopoly corporations began getting their way. Labor unions were forced into giveaways and cities were forced to cut social services, ease environmental restrictions, and attack unions of city employees. By the end of the 1970s, monopoly capital's reactionary circles were poised to fully seize all the levers of government (Boyle, 13, 16–17).

Neighborhood organizations entered the '80s still politically effective in many cities. Their strength and rights were generally recognized in city halls. Sometimes allied with council supporters, they no longer needed only confrontation tactics to be heard; their standing in city politics made possible effective negotiations. Corporations and politicians were no longer free to spring development schemes upon working-class neighborhoods from behind closed doors (Cunningham and Auerbach, 235–38).

In the 1980s, despite reactionary control of the State, neighborhood organizations have grown into sophisticated networks of communitywide and citywide coalitions across race, ethnic and even class lines, struggling over a host of broad people's issues including health, education, transportation, bank redlining, taxation, energy, pollution, toxic waste disposal, and world peace. And they have entered electoral politics at all government levels, extending the class struggle from the work place to the State (Delgado, 5).

By contrast, politics in the metropolitan suburbs have been marked by a virtual absence of working-class input. Their political life, in general, has developed within a constricted democracy. The spatial segregation of classes, class factions and ethnic groups has reduced it to a vapid, low-key set of parochial politics around insular issues, and to low voter turnouts (Newton, 84–89; Sawers, 8). And this has made suburbs vulnerable to easy control by one corporation or one social group promoting its own special interests (Ashton, 55).

23. Summary and Comments

It seems strange and puzzling that the phenomenal urban growth of this century, in so large and advanced a nation as ours, proceeded without the guidance of a national urban policy. In only two brief periods in the managerially adroit age of state monopoly capitalism was there a semblance of national leadership over urban development: one in the Roosevelt New Deal years of the late 1930s, the other in the Johnson Great Society years of the 1960s. Both appeared only when mass, militant people's movements forced a response: the first, to the unemployed marches and the mass organization of industrial workers; the second, to the upheavals of the civil rights and peace crusades (Goldsmith and Jacobs, 62–63).

Why has the federal government presided over this stupendous historic development without a clear urban policy? Surely its enormous yield of profit should have compelled careful guidance. Some said the answer lies in part in the U.S. government structure of 50 states, each with sovereign jurisdiction over its cities, compounded by governmental fragmentation of the modern metropolises. Such divided authority over cities, and the rivalry among municipalities with parochial loyalties, allegedly made a unified urban policy impossible. Further the need to change this admittedly awkward structure did not often arise as long as it functioned passably well (Ianitskii, 1975, 295–96).

Plausible as this may sound, it is contradicted by the two cited exceptions when national urban policies were adopted and carried out, and by the many instances in U.S. history when national policies overrode state sovereignty to meet urgent national ruling-class needs.

Perhaps closer to the answer are those who argue that framing an open national urban policy would have unavoidably focused public attention on the class contradictions in cities. This would subject policy to wide working-class challenge, a hazard ruling circles had to avoid, if possible, by all means (Goldsmith and Jacobs, 58–59). Such reasoning may indeed explain what, in fact, amounts to a covert national urban policy in the ad hoc federal intervention in urban affairs—now by promoting metropolitan highway building, now by urban renewal, now by funding new housing—always disguised as special measures designed to serve the "public interests" when, in fact, intended to aid monopoly capital.

Public transportation is a classic case in point. In almost every advanced industrial country except the United States, high-speed modern trains are the basic elements of metropolitan transport systems. With few exceptions, we have no adequate modern rapid transit in our metropolises. The automobile, oil and rubber monopolies went about the country undeterred, since the 1920s, methodically destroying public rail transport alternatives to autos, buses and trucks.[28] Most of the rapid transit systems the federal government has funded since the 1970s slighted the needs of the densely populated working-class districts—favoring traffic-jammed CBD-bound suburban commuters instead. This bolstered the diminishing vitality of the profitable suburbs and boosted profits in CBDs, but left central-cityites crowded in jammed buses and run-down trains (Goldsmith and Jacobs, 59–60).

Another example: To avoid lowering profits on the real estate market, the State usually refrained from relieving the chronic low-rent housing shortage. Not until the problem had reached crisis proportions threatening production in World War I, did the federal government step in to subsidize a public housing program it quickly terminated after the war (Glaab and Brown, 296–99). The housing problem became critical again in the 1930s, forcing the federal government to act once more to stem home foreclosures, and stimulate home building and ownership.

The prime example, of course, was the Urban Renewal Program in the 1950s, authorizing demolition of working-class and small business districts in central cities to clear urban space for CBD expansion and high-rent housing redevelopment (Fox 88–91).

The State's consistent promotion of monopoly capitalist enterprise in urban development has left the impression that our great cities have been created by the sheer genius of "corporate America." The contributions of enterprising capitalists to urban growth is, of course, undeniable. But the cultivated belief that the "enterprising elite of society" made possible all urban progress is sustained only by obscuring the obvious historical fact that all social wealth is the product of human labor—the labor of the working class.

Nor can the vaunted "elite" of society take credit for the amazing growth of our modern metropolises. Individual capitalists and corporations served mainly as the catalysts in the objectively necessary historical process of decongesting the crowded cities. That they created fabulously luxurious suburban enclaves for the rich in the process attests to their misappropriation and misuse of social wealth. The process of metropolitanization itself, however, albeit perverted, was determined not by the "genius of corporate America" but by the objective necessity to resolve the developed contradiction between the overconcentration of growing production forces in cities and the need for more living space. Biased ruling-class pundits, however, would not acknowledge the star role of the working class in the nation's great urban progress, nor admit their masters' expropriating the nation's urban lands for their own wealth accumulation at the people's expense.

Conversion of public lands to private ownership has remained federal land policy. Only about one-third of our national land is left in the public domain, most of it in forbidding mountains and deserts, the frozen wilderness areas of Alaska, and in national parks. Almost all the rest, especially the most used and valuable urban land, is tied up in private ownership (Clawson, 1964, 946–96. Choice central spaces have gone to the highest bidders, not the socially most rational uses, placing low-rent occupants in central areas under constant pressure from land developers trying to dislodge them for high-rent development. Land distribution by price produced a hierarchy of prestigious urban spaces—from high-rent CBDs to poor commercial and industrial districts, from luxury residential districts to slums—turning our cities into patterns of social segregation and a hodgepodge of discordant uses. Second, healthful green spaces kept shrinking. No city can afford to buy back land needed for parks and recreation at the market's inflated prices. Third, housing costs kept rising. About one-quarter of the cost, or rent, of new urban housing goes to pay the inflated price of the land. Fourth, building and population densities increase to compensate for the rising costs of land. Fifth, cities have tended to sprawl because land developers have "leapfrogged" over high-priced land to cheaper outlying areas, increasing home-to-job distances and extending the length and cost of utility, road, and transportation lines.

In essence, the woes of today's metropolitan suburbs hark back to the "original sin" of committing public land to private ownership. The traffic contradiction that has developed between the suburbs' dispersed homes and concentrated work places turned the dream of private homeownership into a nightmare of costly, nerve wracking, time wasting, air polluting bumper-to-bumper crawl between homes and jobs. Private land ownership, it appears, has begun to prove its social incompatibility.

Private land ownership has also reinforced racism. Racial polarization in suburbia has, in effect, been developing a national urban "apartheid" by confining racial minorities within central cities or designated outer rings. Racism in the guise of fears for real estate values sired the suburbs' exclusionary land zoning laws. So tenacious is suburban racism that it persists even though it is a major cause of the shortage of workers essential to the suburban economy.

This does not argue against suburbanization—the concomitant of the objectively necessary historical process of metropolitanization. But it does indict suburbanization *capitalist style* whose history warns that suburban development is not class neutral. The working class must watch for acts and spatial designs potentially injurious to its class unity. That may not be easily achieved in the admittedly low level of working-class politics in our metropolitan suburbs. Clearly, dispersion, disorientation, delusion by middle class ownership values, and racism have weakened and slowed the progressive political development of the working class in our modern metropolises— paradoxically, at a time of its enormous numerical growth.

The overwhelming majority that is the working class make the terms "working class" and "the people" practically synonymous. That the working class stands numerically dominant yet politically soft hurts not only its interests but those of most of the nation.

The excessive consumption of urban space in a metropolis does not come cheaply. Its cost eventually translates into higher taxes. Both the private car and its accessory the single family home are voracious space eaters. The patterns of scatter they stamp over the metropolitan areas frustrate public transportation, increase paved-area drainage and travel distances, hence water and air pollution. Consider the costly traffic slowdowns of trucks, passenger buses, and cars at bottleneck approaches to destination points. Consider, above all, the terrible loss of life and limb on the highways. In 1983 alone, 29.4 million auto accidents (compared with only 59 for buses) resulted in 30,600 deaths, 4,665,000 injuries, and $62.7 billion in economic losses (Statistical Abstracts, 1986). Finally, consider the effect the dependence on the private auto has had on those unable to use it: the household members left stranded while the family car is in use. The loss of pedestrian movement has dehumanized neighborhood life. Streets no longer function as the places where people meet, walk, talk and socialize. Children, driven to school, miss the learning experience which comes from observing neighborhood life on the way to and from school (Blumenfeld, 1979, 294–96).

Surely, had the working class had stronger political input in urban affairs, the assault by auto, oil, and rubber monopolies on the life, health and welfare of the people could have been checked in good time. The private car need not have become indispensable and public transport need not have declined within the metropolis. One transporation expert wrote: "A thundering herd of interest groups ranging from the Automobile Manufacturers Association to those who build highways and to the great petroleum companies all have a stake in the continued upward spiral of highway construction and the use of the automobile. . . . [they have had] a far more powerful role in policy formation and action on the part of all levels of government than the best interests of the public" (Smerk, 129).

Many today drive autos mainly because they have to. A survey by *Fortune*, taken in the mid-1950s, indicated the degree of involuntary driving. *Fortune* asked 2600 drivers in three major cities "how they liked driving to work, and on what terms they would consider switching to a 'first-class rapid transit system' if one were built in their city." An average of 35 percent said they "did not enjoy driving . . . would almost certainly switch to public transportation if it came reasonably close to competing with auto trips in time, cost and convenience." Sixty-four percent said they would use public transit "if round-trip travel time matched present driving time." An average of 67 percent believed that the "transportation and traffic problem could best be solved by a new public rapid-transit rail system" (Editors of *Fortune*, 59–60).

New and rehabilitated sections of rapid transit systems in Chicago, New York, Boston, Philadelphia, Toronto, San Francisco, Cleveland, Montreal, Atlanta, Washington, D.C., and other metropolises have enjoyed rising riderships. Characteristically, these projects have been planned to serve movement mainly between CBDs and low-density suburbs, which is why their increase in ridership has been relatively modest. Ridership would surely have been greatly increased had the needs of high-density central city districts not been largely ignored (Sawers, 224, 240; Goldsmith & Jacobs, 60).

The dominance of the automobile has determined not only access within the metropolis, it has pervaded many aspects of our culture as well. It inspired, for instance, utopian visions like that of the great architect Frank Lloyd Wright, proposing a future America moving exclusively in private automobiles.

Although Wright's fallacies are transparently obvious, his utopia cannot be lightly dismissed; for it has charmed many young people who, sickened by the decadence and dog-eat-dog world of capitalist cities, attempt, or dream of, escaping to a simple, peaceful life in the countryside. Their romantic fantasy entertains the Wrightian notion that modern society and industry can disperse with impunity and thrive in an idyllic environment. Since people prefer to drive, they ask, why can't economic activities locate along major highways? In the age of the automobile, why can't offices, factories, department stores, colleges, or hospitals go off at will to separate locations? Do not close-circuit television and computers make, or soon will make, coordination within CBDs unnecessary? Why cannot we resurrect our agrarian democracy, enjoying farming, crafts, and doing our "own thing"?

When exposed to the light of reality and reason, however, such illusions soon fade away. Metropolitan development cannot be determined by arbitrary individual will. Rather, it responds to objective laws that individuals are not free to ignore. As Blumenfeld profoundly observed:

Decentralized decision-making, such as prevails in the United States, inevitably leads to ever greater spatial centralization. Spatial decentralization can be brought about only by a central decision maker, who can locate all required establishments simultaneously, or at least in scheduled sequence. This is confirmed by the experience not only of Communist-ruled countries, but also by those Western nations who have achieved some success in spatial decentralization. . . . This dialectic appears to be overlooked by most decentralists who want decentralization both of decision-making and of location (Blumenfeld, 1970, 91–92).

It is noteworthy that utopians in the monopoly-capital stage— Howard, Geddes, The Regionalists, Wright and others—came from the middle class. Curiously, the upperclass produced none. How may this fact be explained? Perhaps from the different social roles the two classes and their members have played. Usurping the lion's share of the surplus value the working class has produced, members of the ruling class have lived in the luxury of their exclusive enclaves, isolated and insulated from the rest of society. Their chief concerns have been how to make the most profit and manipulate the subordinate classes enough to stay in power. Having had access to the best of everything, they have had no motivation to dream up utopias. History has dealt a different fate to the middle class, many of whom have had to earn their keep by managing complex urban problems for the ruling class. The task has fallen especially hard on the shoulders of the officials and intelligentsia responsible for implementing ruling-class policy and indoctrinating the people with its ideology. Buffetted by class conflict from above and below, they have been keenly aware of capitalist society's irreconcilable contradictions, yet driven to resolve them. The anguish of their situation may account for the utopian dreams coming from their ranks.

Note, moreover, the common characteristics of middle class utopians. They share the dream of returning to a romantically glorified past in a rural or small-town life, and the myth that big-city evils distort a basically sound capitalist order. In the few instances when middle-class utopians dared to look ahead, as in Orwell's *1984* or Huxley's *Brave New World*, they were full of foreboding.

Romanticizing the past and fearing the future inheres in the ideology of a class having no prospect in history. Its members can only conjure up pleasant dreams of its historical youth or the nightmares of its impending demise. To many middle-class ideologues, the all-pervading crisis of state monopoly capitalism, manifested in the crises of its cities, looms as the sunset of civilization. Hence their pessimistic, fatalistic, irrational ideas. Still others summon up hope, believing in the ability of technological progress to improve capitalism; they spin scientistic illusions and technocratic utopias (Ianitskii, 1975, 325).

The "post-industrial society" visions widely shared among thinkers today is a case in point. Their prophets diligently describe how modern information processing has been changing the location of production forces in the metropolises. They forecast that these changes will reform capitalism. Progress in information technology, they maintain, will automatically effect revolutionary social changes. But they do not say how, and excuse their omission of class forces by the lack of analytical tools that can be fashioned only as the "post-industrial society" develops. In sum, they forecast a future society whose process of becoming they cannot analyze, but expect that future analytical tools will confirm their forecast.

The post-industrialist notion that capitalism is changing because its executive functions are in the hands of salaried corporate managers, with ownership diffused among many stockholders, confuses appearance and essence. The separation of management from ownership is merely an aspect of the division of labor. It does not abolish capitalist production relations in which the surplus value of labor is appropriated by capitalists—either as individual shareholders or as corporation—through the agency of managers. Other post-industrialist assumptions are equally false. For example, their utopian idea that science and reason are replacing the profit-making drive, and universities are supplanting corporate boardrooms in leading modern capitalism. Need it be said that, in fact, state-monopoly capital's strategies are determined by corporate boards of directors and high-level leaders in the State with fingers poised over the dials and buttons of real economic and political power, not by scholars sweating out ideas in think tanks? (Walker and Goldberg, 21).

Equally false is the presumption that in advanced capitalism the "service economy" has been replacing the "industrial economy"; that is, that advanced capitalism has been less goods producing and increasingly a service rendering and consuming society. In reality, the nation has spent increasingly more in the '60s and '70s on durable goods than on services. Moreover, separating production of goods from the production of services distorts the meaning of the division of labor in a complex society. Even shop floor cleaners or food caterers, who by conventional definition perform a service, are essential to production processes. Many, if not most, "service" functions are necessary to, or derive from, production of goods.[29] The whole "service" structure rests on material production. The fact that the percentage of jobs in manufacturing, mining, transportation, construction and communication has declined in proportion to service and office jobs indicates not that the economy has become less "industrial" and more "service" but that service activities, integrally connected to production, have grown with the prodigious increase in the productivity of labor, producing goods. In fact, the evidence indicates that "the manufacturing share has been relatively stable at slightly less than one-quarter of total output since 1975. The manufacturing share of total employment has shown [only] a modest decline during the 1970s" (Hicks, 7). Thus, "the principal business of modern capitalism is still the production and circulation of commodities, not the provision of . . . services. The modern economy is not only still capitalist, it is still *industrial* capitalist." (Walker and Greenberg, 18–19, 39).

The prophets of "post-industrial society" have also proclaimed the end of city-village differences in the modern capitalist age. It can be argued, however, that despite the wide diffusion of modern technology within the nation's settlement system—despite the automobile and greater mobility, improved education, radio, tapes, and TV—inequalities between the economic, social, and cultural levels of city and village have not only remained but have relatively widened. For advanced urbanization had so greatly centralized social and economic interaction in metropolitan centers that it left the exurban peripheries locked in a state of permanent lag. Concentration of intensive material and non-material production in cities has necessarily left social development simpler and slower in all aspects of rural life.

Most non-Marxist sociologists have concluded that "social technology," that is, progress in the physical and social sciences, will automatically resolve capitalist society's social contradictions, including the one between city and village. In the near future, they predict, the STR will largely eliminate the village as a socio-geographic phenomenon. Granted that physical differences between city and village have been fading, and that many villages have been integrated within metropolitan regions, this evades the core of the issue. The city-village differences are not simply those of socio-geography, they are essentially socioeconomic in nature. The mass migration from the rural Black South to the urbanized North merely shifted southern social villages to the Black ghettos of our cities. The segregated Black ghettos and the ethnic neighborhoods remain "villages in the city," enclaves of isolated people and cultures. For the "village" is not simply a place of rural life and labor, it is the prevalence of archaic forms of social relations; of inequality and oppression of villagers merely moved to a new place (Ianitskii, 1975, 160, 169).

In sum, the anticity utopias and "post-industrial city" illusions only sow confusion, weakening the people's will to get at the real reasons and seek political solution to their cities' problems.

One of the knottiest city problems has been their perennial shortfall of funds. Why are most of our cities gripped by fiscal hardships and crisis? Some urban scholars have simply begged the question, attributing it to continually emerging costly city problems. Others saw the main cause in the burdens cities bear hosting large poor populations. Still others thought the fault lay in national overspending on the military, foreign aid, and space exploration at the expense of social needs in the cities. And some put the main blame on inefficiency and corruption in city government (Bollens and Schmandt, 168–69).

To be sure, all these are contributing reasons, but they are essentially effects of the root cause: the deepening overall crisis of capitalist society. In the state monopoly capital stage, the more the State invests in promoting private profits and itself bears the rising costs of securing the social system, the more society's contradictions appear in the arena of the State. Monopoly capital's demands upon State expenditures have tended to rise faster than the State could finance them, resulting in fiscal, economic, social and political crises (Hill, 1978, 217–18; O'Conner, 9).

Diffusing its effects throughout the government structure of the nation, the general crisis of the State has produced the fiscal crises of cities. The federal government having taken the bulk of national tax dollars and turned over hundreds of billions to the big banks as interest, has left the states and the cities to raise what other monies they could to finance their needs. The cities bear much of the national burdens of unemployment, health, education and welfare. In addition, cities have suffered fiscal effects of the "normal" malfunctions endemic to capitalism. Economic stagnation and periodic recessions have eroded city tax revenues, and the politics of "free enterprise" have exposed city treasuries to corruption and looting. Colluding with city officials and politicians, financiers ripped off cities with usurous interests on loans, real estate moguls got away with tax favors, suppliers padded their bills, and contractors freely overcharged costs. All this has driven most cities into huge debts and fiscal crises and some, like New York and Cleveland, to the brink of bankruptcy (Hill, 183, 244–46).

To extricate cities from their fiscal morass, monopoly capital has favored what it deemed the most sensible "solution"; namely to cut city services to the people, especially to the most "burdensome" poor. "Shrinkage," that is, squeezing out the poor by attrition of city services and harassment, gained a respected hearing in city-planning theory and wide application in administrative practice. Federal "slum clearance" took part in this scheme.

To many, the Urban Renewal Program seemed just that—a renovation of outworn parts of cities. Indeed, it often succeeded in improving the appearance and invigorating the use of old urban spaces, albeit at a high human cost to their dislocated occupants. But few saw its real purpose—restructuring urban spaces from forms cast in the era of industrial capitalism to forms fitting the needs of state-monopoly capitalism. The Urban Renewal Program has played midwife, as it were, to the birth of the new era's urban order of things (Kleniewski, 218; Mollenkopf, 1981, 16).

The working class, however, remembers "Renewal" for its wholesale distruction of precious working-class homes and neighborhood life. It added one more lesson to its experience that its neighborhoods are always potential targets of capitalist schemes to raise the "obsolete" for "rational," that is, more profitable, uses. In a class society, what is "obsolete," and "rational" is often a matter of class values. What the upperclass sees as obsolete structures and urban uses may be affordable shelter and vital communities to the class it exploits. Upperclass market values tend to warp human values. Even its most compassionate pundits have long marked working class areas as "marginal," "ugly," "dangerous" and "expendable" and found it quite conscionable to sentence them to "renewal" by demolition. Our cities need slum clearance, yes. But urban renewal must *follow* social renewal, and abolition of slums the abolition of poverty.

Since the 1970s gentrification, the more benign form of "urban renewal" has been no less destructive to working-class neighborhoods. With a few notable exceptions, gentrification has not generated the widespread organized neighborhood resistance that met Urban Renewal. In part gentrification developers have applied devious tactics to avoid high visibility. They have bought up homes more slowly, snatching a few households at a time in seemingly unrelated locations. By the time a neighborhood awakens to the threat of its imminent destruction, the invaders are well entrenched in their midst with wealth, property laws, and the State on their side. Unorganized, the victims stood defenseless. Insidiously occupying small sections at a time, gentrification can affect large parts of cities. It can make thousands of homes insecure, resegregate integrated neighborhoods, and weaken the political potential of concentrated working-class districts.

Unwittingly, the federal Urban Renewal Program left in its wake two progressive political side effects. One in the form of the legal precedents set by the 1950s U.S. Supreme Court decisions on taking private property to promote public health, safety, welfare and morals—precedents having profound implications for the future of working-class politics. The other, in the arousal of masses of politically inactive neighborhood people to organize and militantly defend their homes, communities, and democratic rights. Those battles led to the precedent-breaking legal recognition of neighborhood representation in the city's planning process. Even more importantly, it led to the emergence of broad alliances among community organizations for struggle on wider political issues in the cities and the nation.

This brings us to the problem of working-class politics.

Organized labor has increasingly realized that to defend its class interests it must fight at once on two fronts. It must fight first, at the point of production for jobs, wages, good working conditions, and the right to organize and bargain collectively—a struggle it must wage directly with employers and indirectly also with their guardian, the State. It must fight secondly, at the point of consumption for affordable housing, education, health protection, safety, transportation, utilities, and social welfare.

The political arena around city government is of special importance to working-class politics because working people greatly depend on the city services that make up a good part of their real income and welfare. Poor public health services, for example, raise the cost of health care or lower health standards, threatening the lives and livelihood of working-class families, for whom staying well means being able to work and subsist. Poor refuse removal and street cleaning spreads gloom and infectious diseases. Poor public transportation reduces access to distant jobs, to friends and to social facilities, lessening opportunities for self improvement, social life, and personal growth. Poor public education threatens the economic future of working-class children, whose ability to get a job in an increasingly complex economy depends on the education they get. Poor park and recreation facilities force children to play in dangerous streets and alleys. Finally, poor social welfare services threaten the unemployed's last chance to endure (Miller and Roby, 93–100).

How large a share, how good a quality, and at how low a price in taxes the working class can get city services depends, in large part, on its weight in city politics. Hence the importance of its organized struggle in the city's political arena. This is not the formidable political task it may seem. City governments being geographically closest, most visible and accessible to the people, and the most responsive to their demands are, in fact, the easiest political arenas to deploy in and win (Friedland et al, 452).

Fred Ellis

PART THREE: *Our Cities' Future*

24. Retrospect, Trends, and Prospects

There has been no dearth of seers and oracles spinning out prophesies on the future of cities. But to what avail? The detailed fortune-telling forecasts of futurologists and other would-be prophets have varied and wavered between boom and doom. Trying to predict the future of cities with only pragmatist tools is a sheer waste of time. For who can possibly foretell the economic and political specifics born of myriad variables that will generate their changes over the years? It is possible, however, to identify today's main socioeconomic-political trends and infer from their general direction a probable future.

We tend to forget how the trends of yesteryear determined the past and the present and influence the events that will be tomorrow's history. Our country has urbanized in three distinct socioeconomic-technological phases. These roughly coincided with, indeed stemmed from, the three development stages of capitalist society: the commercial, industrial and state-monopoly capital.

In the first phase, the main trends in society's development grew out of capital accumulation by commerce. Merchants and petty manufacturers prospered by trading in produce and goods. They developed technology in extractive and manufacturing industries. Most of the population then engaged in agriculture, mining and lumbering, providing food, raw materials and fuels for the production and exchange of goods in the cities. The cities were small, with only crude social facilities and services to fill its most elementary needs. Cities multiplied as new settlements mushroomed at the sites of new primary industries.

In the second phase, the main social trends were based on profiting by industrial production. A large and growing part of the nation labored in factories, warehouses, on building sites, railroads, and ships; a diminishing number stayed in agriculture and the extractive industries; and a smaller but fast-growing part worked in trade, services, and administration. Farmers moved from the countryside to growing cities for jobs, business, and cultural opportunities. Urban growth soared around expanding specialized manufacturing, transport, energy, and building industries. Large cities were populated by growing numbers of skilled and semi-skilled workers requiring greater social, educational, cultural, and service facilities. Competition among capitalists spurred technological progress in every branch of the economy, raised labor productivity, increased production volumes, and sped delivery of goods to developing markets.

In the third phase, the main trends stemmed from employment of labor in mass production industries and corporate mergers on a new scale. Automation gradually reduced the proportion of industrial workers in the labor force. Agriculture and the extractive industries, largely mechanized, employed a dwindling minority of the population. The number of well-educated workers, requiring social, cultural, and service facilities of the highest order steadily increased. Jobs expanded in technology, finance, administration, the media, distribution, education, health, and public services generally. Urban development was driven by increasing specialization and diversity in the production of goods and the growth of a wide range of services. Fusing or linking with neighboring settlements, cities grew into economically (though not politically) integrated, versatile expanding metropolises. Driven by social trends born of a high technological level of production, but facing increased pressures from the TNCs—this is our present reality.

The 1970s' recession marked the new trend with ominous potential effects on the life of our cities—increasing application of computers in production, management, and marketing. The old system employed workers mass-producing large inventories in huge central plants for far-flung unstable markets. It has been yielding to new methods of flexible production in small batches to fill orders at hand, with fewer workers, in small plants geographically distributed close to their markets. The new trend has raised labor productivity and lowered fixed capital investments, inventories and costs; speeded world marketing, and yielded higher profits. But it has closed many large plants, increased unemployment and economic distress, and aided the growth of transnational corporations, thus increasing their inordinate economic-political powers to decide the fate of our cities.

This trend augers an increasing flight of production jobs to national and global locations with lower production costs and high trade advantages. Corporate and auxiliary service activities will probably loom even larger in the economies of the top centers of monopoly capital's hierarchy of cities, reducing material production to second and third rank. This may generate construction of more office towers, high-rent apartments, lavish stores, cultural and recreational facilities in the center, causing further attrition of small business and moderate to low income housing (Williams and Smith, 208–11).

The basic economies of regional and lesser cities will probably stay generally mixed. Although they, too, have tended to develop service activities, many are likely to retain factories producing for their respective regional or local markets. As the national and international division of labor increases, however, the older northeastern industrial cities may expect continued, if uneven, disinvestment, with rising tides of physical decay, while cities in the south and southwest may see continued investment and building. Still, a reverse flow of capital from South to North may occur should disinvestment so depress wages, social services, and land prices in the old industrial centers as to again make them targets for profitable reinvestment (Ibid).

The increasing ability of the TNCs to roam the country and the world, disinvesting and investing at will to maximize profits is likely to advance production, management and living standards in some places, inflict depression and poverty on others, and increase labor exploitation everywhere. The TNCs will continue to blackmail cities into heavy expenditures on CBD infrastructures, tax abatements, social services cuts, and union busting in return for their presence and the jobs they do generate (Harvey, 1987, 32).

The global strategies of transnational corporations have been paying off in the short run but they appear headed to an inevitable fall. Militarizing national economies and fomenting local wars has proved profitable to date. But having pushed even the richest nations into unbearable debts and austerities, they are mounting an economically and politically impossible cost.

What prospects, then, await the cities? Will the transnational corporations continue to expand and dominate their future? Having inevitably emerged out of the process of capital-concentration inherent in capitalism, TNCs are likely to keep growing as long as the capitalist economy develops. Heir to all the contradictions of their social system, however, they are politically vulnerable (Sergeyev, 1983, 32).

Paradoxically, their greatest weakness lies in their seemingly greatest strength—militarization of the national economies they control. Although militarization has yielded fabulous profits, it has tended to exacerbate capitalism's inner contradictions. Having led to superexploitation, regional wars, and the danger of an omnicidal world war, militarization has become a growing political liability in every country. The TNCs must contend with an increasingly powerful world peace movement and the peace initiatives of the socialist countries. The TNCs face rising pressures to demilitarize national economies, revive civilian production, advance social welfare, rehabilitate cities, and protect the natural environment. They also face a more militant and united labor movement, in battle for its rights and for economic gains. They must also cope with growing resistance from the exploited developing countries and pressures for new, more equitable rules in world trade and debt restructuring.

The first signs of this happening have already been recorded. With trends toward world disarmament and peace gaining momentum, the prospects for world peaceful economic expansion may be brightening. As the process unfolds and military budgets shrink, amassed capital is likely to flow into civilian production, services, and trade—expanding, no doubt, the nation's metropolitan centers. Such events would have a regenerative effect on life in our cities.

25. Prospects for Metropolises

In the foreseeable future, the metropolis will continue as the dominant urban form. Historically young, it has yet to run its full evolutionary course. Metropolises will continue to function as the centers upon which their regions' activity lines converge and from which branching activities radiate. And their central cities and suburbs will continue to integrate economically within the limits imposed by their governmental structures.

Metropolises will endure despite the disruptive mobility of the TNCs and other megacorporations. No matter where and why they move their profits, decentralized decision-making and complex division of labor will require concentration of economic activities within metropolises. No matter how much they extend managerial and service activities, these cannot alone sustain any metropolis, for non-production activities must be based on the production activities that created them in the first place (Hill, 1983, 51; Hicks, 133–35).

The nation's natural population growth and continued immigration will increase metropolitan populations, mostly in the suburbs and especially in the Sunbelt—as long as their living and production costs remain relatively lower than in the central cities and the Snowbelt (Bradberry et al, 12).

Further expansion of metropolises will depend, of course, on economic growth. Assuming an average growth across the cyclical hills and valleys, quite possible in the age of the science-technology revolution, further division of labor should spin off new specialized industries that can locate advantageously in outlying metropolitan spaces. New roads into the countryside and the rising trend for recreation outside the metropolis will also tend to expand metropolitan regions.

Will open-ended metropolitan growth ultimately result in a fusion of neighboring metropolises, like those between Boston and Washington, into continuous urban belts and a new "megalopolis" form of settlement? Most urban scholars think not. For unlike their European counterparts, U.S. metropolises have taken mononuclear forms. That is, they are strongly oriented on single central cities separated by open areas (Blumenfeld, 1979, 124–25). Indeed, among urban theorists, visions of future "megalopolises" have been countered with fancies of "metropolitan shrinkage." A possible prolonged future energy shortage, some thought, may cause a movement away from energy-wasting suburbia and toward energy efficient apartments, cluster housing and mass transportation (Woodruff, 41–42). However, during the oil crisis of the 1970s, suburbanites tended to absorb the higher costs, or buy smaller cars, form car pools, take fewer trips, and insulate their homes rather than give up their suburban living (Blumenfeld, 1979, 351).

Both metropolitan expansion and contraction, however, may alternate in the future. In the event of a possible long economic recession or energy crisis, many middle-income households may find maintaining private homes and cars increasingly difficult. This may well cause trends toward higher-density living and public transport and a consequent shrinkage of urban space or, at least, a halt in expansion. On the other hand, economy-boosting technological breakthroughs, like perhaps a revolutionary advance in power delivery may hasten metropolitan spread.

In the latter event, links between city and suburbs will further attenuate and strengthen between suburbs, tending to form large suburban subcenters. Intersuburb auto commuters will steadily outnumber suburb-city commuters, tending to shrivel mass transit. Mutual access between city-based unskilled workers and growing suburban job markets will continue to wither (Bradberry et al, 11; Orski, 9). This will probably harden the metropolitan pattern of spatial segregation by class and race. The high-income households will continue to gravitate to the outer suburbs and gentrified central city districts. More skilled workers will tend to follow industries bound for dispersed suburbs, and more unskilled workers and racial minorities will populate central-city fringes and the first ring of suburbs. This pattern has been jelling, in fact, in many metopolises, weakening their potential for rational integration.

Although urban scholars generally agree that the technical

problems of our metropolises are surmountable, their social problems tend to multiply and get harder to solve. They may be managed or controlled for a time only to emerge with greater intensity later. Take, for example, the technologically advancing economy's increasing dependence on a well-educated, skilled labor force able to operate, improve, and coordinate complex production forces scattered over a metropolitan region. Creating a large labor force of this kind, however, requires raising the living standards and educational level of the working class and drawing it into production, management and executive functions. Thus far, monopoly capital has gotten by with limiting intellectualization of labor to select, relatively small groups of privileged professionals and paraprofessionals, and relegating a growing part of the labor force to an unwanted "surplus" of "unemployables." But the momentum of the science-technology revolution is not likely to tolerate such limitations for very long. In time, the collision between monopoly capital's political strategy and the onward march of science and technology must negatively affect production and increase economic and political tensions in our metropolises (Akhiezer, 84–88).

Another problem lies in the anticity attitudes of the middle and upper classes and their continuing flight to isolated suburbs, thus lowering the capacity of metropolises to generate interaction between its classes and groups. This, too, must ultimately negatively affect the economy. For production in the high-technology age demands that its labor force constantly stimulate its creativity through interaction with the diversity of people, skills and cultures abounding in the metropolis. Clearly, the compact, culturally rich central city—not the scattered, hidebound suburbia—is the most nourishing environment for creative social interaction.

A basic social problem inheres in the private ownership and wasteful use of land in metropolitan regions. It is the main cause of our ineffecient automobile-centered transportation system.

Still another problem resides in the relationship between corporations and suburbs. Suburbs are often forced to bid for the corporation in the first place, offering tax breaks, public land, or cheap utilities. Often, location of a large enterprise in any suburb tends to be temporary. The host suburb's short-term gains from what taxes and jobs it can get often turn into long-term losses when the corporation suddenly decides to move to a more profitable location. In the small suburbs, the loss of even one large workplace often brings on economic misfortune and a municipal crisis.

All these social problems, and more, tend to intensify as new millions of the country's growing population settle mainly in metropolitan suburbs. Scattered land use for more low-density housing will inevitably result in further metropolitan spread, increased auto congestion, and higher costs increasing the frictional losses in the suburban economy. There is apt to be more environmental disruption, a greater tendency to move work places about, and yet poorer access to and integration with the central city. Added together, the debilitating effects of metropolitan social problems and contradictions portend a gradual loss of efficiency in the national economy and a steady deterioration in the national standard of living.

That fragmented metropolitan government has been unable to control—much less try to solve—these contradictions, has troubled some leaders even of monopoly capital. They have favored creating a metropolitan level of government, all the more for bringing rising political influences of central-city working-class populations under the control of the politically more tractable suburban majorities. The metropolitan governments that consolidated central cities and suburbs in southern metropolises like Miami, Richmond, and Jacksonville, and weakened the political strength of city-based Black and working-class majorities, are likely to inspire similar governmental reforms in other southern metropolises. In the Snowbelt, the dominant corporations seem to expect that central-city dependence on the jobs and taxes their activities generate will keep city councils and mayors in check. Should their hopes fail, however, future corporate political strategy may aim for metropolitan government in northern metropolises as well (Markusen, 97).

Will the negative metropolitan trends in the monopoly capitalist stage inevitably lead to urban decline?

Some urban scholars think that they must. They see no end to the conflcit between central cities and suburbs, expect continued class and race polarization, and anticipate the suburbs' ultimately facing the central city's problems of poverty and social ills.[1] Some have concluded that urban decline is inevitable because the crisis of cities merely reflects the chronic crisis and progressive decline of capitalist society.[2]

Such dark prospects are quite plausible under unrestrained monopoly-capital rule. But there would be brighter alternatives were monopoly capital checked by a powerful people's political force. Effective working-class political opposition could arrest and reverse the socially harmful trends and set in motion new trends toward favorable goals.

The ways for healing the metropolis are many. They can be effectively used provided the people's will to use them is strong enough and united.

Despite the badly mismatched land uses in our metropolises, the movement of their people and goods could be greatly improved. Government land-use policies designed to redistribute work places close to homes, and transportation strategies designed to shorten and speed origin-to-destination trips, would gradually minimize the need and maximize the possibility for commuting (Blumenfeld, 1967, 81–82).

Rationally planned ample public transport, providing an attractive alternative to private cars, could significantly lower road congestion and air pollution. The best way to make it attractive is to make it free. A fare-free public transport system is not as radical an idea as it may seem. It has long been used in providing many free roads and highways, and free elevators, escalators and people movers. Its logic has too long been denied to the use of buses and trains. It makes sense because it would benefit all of society through higher economic efficiency and better public health, as do free public schools, libraries, museums, and health clinics (Blumenfeld, 1979, 296).

The most rational transportation system, however, cannot prevent wasteful movement within the metropolis. Only a gradual long-range rearrangement of land uses can reduce waste motion, ease traffic, and improve metropolitan function. Indeed, a rational transportation system would work most efficiently and cost least to run were homes and work places more densely concentrated along its corridors (Blumenfeld, 1967, 57–59). Such concentrations can be created by publicly sponsored metropolitan redevelopment on publicly owned land, and by strict public control over private land owners' use of urban land to protect public interests (Blumenfeld, 1979, 300).

Rational public land-use controls and new development on publicly owned land—that is, building on less land at medium and high densities—would preserve more of the natural environment for parks and recreation, reduce urban sprawl, increase the affordable housing stock, and cut home-to-job distances and travel time. It would gradually convert the sprawling low-density urban areas into a more compact and energy-efficient metropolis knitted together by energy-saving public transportation. It would maximize accessibility to jobs, workers, goods, services and recreation and raise social interaction throughout the metropolis to a higher level and more vigorous tone.

Using their bypassed lands at medium and high densities, the nation's metropolises could comfortably hold within their present areas many more millions of people as well as large open spaces. In Sweden's Stockholm and in the densely populated metropolises of the Netherlands and West Germany's industrial Ruhr, well designed farms, forests and parks separate built up urban areas to provide pleasant landscapes, farm produce, and recreation within easy reach by their inhabitants (Faltermeyer, 152–55). Surely what has been accomplished in other capitalist countries through public planning and rigid public control over urban land use, can be achieved by similar means in our country.

John Heliker

26. Prospects for Central Cities

It is common knowledge that most of our central cities are gripped by an apparently endless crisis. "Crisis" seems to correctly describe them, beset as they are by contradictions and conflicts that cannot be resolved short of basic changes in the principles and rules by which they are governed. Surely the loss of production, loss of population, loss of housing stock, loss in living standards, loss in municipal revenues, loss in city services, decay of infrastructures, rising living costs, increasing poverty, climbing morbidity and crime rates are symptoms of crisis. They may not be visible in the showcase air of CBDs where billions are transacted and visitors applaud, but they glare from most streets in the rest of the city where its people live and strangers seldom go.

It is not common knowledge, however, that the crises of our cities are not of their making; that they stem from the general crisis of capitalist society; that, in fact, they are its local manifestations modified by local historical, political, economic, and geographic specifics. The long chain of causes and effects linking the overall crisis of the larger society with that of our cities may obscure the organic connection between the two. Recognizing it, however, is essential to understanding the true situation. The shift of industries from the Snowbelt to Sunbelt regions and abroad, for instance, has been determined more by global and national than by local economic forces. The postwar world rivalry between capitalist states and the effects of the science-technology revolution influenced the shift as much as did the differences between the wage levels, infrastructures, and land costs of northern, southern and foreign cities.

Urban scholars see no end to the crisis of cities. The prospects, they think, are especially grim for industrial cities like Detroit, St.

Louis, Newark, or Buffalo in the northeast and southern cities like Birmingham, Miami and Atlanta, where growing concentrations of unemployed and poor—the effects of economic restructuring—and spreading urban decay increasingly divert city funds away from profit-yielding activities and increase the potential for social unrest (Hill, 1978, 230; Nathan, 9).

Indeed, they see gloomy prospects for most capitalist cities, even the much glorified capitals of Europe, whose splendors are centered in the special parts writers extol and tourists rave about, but whose pervasive poverty and decay beyond them go either unseen, ignored, or belittled. London, Paris and Rome contain not just the finest urban treasures and amenities, they also harbor mass misery and physical rot (Rodwin, 11, 16; Goering and Lichten, 304). Private wealth and public squalor, affluence and poverty, are the common fortunes and the continued outlook for most capitalist cities, proving the common source of their individual crises.

The fate of our cities, therefore, depends on the fate of the capitalist world's economy which, in turn, depends in large part on the politics of its ruling clases. Should their reactionary wings dominate the policies of their states and aim to maximize exploitation, distribute upward national wealth, and militarize national economies, then the fate of our cities may grow worse. Should, however, their liberal wings rise to power and promote profit through expanded national and world civilian markets, peaceful coexistence, and a downward distribution of national wealth, then the prospects may improve for the world's economies and cities.

Most urban scholars tend to agree, however, that whatever political route our ruling class may take in the future, central-city development will proceed along recent trends. Management and service activities will continue to expand, and manufacturing and populations will continue to shrink. CBDs, growing larger and slicker, will develop into affluent islands amid vast urban areas populated by masses of low-income and unemployed populations beset with all the social maladies that poverty incubates (Morial and Barry, 4). Moreover, they predict a further weakening of the geographic and economic centrality of central cities within their metropolitan systems, for the latter will continue tending to become "increasingly polycentric or multinodal and linear rather than concentric" the more they expand and develop industrial and commercial subcenters among the suburbs (Hill, 1984, 137–38). These trends will also tend to weaken the influence of central cities in Congress, for continued population movement from cities to suburbs will continue shifting the political weight to suburban Congressional districts. And an anti-city Congress will continue to favor suburban and rural development and deny federal funds to central cities (Morial and Berry, 3, 5; Herbers, 175).

These predictions may merely project current trends, yet they seem to accord with the apparent general political-economic drift of capitalist society. Its recurrent economic recessions suggest a bleak prospect of continued economic stagnation and consequent austerity, and decline in the quality of life in central cities (Edel, 242). Left politically unchecked, monopoly corporations and conservative governments will go on restructuring the economy, closing plants and forcing millions into an unstable existence. More losses of industries and upper-income populations will further lower central city revenues, raise taxes, and cut city services (Bradberry et al, 12). More automation will increase unemployment and pressures on wages and salaries. Inflation will further increase the cost of food, shelter, goods, and utilities, squeezing the people in the vise of rising prices and diminishing incomes. Increasing poverty will assail the health, morals and morale of many neighborhoods (Bluestone and Harrison, 82–83). Central business districts will drain more city funds, increase gentrification, and dislocate low-income tenants and home owners (Lang, 12). While the cores of central cities will continue to draw corporate offices, luxury housing, educational institutions, services, high-price stores, and hotels, working-class cityites will be pushed ever more to the outer edges. While shining new towers will continue to rise along the tidy streets in the core, the old housing stock will continue to succumb to the wear-and-tear, low maintenance, and the effects of poverty along the unkempt streets in the rest of the city (Hill, 1984, 135; Berry and Elster, 35). Little, if any, new affordable housing may be built to offset the losses to obsolescence, fire, and gentrification.

Even a political victory of monopoly capital's more liberal wing would present little happier prospects. It might ease the plight of the cities a little, but history warns to expect not much more, for the liberal wing would act for monopoly capital still. Even if it changed course and demilitarized the economy and world politics, it would still be compelled to champion its vital needs to move capital globally to points of highest profitability, caring little over the ill effects that may have on cities and people back home.

Ruling-class callousness to the plight of the nation's cities and continued decline in both national and urban affairs has put the legitimacy of monopoly capital's national leadership into question. Disinvesting at home and investing abroad, closing plants and ruining communities in hundreds of cities has raised deep worries among working people. If the nation faces stagnation at the cyclical crest of the 1980s, millions wonder, what will monopoly-capital rule bring upon the nation in the coming recession of the 1990s?

Growing distress and distrust among the people portend a coming political crisis for monopoly capital and pose before the nation the need for change in class leadership. The current trends need not shape the nation's destiny; they can be changed by a people determined to change them.

27. The Working Class and Political Action

From its infancy in the commercial stage to its aging in the monopoly stage, the capitalist class had called the political shots in the nation. Now, in its declining years and failing ability to look after the people's welfare, the nation needs a new vigorous leadership to challenge the rule of the self-centered monopoly capital.

No class in the nation is more qualified than the working class for the job. For it represents the great majority of the nation, creates its wealth, and maintains its metropolises—the sites of its work places and homes. It alone can defeat the ruling class on the political battlefield for it has the strength of great numbers, the ultimate command over the nation's economy, and the moral force as the nation's defender of human rights and social progress.

Monopoly capital's attacks of the '80s on the people's welfare are at last losing their force. The time is approaching for a people's counterattack to revive the nation's industries, rebuild its cities, and renew its national life. Organized labor has begun to move out of its defensive trenches and onto the broad theater of class and political struggle. The political struggle clearly requires new strategies and allies. If organized labor is to lead the fight for national progress, it must defend not only its own interests but those of all other peoples oppressed by monopoly capital. For alongside the antagonism between it and monopoly capital, to paraphrase Engels, is the general antagonism between all exploited and their exploiters, and it is precisely this circumstance that enables labor to represent not just its special class interest but those of the whole suffering humanity (Engels, 1935, 24).

Monopoly capital's global exploitation behooves organized

labor to lead in organizing millions of unorganized, oppressed working people at home and abroad. Fostering international labor unity is all the more compelling because millions of unorganized national- and racial-minority workers in the U.S. feel a close kinship and sympathy for people in their countries of origin whom the transnational corporations exploit. This modern reality makes necessary a labor strategy based on defense of a nationally and racially diverse working class at home and abroad in a global unity against the common class foe.

The heterogencity of the American working class, however, presents special organizational problems. Even the second and third generations of millions of workers retain the national, religious and cultural prides of their immigrant ancestors, leaving weak seams in the colorful patchwork of the American working class (Fried et al, 12–15; Green, 1976, 69). In cities across the country, its minorities continue to form separate neighborhoods, communities and associations. Many still think of themselves as workers on the job but as national minorities, ethnics, neighbors, and group members outside their work places. This duality of identity is a fact of American working-class life. Political unity of the working class in American cities must therefore arise from a political alliance of trade unions with the racially oppressed as well as with workers in their neighborhoods and organizations.

Organized labor and these people's organizations are natural allies; both have long struggled separately against the same political foes. They stand to gain much from mutual support in strikes against employers and in battles with landlords, redlining banks, hostile government bureaucrats, or prejudiced media. Some examples may illustrate this process. In one, a union helped save a neighborhood. In the 1960's, a strong organization was formed in San Francisco's Yerba Buena neighborhood to defend itself against a devastating Urban Renewal scheme. Drawing on their union experience and connections, veteran longshoremen who lived there organized the neighborhood to oppose the project's proposal to bulldoze their homes. After a long struggle, with active union support, the neighborhood organization won its demands to rehouse the dispossessed at public expense right where they lived, saving the neighborhood's integrity (Weiss, 73–74).

In another, neighborhood organizations helped bring victory to a union. In 1984, Yale University's clerical and technical workers led a successful long strike for union recognition and benefits. During a critical phase of the strike the union sought the help of New Haven's neighborhood and community organizations and got their support—from funds, to organizing, to picketing. The support tipped the scales in the struggle. That experience drew New Haven unions and people's organizations into close cooperation ever since (*Economic Notes*, Nov–Dec., 1985).

This trend has continued. At this writing, there is wide community and ad hoc organization support for the strike of the Pittston coal miners, as well as national labor solidarity. Similarly, around the Eastern Airline strike. On the political level, the Harold Washington Party in Chicago and the even more recent victory of David Dinkins in the New York primary election are evidence of the growing coalition of labor, Black people's organizations, and community activists, with important and growing support from white ethnic workers and their families. Clearly, combining the knowhow and resources of organized labor and organized communities can build a solid working-class power block in city politics. The forming alliance of union and neighborhood organizations can reach out to other ad hoc social movements to forge a political coalition with all who challenge monopoly capital's oppressive power. The movements opposing discrimination against racial and ethnic minorities, against women, the aged, the young, the handicapped, and the poor are, in fact, opposing evils committed by their common class enemy. United in a coalition, the separate movements would augment their individual powers manyfold in united action. Precisely such coalitions have won in the past bigger shares of the national wealth and better city services for the people. True, coalition diversity produces organizational stresses, but problems in struggle are the grindstones on which people's wisdom is sharpened and able leaders are honed (Clawford and Piven, 219–20). Coping with problems, people's leaders gain skill in the art of politics and confidence in dealing with their adversary. Seen up close, officials appear less awesome and the inner weaknesses of the ruling class more obvious. In close combat with their opposites, working class political fighters realize how much better the affairs of the nation and its cities could be run were the people in power.

The leadership in the alliance, however, must logically come from organized labor. Its long history, rich experience, celebrated victories, strength of numbers, and daily struggle for the welfare of working people, place upon it the responsibility (and honor) of leadership. To build and sustain it, organized labor must grow roots in the neighborhoods and the social communities in which the working class minorities live.

The people's alliance might mount a two-pronged political attack: one, to maximize possibilities for making a living in the city; the second, to raise the quality of life in its working-class districts.

The first concern in every working-class home is having well-paying jobs for those who can work and adequate support for those who cannot. Meeting this basic need in our society takes ceaseless political effort. Organized labor has always been prodding city governments to stimulate employment and restrain job-draining corporate disinvestment and plant closings. The alliance could add vigor and political clout to that effort. It might push for federally and state funded employment on socially useful public works, renewing and expanding city infrastructures and cultural life.

People, however, do not live by jobs alone. Urban life sags not only when people lack work, it also loses vigor when they lack decent housing, good transportation, good health care, good sanitation, good schools and, not least, a safe and cheerful environment. What have been sporadic actions by ad hoc groups to relieve such problems, the people's alliance might turn into a systematically organized, unremitting citywide struggle.

Poor physical environments in working-class districts have seemed least offensive only because compared with lacks in housing, transportation, health care, sanitation and schools they seemed more tolerable. Capitalist society has for so long inflicted drabness on working-class districts that it has become accepted as an inescapable evil. It is time that the dreary, joyless environments of working-class residential areas be recognized for the subtle means of oppression they are, for they depress and subdue the human spirit and, with it, the pluck of democratic citizenship. In its extreme, it has acted upon people in the slums and the ghettos as:

> A constant reminder of where they stood in society. If one's dwelling is shabby or worse, if the streets go unkempt and the garbage uncollected; if these rubbished streets are punctuated with abandoned shells of buildings and cars; if play spaces are scarce and unkempt, the

environment does more than assault the senses of sight and smell. It assaults the spirit, especially that portion of the spirit where self-regard is built (Canty, 103–04).

Good maintenance, beautification, and environmental enrichment ought to be an integral part of every city renewal plan to give every working-class neighborhood an upbeat tone. Good housing in a pleasant urban environment is a right of all working people, not the exclusive privilege of the rich. Only redevelopment to this end can be rightly called urban renaissance.

Since most problems of urban rehabilitation are clearly national in scope, their redress must be sought at the national political level. To be more effective, therefore, labor-community coalitions would obviously have to organize and extend their struggle to the national scale. But the strength of the national coalition, like the might of a river, depends on the number, size and vigor of its tributaries—the coalitions of its local units.

But what could be the national coalition's local unit in the modern metropolis? Each city and suburb? The metropolis itself?

Because cities and suburbs continue to govern autonomously within established legal boundaries, they are still perceived as independent entities. The fact, however, that their independence has long been superseded by the reality of the metropolis upon which they are dependent components suggests that the metropolis should be considered as a territorial unit of modern political alliances. The central cities, however, will remain the centers of metropolitan organization for the following cogent reasons. First, because here are concentrated organized masses who can provide adequate response to calls for mass action. Second, because working-class leadership is located in central cities for much the same reasons that other central administrative activities locate there. Their functioning requires face-to-face communication with leaders of other city-based labor and people's organizations and with political, governmental and other institutional representatives. Labor also needs quick access to various central information sources and to the many specialized legal, editorial, media, and distribution services. Third, the same law of polarity that governs production and marketing applies to organized workers as well. The dispersed working class in the vast area of the metropolis can be united politically only from a central point from which all parts of the metropolis can be most easily reached.

Great as the political influence of the working class has been in our national history, it fell far short of its potential. Compared with its economic weight and majority in the nation, it has been lagging in systematic national politics. That lag has put American labor at considerable disadvantage in the class struggle. As one labor writer put it: "For unions to fail to take on the employers in the political arena as well as economics, is like fighting a powerful antagonist with one hand tied behind you" (Green, 1976, 117). Where labor movements have been politically active and formed their own parties, as in most European countries, the working class has won far higher standards of living and positions of power in national and urban affairs.

In the absence of a labor party in our country, individual labor unions have engaged in city politics defensively and limitedly, relying on the temporary convenience, opportunism, or charity of common politicians to fend off employers' attacks. Few have a sustained struggle for broad social benefits. Moreover, lacking their own political party and mass communication media, they could not effectively counteract upperclass propaganda branding unions as troublemaking selfish "special interest groups" while exalting capitalists as constructive "civic minded community leaders." Unions of city workers have been especially vilified as "payroll padding" villains responsible for the high cost of city services and rising taxes when, in truth, city services are by their nature labor intensive and taxes rise because the politically well-organized upper classes manage to evade paying their just share of social costs (Rich, 199). Generally shunning systematic action in city politics, organized labor has forfeited possible advantages had it claimed its rightful place in the political arenas. It could have turned city politics from a field of only upperclass victories to one on which the people could have done battle with telling effect (Bollens and Schmandt, 140–41; Adrian, 112).

The word "politics," however, has evoked loathing in many working people, for whom corrupt antilabor politicians have made "playing politics" a contemptible activity. This, however, ought not twist the meaning of "politics," for the political decisions made daily at every government level affect the working class every day.

Moreover, with labor out of the political arena, the upper classes are free to set the political agenda. Freely deciding which issues are and which are not fit for public attention, they can maintain the illusion that their interests coincide with those of the people. Finally, the widening range of working class concerns in the fast-moving social developments of modern times make its engagement in politics imperative. The evidently endless crises of capitalism, constant threat to living standards, increasing pollution, and the genocidal danger of modern weapons raise workingclass worries not only over jobs and wages but also over the broader issues of housing, taxes, inflation, health insurance, education, urban decline, corporate and government corruption, the global economy and environment, and world peace. These concerns can be dealt with only through politics. Organized labor has therefore increasingly moved into struggle on political issues at the national and local levels. Of the two, it has found that local political power brokers and government officials could be more easily dealt with.

Perhaps the time has come for bold steps to remove the legal restrictions preventing cities from creating jobs and raising revenues through enterprises of their own. That is not a new or as radical an idea as it may sound. It is, in fact, an old practice in some European capitalist countries whose cities draw revenues from nationalized industries and utilities. Why not city owned and operated banks, power and gas companies, or even manufacturing plants in our country? (Friedland et al, 1977, 454).

Or take the matter of city taxes. Although not at once obvious to everyone, the conflict over who pays how much in city taxes is part of the struggle over profits and wages. When capitalists receive city services for their enterprises they in effect transfer a part of their business costs to the city budget—costs they only partly repay in taxes. By far the largest part is paid by the people in income, sales, and real estate taxes (Marcusen, 90). Renters may harbor the illusion that the city real estate tax is no problem of theirs, but it is, for it is built into their rent (Adrian, 112). Thus, the city tax system needs new answers to old questions: How to plug the tax loopholes the upper classes enjoy and set up effective democratic controls to assure progressive tax collection? How to simplify the tax system and eliminate its negative effects on rents and the housing stock? Does the answer lie, as some propose, in replacing the property tax with a progressive income tax?

The growth of central business districts (CBDs) is yet another example. Politicians and the media have trumpeted CBD growth as heralding an urban "renaissance," although outside CBD areas, especially in working-class districts, urban decline has generally continued and even accelerated by diversion of city funds to CBD developments. City officials claim that the CBD investment will generate more jobs than those lost to industrial disinvestment. People's politics must establish its own policy by first answering some practical questions: What are the real credits and debits of CBD growth? Do benefits spin off CBD growth to help the rest of the city? How *can* CBD prosperity be tapped to benefit the rest of the city?

Gentrification in the wake of CBD growth is another concern. Its displacement of low-income people tends to create conflicts between the strata at the opposite ends of the working-class income scale. People's politics must find ways to minimize such conflicts by addressing two basic questions: Can the pain of displacement be reduced by forcing developers and the city to adequately compensate the victims of displacement? More basically, how to control real estate and developer operations to avoid or reduce their negative effects on housing, land use, and the people in the city?

These few examples suggest the wide political field upon which people's politics could challenge monopoly capital to make it pay some of its long overdue debts to the people. The itemized bill would obviously run higher than any city could collect by itself. Clearly, the federal government, which draws the most tax dollars from the cities, must be forced to ante up the difference. A main task of working-class politics, therefore, would be to struggle for a national urban policy addressing the needs of the people in housing, health care, education, social services, and people-oriented urban renewal. Carrying the political struggle from the city to the national level requires merging the people's political alliances and coalitions of all cities for a united national political fight.

28. Toward a National Strategy

To effectively halt and reverse the present state of urban decline, the people's alliances must find ways to unite the cities so as exercise their combined strength at the national level. They must form in essence, if not in organizational form, a people's league of cities to press for urban demands.

Monopoly capital has itself set the agenda for immediate goals: a defense against its abuses of social life in the cities. Each of the groups making up the alliance will have, of course, specific grievances of its own. They could all be included in the struggle program to forge a strong unity around the principle that an injury to one in fact injures all.

The greatest danger in recent times has been the epidemic of plant closings spreading economic and social ruin among industrial communities. No theoretical soothsaying that disinvestment in industry means merely a transition to more progressive forms of production can condone governmental inaction in the face of the consequences they have visited upon hundreds of communities for whom plant closings are an immediate matter of life and death. The peril to millions of working people and the threat to a myriad communities demand that the nation restrain monopoly corporations from wielding their economic power with arrogant disregard for community welfare and human life, and that government declare affected communities disaster areas and provide them accordingly with appropriate relief and renewal.

Equally disastrous is the lot of the thousands of homeless roaming the streets of our cities. Emergency care and housing to comfort and rehabilitate them should be set going at once. Means are not lacking. Vacant apartments, government facilities, mobile homes and other emergency housing can be used until the employable homeless have jobs and are properly housed, and those needing help get decent and constructive care. At the same time, the government should prevent further homelessness by stopping evictions and home foreclosures of unemployed or needy for lapses in rent or mortgage payments. Government should assume responsibility for their housing, heat and light bills for the duration of the unempoyed household's inability to pay them due to circumstances beyond their control. It should also stop all demolitions of low-income housing stock until an adequate rehabilitation and building program meets the market demand for affordable homes.

The people's "league of cities" would press also to reverse the cuts monopoly capital had effected in city health, transportation, sanitation, education, safety, and welfare services, and to increase state and federal aid to the cities so they can maintain and enhance their livability and attractiveness to economic activities.

How many of these goals the cities may achieve will depend partly on the administrations in power in federal, state and city governments; partly on the condition of the national economy; but mainly on how large, united, and militant the people's alliance becomes. Recent experience has shown that even while a people's coalition has been developing, even in 1980s' reactionary Washington, organized labor's and the people's resistance did save most of the programs they had won in earlier struggles—despite relentless attacks. Social Security, unemployment insurance, public housing, the wage-hour law, education and welfare programs—although cut and weakened—remain in force. Should the trend toward electing more progressive leaders at the local level continue, should the economy get into more difficulties—the possibilities for popular gains can increase.

If there are signs of tottering in the national economy, the people's coalition should mount an offensive for national policies to redirect the flow of national funds away from feeding corporate subsidies and wasteful foreign intrigues and toward benefiting the people in our cities and nation.

This is bound to rouse furious monopoly-capital resistance, whose leaders and minions will most likely lurk within the military-industrial complex, the government, and the mass media. To ferret them out, to expose them and to force them to yield ground should constitute the tactics of the people's offensive.

The offensive must also mount an ideological drive against anti-city ideas to break the hold of romantic myths about the "good life" in the country, which political reaction has used to malign the city it fears for its progressive political leanings. Long prevailing anti-city notions have helped to make us the sole advanced nation having no consistant view of its urbanization, no clear idea of its system of cities, no coherent national urban policy, no urban development program, not even a plan to halt urban decline. It is time the nation faced the reality that for most of its people in modern times the "good life" *can* blossom in cities. It must grasp and accept the fact that its cities are vital centers of its life and that the lot of the people who live in them must command its central attention.

Accordingly, a national urban policy should boldly advance a series of essential programs:

1. A public works program to rehabilitate and modernize urban infrastructures and public facilities, especially in decayed urban areas, with emphasis on hiring and training local unemployed—under affirmative action—for the physical, economic, and social renewal of their communities.

2. A massive national housing program to provide affordable low- and middle-income housing throughout metropolitan areas.

3. A program to train or retrain and absorb the chronically unemployed of central cities and old suburbs into the metropolitan suburban economies.

4. A land control program in metropolitan areas restricting land speculation, acquiring unused land for public ownership and development or lease, and regulating land use to increase high- and middle-density development conducive to public transportation.

5. To promote public transportation in metropolises at low or no fares to invigorate metropolitan economic and social life and reduce road congestion, accidents, and air pollution.

6. High-quality free public education, from nursery through university, to assure universal access to employment in the modern technologically advancing national economy.

7. Universal health care, child care for working and ill mothers, and nursing care for the disabled and infirm aged.

8. A poverty-fighting program of nationally uniform welfare standards assuring an adequate income and dignified support system for all who need it.

9. A program for progressive improvement of urban environ-

ments reducing air, land, and water pollution, and enforcing safe waste disposal.

10. A program for beautification of cities, creating ennobling urban amenities inspiring love and pride of place in every neighborhood.

A national urban policy based on such programs would benefit the nation in several ways. It would greatly cut unemployment. Being labor intensive, construction and city services employ many high and low skills and generate many jobs in supporting activities. It would reduce the severity and speed recovery from economic recessions. And it would ease conversion of the military to a civilian economy in the process of world disarmament.

Most people would probably agree that such urban policy is desirable, but many may doubt that it is realizable and ask: Where would the needed money come from?

Ironically, few question the nation's ability to produce great wealth or the wisdom of lavishing it on powerful monopoly corporations, or giving it up for bank bailouts, or pouring it into padded defense contracts and wars. But if the nation can be that productive and extravagant while those whose labor make it rich live in cities too poor to provide good public services, is it not possible, just, and more useful that the wealth they produce be channeled more to improve their condition and less to dubious corporate incentives and questionable "defense needs?" The people's offensive should attack the nation's lopsided priorities and strive to replace the old ways of public revenue raising and spending with a new national policy that would include:

1. Speeding world disarmament: defuse regional wars, cut the military budget, and draw on the saved funds to finance urban revival.

2. Plug the loopholes in federal, state, and local tax laws through which monopoly corporations and the super-rich keep billions in unpaid taxes.

3. Raise corporate and high-income taxes; cut or eliminate regressive home real estate and sales taxes.

4. Finance cities mainly by per-capita share of the national income tax, freeing the central cities from dependence on state governments, and the suburbs from competition for corporate enterprises.

5. Relieve the cities of bearing the cost for the national and state responsibilities of public education, health, and welfare.

6. Lift the bans on cities against engaging in profitable enterprises. Let cities own and profit from public utilities, municipal banks, and like business enterprises.

Significantly, each of the proposed reforms calls for national rather than local programs, yet each deals with local everyday living needs. For in our complex integrated political economy no local community—not a suburb, not a city, not a metropolis, not even a region—can meet its needs alone.

Ironically, monopoly capital's politicians and media hustlers have long labelled the people's organizations "special interest groups." The people allegedly are adequately represented and defended on Capitol Hill and in the White House by "friendly" elected officials. But they have been seldom represented by politicians of and loyal to the people. A people's coalition, based upon its cities, must field its own candidates for public office.

Consistent working-class electoral politics could achieve two advantages not fully realizable by other organizational means. First, electoral struggles would yield bonuses beyond electing candidates to office. They would draw closer and raise the class awareness of masses of people, reaffirm and expand the people's democratic rights, and boost the prestige of labor unions and people's organizations in the nation. Secondly, rallying its majority around its own platform and leaders, the working class would at last begin its historic march toward becoming the leading class and political force in the nation.

In electoral struggles, the working class could beat the upper-class even though the latter can gather huge sums to grease its election campaigns. Only the working class can deliver the votes, as well as raise the needed campaign money through a mass of small contributions. Public financing initiatives can also equalize expenditures and sums raised. These advantages, however, materialize only with the presence of a highly visible permanent political organization having an effective network of communications with its working-class constituency.

Building the base of its own political organization in the cities, working-class electoral activity gives significant leverage in city affairs. At best, it could elect its own to city office. Holding office offers many advantages. It would give its representatives political experience, confer upon them leadership status in the city, and make possible their full-time political activity. Their powers to affect new laws, interpret old laws, push or delay executive action are obvious.

Some ruling class pundits have brazenly declared that "problems of governance in the United States stem from an excess of democracy" (Crozier et al, 113). Such admission confirms monopoly capital's inclination toward totalitarian rule. To the working class, on the contrary, preserving and expanding democracy is vital to its political welfare. The electoral arena is now full of restrictions, exceptions, and exclusions. Every state and city has its own laws and rules barricading the way to the ballot for all but the two major parties. The people's coalition would therefore need to win national electoral reforms to remove the obstacles placed against new parties, introduce proportional representation, institute equal funding of election campaigns, provide free and equal media coverage for all candidates, and remove all restrictions on voting.

Political activity would logically move in the direction of a national party of labor and the people in opposition to the established parties of capital. It would defend and further the common interests of labor, oppressed racial and national minorities, women, youth, seniors and other social groups threatened by monopoly capital's domination. It should not, however, limit itself to electoral and legislative activity but should always engage the people in political action to advance their rights in every area of urban life. High on its agenda should be expanding democracy in city government, opening all its agencies to public view and control.

The recent call of NOW (National Organization for Women) for an independent party, the electoral strength of the Rainbow Coalition led by Jesse Jackson, labor's thrust for its own independent role—all are stirrings in the direction of breakaway from the two-party trap as we have known it.

Reforms won in struggle improve the life of the nation's working people, and, in the process, develop the people's political consciousness, leadership skills, and unity. Reforms, however, have their limits. They can diminish the abuses of a basically unjust society, but they cannot make it just. In the final account, reforms of capitalist society do not exceed the limits of the ruling class to grant them, lest they threaten its existence. Were there no exploitation of labor, no unemployment to keep labor competitive, no profiting from privately owned buildings, no division among its subjects, no public taxation, no freedom to exploit land and natural resources— there would be no capitalism.

Making reforms the ultimate goal would lead the people's coalition into a political dead-end street. For the ruling class would ceaselessly try to withdraw the gains and force the people back to square one, back into a defensive position. Loss of political vigor would inevitably follow, for political struggle brooks no stalemate. Its combatants must either press forward to victory or sustain loss and fall back.

Its forward development would impel the coalition—or a people's labor party—toward becoming an instrument of a struggle to change the social order into one based on a higher democracy and social justice. When it becomes powerful enough to rule, it must move to annul the domination of the capitalist minority and its ownership of the national wealth, and lead the working majority to political dominance and public ownership of the nation's resources. For only by placing the nation's resources in the national keep can it finally free government to fully serve the people's welfare and set its cities moving on the road to unlimited progress.

Eastwood

NOTES

Introduction, pp. 1–11

1. See description and critique of positivism-pragmatism in Wells, pp. 13, 187–190, 200–201; Cornforth, p. v; Osipov, p. 73.

2. Since the mid-1970s, several new philosophic approaches to urban studies (such as idealism, humanism, structuralism and materialism) began to challenge the assumptions and premises of positivism. Their effect on the literature on cities, however, has been quite small. Others (such as behavioralism) try to correct the deficiencies of positivism without altering its basic premises. They merely play obbligato variations around the dominant tune.

3. Robert E. Park, Ernest W. Burgess and Frederick D. McKenzie, *The City*, University of Chicago Press, Chicago, 1925.

4. Louis Wirth, *On Cities and Social Life*, 1948.

5. See, for example, Raymond Williams, *The Country and the City*, Oxford University Press, 1973, pp. 302–303.

6. See V.I. Lenin, *Imperialism: The Highest Stage of Capitalism*, especially chapters 3 and 7. International Publishers, New York, 1939.

Part One, pp. 15–91

1. Steve Talbot, *Roots of Oppression*, chap. 2; International Publishers, New York, 1981.

2. The vestiges of feudal serf-master production relations continued in the early years of commercial capitalism. Indentured servitude and slavery lasted longer in the colonies, especially in the South where a labor shortage and plantation econmy demanded a large stable work force (*See* Foner, 1976, 8–9).

3. The population of Boston, New York, Baltimore and Philadelphia increased between 180 percent and 290 percent.

4. Corporations, i.e., pooled capital, appeared during the commercial stage in the textile, iron and coal industries and in canal and railroad enterprises. No individual or partnership of capitalists could raise the $15,000,000 to build the Baltimore and Ohio Railroad or the $25,000,000 the Erie Canal cost. In 1850 Boston, fifteen associate families controlled 20 percent of the country's cotton spindles, 30 percent of Massachusetts' railroad mileage, 40 percent of the city's banking, and virtually all of the city's economic, political and cultural life (Foner, 1947, 56).

5. While only 77 patents were granted in the United States in 1810 and 544 in 1830, the number had risen to 993 in 1850 and 4,778 in 1860 (Foner, 1947, 53); from 13,000 in 1870 to 21,000 in 1880 (Foner, 1955, 14).

6. The United States value of manufacture rose fourfold between 1840 and 1860 from $483,278,000 to $1,885,861,000; cotton spindles—from 2,284,631 to 5,235,000; value of woolens products—from $20,696,999 to

$68,665,000. From 1850 to 1860, production value of tools and farm machinery rose from $10,500,000 to $21,000,000; furniture and upholstery from $7,000,000 to $28,000,000; and vehicles from $18,000 to $36,000,000 (Foner, 1947, 57).

7. Between 1860 and 1880, the United States doubled its wheat and corn production, and doubled it again by 1900. In 1880, it became the world's largest exporter of wheat (Schlesinger, 1951, 37).

8. Local business districts developed in some sections of cities, serving mainly as distribution centers for household goods and maintenance services, and hosting some spinoffs from CBD production activities. But only the CBD had the remarkable growth dynamics generated by its large external economies of scale.

9. Horse-drawn streetcars, which dominated urban transportation between 1850 and 1890, moved at the rate of 4 to 7 miles per hour serving, within half an hour, areas between 2 and 3½ miles from the center of the city. The electric trolley cars, which dominated urban transportation between 1890 and 1910, more than doubled the speed of movement in the city quadrupling the area reached within half an hour of the city center (Ward, 1971, 125, 131).

10. In the final decades of the 19th century, the concentration of production in large industrial monopolies led to their tendency to merge or coalesce with finance capital. In the process, finance capital increasingly assumed the lead in the economy, politics, government, and urban affairs.

11. In the 1880s, the number of employed child workers increased from 1,000,000 to 1,750,000. Like the men, women and children worked 12 hours a day. As late as 1908, steel mills and railway switch yards in Pittsburgh employed workers in 12-hour shifts of seven days a week (Callow, 1982, 111).

12. The early romantics and the intellectual writers later in the century thought the cities were corrupting those who lived in them and enslaving the nation's rural inhabitants. They echoed the nation's farmers dislike of the big cities—the seats of the new power of capital, the management of railroads, and the production of machines which were revolutionizing agriculture and subjecting it to capitalism (Diamond, 1941, 69–70). Some historians hold that the anti-city attitudes of the nation's intellectuals merely reflected a dominant anti-city attitude in the history of the nation. Others, however, asked how the sentiments of intellectuals, admittedly alienated from the rest of the nation, could be considered representative. These historians argue that antiurbanism has been overstated, obscuring opposite attitudes current at the time, the affirmation of city-boosterism, for example, and the ambivalent attitudes of both liking and distrusting the city (Callow, 1982, 331).

13. The danger of spreading infectious diseases through contaminated water was well known by then, for the germ theory reached the United States in the 1870s. Yet, city governments gave priority to infrastructural projects for industry and commerce; provision of water supply and sewage disposal in residential districts came off second best. In the 1880s, most cities still used the conventional method of discharging household, industrial and business wastes into private cesspools adjoining dwellings, factories and shops. As cities grew, new homes, tenements and work places built the privies and cesspools they needed, increasing soil and water pollution. Only after pollution caused cata-

strophic epidemics did public water supply and sewage disposal become a generally required municipal service. Still, the big cities that had some underground sewer lines discharged their wastes into nearby bodies of water.

The disposal of solid wasates was similarly left to private arrangements. Yards, alleys and street frontages of buildings became holding areas for piles of decaying garbage until their periodic removal in open wagons to municipal dumps, or by scows and barges a few miles out to sea (Peterson, 1981, 15–21).

14. Agents of American corporations offered to prepay passage from Europe to United States ports for immigrants who agreed to work for wages far below those paid to American workers (Schlesinger, 1951, 167). The 13.5 million mostly peasant immigrants to the United Staes in the late nineteenth century had no choice other than to stream to industrial cities. By the mid-1870s, the country had no more free-land frontiers, and mechanization was sending thousands of superfluous farm workers to seek jobs in the cities. By 1910, therefore, the large influx of immigrants changed the composition of our urban population. About two-thirds of the urban population in the North's biggest industrial cities consisted of first and second generation immigrants (Glaab, 1963, 176; McKelvey, 1969, 63; Ward, 1971, 51).

15. The term "ghetto" initially referred to quarters in European cities where oppressed Jews were officially confined, then erroneously used at the turn of the century to describe the concentration of Jewish immigrants on New York's Lower East Side and, by extension, to other concentrations of national minorities in American cities. It has been incorrectly applied to a variety of American ethnic neighborhoods.

White ethnic neighborhoods did not form primarily because of repressive controls, except for a few years after the heavy immigration at the turn of the 20th century when anti-alien prejudices and fears isolated the newcomers. Integration and mobility have since dispersed most of those immigrants within the urban fabric. What white ethnic neighborhoods continue to exist have resulted from voluntary bunching and self-imposed seclusion for religious or nationalist reasons, i.e., the "New Polands" "Little Italys," etc.

Part Two, pp. 95 to 161

1. Based in part on my essay "Transnational Corporations and Urban Decline" in *Political Affairs*, January 1983, 30–37.

2. The tendency of monopoly capital to integrate the capitalist system globally is demonstrated by the increased frequency of corporate mergers and growth of transnational corporations. In 1941, for example, 1000 U.S. manufacturing firms controlled approximately two-thirds of all manufacturing assets. By 1980, only 200 firms did. Concentrated capital enabled key corporations to coordinate, command, and control critical trade, communication, manufacturing and distribution networks throughout the world. Transnational corporations made production location and relocation decisions on the basis of corporate profitability, growth and convenience in disregard for the welfare of *nations*, let alone of local communities (Smith, M. P., 1980, 236–37).

3. Discoveries in electronics, cybernetics and optics led to new means of communication. Lasers revolutionized many fields of technology. Advances in biology and genetic engineering found practical applications in agriculture,

pharmacology and food industries. These and other achievements in science and technology set off a wave of innovations in production and the birth of new industries. The high and growing demand for the new products at high monopoly prices and profits account, in large part, for the shifts in capital from old sectors of industry in long established locations to new ones in more advantageous locations.

4. Metropolitan areas are not to be confused with the *Standard Metropolitan Statistical Areas* (SMSAs) often cited in the literature on the monopolies. The Bureau of the Census bases its SMSAs on county and local government boundaries which do not necessarily represent the real, and changing, areas of metropolises. The SMSA was adopted to compensate for the absence of statistical data in the expanded urban territories when cities failed to expand their political boundaries as they grew. Since June 1983, the Bureau of the Census replaced the term SMSA and SCMSA (Standard Consolidated Metropolitan Statistical Area) with the new terms MSA (Metropolitan Statistical Area), CMSA (Consolidated Metropolitan Statistical Area) and PMSA (Primary Metropolitan Statistical Area—individual within MSAs and CMSAs). The entire territory of the United States is classified as Metropolitan (inside MSAs and CMSAs) or Non-metropolitan (outside MSAs and CMSAs).

5. Not all central cities have been losing jobs. In 1975, only 11 percent of 388 cities of over 50,000 recorded an absolute job loss. Often, growth in nonmanufacturing activities has stimulated central-city industrial growth. While the proportion of central cities who lost population increased between 1960 and 1975, that of cities which lost jobs dropped from 21.1 percent to 10.1 percent over the same period (Hicks, 124).

6. A study of job growth in San Francisco between 1972 and 1984 by Massachusetts Institute of Technology economist David Birch confirmed his similar findings in other cities that "in general, job growth and growth in new office space are inversely related." Central-city office expansion not only did not create the job gain the cities expected, it resulted in a net job loss since the 1980s. Despite that, and climbing office vacancy rates due to overbuilding, office-tower building continues unabated because it has been driven not by demand for office space but by tax shelter considerations. A huge surplus of investment capital and a series of new tax laws have made investment in office-tower construction highly attractive, even if the buildings go largely unrented for many years. When vacancy rates get very high, however, the investors suddenly pull out, as they did in Houston, plummeting construction jobs almost to zero (Redmond and Goldsmith, 18–21).

7. Between 1920 and 1970, capital concentration in agriculture and its mechanization drove about 40 million rural inhabitants to cities. About five million of them were Southern Black farm workers and small farmers (Hill, 1983, 240; Perry and Watkins, 1977, 286–87).

8. In London of the 1960s, young suburban gentry, engaged in doing business in the central business district, began buying up and restoring decaying old homes in blighted central city working-class neighborhoods. The influx of this middle-class gentry raised rents and house prices displacing former

renters and home owners whose old neighborhoods became no longer affordable. Londoners dubbed this process of conversion from working-class to middle-class neighborhoods "gentrification," a term used since for the similar process in our cities.

9. Motor vehicle registration jumped from 9,239,000 in 1920 to 19,941,000 in 1925, to 26,532,000 in 1930, reaching 32,036,000 in 1940.

10. The federal government aided suburban housing construction through guarantees to banks to buy back mortgages the banks did not want to hold for their full term. Mortgages were also offered to buyers at lower interst rates and insured against loss. In addition, home buyers were offered liberal tax credits for mortgage interest payments. These incentives have been estimated to have given $3 billion annually in housing aid to middle- and upper-income households (Goering and Lichten, 310).

11. Real Estate Research Corporation, *The Costs of Sprawl*, 1974, 7, 21.

12. Boris Pashkarev, vice-president in charge of research and planning, New York Regional Plan Association, in a paper read at the 1976 Congress of the American Institute of Planners.

13. A 1967 survey by the AFL-CIO Committee on Political Education (COPE) "found that almost half of those polled lived outside the central city, and of those under 40 years of age nearly three-quarters were suburbanites" (Bollens and Schmandt, 52). In 1977, the Bureau of Labor Statistics showed that while 28 percent of all employed in the United States lived in central cities, 41 percent lived in suburbs and 31 percent lived outside metropolitan areas. In 1980, 60.2 percent of metropolitan workers lived in the suburbs.

14. Suburbanizing industries at first tended to settle on cheap land near transport routes to assure access to markets and labor. In the 1960s and '70s, however, industrial locations were also influenced by middle-class residential suburbs luring industries with cheap land, low tax rates, and other incentives, to boost their tax revenues. In choosing the winning suburbs, industries tended to pick small wealthy municipalities with high zoning requirements and property taxes owning large outlying tracts of land in order to force their workers to live in separate suburbs, away from their plants. The strategy yielded wealthy suburbanites lower property taxes than those paid in neighboring working-class suburbs for the same municipal services, and robbed the workers from having a civic say over the operations of their employers (Hoch, 47–48).

15. Oil and natural gas supplied less than half of United States fuel needs in 1940, 57 percent in 1950, 73 percent in 1960, and 78 percent in 1975 while coal provided only 17 percent. In 1975, the Sunbelt produced 82 percent of the country's oil and 88 percent of its natural gas (Sole, 175).

16. Great Soviet Encyclopedia, 1978, 4:4D-41.

17. Nadel evaluated the 1970 U.S. Census of Population and arrived at approximate proportions of the several social classes in the U.S. labor force. Using Nadel's derived ratios, the approximate size of each class in 1970 may be computed with the aid of this formula: $\dfrac{A \times B \times C}{D} = E$ where: A = Nadel's percentage of the class in the labor force, B = the 1970 labor force, U.S. Bureau of the Census, C = Average 1970 household (1970 population divided by number of 1970 households), D = Total 1970 U.S. Population, E = Percentage

of the class in the 1970 U.S. population. Thus: $\dfrac{.03 \times 79,802,000 \times 3.14}{208,067,000} = .04$

Sources: Nadel (1982) Table 5,94; Statistical Abstracts of the United States, 1986.

18. Repeating the procedure in Note 17, the percentage of the middle class in the 1970 population may be derived thus:

$$\dfrac{.19 \times 79,802,000 \times 3.14}{208,067,000} = .23$$

19. This is based on the total 1970 labor force multiplied by .78 and the 1970 adjusted average household, and divided by the total 1970 population. Allowing for more than one worker in many working-class families, the 1970 average household is here modified to an assumed 2.44. Thus: $\dfrac{79,802,000 \times .78 \times 2.44}{208,067,000} = .73$ of the national population.

Sources: Nadel, 1982, Table 5, 94; U.S. Statistical Abstracts, 1986.

20. Ebenezer Howard, *Garden Cities of To-Morrow,* London: Faber and Faber, Ltd., 1951.

21. Patrick Gedess, *Cities in Evolution: An Introduction to the Town Planning Movement and to the Study of Civics,* New York: Harper and Row, 1968.

22. Frank Lloyd Wright, *The Living City,* New York: Horizon Press, 1958.

23. See Melvin M. Webber, "The Post-City Age," *Daedalus,* vol. 97, no. 4, 1968; Jean Gottman, "Urban Centrality and Interweaving of Quaternary Activities," Brian J. L. Berry, "The Geography of the U.S.A. in the Year 2,000," and others in *Ekistics,* vol. 29, no. 174; and P. L. Meier, *The Communication Theory of Urban Growth,* MIT Press, 1965 and "The Metropolis As a Transaction Maximizing System," Daedalus, vol. 97, no. 4, 1968.

24. The idea of the "post-industrial society" was developed by Daniel Bell in *The Coming Post Industrial Society: A Venture in Social Forecasting,* New York: Basic Books, 1973.

25. See Roger Starr, "Making New York Smaller," *New York Times Magazine,* November 14, 1976.

26. Historically, most state governments have been controlled by rural anti-city politicians. State constitutions, adopted in the predominently agricultural period of their histories, based legislature representation on geography rather than population—a defense the farmers created against political domination by city-based developing capitalism. Most state legislatures have therefore been dominated by minority rural populations guarding their state-financed privileges against the growing cities' rising demands for state financial support.

The 1964 Supreme Court one-man-one-vote decision ended this electoral anachronism. It increased, however, the representation of the more populous suburbs. Anti-city suburban politicians soon allied with their rural counterparts to continue state anti-city policies. The cities have therefore turned to the federal government for help in times of crisis (Rogers, 130–31; Berman, 79–81).

27. Statistical Abstracts of 1986, U.S. Bureau of the Census.

28. In his *American Ground Transportation: A Proposal for Restructuring the*

Automobile, Truck, Bus and Rail Industries (presented before the Subcommittee on Antitrust and Monopoly of the Committee on the Judiciary, United States Senate, pursuant to S. Res. 56, Sec. 4, Feb. 26, 1974, U.S. Printing Office, Washington, D.C.) Bradford C. Snell documents how the powerful automobile, oil and tire monopolies have manipulated all levels of government to methodically destroy intra- and inter-city rail transportation throughout the country to promote the construction of highways and sale of motor vehicles. Snell had charged that between 1932 and 1956 the automobile lobby had spent millions of dollars to gain control of 100 electric rail systems in 45 cities of 16 states and convert their operations to buses. In the 1940s, it bought up and scrapped parts of the Pacific Electric, then a viable interurban electric rail system serving 110 million passengers in 56 Southern California towns, forcing it out of business by 1961. Since 1974, Los Angeles has been trying to reestablish the city's rail transit system the auto lobby had ruined.

29. The "services" theory is badly misconceived. Even in the industrial-capitalist stage, service workers outnumbered manufacturing workers. In 1880, for example, manufacturing jobs accounted for 19 percent while "service" jobs stood at 25 percent of the national work force and 60 percent of the urban work force. Judged by "post-industrial society" criteria, therefore, the United States has always been a "service" rather than an industry society (Walker, 1985, 81–82).

Part Three, pp. 165 to 193

1. Gans, H. J., "The Future of Suburbs," in R. Ehrensaft and· R. Etzioni, eds., *Anatomies of America: Sociological Perspectives.* London: 1969.

2. See D. R. Fusfield, "The Economics of Cities," ch. 42 in *Economics,* Lexington Heath, 1972; D. Netzer, *Economics and Urban Problems,* New York, 1972; J. Lindsay, *The Future of American Cities,* Britanica Book of the Year, 1972.

REFERENCES

Abbott, Carl. *Urban America: Growth and Politics in Sunbelt Cities.* Chapel Hill: University of North Carolina Press, 1981

Abrams, Charles. *Forbidden Neighbors.* New York: Harper and Brothers, 1955.

The City Is the Frontier. New York: Harper and Row, 1965

Adrian, Charles R. and Press, Charles. *Governing Urban America: Structure, Politics, and Administration.* New York: McGraw Hill Book Co., Inc., 1972

Akhiezer, A. S. "Rabochii Klass i Urbanizatsia v Usloviakh Nauchnotekhicheskoi Pevolutsii" [the working class and urbanization under conditions of the science-technology revolution] in Ianitskii, 1972

Alcaly, Roger E. and Mermelstein, David, eds. *The Fiscal Crisis of American Cities.* New York: Vintage Books, 1977

Aptheker, Herbert. *The American Revolution, 1763–1783.* New York: International Publishers, 1960

And Why Not Every Man? Berlin, GDR: Seven Seas Publishers, 1961

Afro-American History: The Modern Era. New York: Citadel Press, 1971

The Unfolding Drama: Studies in U.S. History. Edited by Bettina Aptheker. New York: International Publishers, 1978

Arab-Ogly, E. A. "Sovremionii Mir i Sotsial'nye Problemy Urbanizatsii [The contemporary world and social problems of urbanization] in Ianitskii, 1972

Ashton, Patrick J. "Urbanization and the Dynamics of Suburban Development Under Capitalism," in Tabb and Sawers, 1984

Bensman, Joseph, and Vidich, Arthur J., eds. *Metropolitan Communities: New Forms of Urban Subcommunities.* New York: New Viewpoints, 1975

Berman, David R. *State and Local Politics.* Boston: Halbrook Press, Inc., 1975

Berry, Brian J. L. *Growth Centers in the American Urban System,* Vol. 1, Cambridge, Mass.: Ballinger Publishing Co., 1973

Blackmar, Betsy. "Class Conflict in Canadian Cities," *Journal of Urban History* 10 (February 1984): 211–221

Bluestone, Barry and Harrison, Bennett. *Capital and Communities: The Causes and Consequences of Private Disinvestment.* Washington, D.C.: The Progressive Alliance, 1980

Blumenfeld, Hans. "The Exploding Metropolis," *Monthly Review* 10 (April 1959): 476–486

The Modern Metropolis: Its Origins, Growth, Characteristics and Planning: Selected Essays. Edited by Paul D. Spreiregen. Cambridge, Mass.: The M.I.T. Press, 1967

"The Rational Use of Urban Space as National Policy," in Erber, Ernest, ed., *Urban Planning in Transition.* New York: Grossman Publishers, 1970

The Metropolis and Beyond. New York: John Wiley & Sons, 1979

Bollens, John C. and Schmandt, Henry J. *The Metropolis: Its People, Politics and Economic Life.* New York: Harper & Row, 1975

Boyte, Harry C. *The Backyard Revolution: Understanding the New Citizen Movement.* Philadelphia: Temple University Press, 1980

204 • References

Bradburry, Katherine L.; Downs, Anthony; and Small, Kenneth L. *Urban Decline and the Future of American Cities*. Washington, D.C.: Brookings Institution, 1982

Brownell, Blaine, and Goldfield, David, eds. *The City in Southern History: The Growth of Urban Civilization in the South*. Port Washington, N.Y.: Kennikat Press, 1977

Callow, Alexander B., Jr., ed. *American Urban History: An Interpretive Reader with Comments*. 3rd ed. New York: Oxford University Press, 1982

Canty, Donald. *A Single Society: Alternatives to Urban Apartheid*. New York: Frederick A. Praeger, 1969

Checkoway, Barry. "Large Builders, Federal Housing Programs and Postwar Suburbanization," in Tabb and Sawers, 1984

Claward, Richard A., and Piven, Frances Fox. *The Politics of Turmoil: Essays on Poverty, Race, and the Urban Crisis*. New York: Random House, 1974

Clawson, Marion. *Man and Land in the United States*. Lincoln, Nebraska: University of Nebraska Press, 1964

America's Land and Its Uses. Baltimore: The Johns Hopkins Press, 1972

Clay, Phillip L. *Neighborhood Renewal: Middle-Class Resettlement and Incumbent Upgrading in American Neighborhoods*. Lexington, Mass.: Lexington Books, 1979

Cohen, Barry, "Structural Crisis and Conditions of Labor." *Political Affairs* LXIV (June 1985): 10–16

Cohen, Robert B. "Multinational Corporations, International Finance and the Sunbelt" in Perry and Watkins, 1977

"The New International Division of Labor, Multinational Corporations and Urban Hierarchy" in Dean, Michael, and Scott, Allen J., eds. *Urbanization and Urban Planning in Capitalist Society*. London: Methuen, 1981

Coit, Katherine. "Local Action, Not Citizen Participation," in Tabb and Sawers, 1978

Conzen, Michael P. "American Cities in Profound Transition: The New City Geography of the 1980s. *Journal of Geography* 83 (May–June 1983): 94–102

Cornforth, Maurice. *In Defense of Philosophy: Against Positivism and Pragmatism*, International Publishers, New York, 1950.

The Open Philosophy and the Open Society. New York: International Publishers, 1968.

Cox, Kevin R., ed. *Urbanization and Conflict in Market Societies*. Chicago: Maaroufa Press, Inc., 1978

Crozier, Michael; Huntington, Samuel P., and Watanuki, Joji. *The Crisis of Democracy: Report on the Governability of Democracies to the Trilateral Commission*. New York: New York University Press, 1975

Cunningham, James, and Auerbach, Arnold, Jr. *The Urban Triangle: Corporate Political, and Neighborhood Power: The Pittsburgh Story* (unpublished) Pittsburgh: Hillman Library, University of Pittsburgh.

DeLast, Jacqueline. "Contracting Out Public Services: Some Unanswered Questions." Ph.D. dissertation. University of Pittsburgh, 1962

Delgado, Gary. *Organizing the Movement: The Roots and Growth of ACORN*. Philadelphia: Temple University Press, 1986

Diamond, William. "On the Dangers of Urban Interpretation of History," in

Goldman, Eric F., ed. *Historiography and Urbanization*. Port Washington, NY: Kennikat Press, Inc. 1941

Edel, Matthew. "The New York Crisis as Economic History," in Alcaly and Mermelstein, 1977

Editors of *Fortune*. *The Exploding Metropolis*. Garden City, NY: Doubleday Anchor Books, 1957

Encyclopedia Americana, 1983 ed. s.v. "History of Railroads in the United States" by John F. Stover

Engels, Frederick, *Anti-Duhring: Herr Eugene Duhring's Revolution in Science*. New York: International Publishers Co., 1935; Marx/Engels *Collected Works*, Vol. 25, 1987. "On the Housing Question," Marx-Engels *Collected Works*, Vol. 23, 1988 *Origin of the Family, Private Property and the State*. New York: International Publishers Co., 1942

Ernest, Robert, "The Living Conditions of the Immigrant," in Waksman, *The Urbanization of America*

Etzkowitz, Henry and Mack, Roger. "Corporations and the City: Oligopolies and Urbanization," *Comparative Urban Research* 6 (2–3 1978): 46–53

Fainstein, Norman I. and Fainstein, Susan S., eds. *Urban Policy Under Capitalism*. vol. 22, Urban Affairs Annual Reviews. Beverly Hills: Sage Publications, 1982

Faltermayer, Edmund K. *Redoing America*. New York: Evanston and London, 1968

Fincher, Ruth. "Analysis of the Local Level Capitalist State," *Antipode* 13 (2, 1981): 25–31

Flink, James J. *The Car Culture*. Cambridge, Mass.: The MIT Press, 1975

Foner, Philip S. *History of the Labor Movement in the United States*. Vol. 1: *From Colonial Times to the American Federation of Labor*. New York: International Publishers, 1947

History of the Labor Movement in the United States Vol. 2: From the Founding of the AF of L to the Emergence of American Imperialism. New York: International Publishers, 1955

History of the Labor Movement in the United States. Vol. 3: The Policies and Practices of the American Federation of Labor, 1900–1909. New York: International Publishers, 1964

Labor and the American Revolution. Westpoint, Conn.: Greenwood Press, 1976

History of the Labor Movement in the United States. Vol. 5: The AF of L in the Progressive Era, 1910–1915. New York: International Publishers, 1980

History of the Labor Movement in the United States Vol. 6: On the Eve of America's Entrance Into World War I, 1915–1916. New York: International Publishers, 1982

Fried, Marc; Fitzgerald, E.; Gleicher, P.; and Hartman, C. *The World of the Urban Working Class*. Cambridge, Mass.: Harvard University Press, 1973

Friedland, Roger; Piven, Frances Fox; and Alford, Robert R. "Political Conflict, Urban Structure, and Fiscal Crisis," *International Journal of Urban and Regional Research* 1 (October 1977): 447–471

Friedland, Roger. "Central City Fiscal Strains: The Public Costs of Private Growth," *International Journal of Urban and Regional Research* 5 (September, 1981): 356–375

Gertler, Len. "The Changing Metropolis and the Blumenfeld Blues," in Hitchcock,

206 • References

John R. and McMaster, Anne, eds., *The Metropolis: Proceedings of a Conference in Honor of Hans Blumenfeld*. Toronto: Department of Geography and Center for Urban and Community Studies, University of Toronto, 1985

Glaab, Charles N. *The American City: A Documentary History*. Homewood, Ill.: The Dorsey Press, Inc., 1963

Glaab, Charles, and Brown, Theodore. *A History of Urban America*. 2nd ed. New York: MacMillan Publishing Co., Inc., 1976

Glazerman, G. *Classes and Nations*. New York: Progress Publishers, 1977

Goering, John, and Lichten, Eric. "The Political Economy of Cities and the 'Urban Crisis'" in McNall, Scott, ed. *Political Economy: A Critique of American Society*. Glencoe, Ill.: Scott, Foresman and Co., 1981

Goldsmith, William W. and Jacobs, Henry M. "The Improbability of Urban Policy: The Case of the United States," *Journal of the American Planning Association* 48 (Winter 1982): 53–66

Goodman, Jay S. *The Dynamics of Urban Government and Politics*. New York: Macmillan, 1975.

Gordon, David. "Capitalist Development and the History of American Cities," in Tabb and Sawers, 1978

Gottdiener, M. "The Theory of Metropolitan Expansion: A Reexamination," *Comparative Urban Research* 10 (1 1983): 108–124

Gottman, Jean. "The Evolution of Urban Centrality," Ekistics 39 (April 1975): 220–228

Green, Constance McLoughlin. *The Rise of Urban America*. New York: Harper & Row, 1965

Green, Gil. *What's Happening to Labor*. New York: International Publishers, 1976

Haas, Edward F. "The Southern Metropolis, 1940–1976," in Brownell and Goldfield, 1977

Hall, Peter. *The World Cities*. New York: McGraw Hill Book Co., 1966

Hamilton, Richard F. *Class and Politics in the United States*. New York: John Wiley & Sons, Inc., 1972

Harloe, Michael, ed. *Captive Cities: Studies in the Political Economy Of Cities and Regions*. New York: John Wiley and Sons, 1977

Harring, Sidney L. *Policing a Class Society: The Experience of American Cities, 1865–1915*. Brunswick, N.J.: Rutgers University Press, 1983

Harriss, C. Lowell, ed. *The Good Earth of America: Planning Our Land Use*. Engelwood Cliffs, N.J.: Prentice-Hall, 1974

Harvey, David. *Social Justice and the City*. Baltimore: John Hopkins Press, 1973
"The Geographical and Geopolitical Consequences of the Transition from Fordist to Flexible Accumulation." Paper presented at Rutgers University Center for Urban Policy Research Conference, Washington, D.C., 1987

Hays, Samuel P. "Reform in Municipal Government," in Wakstein, 1970. (Reprinted from *Pacific Northwest Quarterly* 55 (October 1964): 157–169
"The Changing Political Structure of the City in Industrial America," in Callow, 1982. (Reprinted from *Journal of Urban History* 1 (November 1974): 6–38

Herbers, John. *The New Heartland: America's Flight Beyond the Suburbs and How It is Changing our Future*. New York: Times Books, 1986

Hicks, Donald. *Advanced Industrial Development: Restructuring, Relocation and Renewal*. Boston: Oelgeschlager, Gunn & Hain, Inc., 1985

Hill, Richard Child. "Capital Accumulation and Urbanization in the United States," *Comparative Urban Research* 4 (2–3 1977): 39–60
"Fiscal Collapse and Political Struggle in Decaying Central Cities in the United States," in Tabb and Sawers, 1978
"Capital Accumulation and Urbanization in the United States," in Lake, 1983
"Urban Political Economy: Emergence, Consolidation, and Development," in Smith, Michael Peter, ed. 1984

Hoch, Charles. "Social Structure and Suburban Spatio-Political Conflicts in the United States," *Antipode* 11 (3 1979): 44–55

Hoover, Edgar M. *Motor Metropolis: Some Observations on Urban Transportation in America*. Pittsburgh: University of Pittsburgh Center for Regional Economic Studies, 1965

Hymer, S. H. "The Multinational Corporation and the International Division of Labor" in Hymer, S. H., ed. *The Multinational Corporation: A Radical Approach*. Cambridge, Mass.: Cambridge University Press, 1979

Ianitzkii, O. N., ed. *Urbanizatsia, Nauchno-teknicheskaia Revolutsia i Rabochii Klass: Nekotorie Voprosy Teorii, Kritika Burzhuaznykh Kontseptsii* [Urbanization, the science-technology revolution and the working class: some problems of theory, critique of bourgeois concepts]. Moscow: Nauka, 1972
Urbanizatsia i Sotsial'nye Protivorechia Kapitalisma: Kritika Amerikanskoi Burzhuaznoi Sotsiologii [Urbanization and the social contradictions of capitalism: a critique of American bourgeois sociology]. Moscow: Nauka, 1975

Josephson, Matthew. *The Robber Barons: The Great American Capitalists 1861–1901*. New York: Harcourt, Brace & World, Inc., 1934

Kalt, Hans. "Herolded Recovery or Continued Crisis?" *World Marxist Review* 27 (May 1984): 73–79

Kasarda, John D. "People and Jobs on the Move: America's New Spatial Dynamics." Paper presented at Rutgers University Center for Urban Policy Research Conference, Washington, D.C., 1987

Kesselman, Mark. "The State and the Class Struggle," in Ollman, B. and Vernoff, E. *The Left Academy: Scholarship on American Campuses*. New York: McGraw-Hill, 1981

Kleniewski, Nancy. "From Industrial to Corporate City: The Role of Urban Renewal," in Tabb and Sawers, 1984

Kozlov, G. A., ed. *Political Economy: Capitalism*. Moscow: Progress Publishers, 1977

Kotler, Milton. *Neighborhood Government: The Local Foundation of Political Life*. Indianapolis: Bobbs-Merrill, 1969

Ktzanes, Thomas, and Reissman, Leonard. "Suburbia—New Homes for Old Values," *Social Problems* 1 (3 1959–1960): 187–195

Lachman, M. Leanne and Downs, Anthony. "The Role of Neighborhoods in the Mature Metropolis," in Leven, Charles L., ed. *The Mature Metropolis*. Lexington, Mass.: Lexington Books, 1978

Lake, Robert W. *The New Suburbanites*. New Brunswick, NJ: Rutgers University, Center for Urban Policy Research, 1981
ed. *Readings in Urban Analysis: Perspectives on Urban Form and Structure*. Rutgers, NJ: The State University of New Jersey, 1983

Lane, Roger. "Urbanization and Criminal Violence," in Callow, 1982

Lang, Michael H. *Gentrification and Urban Decline: Strategies for America's Older Cities.* Cambridge, Mass.: Ballinger Publishing Co., 1982

Levison, Andrew. *The Working Class Majority.* New York: Penguin Books, 1974

Lineberry, Robert L. ed. *Equality and Urban Policy: The Distribution of Municipal Public Services.* vol. 43, Sage Contemporary Social Science Issues. Beverly Hills: Sage Publications, 1978

Lipsky, Michael, and Levi, Margaret. "Community Organization as a Political Resource," in Hahn, Harlan, ed. *People and Politics in Urban Society.* Beverly Hills: Sage Publications, 1972

Lubove, Roy. *The Urban Community: Housing and Planning in the Progressive Era.* Engelwood Cliffs: Prentice Hall, Inc., 1967

Lupsha, Peter A. and Siembieda, William J. "The Poverty of Public Services in the Land of Plenty: An Analysis and Interpretation," in Perry and Watkins, 1977

Maergoiz, I. M. and Lappo, G. M. "Geografia i Urbanizatsia" [Geography and Urbanization] in Kavalev, S. A., ed. *Urbanizatsia Mira* [World Urbanization]. Moscow: Mysl', 1974

Marcuse, Peter. "The Targeted Crisis: On the Ideology of the Urban Fiscal Crisis and Its Uses," *International Journal of Urban and Regional Research* 5 (September 1981): 330–354

"To Control Gentrification: Anti-Displacement Zoning and Planning for Stable Residential Districts," *New York University Review of Law and Social Change* XIII (4 1984–1985): 931–952

Markusen, Ann R. "Class and Urban Social Expenditure: A Marxist Theory of Metropolitan Government," in Tabb and Sawers, 1984

Martin, Roscoe C. *The Cities and the Federal System* New York: Atherton Press, 1965

McKelvey, Blake. *The Urbanization of America 1860–1915.* New Brunswick, NJ: Rutgers University Press, 1963

The Emergence of Metropolitan America, 1915–1966. New Brunswick, NJ: Rutgers University Press, 1968.

The City in American History. London: George Allen and Unwin, 1969

Miliband, Ralph. *The State in Capitalist Society.* London: Wiedenfeld & Nicolson, 1969

Miller, Seymour Michael and Roby, Pamela A. *The Future of Inequality.* New York: Basic Books, 1970

Mills, Edwin S. "Service Sector Suburbanization." Paper presented at Rutgers University Center for Urban Policy Research Conference, Washington, D.C. 1987

Mollenkopf, John H. "The Crisis for the Public Sector in American Cities," in Alcaly and Mermelstein, 1977

"The Postwar Politics of Urban Development," in Tabb and Sawers, 1978.

"Neighborhood Political Development and the Politics of Urban Growth: Boston and San Francisco 1958–78," *International Journal of Urban and Regional Research* 5 (March 1981): 15–38

Morial, Ernest N., and Barry, Marion Jr., eds. *Rebuilding America's Cities: A Policy Analysis of the U.S. Conference of Mayors.* Cambridge, Mass.: Pallinger Publishing Co., 1986

Morris, David, and Hess, Carl. *Neighborhood Power.* Boston: Beacon Press, 1975

Myers, Gustavus. *History of the Great American Fortunes.* New York: The Modern Library, 1937

Nadel, S. N. *Contemporary Capitalism and the Middle Class*. New York: International Publishers, 1982

Nathan, Richard P. "Living with Harsh Realities," *Planning* 49 (October 1983)

Netzer, Dick; Kaminsky, Ralph; and Strauss, Katherine W. *Public Services in Older Cities*. A project of New York University Graduate School of Public Administration. New York: Regional Plan Association, 1968

Newton, Kenneth. "Conflict Avoidance and Conflict Suppression: The Case of Urban Politics in the United Staes," in Cox, 1978

O'Connor, James R. *The Fiscal Crisis of the State*. New York: St. Martin's Press, 1973

Orski, C. Kenneth. "The Suburbs Grasp the Reins," *Planning* 53 (January 1987)

Osipov, G. *Sociology: Problems of Theory and Method*. Moscow: Progress Publishers, 1969

Parenti, Michael. "Two Faces of the Capitalist State," *Political Affairs* LXIII (June 1984): 14–18

"Monopoly Capital and Culture," *Political Affairs* LXIV (March 1985): 3–12

Perlo, Victor. "On the So-called Middle Class," *Political Affairs* XL (August 1961): 57–59

Perry, David, and Watkins, Alfred J., eds. *The Rise of the Sunbelt Cities*. vol. 14, Urban Affairs Annual Reviews. Beverly Hills: Sage Publications, 1977

"People, Profit, and the Rise of the Sunbelt Cities," in Perry and Watkins, 1977

Peterson, John A. "The Impact of Sanitary Reform Upon American Urban Planning, 1840–1890," in Krueckeberg, Donald A. *Introduction to Planning History in the United States*. New Brunswick, NJ: Rutgers University Press, 1983

Pierce, Bessie L. "Society and Labor in an Expanding City," in Wakstein, 1970

Rabinowitz, Howard N. "Continuity and Change: Southern Urban Development, 1860–1900," in Brownell and Goldfield, 1977

Real Estate Research Association. *The Costs of Sprawl*. Report prepared for the Department of Housing and Urban Development (HUD) and the Environmental Protection Agency (EPA). Washington, D.C.: U.S. Government Printing Office, 1974

Redmond, Tim, and Goldsmith, David. "The End of the High-Rise Jobs Myth," *Planning* 52 (April 1986): 18–21.

Reps, John W. *The Making of Urban America: A History of City Planning*. Princeton, NJ: Princeton University Press, 1965

Town Planning in Frontier America. Princeton, NJ: Princeton University Press, 1969

Cities of the American West. Princeton, NJ: Princeton University Press, 1979

Rich, Richard. "The Political Economy of Public Services," in Fainstein and Fainstein, 1982

Rodwin, Lloyd. *Cities and City Planning*. New York: Plenum Press, 1981

Rogers, David. *The Management of Big Cities*. Beverly Hills: Sage Publications, 1971

Rubin, Julius. "Growth and Expansion of Urban Centers," In Wakstein, 1970

Rumianstsev, A. M. "Urbanizatsia i Obshchestvo" [Urbanization and society] in Ianitskii, O. N., ed., 1972

Sale, Kirkpatrick. "Six Pillars of the Southern Rim," in Alcaly and Mermelstein, 1977

Saunders, Peter R. *Social Theory and the Urban Question*. New York: Holmes & Meier Publishers, Inc., 1981

210 • References

Sawers, Larry. "New Perspectives on the Urban Political Economy," in Tabb and Sawers, 1984

Schlessinger, Arthur M. *The Rise of Modern America, 1865–1951.* New York: The Macmillan Co., 1951

"The City in American Civilization," in Callow, 1969a-

"The Urban World," in Callow, 1969b

Sergeyev, N. "International Monopolies and Capitalism's Deepening Crisis," *Political Affairs* LXII (September 1983): 31–38

Siegel, Adrienne. *The Image of the American City in Popular Literature, 1820–1870.* Port Washington, NY: Kennikat Press, 1981

Smerk, George M. *Urban Mass Transportation: A Dozen Years of Federal Policy.* Bloomington, Ind.: Indiana University Press, 1974

Smith, Michael Peter. *The City and Social Theory.* New York: St. Martin's Press, 1979

ed. *Cities in Transformation: Class, Capital, and the State.* vol. 26, Urban Affairs Annual Reviews. Beverly Hills, 1984

Smith, Neil, "Toward a Theory of Gentrification: A Back to the City Movement by Capital, Not People," in Lake, 1983

Smith, Neil and Williams Peter, eds. *Gentrification of the City.* Boston: Allen and Unwin, 1986

Snell, Bradford C. *American Ground Transport: A Proposal for Restructuring the Automobile, Truck, Bus, and Rail Industries.* Washington, D.C.: U. S. Government Printing Office, 1974

Spear, Alan H. "The Making of the Black Ghetto," in Wakstein, 1970

Steffens, Lincoln. *The Shame of the Cities.* New York: Sagamore Press, Inc., 1957

Stilgoe, John R. *Metropolitan Corridor: Railroads and the American Scene.* New Haven: Yale University Press, 1983

Susser, Ida. *Norman Street: Poverty and Politics in an Urban Neighborhood.* New York: Oxford University Press, 1982

Tabb, William K. "The New York Fiscal Crisis," in Tabb and Sawers, 1978

Tabb, William K. and Sawers, Larry, eds. *Marxism and the Metropolis.* New York: Oxford University Press, 1978

Marxism and the Metropolis: New Perspectives in Urban Political Economy. 2nd ed. New York: Oxford University Press, 1984

Taylor, George Rogers. "Building an Intra-urban Transportation System," in Wakstein, 1970

Turner, Ralph. "The Industrial City and Cultural Change," in Wakstein, 1970

Vernon, Raymond, *The Changing Economic Functions of the Central City.* New York: Committee for Economic Development, 1959

Wade, Richard C. *The Urban Frontier: The Rise of Western Cities, 1790–1830.* Cambridge, Mass.: Harvard University Press, 1959

Wakstein, Allen M. ed. *The Urbanization of America: An Historical Anthology.* Boston: Houghton Mifflin Co., 1970

Walker, Richard A. "The Transformation of Urban Structure in the Nineteenth Century and the Beginning of Suburbanization," in Cox, 1978

"A Theory of Suburbanization: Capitalism and the Construction of Urban Space in the United States," in Dear, Michael, and Scott, Allen J. eds. *Urbanization and Urban Planning in Capitalist Society.* London: Methuen, 1981

"Is There a Service Economy? The Changing Capitalist Division of Labor," *Science & Society* 64 (Spring 1985): 42–83

Walker, Richard A. and Greenberg, Douglas A. "Post-Industrialism and Political Reform in the City: A Critique," Antipode 14 (1 1982): 17–32

Watkins, Alfred J. and Perry, David. "Regional Changes and the Impact of Uneven Urban Development," in Perry and Watkins, 1977

Ward, David. *Cities and Immigrants: A Geography of Change in Nineteenth Century America.* New York: Oxford University Press, 1971

Weiss, Marc A. "The Origins and Legacy of Urban Renewal," in Clavel, Pierre; Forester, John, and Goldsmith, William W., eds. *Urban and Regional Planning in an Age of Austerity.* New York: Pergamon Press, 1980

Wells, Harry K. *Pragmatism: Philosophy of Imperialism.* New York: International Publishers, 1954

White, Morton and Lucia. *The Intellectuals vs. The City: From Thomas Jefferson to Frank Lloyd Wright.* Cambridge, Mass.: Harvard University Press, 1962

Williams, Peter, and Smith, Neil. "From 'Renaissance' to Restructuring: The Dynamics of Contemporary Urban Development," in Smith and Williams, 1986

Wilson, James Q. "Planning and Politics: Citizen Participation in Urban Renewal," Journal of the American Institute of Planners XXIX (4 November 1963): 242–249

Woodruff, A. M. "Recycling Urban Land," in Harriss, 1974

Index

213

A RELUCTANT ASSASSIN

A RELUCTANT ASSASSIN

~ ORDER OF THE MOONSTONE ~

PART 1

JC MORROWS

A Reluctant Assassin
Copyright © 2015 by JC Morrows

This title is also available as an e-book.

S&G Publishing, Knoxville, TN
www.sgpublish.com

Library of Congress Cataloging-in-Publication data
Morrows, JC.
    A Reluctant Assassin / JC Morrows.

ISBN-13: 978-0692482728   (Trade Paperback)
ISBN-10:   0692482725   (Trade Paperback)
1. Teen / Religious / Christian / Action & Adventure.
2. Fiction / Science Fiction / Steampunk.
3. Fiction / Romance / Science Fiction.

                    2015947246

This novel is a work of fiction. Names, characters, places and incidents are either products of the author's imagination or used fictitiously. Any similarities to real persons, locations or events is purely coincidental.

Scripture quotations are from the Holy Bible (KJV)

First Edition 2015

For Mom

ENDORSEMENTS

"*A RELUCTANT ASSASSIN*, THE FIRST BOOK IN THE *ORDER OF THE MOONSTONE* SERIES, IS A MUST-READ."

"IN *A PERILOUS ASSIGNMENT*, JC MORROWS BUILDS SUSPENSE AND AN OMINOUS SETTING THAT WILL LEAVE YOU EAGER TO READ MORE OF HER MOONSTONE SERIES."

"*A PERILOUS ASSIGNMENT* IS A TENSION-FILLED GLIMPSE INTO THE EXCITING STORY WORLD OF THE ORDER OF THE MOONSTONE SERIES."

A NOTE FROM THE AUTHOR

I KNOW WE DON'T ALL LOVE HISTORY, BUT SOMETIMES IT CAN BE HELPFUL . . . AND INTRIGUING.

IN THE FOLLOWING STORY, AURALIUS EXISTS IN PLACE OF WHAT WE KNOW AS THE UNITED STATES OF AMERICA.

DON'T WORRY . . . I'M NOT GOING TO GO INTO A LOT OF DETAIL YET. IT WOULD RUIN THE STORY TO REVEAL EVERYTHING HERE, SO I WILL SIMPLY SAY THE FOLLOWING...

THE PEOPLE OF AURALIUS ARE EVEN MORE OF A MIXTURE THAN THE U.S.A. THAT WE KNOW TODAY. ANY STRANGE SPELLINGS OR ODD PHRASES IN THE FOLLOWING STORY ARE THE PRODUCT OF THAT MIXTURE AND THE INFLUENCES OF A REINSTATED MONARCHY.

ENJOY!

~ JC

PREFACE

SHE STRUGGLED TO FOCUS ON THE WARM BROWN OF HIS EYES AS HE LOOKED DOWN AT HER IN ALARM.

BUT DARKNESS CLOSED IN — STEALING THE MOMENT FROM HER.

HER FINGERS WOULD NOT OBEY AS SHE ATTEMPTED TO REACH OUT TO HIM; NO LONGER ABLE TO FEEL HER LIMBS AS THE BLOOD DRAINED FROM HER BODY . . . TAKING WITH IT ANY HOPE OF RECONCILIATION.

ALL THE FANTASIES SHE HAD ONLY JUST BEGUN TO WEAVE SHATTERED AND BLEW AWAY LIKE ASHES — AND THERE WAS TIME FOR ONLY ONE THOUGHT.

WELL, THIS WASN'T PART OF MY PLAN.

ONE

KAYDEN TILTED HER HEAD SLIGHTLY, LOOKING AT THE PAINTING IN FRONT OF HER — A DEPICTION OF THEIR LAST GREAT BATTLE; AIRSHIPS RESPLENDENT, GUNS BLAZING AS THEY FLEW TO MEET THE ENEMY.

SHE ALMOST EXPECTED THE TINY PUFFS OF SMOKE TO DRIFT OFF THE CANVAS AND FLOAT AWAY RIGHT BEFORE HER EYES.

AND IT WAS OBVIOUS WHY THIS PAINTING WAS HUNG HERE — IN THIS ROOM.

OF COURSE THE ROYAL FAMILY WOULD KEEP THIS HERE, WHERE ONLY THEY CAN SEE AND APPRECIATE IT.

THEY CERTAINLY WOULD NEVER CONSIDER PUTTING IT IN THE CITY MUSEUM, WHERE IT COULD BE APPRECIATED BY THE COMMON FOLK . . .

WITH THE ALMOST CONSTANT STATE OF UPHEAVAL IN AURALIUS OVER THE PAST FIFTY YEARS, IT WAS

3

NO WONDER MOST OF THE PEOPLE DETESTED THE FORTINE FAMILY.

LOOKING AROUND THE GREAT HALL, AT THE OVERWHELMING LUXURY, SHE COULDN'T HELP BUT WONDER . . .

HAVE THEY EVER EVEN SEEN THE CITY — ESPECIALLY THE WORST PARTS OF IT; THE DARK ALLEYS, THE FILTHY DITCHES, THE PITIFUL SHELTERS?

SHAKING HER HEAD TO CLEAR THE IMAGES, SHE LOOKED AROUND AGAIN.

SHE'D BEEN SHOWN PICTURES OF THIS ROOM DURING HER PREPARATION, BUT NOTHING COULD HAVE PREPARED HER FOR THE OPULENCE. IT WAS CERTAINLY NOT SOMETHING SHE WOULD BECOME ACCUSTOMED TO ANYTIME SOON . . . ESPECIALLY CONSIDERING HOW MUCH TIME SHE HAD SPENT IN THOSE DITCHES AND BACK ALLEYS.

THE WALLS OF THE PALACE WERE DRAPED IN SILK THE COLOR OF CHAMPAGNE, THE MARBLE FLOOR INLAID WITH GOLD ACCENT PIECES, THE WINDOWS SPARKLED AS ONLY CRYSTAL COULD — AND THAT WAS JUST THIS ONE ROOM.

AND THE PEOPLE IN THE ROOM WERE EVEN MORE GRANDIOSE . . . IF THAT WAS POSSIBLE.

THE WOMEN WORE EXPENSIVE JEWELS AND HIGH-CLASS COSMETICS. THE MEN SPORTED RIDICULOUSLY HIGH TOP HATS AND DIAMOND-STUDDED WALKING STICKS.

EVEN THOUGH SHE STOOD AMONG THEM, ATTIRED IN THE SAME LUXURY, WEIGHED DOWN BY HEAVY

JEWELS AND BURIED IN THICK MAKE-UP, KAYDEN FELT EVERY INCH THE DIRTY STREET URCHIN SHE HAD BEEN FOR MANY YEARS. IT TOOK EVERY OUNCE OF NERVE SHE HAD DEVELOPED TO STAND HER GROUND.

AT LEAST THE SMILE IS EASY, SINCE EVERYONE IS WEARING THE SAME INSIPID HALF-SMILE.

SHE AFFECTED A CAREFULLY PRACTICED, SLIGHTLY BORED EXPRESSION, WHILE MEMORIZING EVERY DETAIL AROUND HER.

THIS WAS ONE OF THE FIRST LESSONS OPERATIVES WERE TAUGHT WHEN THEY ENTERED THE ORDER — SINCE IT WAS IMPOSSIBLE TO KNOW WHAT INFORMATION THEY MIGHT NEED LATER.

BY NOW HER OWN OBSERVATION SKILLS WERE SO FINELY HONED, IT WAS SIMPLY HABIT.

SHE MOVED SLOWLY TOWARD THE ROW OF BUFFET TABLES THAT COMMANDED ONE END OF THE ENORMOUS ROOM.

HER STOMACH WAS TOO KNOTTED UP TO ACCEPT FOOD, BUT SHE COULD AT LEAST HAVE A GLASS IN HER HAND AS SHE MADE ANOTHER CIRCUIT.

SHE RESISTED THE URGE TO REACH UP AND TUG ON HER HAIR AS SHE LOOKED AROUND.

NO ONE ELSE HAS RED HAIR. AT LEAST HALF THE GIRLS HERE HAVE BLACK HAIR. I COULD BLEND IN SO MUCH BETTER IN MY USUAL BLACK.

IT WAS THE FIRST THING SHE HAD BEEN OVERRULED ON FOR THIS ASSIGNMENT. SHE HAD POINTED OUT THAT HER DARK, RED LOCKS WERE A FLASHING BEACON AND WOULD DRAW FAR TOO

MUCH ATTENTION TO HER.

OF COURSE, DREY HAD INSISTED — NOT ONLY WOULD MAINTAINING THE DARK BLACK RINSE SHE USED FOR COVERT MISSIONS BE TOO MUCH TROUBLE — BUT THE NATURAL RED OF HER HAIR MIGHT BE ENOUGH TO DRAW ATTENTION FROM THE PRINCE.

SO HERE SHE STOOD, HOLDING A RIDICULOUS GOBLET FILLED WITH LIQUID THAT NEARLY MATCHED THE BOLD COLOR OF HER HAIR, TRYING DESPERATELY TO REMAIN INCONSPICUOUS.

SHE HAD LEARNED THE HARD WAY THAT THERE WAS A FINE LINE BETWEEN BEING UNNOTICED AND BEING UNOBTRUSIVE. WHILE THERE WERE BUT A FEW GUARDS IN THE ROOM AT THIS TIME, THERE WOULD SOON BE MANY MORE.

SHE AND THE OTHER GUESTS MIGHT BE IN THE HEART OF THE ROYAL PALACE, BUT THE HEAD OF SECURITY WOULD NEVER ALLOW THE CROWN PRINCE TO WALK INTO A ROOM FILLED WITH THIS MANY PEOPLE — NOT WITHOUT AT LEAST A DOZEN GUARDS.

IF HE WERE A BIT LESS CAUTIOUS, I WOULDN'T EVEN NEED TO BE HERE.

SHE HAD THE SUDDEN URGE TO LAUGH, BUT RECOGNIZED IT AS NERVES AND QUICKLY SUPPRESSED IT.

SLOWLY MOVING AROUND THE ROOM, WORKING TO KEEP UP THE UNINTERESTED, SLIGHTLY HAUGHTY EXPRESSION SHE WAS NOT YET ACCUSTOMED TO, SHE WENT BACK TO EXAMINING THE ARTWORK.

It took perusing several paintings before she realized what she was looking at. And she nearly moved back to the corner to start from the beginning, but knew it might call attention to herself, so she stayed where she was.

From a distance, it was difficult to pick out small details, but she could easily see the first painting was a depiction of the old democracy.

How far we've come . . . have we learned nothing?

A selection of images from the Second Civil War followed the image of the old democracy.

A shudder — cold as ice — trickled down her spine as the reality of the images before her, took hold of her.

How did we manage to survive such insanity?

She shook her head and moved on.

Beyond the Second Civil War images, there was a single portrait of a beautiful landscape. It brought to mind wondrous fairy tales she vaguely remembered from her childhood. She stood looking at it for nearly a minute before moving onto the next one.

When she did, the warmth she had momentarily felt was replaced by another chill — this one reaching her very core.

World War IV had brought with it nothing but decimation. No country or culture had

REMAINED UNSCATHED, AND THE IMAGE BEFORE HER SHOWED IT IN CHILLING DETAIL.

SHE WAS SURPRISED TO REALIZE THERE WERE TEARS ON HER LASHES. BLINKING RAPIDLY, SHE STEPPED HASTILY TO THE NEXT GROUP OF PAINTINGS.

AT LEAST SOCIETY STILL BENEFITS SOMEWHAT FROM THE INDUSTRIAL REVOLUTION THAT FOLLOWED. THANKFULLY, WE FOUND WAYS TO EXIST WITHOUT FOSSIL FUELS AND NUCLEAR ENERGY BEFORE MORE LIVES WERE LOST.

UNFORTUNATELY, THE DEMISE THAT HAD ROCKED THE ENTIRE WORLD HAD ALSO CAUSED UPHEAVAL IN NEARLY EVERY GOVERNMENTAL SYSTEM AS WELL.

THEIR COUNTRY HAD NOT BEEN SPARED THE GRASPING PRETENDERS, DESPOTS OR DICTATORS. THEY HAD SPENT THE NEXT TWO HUNDRED YEARS PLAYING TUG-OF-WAR WITH THEIR COUNTRY, AS WELL AS THE OTHER COUNTRIES INVOLVED IN WORLD WAR IV.

ONLY BY TURNING AGAIN TO A MONARCHY HAD AURALIUS BEEN ABLE TO OVERCOME THE WARLORDS WHO HAD PREYED ON THE INNOCENT AND WEAK — AND MANAGED TO SURVIVE.

ALTHOUGH I'M NOT SURE WE DIDN'T SIMPLY TRADE ONE DICTATOR FOR ANOTHER, ESPECIALLY IF DREY IS RIGHT.

SHE LOOKED UP, REALIZING SHE HAD COME FULL-CIRCLE, TO STAND IN FRONT OF THE PAINTING SHE'D BEEN PRETENDING TO OBSERVE ONLY A FEW MINUTES BEFORE.

A new appreciation for the scene in front of her filled her with unexpected awe. Here was proof of how resilient their people were as a nation.

Some of us anyway . . .

Turning slowly, she looked around the room again at the other guests; twenty-four young women and their families, waiting not-so-patiently for the young prince to arrive.

She already had a good idea of who they were and where they had come from, but observing them in this environment gave her a whole new outlook on each lady.

Each one of them had something she did not; money, prestige, power, popularity, even fame — but not one young woman here had seen what she had. Not one of them had stood against the odds that had been stacked against her since her parents' death.

Not one other person in this room had been forced to fight for their very survival. It made perfect sense to her that they would look right past this wall . . . never seeing the significance that was represented behind her.

She might be at a slight disadvantage in some ways, but she was clearly superior to every other person in this room when it came to a few specific skills.

And I might be made up to look like a princess, but underneath these stupid petticoats and jewels . . .

I. Am. A. Fighter.

She was ready to do whatever she had to do, ready to take on anyone who stood in her way . . . or anyone who tried to deter her from her mission.

Drey himself had chosen her from a selection of over a hundred young women — operatives with more experience, more beauty and more womanly wiles.

He must have seen something special in me; something that would catch the eye of the Prince . . . and I vow that I will not let him down.

She took a deep breath as everyone in the room turned toward the large doors at the other end of the Great Hall.

He's coming.

I have to calm down.

Kayden took a deep breath . . . and then another. She would need all of her wits about her right now.

TWO

DVARIUS STOPPED JUST INSIDE THE DOOR AND TOOK A MOMENT TO APPRECIATE HIS FINAL MOMENTS OF LIFE WITHOUT THE RESPONSIBILITY OF THE CROWN.

ONCE HE STEPPED INTO THE ROOM — ONCE HE TOOK THIS STEP — HIS LIFE WOULD CHANGE FOREVER.

A RECENT CONVERSATION WITH HIS ADVISORS FLOODED HIS MIND. THINKING ABOUT IT, HE WAS CERTAIN THAT, WHILE ANY OTHER MAN MIGHT BE DELIGHTED AT THE THOUGHT OF WHAT HE WAS PREPARING TO DO, HE . . . WAS NOT.

"THIS IS NECESSARY, YOUR HIGHNESS. THE COUNTRY IS IN TROUBLE. THERE IS MUCH GOING ON OUT THERE THAT YOU ARE UNAWARE OF."

DROPPING A FOLDER ON THE DESK BETWEEN THEM, PETERO CONTINUED.

"YOU MUST DO SOMETHING THAT WILL SHOW THE

PEOPLE YOU ARE SERIOUS ABOUT YOUR RESPONSIBILITY AND YOU ARE WILLING TO DO WHATEVER IS NECESSARY TO SECURE THEIR SAFETY."

HE'D LET OUT A SHORT BARK OF LAUGHTER BEFORE CONTINUING, "THIS SHOULD AT LEAST DISTRACT THEM FROM THEIR TROUBLES FOR A TIME."

"AND YOU TRULY BELIEVE THIS IS THE BEST IDEA; BRINGING TWENTY-FIVE YOUNG WOMEN INTO THE PALACE — WOMEN WHOM I'VE NEVER MET — AND EXPECT ME TO JUST . . . CHOOSE A BRIDE?"

HE HADN'T NEEDED TO WAIT FOR A RESPONSE.

BEFORE HE ASKED THE QUESTION, HE'D KNOWN THE ANSWER . . . EVEN THOUGH HE DID NOT YET HAVE THE CROWN, HE WAS STILL EXPECTED TO BEHAVE AS IF HE DID.

HE WAS REQUIRED TO MAKE DECISIONS AS THE KING WOULD, BUT HE WAS NOT CERTAIN HE WAS READY FOR IT. HE HADN'T TOLD ANYONE . . . BUT HE WAS TERRIFIED.

THE LOW HUM OF VOICES BROUGHT HIS ATTENTION BACK TO THE ROOM — AND THE YOUNG LADIES — THAT AWAITED HIM.

EVERYWHERE HE LOOKED, OPULENT GOLD AND GLITTERING JEWELS WINKED BACK AT HIM. HE WAS SURROUNDED BY BEAUTIFUL WOMEN AND THEIR FAMILIES . . .

SO WHY DO I FEEL AS THOUGH I AM THE ONE UP FOR SALE?

WHAT WAS IT ABOUT THIS WHOLE EXPERIENCE THAT GAVE HIM THE WORST POSSIBLE FEELING?

"What are you waiting for?"

The words were accompanied by a light punch on the arm, which brought a reluctant smile to Dvarius' face.

He turned to his long-time friend and confidant. Marek's attitude was expected. He didn't take anything seriously.

"Want to take my place?"

Dvarius thought fondly of the games they had played as children; he being the young nobleman with no responsibilities and Marek taking the mantle of prince. It had been fun — trading places. But it had only been a child's game. This . . . this was for real.

"Just say the word, Var."

Marek laughed again as he slapped the Prince on the shoulder.

"Seriously man, what are you waiting for? Get in there — or I will."

Dvarius tried to allow his friend's enthusiasm to wash over him, hoping he could find an ounce of something other than dread to fill himself with.

If only he could take the crown as a single man. It would make everything so much easier. He could take his time . . . find a wife in a more traditional way, like his father had.

But he could not change the law until he was King . . . and his mother was certainly in

NO SHAPE TO TAKE ON THE HOUSE OF LORDS OR
THE SENATE RIGHT NOW, SO HE WAS LEFT WITH
THIS RIDICULOUS CHARADE.

HIS ADVISORS HAD INSISTED FOR MONTHS THAT
THIS WAS THE BEST WAY TO HANDLE THE
SITUATION. HE MUST SHOW A STRONG PRESENCE.

BEING SO MUCH YOUNGER THAN HIS FATHER HAD
BEEN WHEN HE'D TAKEN THE CROWN, DVARIUS
MUST SHOW THE PEOPLE — BUT MORE THAN THAT,
THEIR ENEMIES — THAT HE WAS FULLY IN CONTROL
OF THE STILL YOUNG, BUT STRONG COUNTRY.

TO SHOW WEAKNESS IN ANY WAY WOULD THROW
THE COUNTRY INTO TURMOIL AND OPEN THEM UP TO
THE POSSIBILITY OF ATTACK. GOD KNEW THIS
COUNTRY HAD SEEN ENOUGH WAR IN THE LAST
THREE DECADES TO LAST SEVERAL LIFETIMES.

THE THOUGHT OF WAR TURNED HIS STOMACH AND
BROUGHT TO MIND THE VIVID PICTURES FROM HIS
YOUTH; LEAVING HIM WITH THE FEELING OF AN ICY
HAND CLAMPED AROUND HIS HEART.

IF THIS WAS THE ONLY WAY TO KEEP THE COUNTRY
FROM BEING PLUNGED INTO ANOTHER WAR, HE
WOULD GLADLY THROW HIMSELF ON THE BLOCK.

WHAT WAS HIS OWN LIFE, EVEN HIS OWN
HAPPINESS, COMPARED WITH AN ENTIRE COUNTRY?

HE DIDN'T KNOW IF HE COULD BE AS WISE A KING
AS HIS FATHER HAD BEEN, BUT HE WAS
DETERMINED TO DO WHATEVER HE MUST TO
ENSURE THAT HE HAD A CHANCE TO PROVE
HIMSELF.

NOT ONLY TO HIS MOTHER AND HIS ADVISORS, BUT

TO THE PEOPLE AS WELL.

STILL . . .

HE HELD ONTO THE IDEA THAT HE MIGHT FIND LOVE. IT WAS A FANCIFUL NOTION IN THE EYES OF MOST, BUT HE KNEW HIS FATHER HAD LOVED HIS MOTHER DEEPLY.

SO, PERHAPS IT WAS NOT AS IMPOSSIBLE FOR HIM AS HE HAD BEEN THINKING FOR SOME TIME NOW.

"HEY MAN, ARE YOU OKAY?"

MAREK SOUNDED MORE SERIOUS THAN DVARIUS HAD HEARD HIM IN A LONG TIME. HE MUST UNDERSTAND MORE ABOUT WHAT WAS AT STAKE HERE THAN HE ALLOWED ANYONE TO SEE.

DVARIUS TURNED TO LOOK AT HIS FRIEND, AND THEN TURNED TO LOOK AROUND THE ROOM AGAIN, AS HE TOOK A DEEP BREATH.

"NO, NOT REALLY . . . BUT THERE'S NOTHING TO BE DONE FOR IT."

"I'M RIGHT HERE. YOU NEED A BREAK, A DIVERSION, WHATEVER . . . JUST SAY THE WORD."

MAREK'S HAND CAME DOWN ON HIS BACK EASIER THIS TIME AND HIS FRIEND'S SUPPORT — MORE THAN ANYTHING ELSE — GAVE DVARIUS THE COURAGE TO MOVE.

GOD, PLEASE HELP ME.

DVARIUS RAISED THE SILENT PLEA AND GRITTED HIS TEETH AS HE MOVED PAST THE DOORWAY.

IMMEDIATELY THE FRUSTRATION THAT HAD BOUND HIM WAS REPLACED BY A CALM ASSURANCE. GOD

HAD HEARD HIS PLEA.

HIS ADVISORS HAD STRONGLY SUGGESTED HE KEEP HIS FAITH TO HIMSELF. HE COULD STILL HEAR THE INSISTENCE IN THEIR VOICES, TELLING HIM THAT FAITH IN SOMETHING THAT DIDN'T EXIST WOULD MAKE HIM LOOK SOFT.

"COME NOW, YOUR MAJESTY; HOW WILL IT LOOK FOR THE KING TO PUT HIS FAITH IN SOMETHING OTHER THAN HIMSELF? YOU ARE AURALIUS. YOU MUST NOT FALTER AND YOU MUST NOT SHOW WEAKNESS. THIS . . . FAITH . . . BELIEVING IN SOMETHING THAT DOES NOT EXIST."

IT WAS ONE AREA HE WOULD NEVER AGREE WITH THEM ON. HIS FAITH WAS AN INTEGRAL PART OF WHO HE WAS; WHO HIS FATHER HAD RAISED HIM TO BE.

GOD MIGHT NOT HAVE LEFT EVIDENCE THAT CONVINCED THOSE WITH THE GREATEST DOUBTS, BUT DVARIUS HAD CERTAINLY BEEN CONVINCED BY IT. AND HE KNEW HIS FAITH WOULD MAKE HIM A BETTER KING, EVEN IF HIS ADVISORS DID NOT.

WHENEVER HE FELT HIS OWN WEAKNESS THREATEN TO OVERWHELM HIM, HE LOOKED TO GOD AND HIS STRENGTH WAS MIRACULOUSLY RENEWED, AS IT WAS NOW.

THANK YOU, LORD.

HE STOOD A BIT TALLER AS HE FELT THAT STRENGTH FLOW THROUGH HIM NOW.

AND THE WARMTH THAT FOLLOWED IN ITS WAKE HELPED DVARIUS TO UNDERSTAND THAT THIS DECISION WAS NOT HIS TO MAKE — ONLY HIS TO

ACCEPT.

THE WOMAN GOD INTENDED FOR HIM TO MARRY WAS IN THIS ROOM SOMEWHERE. HE JUST HAD TO BE STILL AND LISTEN FOR GOD'S INSTRUCTION.

WITH THAT IN MIND, HE LET OUT THE BREATH HE HADN'T REALIZED HE WAS HOLDING . . . AND LOOKED AROUND THE ROOM AGAIN.

IMMEDIATELY, ONE YOUNG WOMAN STOOD OUT TO HIM. SHE WAS STANDING ALONE, BY THE FAR WALL, TURNED TOWARD ONE OF THE LARGER PAINTINGS THAT GRACED THE ROOM.

SHE LOOKED NERVOUS, BUT THE WAY SHE HELD HER SHOULDERS BESPOKE A COURAGE DVARIUS FOUND HIMSELF IMMEDIATELY ENVIOUS OF.

THE MUSCLES IN HIS STOMACH TIGHTENED AND A RUSH OF HEAT WASHED OVER HIM AS HE STUDIED HER.

SHE STOOD NEAR THE PAINTING OF THEIR LAST GREAT BATTLE — AND THOUGH SHE FACED THE PAINTING, SHE TURNED SLIGHTLY TO EACH SIDE EVERY FEW SECONDS, AS IF SHE WERE WATCHING EVERYONE ELSE IN THE ROOM.

SHE WAS DRESSED MUCH LIKE EVERY OTHER YOUNG WOMAN IN THE ROOM, BUT THE WAY SHE HELD HERSELF REMINDED HIM LESS OF A LADY AND MORE OF HIS GUARDS.

THEN SOMEHOW, THOUGH HE HADN'T NOTICED A MOVE OF HER HEAD, HER EYES MET HIS FROM ACROSS THE ROOM.

THE DEEP PEWTER OF HER EYES, SURROUNDED BY A PALE, DELICATE FACE, WAS FRAMED BY A TUMBLE

OF BOLD, AUBURN HAIR.

THE SIGHT OF HER TOOK HIS BREATH AWAY. IT WAS AS IF HER EYES WERE A DAGGER THAT PIERCED HIS HEART — EXCEPT HE HAD NEVER FELT MORE ALIVE THAN HE FELT IN THAT MOMENT.

HE TURNED AND FLASHED A SMILE AT MAREK BEFORE STRIDING PURPOSEFULLY ACROSS THE ROOM, IGNORING THE RECEIVING LINE THAT HAD FORMED AT HIS ARRIVAL.

THREE

KAYDEN'S BREATH CAUGHT IN HER THROAT WHEN SHE REALIZED THAT THE PRINCE HAD NOT ONLY CAUGHT HER CHECKING THE ROOM, BUT HE HAD ACTUALLY MET HER GAZE WITH HIS OWN.

AND NOW HE WAS WALKING IN HER DIRECTION.

HER LUNGS WERE STRAINING WITH THE BREATH SHE HELD. AFTER A MOMENT, SHE LET GO WITH AN EXHALE THAT SOUNDED FAR LOUDER TO HER EARS THAN IT SHOULD HAVE BEEN.

SHE KNEW SHE HAD TO FOCUS ON HER TRAINING, BUT HER NERVES WERE CHURNING WITHIN HER. IT WAS AN UNFAMILIAR SENSATION; ONE SHE'D NOT EXPERIENCED IN YEARS.

VOICES FLITTED THROUGH HER HEAD, REMINDING HER OF THE THINGS SHE HAD BEEN DRILLED IN SINCE SHE'D BEEN CHOSEN FOR THIS MISSION.

"NEVER LET HIM SEE WHO YOU REALLY ARE."

"You do belong there. Remember that. Show him that."

"Always be a lady."

"We're counting on you."

"You can do this."

"Never forget . . ."

The last had come from the only woman she had ever truly considered a friend, whispered as Kayden had walked through the lines of women that had been assembled for Drey's assessment.

Voi had reached out as Kayden walked past her and the woman's hushed voice . . . and whispered words had followed her even as Kayden had moved through a part of the underground complex she hadn't known existed before.

Kayden still wasn't certain what Voi had meant when she'd said the words, but they had stayed with her throughout the intensive training.

Through the fittings and measurements for her new wardrobe; through the endless recitations of information that was being fed to her about the royal family and the other twenty-four girls and their families.

She thought back to those fittings for a moment. She had stood on a raised platform for hours while someone measured her.

Articles of clothing were brought in for

HER TO TRY. DRESSES AND ACCESSORIES WERE TRIED — AND ACCEPTED OR REJECTED IN A FLURRY OF ACTIVITY.

THERE WERE CERTAINLY TIMES SHE WISHED SHE HAD KNOWN SHE WOULD BE SPENDING SO MUCH TIME IN THESE CRAZY DRESSES AND ALL THIS MAKEUP.

SHE MIGHT HAVE RECONSIDERED.

I MIGHT HAVE RECONSIDERED . . .

HA, WHO AM I KIDDING? I NEVER HAD A CHOICE.

KAYDEN HAD NO INKLING OF THE IMPORTANCE OF THIS ASSIGNMENT WHEN SHE'D STOOD IN A ROOM, WAITING FOR DREY TO MAKE HIS CHOICE. NOR HAD SHE BEEN GIVEN ANY DETAILS.

LIKE EVERYONE ELSE, SHE WAS ORDERED . . . AND SHE HAD OBEYED.

EVENTUALLY, LITTLE BY LITTLE, INFORMATION HAD BEEN SHARED WITH HER UNTIL SHE'D BEEN DISPATCHED TO THE PALACE.

TO KEEP HERSELF FROM WORRYING OVER THE POSSIBILITY THAT THIS WOULD BE HER LAST MISSION, SHE CONCENTRATED ON THE LESS SIGNIFICANT DETAILS, SUCH AS HOW SHE LOOKED.

SHE LONGED FOR HER HORSE, HER BOW, AND THE SIMPLER RIDING CLOTHES SHE'D BEEN ISSUED — AND THEN ALTERED — FOR HER OWN USES; BECAUSE EVEN THE STURDY DRESS MADE FOR RIDING WAS NOT DESIGNED FOR HOW ACTIVE SHE PREFERRED TO BE.

I WILL MISS THAT HERE.

THERE WOULD BE NO CLIMBING, NO TARGET PRACTICE, NO SWIMMING, AND NO HIKING DEEP INTO THE DARK MOUNTAINS.

OH WELL, IF THIS WORKS, I'LL ONLY BE HERE A SHORT AMOUNT OF TIME.

SHE COMFORTED HERSELF WITH THE WORDS AND THEN SHOOK OFF THOSE THOUGHTS AS THE PRINCE CAME EVER NEARER.

SHE HAD HOPED HE WAS SIMPLY WALKING IN HER DIRECTION, BUT NO, HE WAS WALKING RIGHT TOWARD HER.

THERE WAS NO DENYING IT NOW.

HE IGNORED EVERY OTHER GIRL IN THE ROOM AND HE'S WALKING RIGHT TO ME.

MAYBE THIS WILL WORK AFTER ALL . . . SHE THOUGHT TO HERSELF, TRYING TO SUPPRESS THE SMILE THAT LEAPED IMMEDIATELY TO HER LIPS.

WHEN HE WAS CLOSE ENOUGH, SHE SWEPT INTO THE DEEP CURTSY SHE'D PRACTICED SO MANY TIMES SHE COULD HAVE DONE IT IN HER SLEEP.

HOWEVER, BEFORE SHE'D EVEN DROPPED COMPLETELY, THE PRINCE TOOK HER HAND AND PULLED HER BACK UP.

HIS EYES MET HERS AS HE LEANED OVER HER HAND AND BRUSHED A KISS ACROSS HER KNUCKLES.

HIS LIPS HAD BARELY MADE CONTACT WITH HER SKIN WHEN EVERY NERVE ENDING FROM HER FINGERTIPS TO HER ELBOW BEGAN TINGLING.

THE BREATH STUCK IN HER THROAT AS SHE TRIED DESPERATELY TO REMEMBER WHAT SHE WAS

SUPPOSED TO SAY.

"MY DEAR."

HE SAID THE WORDS LIKE AN ENDEARMENT, BUT THE TONE WAS COMPLETELY LOST ON HER, AS FLASHES OF A DARK STREET AND THE SMELL OF BLOOD AND ROTTING GARBAGE INVADED HER SENSES.

A CHILL ERASED THE TINGLE THAT HAD BEGUN IN HER ARM AS IT RUSHED FROM HER HEART AND SENT WEAKNESS CRASHING THROUGH HER.

REMEMBERED SOUNDS OF THE CITY AND A DARK ALLEY DROWNED OUT THE MUSIC PLAYING QUIETLY IN THE BACKGROUND OF THE GREAT HALL. THE MEMORY OF SUCH STRONG, RANCID SMELLS TURNED HER STOMACH — AND THE PANIC THAT HAD FLOODED HER BODY IN THAT MOMENT, SURGED THROUGH HER LIMBS.

IT TOOK EVERY BIT OF TRAINING TO FORCE HERSELF BACK TO THIS MOMENT.

TRULY, SHE THOUGHT SHE HAD LET GO OF THAT MEMORY YEARS AGO, BUT IT WAS ALL TOO CLEAR IN HER MIND, AND SHE SPOKE THROUGH GRITTED TEETH . . .

"MY. NAME. IS. KAYDEN."

THE PRINCE LOOKED AT HER WITH AN ODD TILT TO HIS HEAD AS HE STEPPED BACK AND RELEASED HER HAND. THE SUDDEN LOSS OF CONTACT SOMEHOW BROUGHT HER BACK TO HER SENSES.

SHE HAD TO GET A GRIP ON HERSELF OR SHE WOULD MISS THIS CHANCE.

Taking a quick glance around the room, trying to gauge how close everyone was, she breathed a sigh of relief when she saw there was no one near enough to have heard her words, or worse, the tone of them.

She opened her mouth to apologize, but the Prince spoke first.

"My apologies . . . Kayden."

The Prince inclined his head in her direction, and it was all Kayden could do to keep her mouth from dropping open.

Wait.

I just insulted him and he's giving me the honour of a royal bow.

Nothing — absolutely nothing — she had been taught could have prepared her for this. The smooth apology she had planned to deliver slid away and she did what came much more naturally to her — she stuttered.

"Your Majesty . . . I . . . I . . . I am so very sorry."

Well, now I've done it.

Shame burned her cheeks as she looked down at the floor.

I'm supposed to be making a good impression on the Prince.

She had been given an amazing opportunity — and she was messing it all up.

FOUR

STILL WAITING TO BE SOUNDLY SCOLDED, KAYDEN WAS SURPRISED TO HEAR LAUGHTER COMING FROM THE PRINCE.

NOT THE SCORNFUL LAUGHTER SHE WOULD HAVE EXPECTED AT HER BUMBLING APOLOGY, BUT THE DEEP, WARM, DELIGHTED LAUGHTER OF A MAN WHO WAS GENUINELY ENJOYING HIMSELF.

IT SHOCKED HER.

EVEN MORE SURPRISING WAS THE FEEL OF HIS HAND ON HER CHIN. AT THE GENTLE PRESSURE SHE LIFTED HER CHIN, WITH SURPRISE AND EMBARRASSMENT STILL AT WAR WITHIN HER.

WHEN HER EYES MET HIS, SHE WAS SHOCKED TO SEE SUCH WARMTH FILLING THE CHOCOLATE DEPTHS.

WHY DID IT HAVE TO BE CHOCOLATE?

SHE HAD SEEN DOZENS OF PICTURES OF THE PRINCE, BUT NONE OF THEM HAD PREPARED HER FOR THE VELVETY CHOCOLATE COLOR OF HIS EYES. SHE COULDN'T SEEM TO LOOK AWAY FROM THEM.

WHEN DID HE GET SO CLOSE TO ME?

LOOKING UP INTO HIS EYES — FULL OF CURIOSITY AND INTEREST — SHE REALIZED SOMETHING ELSE.

THIS IS NOT THE MAN I WAS EXPECTING.

THERE WAS NO COLD IN HIS EYES, NO DISDAIN, AND NO AIR OF SUPERIORITY. HE EXUDED WARMTH AND A CONFIDENCE THAT SURPRISED HER.

AND THERE WAS . . . SOMETHING ELSE AS WELL; SOMETHING SHE COULD NOT IMMEDIATELY IDENTIFY.

SHE TRIED TO THINK . . . TO ANALYZE . . . TO PUT HERSELF INTO A DETACHED STATE OF MIND, BUT THE FEEL OF HIS FINGERS GENTLY RESTING ON HER SKIN WAS SENDING SOME UNEXPECTED SENSATIONS THROUGH HER.

EVERY NERVE ENDING ALONG HER CHIN AND THROAT WAS ON FIRE; SO MUCH MORE INTENSE THAN THE LIGHT TINGLE SHE'D FELT A FEW MOMENTS BEFORE.

SHE WAS INTENSELY AWARE OF HIS TOUCH, AND SHE WAS CERTAIN EVERYONE NEARBY MUST BE ABLE TO HEAR HER SPEEDING HEART.

THE EMOTION CHURNING WITHIN HER IN THAT SEEMINGLY ENDLESS MOMENT WAS NEARLY TOO MUCH TO CONTROL.

FOR A MOMENT — JUST A MOMENT — SHE FORGOT

WHO SHE WAS AND WHAT SHE WAS HERE TO DO; HER MISSION, HER TRAINING, EVERYTHING WAS GONE.

HER MIND EMPTIED . . . AND IN CREPT AN EMOTION SHE HAD NOT ALLOWED FOR MANY YEARS. SHE COULDN'T REMEMBER THE LAST TIME SHE HAD EXPERIENCED IT . . . BUT SHE FELT IT NOW. IT EXPLODED IN HER HEART AND FLOODED HER SOUL.

HOPE.

IT TOOK OVER HER SENSES AND SHE FELT A SMILE BLOOM ON HER LIPS AND SPREAD ACROSS HER ENTIRE FACE.

THE HAND ON HER CHIN SLIPPED UP TO CUP HER CHEEK AND THERE WAS SOMETHING IN THE PRINCE'S EYES THAT MADE HER FEEL EXCITED AND WARY ALL AT ONCE.

THE WAY HE WAS LOOKING AT HER NOW SENT SHIVERS DOWN HER SPINE. AND, CONTRARILY, THERE WERE FLICKERS OF FIRE JUMPING IN HER STOMACH.

SHE COULD FEEL AN INTENSE HEAT SPREADING ALONG HER ENTIRE BODY; EVERY MUSCLE TENSED IN ANTICIPATION, EVERY NERVE ENDING WAS ON FIRE.

AN OVERWHELMING DEPTH OF EMOTION ROBBED HER OF SPEECH AND THOUGHT . . . UNTIL HER MOTHER'S FACE — INEXPLICABLY — FLOATED INTO HER MIND, BRINGING WITH IT A DEEP LONGING AND HEARTBREAK.

A WARM TEAR SLIPPED DOWN HER CHEEK AS HER EMOTIONS AGAIN OVERWHELMED HER. THE MEMORY

THAT CAME TO HER WAS ONE THAT SHE HAD THOUGHT WAS FOREVER LOST TO HER.

SHE WAS LOOKING UP AT HER MOTHER'S SMILING FACE — A FACE SO INCREDIBLY BEAUTIFUL, IT WAS BREATH-TAKING.

KAYDEN VAGUELY WONDERED HOW SHE COULD POSSIBLY BE RELATED TO THIS WOMAN, WHO LOOKED MORE LIKE AN ANGEL THAN SOMEONE'S MOTHER.

SHE CLOSED HER EYES SO THAT SHE COULD SAVOR EVERY MOMENT OF THE MEMORY SHE HAD THOUGHT WAS LOST TO HER FOREVER.

AS SHE DID, SHE TURNED HER HEAD SLIGHTLY, BREAKING HER CONTACT WITH THE PRINCE — AND THE SHOCK WAS NEARLY PAINFUL.

REALITY CRASHED IN ON HER, SMOTHERING ANYTHING ELSE AND REMINDING HER OF WHO SHE WAS AND WHAT SHE WAS DOING HERE.

BEFORE SHE COULD FULLY REGAIN HER BALANCE IN THE SITUATION, SHE FELT THE PRINCE'S FINGERS BRUSHING AWAY THE ONE TEAR THAT HAD ESCAPED.

"TRULY YOU ARE A PUZZLE, MISS."

HE SAID THE WORDS SOFTLY, WITH UNCERTAINTY, BUT THERE WAS SOMETHING ELSE IN HIS WORDS AS WELL — SOMETHING SHE DIDN'T WANT TO ANALYZE.

SHE WOULD THINK ABOUT IT — AND WHAT IT MIGHT MEAN — LATER, BUT FOR NOW SHE NEEDED TO GET HERSELF BACK UNDER CONTROL.

"YOU NEARLY SNAP MY HEAD OFF . . ."

Her eyes fluttered open when his breath tickled her cheek.

"Then you apologize, unnecessarily I might add."

A short laugh accompanied those words.

"And finally . . . you smile so unexpectedly that somehow I feel I've been granted a very precious gift."

His fingers dropped away and she finally felt as if she could breathe again.

"Now, I see a tear on your cheek and that breathtaking smile has disappeared . . . Yes, a puzzle indeed."

She risked a look at him. He was smiling . . .

Good. Now I just have to figure out how to answer him.

She was saved from coming up with anything because at that moment, someone walked up and whispered something in the Prince's ear.

The amused look that had been on his face disappeared and was replaced by an expression much more in line with what she had been prepped for. Here was the ice-cold demeanor she'd been told to expect.

An involuntary shiver raced down her spine and it was all she could do to keep still; confused all the more, because she had no idea if she was at last seeing the real Prince Dvarius now, or not.

She took a moment to study the man beside

HIM. THIS WAS ONE OF THE ADVISORS SHE HAD BEEN WARNED ABOUT. SHE FLIPPED THROUGH HER MENTAL FILES UNTIL SHE LANDED ON HIS.

AH, YES . . .

PETERO.

HE HAD BEEN WITH DVARIUS' FATHER, AND HIS UNCLE BEFORE THAT.

THIS MAN HAD BEEN A PART OF THE PALACE STAFF FOR A VERY LONG TIME. HE WOULD EITHER BE AN INVALUABLE ASSET OR AN IMMOVABLE IMPEDIMENT.

TIME WOULD TELL . . .

THE PRINCE TURNED BACK TO HER AND INCLINED HIS HEAD AGAIN, CONFUSING HER ALL OVER AGAIN. THE COLD WAS GONE, REPLACED BY THE WARM, FRIENDLY, INTRIGUING MAN SHE HAD BEEN SPEAKING TO ONLY A FEW MOMENTS AGO.

"WITH APOLOGIES, I MUST TAKE MY LEAVE. I TRUST WE WILL SPEAK AGAIN SOON."

HE TURNED TO EVERYONE ELSE IN THE ROOM THEN, AND SPOKE A BIT LOUDER TO THE REST OF THEM, AS KAYDEN STRUGGLED TO FIGURE OUT WHAT HAD CAUSED THE SUDDEN CHANGE — FIRST TO COLD — AND THEN BACK TO WARM.

NOTHING WAS IMMEDIATELY APPARENT, EXCEPT THE APPEARANCE OF PETERO.

"I REGRET THAT I AM REQUIRED ELSEWHERE. I DO LOOK FORWARD TO MEETING EVERYONE . . . IT SIMPLY IS NOT POSSIBLE AT THE MOMENT."

THE PRINCE SWEPT A HAND AROUND THE ROOM AS HE SPOKE.

"YOU ARE ALL WELCOME TO STAY, ENJOY THE REMAINDER OF THIS LITTLE WELCOMING SOIRÉE. WHEN YOU ARE READY . . . ." HE NODDED HIS HEAD IN THE DIRECTION OF LADIES GATHERED IN SMALL GROUPS ALL AROUND THE ROOM, AND THEN BACK AT KAYDEN FOR JUST A MOMENT BEFORE GOING ON, "THE STAFF WILL ESCORT OUR LOVELY LADIES TO THEIR ROOMS."

HE LOOKED OVER AT ONE OF THE SERVANTS, WHO BOWED DEEPLY IN RETURN.

"I DO WISH I HAD TIME TODAY TO MEET WITH EACH FAMILY, BUT I AM CERTAIN THERE WILL BE ANOTHER OPPORTUNITY SOON."

AND PRINCE DVARIUS SWEPT OUT OF THE ROOM, A LONG LINE OF ADVISORS IN HIS WAKE.

FIVE

LATER THAT SAME EVENING, KAYDEN STOOD AT THE RAILING ON HER PERSONAL BALCONY AND LOOKED OUT OVER THE CITY SHE HAD GROWN UP IN.

SHE MARVELED AT THE SURREAL QUALITY WHICH SETTLED OVER AURALIUS' CAPITAL CITY FROM SUCH A HEIGHT.

ORUM MIGHT BE NOWHERE NEAR AS PERFECT AND BEAUTIFUL AS IT APPEARED FROM SO FAR AWAY; THE DIRTY STREETS AND CRUMBLING BUILDINGS THAT HAD YET TO BE REBUILT, BUT IT WAS HOME.

THERE WERE STILL BRIDGES AND ROADS THAT WERE IMPASSABLE BY VEHICLE OR FOOT TRAFFIC ALIKE, YET IT APPEARED IN THE NIGHT SKY TO BE A SLEEK, CLEAN, DARK JEWEL ON THE HORIZON.

SHE HAD NOT WANTED TO BELIEVE AFTER MEETING HIM, THAT THE PRINCE WAS THE SAME COLD, ALOOF MAN SHE'D BEEN TOLD ABOUT. BUT HERE WAS

UNDENIABLE PROOF, RIGHT IN FRONT OF HER. HIS PALACE WAS FILLED WITH JEWELS AND ART AND SILK DRAPERIES, AND LAVISH FOOD LAID OUT TO IMPRESS THEIR GUESTS.

AND THE CLOTHES . . .

OH, THE CLOTHES . . . I HAVE TO BE DECKED OUT IN SILK AND IMPORTED LACE TO FIT IN WITH THE KIND OF WOMEN HE MINGLES WITH.

KAYDEN GRITTED HER TEETH WHILE SHE SQUIRMED IN THE TOO-TIGHT DRESS. DURING OTHER MISSIONS, SHE HAD WORN EVERYTHING FROM A MAID'S UNIFORM TO COVERALLS SEEN ON ROAD CREW WORKERS.

SHE'D NEVER BEFORE NEEDED TO WEAR SUCH EXPENSIVE, LUXURIOUS ENSEMBLES WHICH WERE NECESSARY TO FIT IN AT THE PALACE.

AND I WILL BE STUCK IN THEM EVERY DAY . . . ALL DAY.

REACHING DOWN TO HER SKIRT, SHE PULLED AT ONE OF THE LAYERS OF LACE AND RUBBED IT BETWEEN HER FINGERS FOR A MOMENT BEFORE DROPPING IT AGAIN.

HOW DO WOMEN LIVE LIKE THIS ALL THE TIME — WITH SO MANY LAYERS AND HOOPS AND STOCKINGS?

. . . AND THE HIGH HEELS? WHAT WAS I THINKING!

SHE SAT DOWN AND STRUGGLED TO REACH BENEATH HER FULL SKIRTS. AFTER SEVERAL FUTILE SECONDS, SHE GAVE UP.

SHE COULDN'T EVEN GET TO HER WEAPON. WHAT WAS THE POINT OF EVEN HAVING IT?

Better hidden under my skirt than discovered by one of the maids running around this place.

There were servants everywhere.

Can't the people in this place do anything for themselves?

There is so much pain and death out there . . .

Yet the Prince sits here in his glass and marble palace, living in luxury while his people starve and freeze to death on the streets of Orum . . . and every other city like it in Auralius.

She struggled for a long moment with the anger building inside of her.

She'd spent too much time on those streets, witnessed too many brutal acts against other citizens, and seen too much death — to believe that the Prince was ignorant of what it was truly like out there. It simply was not possible.

He must know. He is "The Prince" after all. How could he not!

Unless, of course, he did not care to know.

Yes, that makes much more sense. He sits up here and looks down on the glittering jewel that is but a reflection of the city below.

Why would he take time to discover what truly goes on in the back alleys and ditches — if he does not have to see it . . .

WITH NO KNOWLEDGE OF THE TRUTH, THE PRINCE COULD PRETEND EVERYTHING WAS PERFECT. HE COULD ACT AS IF AURALIUS WAS PERFECT.

ALFREID'S WORDS CAME BACK TO HER.

"LIKE YOUR OWN PERSONAL FAIRY TALE . . ."

AT THE TIME SHE HAD SNEERED AT HIS WORDS.

NOW . . . HERE . . . IN THIS PLACE, SHE WAS SURROUNDED BY THE CONFINEMENT OF THE PALACE; THE OSTENTATIOUS DÉCOR, THE FANCY FOOD, THE RIDICULOUS ENSEMBLES . . .

FAIRY TALE INDEED . . . BITING OFF THE REST OF WHAT SHE HAD BEEN THINKING, SHE TURNED TO PACE, NOT REALIZING SHE HAD BEGUN TO MUTTER ALOUD.

"WHAT KIND OF STUPID GIRL WANTS THIS SORT OF FAIRY TALE? NOT THIS ONE; THAT'S FOR SURE. WHY WOULD ALFREID THINK I WANT A FAIRY TALE?"

SHE LET OUT A HUFF OF FRUSTRATION.

"WHAT IF CINDERELLA HAD BEEN SENT TO KILL THE PRINCE?"

NOW THAT'S MY KIND OF FAIRY TALE . . .

THE SOUND OF HER LAUGHTER ECHOED BACK AT HER AS IT BOUNCED OFF THE MARBLE WALLS.

SHE HAD NOT BEEN ABLE TO TRULY APPRECIATE THE DIFFERENCE BEFORE ARRIVING HERE. SHE'D THOUGHT THERE WAS SOMETHING MISSING FROM HER PREPARATION.

BUT NO. MOST EVERYTHING WAS JUST AS SHE HAD EXPECTED IT TO BE.

BITS AND PIECES FROM HER TRAINING FLOWED THROUGH HER MIND AS SHE STOOD LOOKING OUT OVER THE CITY, THINKING ABOUT THE LUXURY SHE WAS STANDING IN; THINGS DREY HAD TOLD HER IN PREPARATION FOR THIS ASSIGNMENT.

HE HAD TOLD HER OF THINGS THE ROYAL FAMILY CHANGED FOR THE PEOPLE . . . MOSTLY THINGS THEY HAD CHANGED TO THE DETRIMENT OF THE PEOPLE.

A PICTURE SHE HAD ONCE SEEN OF A WOMAN IN PANTS AND A STRANGE-LOOKING TOP CAME TO MIND.

THE PICTURE HAD BEEN IN ONE OF THE LAST MUSEUMS LEFT STANDING AFTER THE FOURTH WORLD WAR.

KAYDEN HAD WANTED TO ASK SOMEONE ABOUT THE IMAGE, BUT SHE'D BEEN THERE ON ASSIGNMENT AND WASN'T SUPPOSED TO BE NOTICED, SO SHE'D WALKED AWAY FROM IT WITH NO ANSWERS . . . BUT SHE HAD ALWAYS REMEMBERED IT.

COULD THAT HAVE BEEN ONE OF THE THINGS THE ROYAL FAMILY HAD CHANGED? HAD THERE BEEN A TIME IN THEIR HISTORY WHEN WOMEN WORE PANTS JUST LIKE MEN DID?

HAD THE ROYAL FAMILY DECIDED TO DO AWAY WITH THAT IDEA?

COULD THAT EXPLAIN THIS RIDICULOUS GETUP I'M STUCK IN?

WERE THEY TAKING AWAY PERSONAL FREEDOMS — AS WELL AS FOOD — FROM THE PEOPLE? SHE PICKED AT THE LACE ON HER SKIRT AGAIN.

NOT THAT I WOULD WANT TO WEAR PANTS ALL THE

TIME . . . EXCEPT THAT IT WOULD MAKE RIDING EASIER.

HOWEVER, AS MUCH AS SHE DISLIKED THE EXTRA LAYERS AND TRIMMINGS, SHE KNEW IT WOULD FEEL STRANGE TO WEAR PANTS EVERY DAY; JUST LIKE A MAN.

SHE HAD SOME EXPERIENCE WITH IT, AS SHE'D BEEN UNDERCOVER AS A BOY SEVERAL TIMES IN THE PAST, AND SHE COULD REMEMBER THE STRANGE FEELING . . . THE DISCOMFORT.

NOT THAT I HAVE TO WORRY ABOUT IT ANYWAY . . . KAYDEN REMINDED HERSELF . . . *SINCE IT HAS BECOME ALL TOO APPARENT THAT I'M A GIRL.*

THAT THOUGHT LEFT HER FEELING ANGRY AND RAW.

JUST BECAUSE I'M A WOMAN . . .

SIX

REALIZING HOW SILLY HER WHOLE, INTERNAL DEBATE WAS, SHE SHOOK OFF HER THOUGHTS. IMMEDIATELY, OTHER THOUGHTS — OF INFINITELY MORE IMPORTANCE — TOOK THEIR PLACE.

WHAT OTHER CHANGES DID THE ROYAL FAMILY MAKE?

ARE THEY REALLY SO TERRIBLE? OR — ARE THEY SMALL AND SEEMINGLY INSIGNIFICANT, BUT CLEARLY UPSETTING TO SOMEONE LIKE DREY?

AND WHAT IS IT ABOUT THE CHANGES THAT MAKES EVERYONE SO UPSET?

WAS IT SIMPLY BEING DENIED PERSONAL FREEDOMS OR DID THE ISSUE GO DEEPER THAN THAT?

AND WHY DON'T THEY SPEND THEIR TIME ON MORE IMPORTANT THINGS? IT'S NOT AS IF THERE IS A SHORTAGE OF PROBLEMS IN AURALIUS RIGHT NOW.

OH, THIS IS RIDICULOUS.

SHE SHOOK HER HEAD, TRYING TO DISPEL THE THOUGHTS. SHE WAS HERE TO DO A JOB, PLAIN AND SIMPLE. SHE WOULD GET THE JOB DONE AND THEN SHE WOULD GO BACK TO HER OTHER LIFE . . . HER NORMAL LIFE.

DO I EVEN HAVE A NORMAL LIFE?

RESTLESSNESS SWEPT THROUGH HER AND SHE FOUND HERSELF PACING BACK AND FORTH FROM THE BALCONY — TO THE BED — AND BACK AGAIN.

AFTER SEVERAL MINUTES, SHE WALKED OVER AND SAT DOWN AT THE ENORMOUS DESK THAT SAT ACROSS THE ROOM FROM HER BED.

PICKING UP A PEN THAT HAD BEEN LAYING ON THE SATINY SMOOTH SURFACE OF THE DESK, SHE ABSENTLY TRACED THE ROYAL CREST THAT WAS PRINTED ON THE TOP OF THE PAGE, WHILE SHE TRIED TO FIGURE OUT EXACTLY WHAT TO WRITE.

SHE KNEW THE SUDDEN DEPARTURE OF THE PRINCE HAD TO BE REPORTED, BUT SOMETHING WAS STOPPING HER.

HER RELUCTANCE MADE NO SENSE — ESPECIALLY GIVEN WHAT SHE HAD LEARNED ABOUT THE PRINCE AND HIS LIFE HERE IN THE PALACE.

AND YET, SOMETHING WAS STOPPING HER . . .

COULD SHE IGNORE THE VOICE IN HER HEAD, TELLING HER TO STAY QUIET, OR WOULD SHE IGNORE HER TRAINING?

SHE SAT FOR SEVERAL MINUTES THINKING IT OVER. WHY SHOULD SHE CONSIDER IGNORING HER TRAINING OVER A TARGET — AND THE CONFUSION

THAT HIS TOUCH BROUGHT HER?

SHE'D NEVER HAD A PROBLEM OVERRIDING HER TRAINING WHEN SHE HAD A BETTER WAY OF DOING SOMETHING; WHICH WAS MORE OR LESS WHAT SHE HAD ALREADY DONE WITH THE PRINCE ANYWAY, SNAPPING AT HIM INSTEAD OF FAWNING.

BUT THAT HAD NOTHING TO DO WITH HER SUDDEN RELUCTANCE.

WELL, PERHAPS IT DID . . . A LITTLE.

DREY HAD SAID THAT HE'D SEEN SOMETHING SPECIAL IN HER AND THAT WAS WHY HE'D CHOSEN HER.

AND SHE'D BEEN PUZZLING OVER IT EVER SINCE. CERTAINLY HE KNEW OF HER RECORD WITH THE ORGANIZATION.

HE'D CHOSEN HER IN SPITE OF IT.

THERE MUST BE A REASON.

HAD HE SEEN SOME VALUE IN HER DETERMINATION TO DO THINGS HER OWN WAY WHEN SOMETHING WAS NOT GOING THE WAY IT WAS SUPPOSED TO?

AFTER ALL, SHE ALWAYS GOT THE JOB DONE . . . ONE WAY OR ANOTHER.

SOMETHING ELSE WAS GOING ON HERE. SHE WAS CERTAIN OF IT . . . AND UNTIL SHE GOT TO THE BOTTOM OF IT, SHE WAS GOING TO FOLLOW INSTRUCTIONS.

NOT THAT SHE HAD MUCH CHOICE . . . SHE MIGHT HAVE GOTTEN THE PRINCE'S ATTENTION, BUT SHE WAS HARDLY IN A POSITION TO CARRY OUT HER MISSION . . .

Yet.

So she would wait, and watch until an opportunity presented itself.

With that in mind, she leaned over the paper and carefully began composing the coded message that would be delivered to headquarters.

Under normal circumstances, she would be responsible for getting to the first drop point. However, she was not allowed to leave the palace grounds by herself, so arrangements had been made for a change in the first drop point.

She would have the letter sent to the residence she had temporarily taken command of, and the operatives there would pass it along to the next point.

Secretly, she had railed against the change in her routine.

Even though she enjoyed flouting the rules now and then when it suited her, it felt as if her skills had been called into question.

As if I couldn't possibly sneak past the palace guards if I chose to.

She was tempted to do it — just to prove she could; not to mention the opportunity to get away from this suffocating palace.

To be out in the fresh air . . . to be running along silent streets or climbing the enormous walls that surrounded the Palace.

Ahh, now that is true freedom . . .

HMM . . . BUT WHERE WOULD I GO?

SHE THOUGHT IT OVER WHILE THE INK DRIED ON HER FINISHED CORRESPONDENCE.

SEVEN

DVARIUS COULD BARELY BELIEVE THE WORDS HE WAS HEARING. THIS . . . THIS WAS THE REASON HE HAD BEEN DRAGGED AWAY FROM KAYDEN?

"YOUR HIGHNESS, PLEASE CONSIDER LADY CELESTIA."

LEONAL SPOKE SOFTLY, ALMOST AS IF HE WAS PLEADING.

DVARIUS SIMPLY GRITTED HIS TEETH.

"SIRE, YOU MUST TAKE THIS SERIOUSLY. YOU SIMPLY CANNOT AFFORD TO ALIENATE OUR MOST PRESTIGIOUS FAMILIES. THEY WILL BE YOUR GREATEST ALLIES IN THE YEARS TO COME."

THIS FROM PETERO.

DVARIUS BRISTLED AT THE MAN'S WORDS. AS IF HE WAS UNABLE TO RUN THE COUNTRY WITHOUT THE

SUPPORT OF THE WEALTHIEST FAMILIES IN THE COUNTRY.

"PERHAPS HIS HIGHNESS DID NOT REALIZE JUST HOW STRONG HIS FAUX PAS . . ."

ALAIN, ONE OF THE YOUNGER ADVISORS, ATTEMPTED TO DEFEND DVARIUS, BUT PETERO CUT THE MAN OFF WITH A SHARP LOOK.

DVARIUS MADE A POINT TO LOOK OVER AT ALAIN AS THE YOUNG MAN BEGAN TO LOOK DOWN.

WHEN HE SAW THE PRINCE WAS LOOKING AT HIM, HE LOOKED UP AND DVARIUS GAVE HIM A NOD AND A SMILE.

EMBARRASSMENT STILL COLORED THE MAN'S FACE, BUT HE DID NOT LOOK DOWN AGAIN. HE NODDED AND INCLINED HIS HEAD TO THE PRINCE IN A CLEAR SIGN OF GRATITUDE AND RESPECT, WHICH GAVE DVARIUS THE COURAGE TO SPEAK UP.

"ENOUGH, PETERO. I NEVER WANTED THIS RIDICULOUS CHARADE . . . AND I PROMISE YOU THIS. IF I FIND THE FUTURE QUEEN AMONG THESE WOMEN, IT WILL NOT BE DUE TO YOUR MANIPULATIONS."

HE LOOKED AROUND THE TABLE AND WAS SURPRISED TO SEE THE CHANGED EXPRESSIONS ON HIS ADVISORS' FACES.

A MOMENT AGO, THEY HAD BEEN LOOKING AT HIM LIKE A BOY. NOW A FEW WERE ACTUALLY LOOKING AT HIM AS IF HE WAS A MAN, AND IT FED HIS COURAGE.

"I WILL MEET ALL THE YOUNG WOMEN EVENTUALLY — AND I WILL CHOOSE FOR MYSELF. I MAY NOT

HAVE THE LUXURY OF MARRYING FOR LOVE, BUT I WILL NOT SHACKLE MYSELF TO SOMEONE WHOM I CANNOT ABIDE; NOT EVEN FOR THE SAKE OF POLITICAL ALLIANCES."

PETERO LOOKED AS IF HE WANTED TO ARGUE. HIS FACE WAS AN UNBECOMING SHADE OF RED, BUT HE HELD HIS TONGUE.

DVARIUS LOOKED AROUND AT THE ADVISORS WHO HAD BEEN FORCED UPON HIM.

EVERY WORD THEY HAD SPOKEN IN THIS ROOM HAD BEEN INTENDED TO REMIND HIM OF HOW FOOLISH HE'D BEEN THIS EVENING.

HE SHOULD NOT HAVE IGNORED THE RECEIVING LINE; THIS HE KNEW . . . BUT HE WAS HAVING DIFFICULTY FINDING ANY REGRET WITHIN HIMSELF.

OF COURSE, NOW HE MUST SOOTHE THE RUFFLED FEATHERS OF THE OTHER FAMILIES.

"YOUR HIGHNESS."

BUT DVARIUS CUT LEONAL OFF. HE WAS WEARY OF THE TIRADE.

NOT ONE OF THEM HAD COME RIGHT OUT AND SAID IT, BUT IT WAS CLEAR THAT FOR SOME REASON HE COULD NOT FATHOM, THEY WERE DETERMINED HE SHOULD NOT CHOOSE KAYDEN.

IT MADE NO SENSE. THE VERY FACT THAT SHE WAS HERE, SHOULD HAVE BEEN GOOD ENOUGH — FOR EVEN PETERO.

PERHAPS IT WAS MORE TO THE POINT THAT HE HAD IGNORED EVERYONE ELSE IN FAVOR OF HER. WHATEVER THE REASON, HE WAS TIRED OF

LISTENING TO THEM.

THE MORE DVARIUS HEARD, THE MORE DETERMINED HE WAS THAT THIS WHOLE EXPERIMENT WAS A MISTAKE . . .

EXCEPT FOR THE FACT THAT, IF NOT FOR THIS . . . THIS . . . RIDICULOUS CHARADE, HE WOULD MOST LIKELY NEVER HAVE LAID EYES ON THE FEISTY REDHEAD WHO HAD ALREADY NEARLY CAPTURED HIS HEART.

SINCE HE HAD ENTERED THE ROOM, HE HAD BEEN BOMBARDED WITH INFORMATION ABOUT EVERY SINGLE YOUNG WOMAN, EXCEPT FOR THE ONE WHOM HE WAS MOST CURIOUS ABOUT.

EACH ADVISOR HAD PRESENTED HIM WITH A FILE STUFFED WITH INFORMATION ABOUT EACH OF THE CANDIDATES WHO HAD BEEN PRESENTED TO HIM AS A POSSIBLE WIFE.

INFORMATION THAT TOLD HIM NOTHING. NOT ONE FILE MENTIONED RELIGIOUS BELIEFS, PERSONAL CONVICTIONS OR IDEALS, POLITICAL OPINIONS, OR EVEN SUCH THINGS AS HOBBIES AND INTERESTS.

"YOUR HIGHNESS, I ASSURE YOU THAT MANIPULATION IS NOT MY AIM. I AM MERELY TRYING TO DO MY JOB; WHICH INCLUDES BEING CERTAIN YOU HAVE THE CORRECT INFORMATION SO THAT YOU MAY MAKE THE BEST POSSIBLE DECISION."

PETERO'S WORDS MIGHT SOUND INNOCUOUS TO THE OTHERS, BUT TO DVARIUS, THEY WERE A CLEAR CHALLENGE. EITHER HE THOUGHT THE PRINCE NEEDED A STRONG PUSH OR HE HAD HIS OWN AGENDA TO PURSUE.

"Sire, we are simply asking that you consider the other ladies," and there was something in the way Petero said the next words that made Dvarius grit his teeth again, "before you make a decision that cannot be undone."

Adin gestured to the stacks of folders arranged on the table in front of Dvarius, but it was Petero who spoke again.

"We have assembled detailed reports on each prospect. They will tell you everything you desire to know."

Dvarius knew there were personal things about each lady in the files, but the pages also pointed to areas where the advisors were certain the *"prospects"* would prove most valuable — political connections, social position, and monetary value of family holdings — which meant nothing to him.

The Prince vowed that not one of those things would have any part in his decision.

He had decided, when this suggestion had been presented to him, that he would need to take time to get to know each individual, not just the persona that everyone saw.

Looking over the thick stack of files in front of him, he realized how daunting a task he had given himself.

Not one of these women would voluntarily show me her true self — well, not until she has a crown on her head.

The moment the thought occurred to him, he

KNEW HE WAS WRONG.

THERE IS ONE LADY IN THE CASTLE RIGHT NOW WHO HAS ALREADY SHOWN ME EXACTLY WHO SHE IS.

IT MATTERED NOT A WHIT TO HIM THAT SHE HAD NOT MEANT TO SHOW HIM HER TRUE FEELINGS.

SHE HAD . . . AND HE WAS FASCINATED.

AND, NO MATTER THE OPINION OF HIS ADVISORS, HE WAS DETERMINED TO GET TO KNOW HER BETTER.

IN THE ROYAL WING OF THE PALACE, THE MAN WALKED ALONG THE HALLWAY WITH QUIET STEPS — NOT HIS NORMAL, SILENT STEPS BUT HUSHED IN THE WAY OF A DIGNIFIED BUTLER.

IT HAD TAKEN NEARLY A DECADE TO FIND HIS WAY INTO THIS PART OF THE PALACE, BUT HE WAS FINALLY HERE AND HE WOULD SHOW THEM ALL.

HE WALKED THE HALLS THAT HE NOW KNEW SO WELL HE COULD WALK THEM BLINDFOLDED. HE COULD SKETCH EACH HALLWAY AND SECRET PANEL WITH PERFECT DETAIL, BUT HE DIDN'T DARE.

IF HE GAVE AWAY TOO MUCH INFORMATION NOW, HE MIGHT BE PULLED OUT.

HE STILL COULD NOT BELIEVE THEY HAD SENT A GIRL . . . A TINY SLIP OF A GIRL, NO LESS . . . TO CARRY OUT THE ASSIGNMENT THAT SHOULD HAVE BEEN HIS.

INSIDE MAN INDEED . . .

He would show them that he was much more than they thought.

He might be scarred . . .

He might be broken . . .

But he was far from useless.

And he would show them all . . . soon.

After all, it wouldn't be the first time he had killed a king.

EIGHT

KAYDEN FOLLOWED THE YOUNG GROOM TO THE STABLES. HE COULD NOT HAVE BEEN MORE THAN TWELVE, BUT HE CARRIED HIMSELF WITH THE BEARING OF A MUCH OLDER LAD.

SHE REMEMBERED THOSE DAYS. SHE WOULD HAVE DONE ANYTHING — *AND DID IN MANY CASES* — TO BE NOTICED.

IF IT HAD NOT BEEN FOR ALFREID . . .

SHE DIDN'T WANT TO CONSIDER WHAT MIGHT HAVE BECOME OF HER. HE HAD TAKEN HER UNDER HIS WING . . .

KEPT ME OUT OF TROUBLE AND . . . SHE GRITTED HER TEETH.

WHY IS THIS STUPID MEMORY COMING UP NOW, AGAIN . . . AFTER ALL THIS TIME?

It wasn't easy, but she forced herself to shake off the memory.

After too many years of allowing the past to have power over her, Kayden had learned not to dwell on the past, having long ago discovered it was always best to leave it there.

She could never have anticipated the Prince's words would bring that memory to the surface, as fresh and clear as if it had happened yesterday.

There was just something about the way he had said "my dear" when he kissed her hand, that had brought the event to mind.

She was even more confused because, though she'd been annoyed, it had not elicited the response she'd expected.

Which is probably a good thing.

It certainly would not have been a good idea to punch the Prince in front of everyone.

It had taken her years to learn how to deal, and on at least one occasion, it had nearly cost her life.

Since that unfortunate incident, she had worked diligently to overcome the effects those words had on her.

Perhaps that was the answer after all — her hard work was paying off — which would certainly help with her missions. Those words seemed to be a favorite among men when it came to the women they were trying

TO IMPRESS.

"ARE YOU SURE ABOUT THIS, MISS?"

SHE LOOKED AROUND, SURPRISED THAT THEY HAD REACHED THE STABLES ALREADY. THIS WAS NOT GOOD.

TWO MISTAKES IN TWO DAYS IS NOT THE WAY I WANT TO START OFF A JOB . . . ESPECIALLY THIS JOB.

THE ORDER PUT THEIR TRUST IN ME — AND I AM NOT GOING TO LET THEM DOWN. ONE WAY OR ANOTHER, I WILL FINISH THIS JOB.

AFTER THAT . . . WELL, AFTER THIS JOB, I'LL SEE ABOUT BUYING MY WAY OUT.

FOR NOW, SHE HAD BETTER STOP DAYDREAMING AND PAY ATTENTION, STARTING WITH ANSWERING THE LAD.

"YES, I'M QUITE SURE."

SHE NODDED TO THE YOUNG GROOM, TRYING TO REASSURE HIM.

SERIOUSLY, HAS NO WOMAN OTHER THAN ME EVER REQUESTED TO RIDE BEFORE?

"REMEMBER THAT YA CAN'T RIDE CLOSE TO THE WALLS . . . THE GUARD WOULD HAVE ME HEAD IF SOMETHING WERE TO HAPPEN TO YOU."

HIS WORDS TOLD HER WHERE SHE HAD ERRED IN HER CONCLUSION. IT WASN'T ABOUT WHETHER OR NOT SHE COULD RIDE. IT WAS ABOUT THE RIDICULOUS SECURITY PROTOCOLS.

KAYDEN WAS TEMPTED TO TELL THE LAD JUST HOW

WELL SHE WAS ABLE TO TAKE CARE OF HERSELF, BUT HELD HER TONGUE.

NO LADY SHOULD BE ABLE TO TAKE CARE OF HERSELF — ESPECIALLY AS WELL AS SHE COULD.

"I PROMISE I WILL STAY WELL WITHIN THE PALACE GROUNDS. I'LL NOT GET NEAR A SINGLE WALL OR EVEN A PALACE GUARD. YOUR HEAD WILL BE SAFE, I SWEAR IT." SHE SMILED AT HIM, TRYING TO REINFORCE HER WORDS.

HE NODDED AND TURNED TOWARD THE STABLES AGAIN. GRATEFULLY, SHE FOLLOWED CLOSE ON HIS HEELS.

HE WALKED THROUGH THE STABLES. SHE CONSIDERED MENTIONING TO HIM THAT SHE WAS PERFECTLY CAPABLE OF SADDLING THE HORSE BY HERSELF. BUT AGAIN . . . SHE WOULD RATHER NOT HAVE TO ARGUE WITH ANYONE ABOUT WHETHER OR NOT SHE WAS ALLOWED TO RIDE AFTER TODAY.

SHE KNEW IT WOULD BE BETTER TO MAKE A FRIEND OF THE LAD THAN AN ENEMY . . . ESPECIALLY AFTER HER ENCOUNTER WITH THE PRINCE'S HUNTSMAN.

IF THE MAN HADN'T BEEN SO STUBBORN.

SHE HAD TRIED CHARM, THEN SHE'D TRIED SWEETNESS. BUT IN THE END, SHE HAD TURNED TO INTIMIDATION.

EXPERIENCE HAD TAUGHT HER THAT A SMALL THREAT WORKED AS WELL AS PLEADING . . . BETTER IN MOST CASES.

"YOU WOULDN'T WANT ME TO HAVE TO GO AND HUNT DOWN THE PRINCE, WOULD YOU?"

"No m'lady."

"I'm certain he would prefer knowing that I am protected. How would he feel if something were to happen to me . . ."

She had let the threat hang in the air a moment before going on, *"and that you refused me protection?"*

The fear in the man's eyes would stay with Kayden for a long time — and now she was questioning her motives.

Just because I wanted some fresh air . . .

Guilt ate away at her, even now.

Alfreid might have been able to teach her how to intimidate, but he'd not been successful in teaching her how to keep her emotions at bay.

The young man in front of her stopped at the stall of a beautiful mare.

"Sweetie here'll take good care o' ya, Miss."

"Sweetie, huh?"

Kayden stepped forward and reached up slowly to give the horse a chance to catch her scent.

"You know what you're 'bout then, Miss?"

Kayden laughed at the surprise in the lad's tone.

"Is it such a surprise?"

"It is around 'ere miss. Only lady I ever seen

ON A HORSE HERE IS THE QUEEN, AND A LONG TIME AGO, THAT WAS."

HIS WORDS WERE NOT NEWS TO HER, BUT SHE PURPOSELY PASTED A LOOK OF SURPRISE AND AWE ON HER FACE BECAUSE SHE WASN'T SUPPOSED TO KNOW ABOUT THINGS THE QUEEN HADN'T DONE IN YEARS.

"SHE RIDES SWEETIE ON OCCASION, MISS."

AT THAT, KAYDEN STEPPED BACK. THERE WASN'T ANYTHING IN HER PROTOCOL ABOUT THAT.

WAS SHE SUPPOSED TO RIDE THE SAME HORSE THE QUEEN HAD RIDDEN ON OCCASION OR SHOULD SHE FIND SOME REASON NOT TO? WOULD SHE CAUSE A PROBLEM IF SHE REFUSED?

"YOU A'RIGHT, MISS? I SAY SOMETHIN' WRONG?"

"NO. NO. YOU DIDN'T SAY ANYTHING WRONG."

SHE WANTED TO ASK, BUT THE WORDS STUCK IN HER THROAT. FORTUNATELY, THE LAD MUST BE ACCUSTOMED TO FIGURING THINGS OUT ON HIS OWN. NOT A MOMENT LATER, HE LOOKED UP AT HER AND SMILED.

"I SEE WHAT YER WORRIED 'BOUT. DON'T WORRY, MISS. THIS AIN'T THE QUEEN'S HORSE. SHE USUALLY RIDES SPIRIT OVER THERE."

HE MOTIONED BEHIND THEM WITH HIS SHOULDER AND KAYDEN LOOKED OVER AT THE STALL.

JUST BEYOND THEM, THE STABLES CHANGED. THE FLOOR WAS CLEANER, THE STALLS FANCIER, AND THE HORSES LOOKED TO BE A MUCH BETTER BREED.

AH YES, THAT MAKES MORE SENSE. THE QUEEN MIGHT OCCASIONALLY RIDE A DIFFERENT HORSE TO GIVE THEM A WORKOUT AS WELL.

KAYDEN KNEW THE QUEEN TO BE QUITE THE ACCOMPLISHED HORSEWOMAN. WITH THAT IN MIND, IT MADE PERFECT SENSE.

"VERY WELL, YOUNG SIR. I SHALL TAKE YOUR ADVICE. SWEETIE IT IS."

"EXCELLENT, MISS. I'LL JUST SADDLE HER UP THEN. WON'T BE A MOMENT."

KAYDEN STOOD WAITING, TRYING TO LOOK BORED, WHEN IN FACT SHE COULD NOT BE MORE EXCITED. TO BE OUT IN THE OPEN WITH NO SCHEDULE, OR FITTINGS, OR A MINDLESS TEA PARTY TO DEAL WITH.

NINE

WIND WHIPPED THROUGH THE DARK, SILKY BRAIDS SHE HAD CAREFULLY ARRANGED TO KEEP HER YARDS OF HAIR MANAGEABLE ON HER RIDE, AS SHE TURNED HER FACE INTO THE BRIGHT SUNSHINE.

THERE WAS NOTHING MORE REFRESHING ON A BEAUTIFUL, FALL MORNING AS FAR AS SHE WAS CONCERNED . . . UNLESS SHE COULD BE RIDING IN THE OPEN WITHOUT THE RESTRAINT OF WALLS AND BOUNDARIES THAT THREATENED TO SMOTHER HER.

OPENING HER EYES, SHE SEARCHED FOR A TARGET OF SOME SORT. SHE MUST TRY THIS INTRIGUING LITTLE BOW; IT WAS SMALLER THAN SHE WAS ACCUSTOMED TO AND MUCH LIGHTER, TOO.

SHE HAD ALWAYS THOUGHT MOONSTONE HAD POSSESSION OF THE FINEST WEAPONS AVAILABLE, BUT THIS BELAYED THAT NOTION. IT WAS LIGHTWEIGHT AND SLEEK AND WOULD BE EASILY

CONCEALED.

SHE WAS TEMPTED TO SNEAK IT BACK TO HER ROOM AND SKETCH IT OUT SO SHE COULD COPY IT LATER.

PROBABLY A BAD IDEA, BUT IT MIGHT BE WORTH TRYING.

SHE TOOK AIM ON A SMALL TREE AND LET THE FIRST ARROW FLY. SHE HIT THE GENERAL AREA SHE'D BEEN AIMING FOR, BUT MISSED DEAD CENTER BY SEVERAL INCHES, WHICH SET HER TEETH ON EDGE.

I HATE TO MISS.

TAKING AIM ON ANOTHER SMALL AREA, SHE LET THE SECOND ARROW FLY. SUDDENLY SHE HEARD A SCREAM AS A HORSE EMERGED FROM THE THICK FOREST AND STEPPED IN FRONT OF THE TREE.

WHERE HAD THE SOUND — THAT SCREAM — COME FROM . . . CERTAINLY NOT FROM HER?

SURELY NOT . . . SHE TOLD HERSELF, EVEN AS SHE REALIZED IT MUST HAVE BEEN HER, AS THE ONLY OTHER PERSON NEARBY HAD COME WITHIN A SECOND OF BEING STRUCK WITH AN ARROW — AND THEY DIDN'T EVEN KNOW IT YET — THEY COULDN'T.

THE RIDER TURNED HIS HEAD THEN, AND LEANED FORWARD JUST ENOUGH SO THE ARROW MISSED HIM BY A HAIR'S BREADTH, CATCHING HIS SLEEVE AS IT FLEW PAST.

IT WAS THE SLEEVE THAT MADE HER REALIZE THE PRINCE SAT IN THE SADDLE. IT WAS THE SAME SLEEVE HE'D BEEN WEARING IN SEVERAL OF THE PICTURES SHE HAD STUDIED EXHAUSTIVELY.

AND SHE NEARLY LOST HER SEAT WHEN SHE THOUGHT OF WHAT SHE COULD HAVE DONE.

A FEELING WAS CLAWING ITS WAY UP HER THROAT, TURNING HER BLOOD TO ICE AND HER NERVES TO MUSH. HER THOUGHTS WERE ALL BUT INCOHERENT AS THE SCENE PLAYED OUT IN HER MIND.

HER ARROW HAD COME WITHIN LESS THAN AN INCH OF PIERCING THE PRINCE'S HEART. SHE WAS OUT IN THE OPEN. THAT COULD NOT HAVE BEEN EXPLAINED AS AN ACCIDENT IN ANY WAY.

AND THE PRINCE WOULD BE DEAD . . .

THE WAVE OF HURT, OF ANGUISH, THAT RUSHED THROUGH HER MADE ABSOLUTELY NO SENSE. BUT HER THOUGHTS WERE STILL TRIPPING OVER EACH OTHER AND NOTHING SEEMED TO MAKE SENSE.

A STRANGE NOISE FILLED HER EARS, BLOCKING OUT EVERY OTHER SOUND AND SPOTS DANCED IN HER VISION, MAKING HER DIZZY.

SUDDENLY, THE PRINCE WAS BESIDE HER, REACHING OUT TO HER, BUT SHE SHIFTED IN HER SADDLE, PULLING AWAY FROM HIM IN PANIC. FRIGHTENING THOUGHTS CAME CRASHING BACK IN ON HER.

THE ARROW . . .

THE HORSE . . .

THE PRINCE.

I NEARLY . . . HE ALMOST . . . I MIGHT HAVE . . . AND HE WOULD BE . . . AS SHE PUSHED DOWN THE RIDICULOUS ANGUISH AGAIN, SHE COULDN'T HELP HERSELF, HER TEMPER EXPLODED.

"WHAT WERE YOU THINKING!"

SHE SHOUTED THE WORDS, NOT CONSIDERING FOR EVEN A MOMENT THAT SHE WAS ADDRESSING THE PRINCE — OR WHO ELSE MIGHT HEAR HER.

"WHAT THE BLAZES WERE YOU DOING? YOU COULD HAVE BEEN KILLED. YOU IDIOT! DID IT OCCUR TO YOU EVEN FOR A MOMENT TO LOOK WHERE YOU WERE GOING? NO, OF COURSE IT DIDN'T. AND JUST WHERE ARE YOUR GUARDS?"

WITH THOSE WORDS, SOMETHING CLICKED IN HER BEFUDDLED BRAIN, REMINDING HER WHERE SHE WAS AND WHO SHE WAS SPEAKING WITH . . . SHOUTING AT. SHE QUICKLY SNAPPED HER MOUTH CLOSED AND DUCKED HER HEAD, ANTICIPATING HIS REACTION.

SHE EXPECTED ANGER, SCREAMING . . . OR WORSE, THE SORT OF CALM AND TERRIFYING FURY SHE HAD BEEN ON THE RECEIVING END OF — ONLY ONCE — FROM DREY.

HE MIGHT EVEN CALL FOR HIS GUARDS AND HAVE ME LOCKED AWAY.

SHE QUIETLY BEGAN TO CALCULATE HOW CLOSE SHE WAS TO THE NEAREST EXIT.

COULD I GET OVER THE WALL? I KNOW IT'S NEARBY BUT WITH HIM SO CLOSE . . . HER THOUGHTS WERE INTERRUPTED BY LAUGHTER; DEEP, FULL, ROBUST LAUGHTER.

SHE FOUND HERSELF SEARCHING HIS FACE TO SEE IF HE HAD POSSIBLY SUSTAINED AN INJURY SOMEHOW . . . SOMETHING SHE HADN'T SEEN IMMEDIATELY . . . PERHAPS FROM HITTING HIS

HEAD, BUT HE APPEARED TO BE IN PERFECT
HEALTH.

"PLEASED TO AMUSE YOU, SIRE."

"YOU DO INDEED, MILADY."

THE SHOCKED GASP THAT ESCAPED THROUGH HER
LIPS TURNED QUICKLY INTO A HISS BEFORE SHE
MANAGED TO CLOSE HER MOUTH AND REGAIN
CONTROL OF HERSELF.

*DID I TRULY SPEAK ALOUD? WHAT IS WRONG WITH
ME?*

ONE OF HIS PERFECT EYEBROWS TILTED AT AN ODD
ANGLE AS HE STUDIED HER AND SHE WAS
SURPRISED AT HOW MUCH A STRUGGLE IT WAS NOT
TO SQUIRM IN HER SADDLE UNDER HIS SCRUTINY.

"HAVE YOU NOTHING ELSE TO SAY?"

"MY DEEPEST APOLOGIES, YOUR HIGHNESS."

HE SURPRISED HER AGAIN WITH MORE LAUGHTER.

"YOU ARE THE ONLY PERSON I KNOW THAT IS
CAPABLE OF DELIVERING A SMOOTH APOLOGY THAT
SOUNDS MORE LIKE A THREAT."

*UH OH, HERE IT COMES. IF HE'S ONLY GOING TO
THROW ME OUT, IT'S TOO BAD I MISSED.*

"A PUZZLE MOST INTRIGUING." HIS WORDS
CONFUSED HER FURTHER.

WAS HE KICKING HER OUT OR NOT?

NOTHING ABOUT THIS MAN MAKES SENSE.

SHE SAT THERE, STARING ACROSS AT HIM, WAITING
TO SEE WHAT HIS NEXT ACTION WOULD BE,

DETERMINED NOT TO BE SURPRISED, NO MATTER WHAT HE DID.

"YOU ARE A VERY GOOD SHOT." HE LOOKED OVER HIS SHOULDER AT THE TREE, "UNLESS OF COURSE, YOU WERE AIMING FOR ME . . ."

"IF I HAD AIMED FOR YOU, YOUR HIGHNESS, I WOULD HAVE HIT YOU."

HE LET OUT ANOTHER LOW, SELF-ASSURED LAUGH BEFORE LOOKING BACK AT HER.

"OF THAT I HAVE NO DOUBT, MY . . . MILADY."

SHE HEARD THE WORDS HE HAD INTENDED TO USE AS SURELY AS IF HE HAD SAID THEM — BUT HE HADN'T, SO SHE CLAMPED DOWN TIGHT ON AN EMOTION THAT RUSHED THROUGH HER AS A MEMORY SURGED INTO HER THOUGHTS — AND THREATENED TO PLUNGE HER INTO PANIC AGAIN.

"KAYDEN!"

HE VAULTED FROM HIS HORSE AND WAS BESIDE HER SO QUICKLY; SHE BARELY HAD TIME TO REGISTER THE MOVEMENT BEFORE HE WAS REACHING UP TO HER.

"I AM WELL."

SHE PROTESTED BUT HE IGNORED HER, PLACING HIS HANDS GENTLY AROUND HER WAIST TO PULL HER FROM THE HORSE.

"YOU ARE AS WHITE AS THE CLOUDS ABOVE." HIS VOICE WAS LOW, SOOTHING — AND SHE FELT HERSELF RELAXING AS HE GENTLY SAT HER BENEATH THE SHADE OF A LARGE MAPLE TREE.

"RELAX."

"I TOLD YOU — I AM WELL."

"SO YOU SAID . . . BUT IT IS NOT TRUE."

HE BRUSHED A HAND SLOWLY DOWN THE SIDE OF HER FACE AS HE SPOKE AND A SLOW BURN BLOOMED WHEREVER HIS SKIN TOUCHED HERS; THROWING HER EMOTIONS INTO EVEN MORE CHAOS.

"YOU DO NOT ALWAYS HAVE TO BE SO BRAVE, KAYDEN." AND HIS VOICE WAS SOFT BUT NO LONGER SOOTHING.

THE BURN WAS WITHIN HER NOW, STIRRING UP EMOTION, SENDING A RUSH OF LONGING THROUGH HER, STARTING WHERE HIS HAND TOUCHED HER FACE AND SPREADING OUT FROM THERE.

RESTING A HAND ON THE SOFT GRASS BENEATH HER, SHE LOOKED UP AT THE PRINCE, WONDERING WHAT IT WAS ABOUT HIM THAT AFFECTED HER IN A WAY THAT NO ONE ELSE EVER HAD.

"I SEE THE COLOR IS RETURNING. GOOD."

HIS HAND LEFT HER CHEEK THEN. KAYDEN WAS CERTAIN HER THOUGHTS WOULD RETURN TO NORMAL THEN . . .

BUT THEY DID NOT.

TEN

DVARIUS COULD NOT REMEMBER THE LAST TIME HE HAD FELT SO ALIVE. IRONIC, SINCE ONLY A FEW MOMENTS AGO HE HAD NEARLY BEEN SHOT — GRANTED, BY AN ARROW — BUT SHOT, NONETHELESS.

THE YOUNG WOMAN WHO WAS CURRENTLY STARING DAGGERS AT HIM WAS A TRUE FASCINATION. NOT QUITE WHAT HE EXPECTED — AND A PUZZLE AS WELL. HE WAS DELIGHTED TO REALIZE THAT NOT ONLY COULD SHE RIDE, SHE COULD SHOOT AS WELL.

SHE WILL BE A CONSTANT CHALLENGE.

IT WAS ODDLY EXCITING TO REALIZE THAT THIS WAS PRECISELY WHAT HE WANTED. A CHALLENGE WOULD BE BETTER THAN BLIND OBEDIENCE, OF THIS HE WAS CERTAIN.

"DID YOU ENJOY YOUR RIDE?"

She looked up at him with shock on her face. Her expression made it clear she expected some sort of punishment — or even a lecture.

It piqued his curiosity, but there were more important things to be said, so he let it pass for the moment.

"Before it ended abruptly, that is . . ."

She let out a low laugh at his words, causing the muscles of his stomach to tighten in reaction.

"It was rather nice, yes. I enjoy riding. Do you?"

Her question took him by surprise. None of the other ladies he had spoken with so far had asked him anything of the sort.

And why should it surprise me that she is different in this as well?

"I do. There is not as much time for it as I would like, but it is a favorite activity. I am delighted to see someone else taking advantage of our wonderful stables."

Since her horse had wandered away to munch on the nearby grass, he settled on the ground beside her and watched the range of emotions that fluttered across her features.

Whatever she was struggling with appeared to be quite serious.

"Kayden?"

She looked up at him, one delicate eyebrow winging up in surprise.

"Your Highness?"

"When we first met — and a few moments ago — you reacted quite strongly to the phrase . . . well, I won't use it, but I'm certain you know the one I mean."

"Yes, Your Highness."

He watched her eyes cloud over and worried that she might not respond if he kept pushing. She was unpredictable at best. And he was quite certain by now that she would not answer unless she wanted to.

He had no illusions that she would tell him what he wanted to know just because he was the Prince, but he needed . . . no, he wanted to know what it was about the phrase "my dear" that bothered her so much.

"Would you tell me about it?"

"It's nothing, really."

"I find that difficult to believe."

She looked down at the blade of grass between her fingers. He watched as she twirled the green blade around and around and waited for her to say more.

"It happened a long time ago, Your Highness. I apologize for my reaction. I truly thought I'd moved beyond it."

Recognizing that she was not going to say more, Dvarius decided it would be best to

STOP PUSHING.

"I KNOW SOMETHING ABOUT THAT. MY ADVISORS TELL ME THAT I SHOULD HAVE ALREADY MOVED ON, BUT HOW DOES ONE SIMPLY STOP MOURNING THE LOSS OF A FATHER?"

SHE NODDED, BUT DID NOT SAY ANYTHING ELSE. THERE WAS A HINT OF SOMETHING IN HER EYES FOR A MOMENT, BUT IT WAS GONE BEFORE HE COULD BEGIN TO FIGURE IT OUT.

WITH EACH MOMENT, HE BECAME MORE FASCINATED BY HER, MORE DETERMINED TO LEARN EVERYTHING ABOUT HER . . . BUT FOR NOW, HE DECIDED TO SWITCH TO A MORE NEUTRAL TOPIC — DESPITE HIS DISLIKE OF MEANINGLESS SMALL-TALK.

"ARE YOU ENJOYING THE PALACE?"

A LAUGH ESCAPED HER BEFORE SHE STIFLED IT.

"NOT ENJOYING THE PALACE, THEN?"

SHE QUIRKED AN EYEBROW AT HIM BEFORE ANSWERING.

"NO, YOUR HIGHNESS. I MEAN, YES, YOUR HIGHNESS."

SHE LOOKED DOWN AND LET OUT A LITTLE HUFF AS A BECOMING BLUSH SPREAD OVER WHAT LITTLE HE COULD STILL SEE OF HER FEATURES.

HE WANTED TO LAUGH AT THE RIDICULOUSNESS OF IT ALL, BUT HE SENSED THAT IT WOULD NOT BE WELL-RECEIVED, SO HE HELD HIS TONGUE.

AFTER SEVERAL MOMENTS, SHE LIFTED HER HEAD, A DEEP SCARLET STILL COLORING HER CHEEKS, AND SPOKE AGAIN, CLEARLY MEASURING EACH

WORD.

"I AM ENJOYING THE PALACE, YOUR HIGHNESS. IT IS NOT AT ALL WHAT I AM ACCUSTOMED TO . . ." SHE LOOKED DOWN AGAIN AND DVARIUS WONDERED IF SHE HAD TRULY MEANT TO SAY THOSE WORDS.

SOMETHING TOLD HIM SHE HAD NOT.

"IT IS BEAUTIFUL. MY ROOMS ARE MAGNIFICENT, AND THE VIEW FROM MY BALCONY IS BREATHTAKING."

SHE SNAPPED HER MOUTH SHUT AGAIN RATHER QUICKLY AND DVARIUS FOUND HIMSELF STIFLING A LAUGH.

SHE MUST HAVE REALIZED JUST HOW HER WORDS MIGHT SOUND. HE WAS TEMPTED TO RESPOND TO THE UNSPOKEN INVITATION, BUT SINCE HE WANTED TO KNOW MORE ABOUT HER, HE CHOSE TO STEER HER ATTENTION AWAY FROM HER FAUX PAS.

"TELL ME ABOUT YOUR HOME. YOU GREW UP NOT FAR FROM THE PALACE, YES?"

"I DID INDEED. HOWEVER, IN MANY WAYS, MY CHILDHOOD FEELS WORLDS REMOVED FROM ALL OF THIS."

SHE WAVED A HAND IN THE AIR; GESTURING BEHIND THEM TO THE PALACE.

"I BELIEVE I KNOW WHAT YOU MEAN. ON THE TRIPS WHERE I ACCOMPANIED FATHER INTO THE CITY, IT WAS LIKE STEPPING INTO ANOTHER WORLD."

"YOU WENT INTO THE CITY WITH YOUR FATHER? HOW OFTEN?"

HER FACE WAS A MASK OF SURPRISE. DVARIUS

WONDERED IF SHE KNEW HOW EAGER SHE
SOUNDED.

IS THIS THE SAME YOUNG WOMAN?

SHE WAS MORE OF A PUZZLE EVERY MOMENT HE
SPENT WITH HER.

"HE WENT OUT INTO THE CITY NEARLY EVERY
WEEK, TO CHECK ON HIS CHAPELS. THEY WERE
VERY IMPORTANT TO HIM. I ADMIT; I DID NOT SEE
THE MERIT UNTIL IT WAS ALMOST TOO LATE. I
ACCOMPANIED HIM NO MORE THAN A HANDFUL OF
TIMES."

HE LOOKED DOWN AS THE GRAVITY OF HIS WORDS
TOOK HOLD. THANKFULLY, KAYDEN'S EXPRESSION
DISTRACTED HIM BEFORE HE COULD BECOME LOST
IN HIS ANGUISH.

"WHAT WAS THE KING DOING WITH THE CHAPELS?"

THE CURIOSITY BURNING IN HER VOICE WAS JUST
THE DISTRACTION HE NEEDED, SO HE HELD TIGHT
TO IT.

IT WAS NO SURPRISE SHE KNEW NOTHING OF HIS
FATHER'S PROJECT. MANY OF THE WEALTHIER
FAMILIES ESCHEWED WHAT THEY CONSIDERED AN
UNNECESSARY EXPENSE ON THE PART OF THE
GOVERNMENT; HER FAMILY MUST HAVE BEEN ONE
OF THEM.

"HE REFURBISHED MANY OF THE CITY'S CHAPELS SO
THAT THE FEW REMAINING CLERGYMEN COULD
MINISTER TO THE PEOPLE."

"I HAD NO IDEA . . ." HER WORDS DRIFTED OFF AND
THERE WAS SOMETHING IN HER EYES — SURPRISE
AND PERHAPS . . . WORRY.

MORE AND MORE OF A PUZZLE . . .

SHE SHOOK HER HEAD AND SPOKE AGAIN, HER VOICE FULL OF CURIOSITY AGAIN.

"HAVE YOU VISITED MANY OTHER CITIES IN AURALIUS?"

"OH YES. FATHER'S PROJECTS EXTENDED INTO MORE THAN JUST OUR CAPITAL. THERE IS NEED EVERYWHERE . . ." HIS VOICE TRAILED OFF AS HE THOUGHT OF HOW CLOSE HE HAD COME TO MISSING OUT ENTIRELY ON THAT TIME WITH HIS FATHER.

IF ONLY I HAD REALIZED EARLIER . . . I COULD HAVE HAD SO MUCH MORE TIME WITH HIM.

"YOU MISS HIM."

HER WORDS DID NOT GET HIS ATTENTION AS MUCH AS THE HAND SHE LAID ON HIS ARM AND HE FOUND HIMSELF SAYING THE FIRST THING THAT CAME TO MIND.

"HOW ARE YOU SO ABLE TO SEE PRECISELY WHAT IS GOING ON WITHIN ME, AND YET YOU ARE A MYSTERY . . . IN EVERY WAY?"

"PERHAPS I SEE IT MORE EASILY BECAUSE I FEEL IT EVERY DAY MYSELF."

"HOW COULD I HAVE FORGOTTEN? OF COURSE, YOU KNOW EXACTLY HOW IT FEELS."

HE MENTALLY KICKED HIMSELF. *I SHOULD HAVE REMEMBERED THAT.*

"IT WAS ALSO . . . A LONG TIME AGO, YOUR HIGHNESS. NOT SO FRESH FOR ME AS IT WOULD BE FOR YOU."

Her voice was so quiet, he could hardly make out her words, but the misery in them was enough to tell him everything he needed to know.

"Does it ever get any better?"

Dvarius turned his hand over, sliding his fingers gently around Kayden's wrist, rubbing his thumb along the soft skin there.

"No, it doesn't."

She looked down at their hands, but he didn't miss the break in her voice.

"I should not be glad we have such a thing to share, but . . . I find myself pleased to know that you understand what I've been going through these past few months. None of the others have any idea."

Kayden looked up at him then, and he was surprised to feel such a strong pull building between them.

Given what he had already felt every time he'd been near her, it shouldn't have been a surprise — but it was.

As he looked into her dark, soulful eyes, he felt himself leaning toward her, almost as if the pull was physical.

This was much more than holding a shared past; this was something from deep within.

He looked down at her lips for a moment and he could feel the muscles in his stomach tighten in anticipation.

What would it feel like to capture that full, lower lip in mine . . .

Will I shock her if I simply lean in and take a kiss?

Should I ask?

THOUGHTS TUMBLED THROUGH HIS MIND AS WHAT HE WAS CONTEMPLATING BEGAN TO SINK IN.

SHE WOULD BE THE FIRST WOMAN HE HAD KISSED.

HIS ADVISORS HAD BEGGED HIM TO KEEP THAT INFORMATION TO HIMSELF, BUT SOMEHOW HE KNEW IT WAS SOMETHING HE WOULD NEED TO TELL HER.

HOWEVER, BEFORE HE COULD DO EITHER, HER HORSE'S LEAD LINE DROPPED BETWEEN THEM AND SHATTERED THE MOMENT.

SHE LET OUT WHAT SOUNDED LIKE A VERY NERVOUS LAUGH.

HE WANTED . . . DESPERATELY . . . TO ASK IF SHE WAS EXPERIENCING THE SAME EMOTIONS THAT HE WAS FEELING.

HE OPENED HIS MOUTH TO SPEAK, BUT CLOSED IT AGAIN NO MORE THAN A SECOND LATER, WITHOUT UTTERING A WORD.

"WE SHOULD GET BACK."

HE LOOKED UP AT HER, BUT HER EYES HAD CLOUDED OVER AGAIN AND HE WAS LEFT WITH HIS CONFUSION AND NO ANSWERS.

ELEVEN

AS MUCH AS HE DETESTED ADMITTING IT, SHE WAS RIGHT. THEY SHOULD GET BACK TO THE PALACE.

HE KNEW THAT — BUT IT WAS THE LAST THING HE WANTED TO DO.

RELUCTANTLY, DVARIUS STOOD AND BRUSHED HIMSELF OFF, LEANING DOWN TO OFFER KAYDEN HIS HAND.

FOR A MOMENT, IT APPEARED SHE MIGHT NOT TAKE IT, BUT THEN SHE SLID HER FINGERS INTO HIS OPEN HAND AND HE PULLED HER TO HER FEET.

SOMEHOW HE OVERCOMPENSATED AND SHE ENDED UP PRESSED AGAINST HIS CHEST INSTEAD OF SAFELY ON HER FEET.

HE IMMEDIATELY MOVED HIS HANDS, ENCIRCLING HER WITH HIS ARMS TO STEADY HER AND THEY WERE PRESSED EVEN CLOSER.

He looked down at her just as she looked up at him, and his attention was again drawn to her lips.

Heat traveled up the length of his chest. Everywhere she was pressed against him felt too hot . . . and the muscles that had been tight felt now as though they might snap.

She cleared her throat and quickly stepped back, putting far too much — yet at the same time, not nearly enough — distance between them.

"Your Highness."

He turned away to take her horse's reins and rubbed a frustrated hand over his face.

As he turned back to help lift her into the saddle, he was shocked to see her swinging herself — skirts and all — into place.

He looked at her for several seconds before he moved away to retrieve the bow she'd dropped earlier.

As he walked back, he examined the small weapon. It was clearly a palace weapon. How had this slip of a girl managed to convince the huntsman she could handle such a thing?

"You seem to have dropped this."

Her expression gave nothing away as she reached down to take the slim weapon.

"I'm curious. Just how did you manage to . . . convince . . . Gelford to release this to you?"

His reaction to the very feminine smile she

SHOT BACK AT HIM AS SHE SHIFTED IN THE SADDLE WAS SWIFT AND REMINDED HIM STRONGLY OF THE TIGHTENING IN HIS GUT ONLY A MOMENT AGO.

IT FORESTALLED ANY FURTHER QUESTIONS.

ONCE SHE WAS SETTLED IN THE SADDLE, THE MINX TURNED TO HIM AND WITH A VERY SELF-SATISFIED SMILE, TOOK OFF TOWARD THE PALACE STABLES, TOSSING A CHALLENGE OVER HER SHOULDER AS SHE WENT.

"RACE YOU BACK . . . YOUR HIGHNESS." HER LAUGHTER RANG OUT AS SHE GAVE THE MARE HER HEAD.

DVARIUS FOUND HIMSELF LAUGHING WITH HER, EVEN AS HE URGED HIS STALLION TO CATCH UP.

HE KNEW MOST OF THE HORSES IN HIS STABLES WELL — AND THE MARE SHE RODE WOULD CERTAINLY PROVIDE A CHALLENGE FOR DESTINY, BUT NOT ENOUGH TO CAUSE HIM ANY CONCERN.

THEY GALLOPED THROUGH THE CAREFULLY SPACED TREES OF THE SPARSE FOREST, WITH HIM STILL FIRMLY IN PURSUIT OF HER.

AFTER A FEW MINUTES, THE FOREST THINNED, GIVING WAY TO GREEN FIELDS, GIVING THEM BOTH THE OPPORTUNITY TO INCREASE THEIR PACE.

DVARIUS LET HIS LAUGHTER RING OUT AS HE ENJOYED THE FEEL OF THE WIND WHIPPING THROUGH HIS HAIR. AND THE SIGHT OF THE DARK RED BRAIDS THAT HAD COME LOOSE FROM THE KNOT KAYDEN HAD SECURED AT THE BASE OF HER NECK EXCITED HIM.

HERE . . . FINALLY, WAS THE CHALLENGE HE'D

BEEN CRAVING. HERE WAS THE REAL PERSON — THIS WAS NO FACADE.

SHE NEARLY RAN ME THROUGH WITH AN ARROW, FOR GOODNESS SAKE.

HE THOUGHT OF WHAT LITTLE HE KNEW ABOUT HER AS THEY RACED ACROSS THE EXPANSE OF WELL-MANICURED LAWN.

HIS ADVISORS HAD GIVEN HIM FILES ON EVERY YOUNG WOMAN HERE, BUT HE'D LEARNED MORE ABOUT KAYDEN IN THEIR TWO SHORT ENCOUNTERS THAN HE COULD FROM ANY FILE.

SHE HAD A FIERCE TEMPER AND A BEAUTIFUL SMILE.

HE COULD SEE THAT SHE SAW HIM AS A PRINCE, BUT SHE ALSO SAW HIM AS JUST A MAN . . .

OTHERWISE SHE WOULD NEVER HAVE SHOUTED AT ME.

ANYONE ELSE WOULD HAVE JUST APOLOGIZED — AGAIN AND AGAIN.

THEN THERE WAS THE FACT THAT SHE'D NEARLY FAINTED. THAT HAD TO MEAN SHE WAS CONCERNED FOR HIS LIFE; AT LEAST A LITTLE.

SHE CLEARLY HAS STRONG FEELINGS FOR ME.

THEY MIGHT ONLY CONSIST OF ANNOYANCE AT THE MOMENT, BUT HE HAD HIGH HOPES THAT HE COULD CHANGE THAT.

WHEN SHE LOOKED OVER HER SHOULDER AND SENT HIM THAT BEWITCHING SMILE, HE LEANED LOW OVER DESTINY'S NECK AND URGED HIM EVEN FASTER.

THE RACE WAS EVEN MORE OF A THRILL BECAUSE HE FELT QUITE CERTAIN SHE WOULD NOT THROW THE RACE JUST BECAUSE HE WAS *THE PRINCE*.

STILL . . . HE WAS DETERMINED TO WIN.

SHE LAUGHED WHEN HE CAME ABREAST OF HER HORSE — AND THEN LEANED OVER HER OWN SADDLE, HAIR BLOWING FREE NOW IN THE WIND THAT WHIPPED BETWEEN THE TWO OF THEM.

HOOVES THUNDERED OVER THE SMOOTH, GREEN LAWN IN THE EARLY MORNING STILLNESS AS THE TWO OF THEM RACED, NECK AND NECK.

JUST AS THEY REACHED THE FINAL RISE BEFORE THE GROUNDS SLOPED DOWN TO THE STABLES, SHE PULLED AHEAD AND STAYED THERE.

NO MATTER HOW HE URGED DESTINY, KAYDEN PUSHED A HALF-LENGTH AHEAD EVERY TIME DVARIUS GAINED EVEN AN INCH.

THEY CRESTED THE HILL AT A DEAD RUN AND SHE TOOK FULL ADVANTAGE OF HER HORSE'S SMALLER FRAME IN THOSE FINAL LENGTHS TO THE STABLES.

THEY RACED ALL THE WAY TO THE MAIN STABLE DOOR — PULLING UP JUST SHORT OF RUNNING OVER THE YOUNG STABLE HAND WHO WALKED OUT, CARRYING FEED BUCKETS.

AT THE SUDDEN STOP OF THE HORSES, HE STEPPED BACKWARD AND DROPPED BOTH BUCKETS, STUMBLING OVER A PAVING STONE.

DVARIUS DISMOUNTED AND WENT TO CHECK ON THE LAD, ONLY TO FIND KAYDEN ALREADY LEANING OVER HIM AND CLUCKING VERY MUCH LIKE A MOTHER HEN.

The young man looked from Kayden to Dvarius and his eyes widened in terror.

Before he'd even gotten to his feet, he changed position as he tried to bow and ended up back on his rear.

Kayden turned her head and threw a look behind her at Dvarius that was completely unreadable, before turning back to the lad and giving him her hand.

The lad looked up at the Prince and then back to Kayden, shaking his head — but Kayden took his arm and pulled him up anyway, before turning to look at Dvarius again.

"Does everyone react this way around you?"

He found himself struggling to not laugh at her fierce tone.

"Aside from you . . . yes, generally."

One side of her lips twitched, but that was the only reaction he could see.

"My apologies, Your Majesty . . ." the lad began, but Dvarius waved away his words.

"Not to worry young man. She has that effect on everyone."

Dvarius looked over at Kayden and was not surprised to see her wearing that same smile he was quickly becoming quite fond of.

There was no shame in the girl . . . not one bit.

He was not at all surprised to see that she had one arm companionably slung over the shoulders of the stable boy — as if he were a younger brother instead of a servant.

That would be why his advisors had done everything they could to steer him away from her — and it was certainly one of the reasons he was so fascinated by her.

This was the woman he needed by his side when the Prime Minister placed the crown on his head.

She did not look at him and see a prince.

She didn't look at the stable boy and see a servant.

She simply saw people.

She would help him remember, even when everyone else around him would strive to make him forget, that his subjects were people — not just servants . . . and certainly not pawns in some massive chess game.

Drey looked over at the spineless excuse for an operative who lay on the ground before him.

What he wouldn't give to have more operatives like the girl he'd sent into the palace.

She knew when to obey . . . but she also had a

WAY OF GOING AROUND THE RULES WHEN THEY DIDN'T SUIT HER. AND SHE DID THINGS HER OWN WAY, WHICH DID NOT ALWAYS SUIT HIS PURPOSES, BUT HER TRACK RECORD WAS QUITE IMPRESSIVE.

GRANTED, THIS WAS THE MOST DELICATE ASSIGNMENT SHE HAD BEEN GIVEN TO DATE, BUT THAT WAS ONE THING THAT MADE IT SO PERFECT.

IF SHE FAILED, THE PALACE GUARD WOULD TAKE CARE OF HER, AND IF SHE SUCCEEDED . . . WELL HE MIGHT HAVE TO REWARD HER QUITE HEAVILY.

THE SOUND OF WHIMPERING MET HIS EARS AND HE FELT A MUSCLE IN HIS JAW TWITCH.

IT WAS THE ONLY THING ABOUT HIMSELF HE HAD NEVER BEEN ABLE TO TRAIN OUT AND IT REMINDED HIM FORCEFULLY THAT HE WAS ONLY HUMAN.

THEREFORE, ANYONE WHO CAUSED IT TO HAPPEN MET WITH SWIFT JUSTICE.

HE TURNED BACK TO THE QUIVERING GIRL WITH A TIGHT SMILE THAT WOULD HAVE TERRIFIED ANYONE UNFORTUNATE ENOUGH TO WITNESS IT.

TWELVE

DVARIUS STRODE PURPOSEFULLY DOWN THE HALL. EVERY MEETING HIS ADVISORS HAD SCHEDULED IN THE LAST WEEK HAD BEEN CENTERED AROUND YET ANOTHER GIRL THEY WERE CERTAIN WOULD BE THE PERFECT CHOICE FOR HIM.

HE WAS BEGINNING TO LOATHE AGREEING TO THIS ENTIRE CHARADE. HE WAS THRILLED TO HAVE MET KAYDEN, BUT HE WAS PERTURBED AT BEING KEPT FROM HER.

THEIR EXHILARATING RIDE HAD BEEN ON HIS MIND ALL WEEK AND HE HAD BEEN THINKING OF LITTLE ELSE DURING THESE MEETINGS. IN EVERY BORING SESSION HIS ADVISORS HAD DRAGGED HIM THROUGH, HE HAD BEEN THINKING ABOUT WATCHING KAYDEN RIDE AHEAD OF HIM, RED HAIR WHIPPING IN THE WIND, HER DELIGHTED LAUGHTER BOUNCING BACK TO HIM.

THE MEMORY HAD TWO EFFECTS ON HIM.

FIRST, HE COULD HARDLY WAIT TO SEE HER AGAIN; TO HAVE HER BY HIS SIDE.

SECOND, HE WORRIED ABOUT THE EFFECT SHE HAD ON EVERY OTHER MALE AROUND. NO DOUBT THERE WERE A DOZEN SUITORS ACTIVELY VYING FOR HER HAND.

THE THOUGHT OF KAYDEN WITH ANOTHER MAN HAD HIM INCREASING HIS PACE.

AND AFTER A MOMENT HE FORCED HIMSELF TO SLOW DOWN AGAIN WHEN HE REALIZED HOW MUCH NOISE HE WAS MAKING AS HE MOVED QUICKLY THROUGH THE HALLS.

WHY DID I WEAR THE ENTIRE UNIFORM? IT MAKES MORE NOISE THAN AN ENTIRE SQUAD OF GUARDS.

IT WAS A SILLY QUESTION BECAUSE HE KNEW PRECISELY WHY HE HAD WORN IT. HE WANTED TO MAKE THE BEST IMPRESSION HE COULD ON HER.

THE CHOICE MIGHT ULTIMATELY BE UP TO HIM BUT HE KNEW THAT HE WANTED HER TO CHOOSE HIM — AS HE HAD ALREADY CHOSEN HER.

MORE THAN ANYTHING ELSE, HE WANTED THAT.

WITH THIS WOMAN, HE KNEW IF SHE CHOSE HIM, IT WOULD BE ABOUT INTEREST, LOVE, EMOTION, ATTACHMENT — NOT A CROWN.

SHE WAS NOT SOMEONE WHO WAS ONLY OUT FOR HIS CROWN . . . HE WAS CERTAIN OF THAT.

WITH KAYDEN, HE COULD SEE MARRIAGE AS A PLACE OF HAPPINESS AND LOVE; WHICH WAS PRECISELY WHAT HE WANTED.

He desired what his parents had achieved; not a marriage that was cold and loveless, not something that had more to do with connections or money than love and attachment.

He was certain God meant that for him, with Kayden. Dvarius had been praying diligently about it since he'd first walked into the Great Hall that evening and spotted her.

Everything about Kayden intrigued him; he wanted her to be his choice, and he wanted to be her choice, but above all he wanted what God had been planning for him because he knew that would be the best choice for both of them.

It certainly had been in his parent's case — he'd heard those very words many times.

"It all had to be God's plan, son. If I had been King first, I would never have been allowed to marry your mother. This is why I have always been grateful I was not the King when I met her."

Of course, his mother had always said that was nonsense. God had meant them for each other and one way or another, He would have brought the two of them together; which was essentially what his father had said.

Dvarius thought about the look that had always passed between the two of them when the subject came up. They would reach for each other and smile over their clasped hands.

That . . . was precisely what he wanted from marriage.

Thinking of his parents made him think about Kayden — and the thought of seeing her again made him feel excited, impatient, and more than a little nervous.

He smiled as he was turning the corner, but the smile disappeared when he collided with a small, female form. He reached out instinctively as they fell; wrapping his arms around the girl, he turned so that he could cushion her fall.

For a moment, he was amazed to feel a bit guilty — thinking that he would be tangled up with a young woman other than the one he intended to marry.

However, the guilt lasted only a moment, until he saw a glint of red out of the corner of his eye and turned his head just in time to catch sight of that bewitching smile of hers.

Kayden. He nearly breathed her name but caught himself just in time.

They landed in a heap on the floor and he took full advantage of the opportunity to enjoy being close to her.

He hadn't appreciated having her in his arms yesterday nearly enough and he was determined to do so now.

Surprisingly, she didn't immediately scramble away. She even looked mildly amused as she lay sprawled across his stomach. After a few

MOMENTS, SHE PULLED HER ARMS UP AND PLANTED BOTH ELBOWS ON HIS CHEST . . . AND THEN SHE RESTED HER CHIN ON HER TINY FISTS.

"YOU PLANNED THIS, DIDN'T YOU?"

HE WAS DELIGHTED TO SEE LAUGHTER IN HER EYES AS SHE SAID IT.

"YOU WOULD NOT BELIEVE ME IF I SAID NO, SO I MAY AS WELL TAKE CREDIT FOR IT," HE TEASED BACK AND WAS REWARDED WITH ANOTHER LAUGH FROM HER.

THE SOUND OF HER LAUGHTER WAS POSITIVELY DELIGHTFUL.

THE THOUGHT THAT HE COULD HAPPILY STAY RIGHT WHERE HE WAS ALL EVENING CROSSED HIS MIND; HOWEVER, HE WAS CERTAIN SOMEONE WOULD COME ALONG AT SOME POINT AND IT WOULD NOT LOOK PROPER FOR HIM TO BE ON THE FLOOR WITH HER ON TOP OF HIM — SO, HE RELUCTANTLY BEGAN TO SHIFT.

SHE WAS QUICKER, SPRINGING UP WITH AGILITY THAT HE COULD NOT IMAGINE HER HAVING, ESPECIALLY UNDER THE YARDS OF FABRIC HER DRESS MUST HAVE.

WHEN SHE GAINED HER FOOTING, SHE REACHED DOWN A HAND TO HIM AND HE HAD TO SMILE AT THE LOOK ON HER FACE. AS THE EXPRESSION IMPLIED, IT APPEARED THAT SHE HAD INDEED TUCKED HER TONGUE INTO HER CHEEK.

"ENJOYING YOURSELF?"

"YES, AS A MATTER OF FACT I AM. IT'S A RELIEF TO FIND THAT YOU ARE NOT, IN FACT, PERFECT."

She placed her fisted hands on her tiny waist — since he did not take her hand to help him up.

"Oh Kayden, I'm far from perfect, I assure you."

He sat there looking at her for a long moment before getting to his feet.

Does she have any idea of how appealing she is — standing there, behaving more like a scolding mother hen than a young woman vying for . . . well, me.

Of course, that was the very reason he was so determined to impress her, choose her, keep her for his own . . . forever. because she was not vying for him — or his crown.

She was simply being herself — and who she was impressed him more than she would ever know.

Looking at her, the possibility of other suitors came to mind again and he felt fresh determination well up within him at the very least, to hold on to her as much as possible this evening.

With that in mind, he bowed and held out his arm to her.

"Milady, may I escort you?" and she reached out her hand, but snatched it back immediately with a smile.

"Do you promise to watch where you're going?"

He couldn't help himself — he laughed — delighted to see the sparkle in her eyes.

"Technically speaking, the fault is as much yours as it is mine. Even in heels, you make no noise when you walk, so it is clearly not my fault that I did not hear you."

"Yes, but you walked right into me. I was watching where I was going, but you were moving so fast, I couldn't get out of the way in time."

She said the words earnestly — and he laughed again.

"All true."

"Very well. I promise to be very careful. After all, I will be escorting someone precious."

He looked at her face as he said the last words, but there was no change in her expression that he could see.

Clearly I have a lot of work to do yet.

She surrendered her hand, which he firmly tucked through his bent arm, and they walked slowly toward the grand ballroom.

THIRTEEN

AS SHE AND THE PRINCE WALKED INTO THE GRAND BALLROOM, KAYDEN HAD TO WORK TO KEEP HER EXPRESSION IN PLACE.

EVERYWHERE SHE LOOKED, SHE COULD SEE JEWELS GLINTING, GOLD SHIMMERING, AND SILKS SWISHING AS PEOPLE MOVED ABOUT THE ENORMOUS ROOM.

SHE COULD FEEL THE BREATH CATCH IN HER THROAT. SHE WASN'T READY FOR THIS. ALL THE TRAINING IN THE WORLD COULD NOT HAVE PREPARED HER FOR THIS.

SOMETHING MUST HAVE SIGNALED THEIR ENTRANCE BECAUSE SUDDENLY EVERY EYE WAS ON THEM AND SHE STRUGGLED TO KEEP A BLUSH FROM SPREADING ACROSS HER CHEEKS.

THE HEAT THAT BLOOMED THERE TOLD HER SHE'D BEEN UNSUCCESSFUL, SO SHE SIMPLY INCLINED HER HEAD AS THE PRINCE ESCORTED HER TO THE MIDDLE OF THE ROOM.

WHETHER SHE FELT CONFIDENT OR NOT, SHE WAS DETERMINED TO SHOW THE REST OF THEM THAT SHE WASN'T THE SLIGHTEST BIT INTIMIDATED.

NOT THAT I HAVE ANY REASON TO BE, SHE MUSED; BEING THAT SHE WAS NOT HERE FOR THE SAME REASON AS THE OTHERS.

NO; HER REASONS WERE MORE IMPORTANT.

MORE URGENT.

AND MORE — MUCH MORE — DANGEROUS.

REMEMBERING WHERE SHE WAS AT THE MOMENT, SHE PURPOSELY MADE HER SMILE A BIT BRIGHTER, ENOUGH TO REACH HER EYES. IF ANYONE WAS WATCHING HER, THEY WOULD SEE THE SPARKLE AND BELIEVE IT WAS THERE FROM HER EXCITEMENT AT BEING NEAR THE PRINCE.

THE PRINCE STOPPED IN THE MIDDLE OF THE WIDE, GLEAMING FLOOR AND NODDED TO THE ORCHESTRA. JUST BEFORE THE MUSIC BEGAN, SHE REALIZED WHAT HE WAS DOING . . . HE INTENDED TO DANCE WITH HER — RIGHT NOW.

SHE HAD THOUGHT HE WAS LEADING HER INTO THE BALLROOM TO BE POLITE. SUDDENLY, PANIC SURGED UP FROM THE PIT OF HER STOMACH.

HE CAN'T DANCE WITH ME — NOT TO OPEN THE BALL.

SHE REALIZED IT WAS TOO LATE TO DO ANYTHING ABOUT IT NOW. HE SPOKE AS HE WAS TURNING HER IN HIS ARMS AND THE MUSIC BEGAN.

"SHALL WE?"

HE STEPPED FORWARD — AND SHE REALLY HAD NO

CHOICE BUT TO FOLLOW — SO SHE DID. SHE HELD HER HEAD HIGH, HER EYES NEVER LEAVING HIS.

SHE WAS THANKFUL NOW FOR THE HOURS OF DANCING SHE'D ENDURED.

WITH EVERYONE IN THE ROOM WATCHING HER, SHE DID NOT WANT TO MESS THIS UP. IT WOULD LOOK SUSPICIOUS AND COULD HURT HER CHANCE TO GET CLOSE TO HIM.

WELL . . . I'M NOT REALLY SURE THAT'S TRUE.

HE SEEMS TO BE INTERESTED IN ME . . . EVEN PURSUING ME. I MUST BE DOING SOMETHING RIGHT. DREY WOULD BE PLEASED. THE THOUGHT BOTH ELATED AND TERRIFIED HER.

THEY SPUN TOGETHER ACROSS THE FLOOR IN A WIDE, SWEEPING ARC.

ODDLY, SHE WAS THANKFUL THEY WERE SPINNING TOO FAST FOR HER TO TAKE NOTE OF THE FACES SURROUNDING THEM.

JEALOUSY WASN'T SOMETHING SHE HAD EXPERIENCED BEFORE, BUT SHE WAS CERTAIN THERE WAS MORE THAN A LITTLE OF IT COLORING THE FACES OF HER RIVALS.

AS THE PRINCE TURNED HER AROUND SHE PAUSED, BEFORE SPINNING BACK TOWARD HIM.

WHEN SHE DID, KAYDEN CAUGHT SIGHT OF ONE OF THE OTHER GIRLS — A LOVELY GIRL, REALLY — WHO WAS WATCHING HER, LOOKING PLEASED.

IT COMPLETELY THREW HER OFF.

WHAT POSSIBLE REASON COULD SHE HAVE TO LOOK HAPPY THAT I AM IN THE PRINCE'S ARMS?

Especially when every other girl would prefer to see me strung up from the nearest tree . . .

The conflicting response made no sense. Kayden puzzled over it for several seconds, until she looked up and met the Prince's gaze.

Once she looked into his eyes, every other thought melted away. The ballroom disappeared, leaving only the two of them — dancing in the clouds somewhere.

No one was watching, no one judging . . . no orders, no mission, nothing but the two of them and the music.

It had only taken a glance to find herself caught. The intensity of his expression held her attention and even the music vanished into the thick fog of passion that enveloped them.

As they twirled, she became aware of his hand at her back. His hold was gentle but firm as he swept her across the dance floor.

Even through the thick, voluminous layers of her dress, she could feel the heat of his body — the thrill of being so close.

The sensations that coursed through her were more than a little confusing. She had never experienced anything like it; the feel of him against her was exhilarating, yet frightening.

She continued to move with him, looking into

THOSE AMAZING EYES, WHILE TRYING TO FIGURE
OUT WHAT WAS GOING ON INSIDE OF HER.

"NO WONDER I CAN NEVER HEAR YOU WALKING.
YOU ARE SURPRISINGLY LIGHT ON YOUR FEET." HIS
WORDS SURPRISED HER.

"WHY DO YOU SOUND SO SURPRISED?"

"I'M NOT . . . WELL, NOT REALLY," HE ANSWERED
WITH A LAUGH.

"YOUR HIGHNESS IS QUITE GRACEFUL AS WELL."

"AM I? THEN WHY DO I FEEL AS CLUMSY AS I WAS
IN MY YOUTH?"

HIS WORDS CONFUSED HER, AND THE LAUGH THAT
ACCOMPANIED THEM; EVEN MORE SO.

*IS HE ASKING ME A QUESTION OR IS HIS QUERY
MEANT TO BE PURELY RHETORICAL?*

"I DON'T WANT YOU TO SLIP AWAY FROM ME,
KAYDEN."

THE WORDS WERE WHISPERED IN HER EAR; THE
BRUSH OF WARM BREATH SENT A SHIVER DOWN
HER SPINE AS THE MEANING BEHIND THEM CAUSED
THE MUSCLES IN HER STOMACH TO TIGHTEN.

*COULD HE POSSIBLY MEAN WHAT I THINK HE
MEANS?*

SOMEHOW SHE FELT THE ANSWER SHOULD BE
OBVIOUS, BUT THERE WERE SO MANY THOUGHTS
SWIRLING AROUND IN HER MIND, SHE WAS TOO
CONFUSED TO FIGURE IT OUT.

LOOKING UP AT THE PRINCE'S FACE, THE DEPTH OF
EMOTION SHE SAW IN HIS EYES ONLY CONFUSED

HER FURTHER.

SOMEONE BUMPED HER LIGHTLY, BUT SHE BARELY REGISTERED THE MOTION. IT WAS CERTAINLY NOT ENOUGH TO PULL HER FROM THE HAZY CLOUD SHE WAS STILL FLOATING ALONG IN WITH THE PRINCE, BUT IT MADE HER REALIZE THAT, AT SOME POINT, OTHER PEOPLE MUST HAVE BEGUN TO MOVE ONTO THE DANCE FLOOR.

SHE WANTED TO LOOK AWAY, TO SEE WHO HAD BUMPED HER . . . WHO HAD JOINED THEM ON THE FLOOR, BUT THERE WAS NO CHANCE OF THEM BECOMING ENOUGH OF A DISTRACTION TO PULL HER FROM THE PASSION IN THOSE DEEP, CHOCOLATE EYES.

AS KAYDEN BEGAN TO TREMBLE, DVARIUS' ARM TIGHTENED AROUND HER, BRINGING HER EVEN CLOSER TO HIM.

"WHERE HAVE YOU BEEN ALL MY LIFE?"

THE PRINCE WHISPERED IN HER EAR, ALLOWING HIS CHEEK TO REMAIN PRESSED AGAINST HERS.

THE SOFT, WHISPERED, WORDS REMINDED KAYDEN WHY SHE WAS HERE.

DID MY MISSION JUST GET EASIER . . . OR IMPOSSIBLE?

FOURTEEN

AFTER ANOTHER MINUTE THE SONG ENDED AND KAYDEN EXPECTED THE PRINCE TO STEP AWAY FROM HER — BUT HE DID NOT.

HE SURPRISED HER BY SWEEPING HER INTO THE NEXT DANCE AS WELL. IT WAS A MORE EXUBERANT TUNE, SO SHE WAS PRESSED AGAINST HIM EVEN MORE TIGHTLY BY THEIR NEAR-CONSTANT SPINS AND TWIRLS.

HIS SMILE WIDENED WHEN SHE LOOKED UP AT HIM AGAIN. HE MUST BE ENJOYING HIMSELF; PERHAPS THAT WAS WHY HE HAD CONTINUED TO DANCE WITH HER. SHE TOLD HERSELF THAT IT COULDN'T BE MORE THAN THAT.

THANKFULLY HER HEART RATE HAD RETURNED TO NORMAL, AND SHE COULD CONCENTRATE ON THE MISSION ONCE AGAIN.

AND ONCE SHE COULD THINK CLEARLY, SHE WAS REMINDED OF THE INCIDENT FROM YESTERDAY.

At the thought of nearly skewering him with an arrow, she felt heat rush across her cheeks again.

It was all she could do to not pull away and run to find a hiding place. The ramifications of such an incident would have been swift and harsh and did not bear thinking of.

The palace guard would have done everything possible to keep her from escaping the palace grounds.

Even if, somehow she had managed to escape, she would have been swiftly hunted down.

It was at least one reason Drey had ordered her mission to look like an accident.

Of course . . . Drey wouldn't exactly mourn my death. And he would get what he wants — just not quite how he wants it.

The pain that pierced her when she thought of the Prince's body lying on the ground — the life slowly leaving him — was sudden, sharp and shocking.

Kayden shook her head to clear her muddled thoughts, but the image persisted. She had visualized that one moment over and over again.

Each time, her heart had jumped into her throat when she remembered seeing his horse step in front of the tree. And then she would calm as he leaned forward and the arrow missed him . . . by a hair's breadth.

She remembered too, the reaction they had

GOTTEN FROM THE STABLE BOY, WHOSE NAME SHE HAD COMPLETELY FORGOTTEN, BUT WANTED TO LEARN, ESPECIALLY IN THE FACE OF WHAT HAD HAPPENED WITH THE PRINCE.

THE LAD HAD SQUEAKED IN ALARM WHEN HE SAW THE RIP IN THE PRINCE'S SLEEVE; BEFORE EITHER OF THEM COULD EVEN SAY A WORD, HE HAD RUSHED OFF TO FIND HIS MASTER.

NOT A MINUTE LATER, THE STABLE MASTER HAD SKIDDED TO A HALT BESIDE THEM — CLEARLY CONFUSED WHEN HE FOUND THE TWO OF THEM INVOLVED IN FITS OF LAUGHTER AT THE RIDICULOUSNESS OF THE SITUATION.

HE'D RECOVERED QUICKLY ENOUGH THOUGH AND DROPPED A BOW TO THE PRINCE BEFORE HE NOTICED THE RIPPED SLEEVE AS WELL.

THEN HIS COMPOSURE HAD VANISHED AS WELL AND HE HAD RUSHED BACK INTO THE STABLES IN SEARCH OF A MEDICAL KIT — WHICH HAD ONLY SERVED TO INSPIRE ANOTHER ROUND OF LAUGHTER FROM HER AND THE PRINCE.

IT HAD TAKEN SEVERAL MINUTES FOR THEM TO RELAY THE STORY — MOST OF IT ANYWAY — WITH THE PRINCE REASSURING THE MAN HE WAS NOT INJURED AND THAT THE ENTIRE THING HAD BEEN NOTHING BUT AN ACCIDENT.

THE STABLE MASTER HAD LOOKED AS IF HE WANTED TO ARGUE, OR PERHAPS AS IF HE'D BEEN TEMPTED TO CARRY THE PRINCE TO A DOCTOR HIMSELF . . . JUST TO BE SURE. BUT HE EVENTUALLY ACCEPTED THE PRINCE'S CONTINUED REASSURANCES.

THE TWO OF THEM HAD WALKED BACK TO THE PALACE TOGETHER . . . WITHOUT AN ESCORT, LAUGHING ABOUT THE INCIDENT UNTIL THEY HAD REACHED HER ROOMS — WHERE THE PRINCE HAD LEFT HER WITH A SWEEPING, EXAGGERATED BOW AND . . . ANOTHER KISS ON THE HAND.

ALL OF IT HAD LEFT HER VERY CONFUSED.

SHE STILL DID NOT KNOW WHAT TO MAKE OF THE PRINCE'S BEHAVIOUR. NONE OF IT LINED UP WITH WHAT SHE HAD BEEN TOLD TO EXPECT, EXCEPT FOR THE ONE MOMENT AFTER THEY HAD MET — WHEN HIS ADVISOR HAD PULLED HIM AWAY.

IT WAS OBVIOUS THERE WAS SOMETHING GOING ON BEYOND WHAT SHE WAS PREPARED FOR, AND IT WOULD BE UP TO HER TO FIGURE OUT WHAT TO DO ABOUT IT.

PERHAPS THIS WAS ONE OF THE REASONS DREY HAD CHOSEN HER — FOR HER ABILITY TO THINK ON HER FEET, TO REACT TO A SITUATION WHICH WAS NOT GOING ACCORDING TO PLAN AND MAKE A SPLIT-SECOND DECISION.

IF IT WASN'T . . . WELL, THAT REALLY WAS NOT SOMETHING SHE WANTED TO CONSIDER.

UNBIDDEN, AN IMAGE FROM SEVERAL MONTHS PAST CAME BACK TO HER. THE POSSIBILITY OF DREY BEING UNHAPPY WITH HER SENT A CHILL DOWN HER SPINE.

IT WAS ALL SHE COULD DO NOT TO REACT PHYSICALLY TO THE MEMORY. IF SHE SHIVERED, THE PRINCE WOULD CERTAINLY NOTICE . . . ESPECIALLY SINCE THEY WERE SO CLOSE.

INSTEAD, SHE FOCUSED HER ATTENTION ON THE PRINCE AGAIN.

HIS PUZZLING BEHAVIOUR ASIDE, SHE HAD A JOB TO DO — AND THE QUICKER SHE GOT TO IT, THE SOONER SHE COULD GET OUT OF THESE CRAZY SURROUNDINGS AND ON TO HER NEXT ASSIGNMENT.

SHE WANTED TO THINK ABOUT WHERE THEY MIGHT SEND HER NEXT, BUT THERE WERE TOO MANY THOUGHTS FLOATING AROUND IN HER HEAD; THE MEMORY OF BEING SPRAWLED ON TOP OF THE PRINCE IN THE HALLWAY EARLIER, THE WAY HER HEART HAD JUMPED INTO HER THROAT WHEN HE'D STEPPED IN FRONT OF HER ARROW, THE WARMTH THAT FLOWED FROM EVERYWHERE HIS BODY BRUSHED UP AGAINST HERS.

KAYDEN THOUGHT ABOUT HOW STRANGE IT HAD FELT TO BE LYING THERE ON TOP OF HIM AFTER HE HAD KNOCKED HER DOWN.

HIS ACTIONS THEN WERE CONFUSING FOR HER AS WELL.

HE HAD TWISTED AT THE LAST MOMENT AND TURNED HER SO THAT HE DIDN'T FALL ON HER . . . BUT WHY HE WOULD CARE IF HE FELL ON HER?

AM I NOT JUST ANOTHER GIRL TO HIM?

WAS SHE NOT JUST ONE OUT OF TWENTY-FIVE YOUNG WOMEN BROUGHT TO THE PALACE FOR HIM TO CHOOSE A BRIDE?

AND WHY HAD HE ESCORTED HER PERSONALLY TO HER DOOR YESTERDAY . . . ESPECIALLY AFTER SHE HAD NEARLY SHOT HIM WITH AN ARROW?

HE HAD ESCORTED HER TO THE BALL TONIGHT; OF

COURSE, HE MIGHT HAVE DONE THAT AS AN APOLOGY FOR RUNNING INTO HER. BUT HE'D ALSO DANCED WITH HER; NOT ONLY THE FIRST — AND MOST IMPORTANT — DANCE, BUT THE NEXT TWO AS WELL.

THE FEEL OF HIS ARMS AROUND HER RIGHT NOW WAS EQUALLY CONFUSING.

SHE TRIED TO IGNORE THE TINY VOICE INSIDE THAT TOLD HER IT WAS A MISTAKE — THAT HER MISSION MIGHT NOT BE WORTH CARRYING OUT.

SHE NEEDED TO GATHER MORE INFORMATION BEFORE SHE MOVED FORWARD WITH ANYTHING, BUT THERE WAS ANOTHER VOICE INSIDE, TELLING HER TO STOP ASKING QUESTIONS, DO HER JOB AND GET OUT OF THE PALACE.

THE WORRISOME QUESTION IN HER MIND WAS . . . IN THE END, WHICH VOICE WOULD SHE LISTEN TO?

HOW COULD I HAVE LET MY GUARD DOWN SO QUICKLY — SO COMPLETELY?

WHAT HAVE I DONE?

FIFTEEN

DVARIUS WATCHED KAYDEN AS THEY
DANCED. HE WAS ACCUSTOMED TO PEOPLE
OFTEN BEING DIFFICULT TO READ, BUT HE
FOUND HER NEARLY IMPOSSIBLE.

SHE HAD CLEARLY BEEN ANNOYED WITH HIM WHEN
HE'D KNOCKED HER DOWN IN THE HALL, BUT SHE
HAD ALLOWED HIM TO ESCORT HER INTO THE
BALLROOM AND PUT FORTH NO PROTEST WHEN HE
LED HER IMMEDIATELY ONTO THE DANCE FLOOR.

THROUGH THREE SONGS, THEY HAD MOVED
TOGETHER, ALMOST AS ONE.

HOWEVER, NOW SHE HAD PULLED AWAY FROM HIM
AND WAS STIFF IN HIS ARMS.

THERE WAS A SLIGHT SMILE ON HER FACE, BUT NOT
THE ONE HE WAS ESPECIALLY FOND OF. THE SMILE
THERE NOW LOOKED STRAINED, FORCED, NOT AT
ALL SINCERE.

IT WAS COMPLETELY AT ODDS WITH HER EARLIER

BEHAVIOUR.

"DO YOU REALIZE HOW THIS LOOKS?"

HER WORDS TOOK HIM BY SURPRISE, AS DID THE EXPRESSION ON HER FACE. THOSE AMAZING EYES OF HERS WERE FULL OF ICE AND ANGER.

"I AM UNSURE OF WHAT YOU ARE REFERRING TO."

HE KNEW PRECISELY WHAT SHE MEANT THOUGH. IN THE DAYS OF HIS GRANDFATHER, OPENING A ROYAL BALL TOGETHER WOULD HAVE BEEN A VERY PUBLIC WAY TO ANNOUNCE THEIR ENGAGEMENT.

PETERO MUST BE LIVID.

"I DON'T SEE THIS BEING SOMETHING TO SMILE ABOUT, YOUR HIGHNESS."

HE HADN'T INTENTIONALLY SMILED BUT IT WAS NOT A SURPRISE THAT THINKING OF THE SOUR LOOK ON PETERO'S FACE WOULD BRING A SMILE TO HIS FACE.

"YOU'RE RIGHT, OF COURSE."

HE DUCKED HIS HEAD BUT COULD FEEL THE SMILE SPREADING SO IT MOST LIKELY SPOILED HIS ATTEMPT AT AN EXPRESSION OF PENANCE.

"WE HAVE ONLY BEEN HERE TWO WEEKS. DO YOU NOT REALIZE HOW THIS WILL MAKE YOU LOOK TO THE PUBLIC?"

"TO BE HONEST KAYDEN, I CARE NOT HOW IT LOOKS OR WHAT ANYONE THINKS OF ME."

THE EXPRESSION IN HER EYES CHANGED THEN, AND AN UNEXPECTED WARMTH SPREAD SLOWLY THROUGH HIM AS THEY CONTINUED TO MOVE

AROUND THE DANCE FLOOR.

SHE'D LOOKED AT HIM WITH ANNOYANCE OR FEAR IN HER EYES. HE HAD SEEN CONFUSION AND EVEN ATTRACTION IN THEIR PEWTER DEPTHS — BUT THIS WAS THE FIRST TIME SHE HAD LOOKED AT HIM WITH RESPECT.

IT WAS NOT THE RESPECT HE SAW EVERY DAY IN THE EYES OF HIS SERVANTS, IT WAS THE RESPECT HE HAD SEEN ONLY ONCE IN HIS FATHER'S EYES; AN EMOTION BORNE OF PRIDE, WHICH HUMBLED HIM.

IN THAT MOMENT — STARING INTO HER EYES, SPINNING WITH HER AROUND THE ROOM; SURROUNDED BY DIGNITARIES AND HEADS OF STATE AND TWENTY-FOUR OTHER GIRLS WHO HAD BEEN BROUGHT TO THE PALACE FOR THE SAKE OF A CROWN — HE KNEW HE HAD FALLEN IN LOVE WITH HER.

AND IN THE NEXT MOMENT, HE WAS SURPRISED TO FEEL FEAR TAKING HOLD OF HIM.

WHAT IF SHE DOESN'T RETURN MY FEELINGS?

WHAT IF SHE IS ONLY HERE BECAUSE SHE HAS TO BE?

WHAT IF SHE'S NOT THE LEAST BIT INTERESTED IN ME?

WHAT IF SHE DOES NOT SHARE MY FAITH?

HOW CAN I JOIN MYSELF WITH SOMEONE WHO DOES NOT BELIEVE AS I DO — WHO HAS NOT GIVEN THEIR HEART TO GOD.

SO MANY OF HIS PEOPLE HAD LOST TOUCH WITH THEIR FAITH DURING THE PAST SEVERAL HUNDRED

YEARS OF WAR, HUNGER, COLD AND FEAR.

HE WAS BLESSED TO HAVE HAD THE LEGACY PASSED DOWN TO HIM FROM HIS PARENTS, BUT HE UNDERSTOOD THAT MANY PARENTS OUT THERE IN THE PROVINCES; WHICH WERE STILL RECOVERING — TAUGHT THEIR CHILDREN QUITE THE OPPOSITE.

BUT HOW CAN I NOT . . . CHOOSE KAYDEN?

HE LOOKED DOWN AT HER AGAIN. SHE WAS LOOKING AWAY FROM HIM, ATTEMPTING TO AFFECT DISINTEREST, BUT THE BLUSH IN HER CHEEKS GAVE HER AWAY.

"IGNORING ME WON'T CHANGE THEIR MINDS, YOU KNOW."

HER LIPS TWITCHED, BUT SHE DIDN'T LOOK BACK AT HIM.

DETERMINED TO GET HER ATTENTION AGAIN, HE PULLED HER A BIT CLOSER AND MOVED THEM TOWARD THE EDGE OF THE DANCE FLOOR.

IT TOOK ONLY A MOMENT, ONCE THEY WERE CLOSE ENOUGH, TO SLIP THROUGH THE SIDE DOOR.

EVERY BALCONY DOOR WAS OPEN TO ALLOW THE BREEZE TO WIND ITS WAY INSIDE SO THE MUSIC FOLLOWED THEM AS THEY MOVED SLOWLY ALONG THE WIDE, STONE BALCONY.

SOMETHING CHANGED THEN, IN THE WAY THEY MOVED TOGETHER. AS SOON AS THEY WERE AWAY FROM THE CROWD OF PEOPLE, THE AIR AROUND

THEM HEATED UP — SIZZLED.

A MOMENT LATER, KAYDEN FELT THE PRINCE'S BREATH AT HER EAR AGAIN. SHE TRIED TO MAKE OUT WHAT HE WAS SAYING BUT IT WAS DIFFICULT TO UNDERSTAND HIM.

IT TOOK A MOMENT FOR HER TO FIGURE OUT THAT HE WAS HUMMING ALONG WITH THE SONG THEY WERE DANCING TO.

THE FEEL OF HIS BREATH AT HER EAR AND THE VIBRATIONS HIS HUMMING SENT THROUGH THEIR CONNECTED BODIES, BROUGHT WITH IT A WHOLE NEW ROUND OF CONFUSION AS HEAT COILED IN HER GUT.

UNDER THE NIGHT SKY, LIT ONLY WITH STAR-SHINE, SHE BECAME EVEN MORE AWARE OF EVERY PART OF HER THAT WAS PRESSED UP AGAINST THE PRINCE.

THERE WAS HEAT CRAWLING ALONG HER SKIN, POOLING ANYWHERE THEY TOUCHED — EVEN THROUGH THE BARRIER OF CLOTHING.

SHE WAS A FLAME — AND HE WAS THE OXYGEN.

SHE LOOKED UP AT HIM AGAIN.

HIS SMILE HAD NOT DISAPPEARED BUT IT HAD CHANGED. THERE WAS SOMETHING IN HIS EYES THAT MADE THE BREATH CATCH IN HER THROAT.

HE HELD HER TIGHTLY TO HIM, POSSESSIVELY . . .

AM I MISREADING THINGS? COULD HE REALLY BE FEELING THIS SAME HEAT AND CONFUSION?

OR IS HE AS COLD AND UNFEELING AS DREY TOLD ME?

She wanted to speak, but no words came. She felt as if there was something she needed to tell him, but her thoughts were too jumbled to form coherent speech.

A moment later she was horrified when the thoughts cleared in her mind and she realized what she had been trying desperately to say.

She started to pull away, but his hold was tight enough that she would have to forcibly remove herself.

She was certain that would draw too much attention so she stayed where she was; cautious to keep herself separated as much as possible.

She would have to get a handle on this — not to do so would be disastrous.

SIXTEEN

THIS WAS PRECISELY WHERE DVARIUS WANTED TO BE — AND THAT WAS ENOUGH. UNFORTUNATELY IT WAS NOT MEANT TO BE FOR LONG.

THE MOMENT THE SONG ENDED, HE FELT A HAND ON HIS SHOULDER.

TRULY.

DVARIUS STRUGGLED WITH HIS TEMPER. HE KNEW THIS WAS NOT THE PLACE TO CAUSE A SCENE BUT IT WAS A MIGHTY STRUGGLE.

"YOUR HIGHNESS, THERE ARE TWENTY-FOUR YOUNG LADIES WHO ARE WAITING TO DANCE WITH THE PRINCE; MOST LIKELY A BIT IMPATIENTLY BY NOW."

HE WANTED TO ARGUE WITH THE MAN BUT KNEW IT WOULD BE A WASTE OF BREATH, SO DVARIUS RESIGNED HIMSELF TO SEVERAL HOURS OF BOREDOM, ESPECIALLY SINCE HE KNEW — IF

PETERO HAD HIS WAY — THERE WOULD NOT BE ANOTHER CHANCE TO DANCE WITH THE ONE WOMAN HE REALLY WANTED TO.

NODDING TO HIS LEAST FAVORITE ADVISOR, HE TURNED BACK TO KAYDEN.

"I APOLOGIZE, MILADY. IT APPEARS MY PRESENCE IS REQUIRED ELSEWHERE."

WITH A SIGH, HE SWEPT A DEEP BOW TO HER AND TURNED AWAY BEFORE HE COULD TALK HIMSELF OUT OF LEAVING HER SIDE.

"YOUR MAJESTY, I REALLY MUST PROTEST YOUR SPENDING SO MUCH TIME WITH THAT PARTICULAR YOUNG WOMAN." PETERO WAS SAYING AS THEY WALKED AWAY FROM KAYDEN.

DVARIUS LOOKED BACK AT HER AS THEY WENT. SHE STOOD IN PLACE FOR A FEW SECONDS BEFORE MOVING AWAY, FOLLOWING THE BALCONY AND AVOIDING THE BALLROOM THAT WAS CROWDED WITH DANCING COUPLES.

HE LOST SIGHT OF HER AS SOON AS HE AND PETERO PASSED BACK THROUGH THE BALCONY DOORS.

HE WAS NOT AT ALL SURPRISED AT THE SENSE OF LOSS HE FELT AT LOSING EVEN THAT TREMULOUS CONNECTION WITH HER.

HE TURNED BACK TO PETERO AND TRIED TO IGNORE THE STEADY LITANY OF EXPLANATIONS THE MAN WAS RECITING — MOSTLY CONSISTING OF WHY KAYDEN WOULD NOT BE A GOOD CHOICE.

WHEN HE EXHAUSTED THOSE, HE CONTINUED WITH ARGUMENTS FOR THE YOUNG LADIES THAT MUST BE

PETERO'S PERSONAL FAVORITES — ONE WHOM THEY WERE CERTAINLY HEADED TOWARD.

NOT A MOMENT LATER, PETERO STEPPED UP TO A YOUNG LADY WHO HAD CLEARLY BEEN WAITING FOR THEM TO APPROACH.

SHE SWEPT INTO A GRACEFUL CURTSY AT THEIR APPROACH, RISING JUST AS SMOOTHLY AFTER A FEW MOMENTS.

"YOUR MAJESTY, MAY I PRESENT LADY CATARINE EGERIA OF THE HOUSE OF COTTSWOLL."

PETERO INCLINED A RESPECTFUL HEAD TO THE PRINCE BEFORE TURNING TO THE YOUNG WOMAN AND HER PARENTS, WHO STOOD JUST BEHIND HER.

"MADAM, MAY I PRESENT HIS ROYAL HIGHNESS, PRINCE DVARIUS REGALD MAXILLAN FORTINE IV," AND WITH ANOTHER BOW, HE STEPPED BACK AND LEFT DVARIUS TO THEIR MERCY.

DVARIUS LOOKED AT THE YOUNG WOMAN AND WAS SURPRISED AT WHAT HE SAW.

SHE WAS ATTRACTIVE ENOUGH, AND SHE WAS CERTAINLY WEARING FINERY JUST AS THE OTHER GIRLS, BUT SHE WAS NOT SPORTING GARISH JEWELS OR ENOUGH PAINT TO MAKE HER LOOK LIKE AN ENTIRELY DIFFERENT PERSON.

SHE HAD A QUIET BEAUTY WHICH APPEALED TO HIM. HER CLOTHING WAS OF THE FINEST MATERIAL, BUT UNDERSTATED AND DEMURE.

EVEN HER PARENTS WERE NOTHING LIKE HE HAD BEEN EXPECTING. UNLIKE SOME OF THE OTHERS, THEY WERE NOT LOOKING AT HIM AS IF HE WERE A PRIZE TO BE WON.

THERE WAS INTEREST, BUT IT WAS MORE OF A RESPECTFUL MANNER, WHICH IMMEDIATELY CAUGHT HIS ATTENTION AND HELD IT.

SINCE HE HAD ALREADY BEEN INTRODUCED, THE NEXT LOGICAL THING TO DO WAS ASK THE YOUNG LADY TO DANCE.

"MILADY, WOULD YOU GRACE ME WITH A DANCE?"

"IT WOULD BE MY HONOUR, YOUR HIGHNESS."

SHE GAVE HIM A SHY SMILE AND LOOKED BACK AT HER PARENTS FOR APPROVAL BEFORE TAKING HIS ARM.

THE YOUNG LADY'S GENTILE MANNER WAS IMPRESSIVE — AS WAS THE APPRAISING PERUSAL HER FATHER GAVE BEFORE NODDING TO HIS DAUGHTER.

DVARIUS LED LADY CATARINE OUT ONTO THE FLOOR AND SWEPT HER INTO THE MORE TRADITIONAL DANCE THAT WENT WITH THE SONG THAT HAD JUST BEGUN.

HE COULD NOT HELP BUT NOTICE HOW LIGHT ON HER FEET SHE WAS — EVERY STEP SURE AND SMOOTH; SHE FELT COMFORTABLE IN HIS ARMS.

IT WAS CLEAR WHY PETERO, AND PROBABLY MOST OF THE OTHER ADVISORS, WOULD PUSH THIS YOUNG LADY FORWARD.

SHE WOULD BE AN EXCELLENT QUEEN, AND THE PEOPLE WOULD SURELY LOVE HER. SHE HAD A QUIET, CALM AIR ABOUT HER THAT WOULD ENDEAR HER TO ANYONE WHO MET HER. THAT WOULD UNDOUBTEDLY BE AN ASSET TO HIM POLITICALLY.

I suppose I should at least get to know the young lady — and the others, too — if I am to make an informed decision.

He knew his thinking was correct — as much as he detested the idea — especially if Kayden did not happen to be the one for him.

Not be the one . . . what am I thinking?

I've already chosen her. I cannot imagine . . .

But what if she refuses me?

What if . . .

I suppose I must get to know the others — and at least try to see one of them as a wife — or a partner.

It would not do to have no knowledge of the other girls if that turned out to be the case.

Careful to suppress the sigh that wanted to escape, he resigned himself to small talk.

"Lady Catarine, how are you enjoying the palace?"

"Very well, Your Highness. Our family's estate is quite lovely, but of course it does not compare to the beauty here in the palace."

Her soft, cultured voice was so completely different from Kayden's — he was tempted to take note of every other difference between the two, but he was determined to give Lady Catarine a chance so he forced himself to push those desires aside.

"You are enjoying the palace then?"

"Yes, Your Highness. My room is quite lovely and I have the most spectacular view of the gardens."

Her words gave him the perfect opening, though he was certain she had not intended it that way. However, as he had no desire to give her the wrong idea, he let the opening go and instead opted for the safer course she had presented.

"Could I interest you in a walk through the gardens tomorrow?"

Her face lit up at the suggestion. Dvarius knew he had taken the right tack.

"I would enjoy that ever so much, Your Highness. Thank you. I confess . . ." she stopped suddenly and dropped her head a bit.

The slight blush that crept its way up her cheeks intrigued him and curiosity got the better of him.

"You confess . . . what, Milady?"

She looked up at him, but it was still several moments before she answered.

"I have wanted to explore the gardens since I arrived, but was uncertain if I was allowed."

She lowered her head again before going on.

"I very nearly sneaked into them this very afternoon."

It was not easy to do, but Dvarius managed to

RESTRAIN THE LAUGHTER THAT WAS DESPERATE TO ESCAPE. IT WOULD ONLY WOUND THIS INNOCENT YOUNG WOMAN.

"LADY CATARINE, THE GARDENS ARE OPEN TO YOU ANY TIME YOU WISH TO EXPLORE THEM."

"TRULY, YOUR HIGHNESS?"

HER EYES WERE SO FULL OF GRATEFULNESS AND EXCITEMENT WHEN SHE LOOKED UP AT HIM AGAIN; HE KNEW HE'D BEEN RIGHT TO CONTAIN HIS LAUGHTER.

"OF COURSE, I WOULD PREFER YOU TAKE A GUARD OR SOMEONE ELSE WITH YOU FOR SAFETY, BUT YES — THE GARDENS ARE ALWAYS OPEN TO YOU, MILADY."

"OH THANK YOU, YOUR HIGHNESS. I WILL ENJOY THAT VERY MUCH."

THEY DANCED FOR SEVERAL MINUTES IN SILENCE AND DVARIUS FOUND HIS THOUGHTS STRAYING TO KAYDEN AGAIN.

HE WAS CERTAIN SHE WOULD NEVER HAVE ASKED PERMISSION TO VISIT THE GARDENS. SHE'D HAD NO DIFFICULTY AT ALL IN PROCURING A WEAPON, AND A HORSE FROM HIS STABLES.

SHE HAD THEN PROCEEDED TO GO RIDING — AND SHOOTING — IN THE FOREST AREA OF THE PALACE GROUNDS; NEARLY SKEWERING HIM IN THE PROCESS.

THE THOUGHT OF THAT EXPERIENCE STILL BROUGHT A SMILE TO HIS LIPS; THE SCREAM THAT HAD COME FROM HER, THE WAY SHE HAD NEARLY SLIPPED FROM HER SADDLE, AND THEN THE SOUND

SCOLDING SHE HAD DELIVERED . . . ONCE HE HAD MANAGED TO KEEP HER FROM FALLING FROM HER HORSE AND LOSING CONSCIOUSNESS.

AND EVEN THAT WAS DIFFERENT FROM ANY OTHER WOMAN HE HAD EVER KNOWN.

WITH THE TYPICAL YOUNG WOMAN, HE WOULD HAVE SIMPLY CONSIDERED HER REACTION A SWOON. WITH KAYDEN — HE FELT NO HESITATION IN THE ASSUMPTION THAT SHE WOULD BRISTLE AT SUCH A DESCRIPTION.

THE MUSIC CHANGED AND TOOK DVARIUS' ATTENTION FROM HIS THOUGHTS OF THE FEISTY KAYDEN.

DO I WANT TO DANCE WITH LADY CATARINE AGAIN OR MOVE ONTO THE NEXT YOUNG LADY?

THE DECISION WAS NOT AN EASY ONE.

IF HE DANCED MORE THAN ONCE WITH LADY CATARINE, IT MIGHT SEND HER THE WRONG MESSAGE.

IF HE MOVED ON TO ANOTHER, HE WOULD HAVE TO START ALL OVER AGAIN.

THE DECISION WAS MADE FOR HIM WHEN HE SAW PETERO ESCORTING A YOUNG WOMAN TO THE DANCE FLOOR.

EITHER HER DRESS HAD BEEN PURCHASED TOO SMALL FOR HER OR SHE WAS THE TYPE WHO THOUGHT SHE COULD ONLY GET ATTENTION BY SHOWCASING HER CHARMS.

EITHER WAY, SHE WAS NOT THE TYPE OF YOUNG WOMAN HE WAS THE LEAST BIT INTERESTED IN

MAKING HIS QUEEN.

SO, IN A MOMENT OF REBELLION, HE TURNED LADY CATARINE BACK TO THE MIDDLE OF THE FLOOR AND LED HER INTO THE NEXT DANCE.

WHILE THEY MOVED AROUND THE FLOOR, THEY DISCUSSED THE MUSIC AND HOW LOVELY THE WEATHER HAD BEEN OF LATE. THE CONVERSATION WAS COMFORTING . . . NOT VERY STIMULATING BUT ENJOYABLE ALL THE SAME.

WHEN THAT DANCE ENDED, DVARIUS WAS ALMOST SORRY TO MOVE ON.

LADY CATARINE DROPPED INTO A DEEP CURTSY — AND HE INTO A FORMAL BOW, BEFORE PETERO APPEARED AT HIS ELBOW AGAIN TO ESCORT HIM TO THE NEXT YOUNG WOMAN.

"UNTIL TOMORROW, LADY CATARINE." DVARIUS REMINDED HER AS THEY PARTED — TO WHICH SHE NODDED SWEETLY AND THEN TURNED QUICKLY AWAY AS A BLUSH MADE ITS WAY ACROSS HER CHEEKS.

AS PETERO LED THE WAY TO THE NEXT YOUNG WOMAN, DVARIUS THOUGHT ABOUT LADY CATARINE AGAIN.

SHE WAS OBVIOUSLY FROM A WELL-TO-DO FAMILY, AS SHE HAD CLEARLY RECEIVED THE PROPER INSTRUCTION AS TO HOW A LADY WAS TO CONDUCT HERSELF.

SHE WOULD MAKE AN EXCELLENT QUEEN, AND HER SOOTHING MANNER WOULD MAKE HER VERY EASY TO LIVE WITH — BUT THERE WAS NO SPARK OF INTEREST BEYOND THAT ON HIS PART . . . AT LEAST

FOR NOW.

HE DETERMINED TO GIVE HER MORE OF HIS TIME — AND ATTENTION — BEFORE DISCOUNTING HER AS AN ALTERNATIVE TO KAYDEN.

IF HE COULD FIND SOME COMMON GROUND BETWEEN THE TWO OF THEM, HE MIGHT DISCOVER A YOUNG WOMAN WHO COULD BE A GOOD MATCH PERSONALLY, AS WELL AS A PROPER CHOICE FOR QUEEN.

SEVENTEEN

KAYDEN WATCHED AS PRINCE DVARIUS WALTZED WITH GIRL . . . AFTER GIRL . . . AFTER GIRL.

SHE WAS SURPRISED TO REALIZE, AFTER SEVERAL GIRLS HAD COME AND GONE, THAT SHE WAS JEALOUS, WHICH MADE NO SENSE AT ALL.

WHY SHOULD I FEEL EVEN THE SLIGHTEST BIT OF ENVY? I HAVE ABSOLUTELY NO INTEREST IN THE PRINCE. SHE WAS HERE FOR ONLY ONE THING — TO DO HER JOB.

AT LEAST THAT WAS WHAT SHE'D BEEN TELLING HERSELF FOR SEVERAL DAYS.

NO, HE CLEARLY WAS NOT WHAT SHE'D BEEN PREPPED TO BELIEVE, BUT SHE STILL HAD A JOB TO DO — AND PART OF THAT JOB WAS TO DO WHAT SHE WAS TOLD — WITHOUT QUESTION.

SHE DIDN'T NEED TO KNOW WHY. SHE JUST NEEDED

TO KNOW WHO . . . HOW . . . WHEN . . . AND WHERE.

BUT SHE HAD TO ADMIT TO HERSELF THAT SHE WAS NOT CONVINCED IT WAS REALLY TRUE THIS TIME.

YESTERDAY, WHEN THAT ARROW HAD COME WITHIN A HAIR'S BREADTH OF HITTING THE PRINCE, HER HEART HAD STOPPED. AND YES, IT HAD BEEN FROM FEAR, BUT NOT THE FEAR SHE'D EXPECTED.

WHEN THE HORSE HAD STEPPED OUT OF THE TREES, SHE HAD FELT FEAR FOR WHAT MIGHT HAPPEN TO AN INNOCENT PERSON WHO JUST HAPPENED TO GET IN HER WAY.

WHEN SHE HAD REALIZED WHO WAS ON THE HORSE, IT HAD FELT LIKE SHE WAS ACTUALLY THERE ON THE HORSE WITH HIM — AS IF SOMETHING WOULD HAPPEN TO HER BY CONNECTION.

BUT THAT'S RIDICULOUS . . . ISN'T IT?

HE IS AN ASSIGNMENT — NOTHING MORE.

IT'S NOT MY PLACE — HAS NEVER BEEN MY PLACE — TO QUESTION THE DETAILS OF AN ASSIGNMENT.

HE MEANS NOTHING TO ME . . . DOES HE?

"MIGHT I HAVE THIS DANCE, MILADY?"

THE DEEP VOICE INTERRUPTED HER THOUGHTS AND KAYDEN SCOLDED HERSELF FOR NOT PAYING BETTER ATTENTION TO WHAT WAS GOING ON AROUND HER.

SHE TURNED TO THE MAN WHO HAD SPOKEN AND WAS SURPRISED TO SEE THE PRINCE'S BEST FRIEND; MAREK MONTVENE.

I'VE NOT SEEN HIM SINCE HE CAME TO THE

WELCOMING PARTY WITH PRINCE DVARIUS.

She knew she should keep her focus on the job at hand, but curiosity got the better of her and she placed her hand in his, following him onto the dance floor.

"Certainly, m'lord."

Watching her companion carefully, Kayden studied the man she was dancing with. She knew from the files she had read, when preparing for the mission, that he was something of a Lothario.

She couldn't be certain how much of that was common knowledge and how much was just good investigation on the Order's part so she would have to tread carefully.

"I was watching you with Dvarius earlier." His deep voice got her attention . . . as did his words.

Kayden nodded, but made a point to say nothing in return.

"You make a handsome couple; striking."

"As you say, sir."

Ducking her head seemed the safest reaction, so she did; while still watching and waiting for the true reason for this interview — for she was certain now of his intent.

"I wonder if you might be having some difficulty watching the Prince spread himself around quite so much."

WHAT EXACTLY IS HE GETTING AT?

"JUST SO YOU KNOW . . . HE IS NOT ANY HAPPIER ABOUT IT THAN YOU ARE. THAT I CAN PROMISE YOU."

THE GASP THAT ESCAPED HER LIPS WAS CERTAINLY A CLEAR GIVEAWAY — HOWEVER, LOOKING UP AT HIM, SHE COULD SEE HE HADN'T REALLY NEEDED THE AFFIRMATION.

SHE TRIED TO COVER HER ERROR AS BEST SHE COULD, ESPECIALLY SINCE THE REALIZATION WAS SOMETHING SHE DIDN'T WANT TO ANALYZE AT THE MOMENT.

"I'M NOT CERTAIN I KNOW WHAT YOU ARE REFERRING TO, SIR."

MAREK NODDED AND SMILED, BUT SAID NOTHING ELSE, EVEN AFTER THE DANCE WAS OVER — WHEN HE SWEPT INTO A BOW BEFORE LEAVING HER WITH A QUICK KISS ON THE CHEEK . . . AND A WINK.

WHAT WAS ALL THAT ABOUT? IF MAREK IS SUCH A LADIES' MAN, WHY IS HE TRYING TO TALK ME INTO A RELATIONSHIP WITH THE PRINCE?

AND WHY WOULD HE CARE IF I'M JEALOUS . . .

KAYDEN TRIED TO REMIND HERSELF THAT SHE HAD NO RIGHTS TO ANY FEELINGS ABOUT PRINCE DVARIUS — JEALOUSY OR ANY OTHER.

HER JOB HELD NO ROOM FOR EMOTIONS. FEELINGS WOULD MAKE HER SLOPPY — AND JUST MIGHT GET HER KILLED.

DESPITE ALL OF THAT, SHE FOUND HERSELF SEARCHING THE ROOM FOR THE PRINCE — AND

WHEN SHE DISCOVERED HIM DANCING WITH THE LADY PADUA, IT TOOK EVERYTHING WITHIN HER NOT TO MARCH ACROSS THE FLOOR AND FORCE THE TWO OF THEM APART.

WHETHER SHE WANTED TO ADMIT IT OR NOT, THE FEELING THAT WAS COURSING THROUGH HER VEINS AT THIS MOMENT WAS CLEARLY THE PANGS OF ENVY . . . JEALOUSY . . . AND IT WAS DIRECTED AT WHOMEVER THE PRINCE HAPPENED TO BE DANCING WITH AT THE MOMENT.

ONE THING WAS CERTAIN; SHE HAD SOME THINKING TO DO.

AND I WILL HAVE TO TREAD VERY CAREFULLY.

SHE KNEW EXACTLY WHAT HAPPENED TO ANYONE WHO CROSSED THE ORDER OF THE MOONSTONE. IT WAS NEVER PRETTY AND IT ALMOST ALWAYS ENDED IN DEATH; BEFORE . . . OR AFTER.

AS MUCH AS SHE MIGHT DISLIKE HER LIFE SOMETIMES, SHE DID NOT WISH THIS ASSIGNMENT TO END IN DEATH.

AT LEAST . . . NOT MY OWN.

AND CERTAINLY NOT OVER A WHINY PRINCE WHO COULDN'T EVEN FIND A WIFE WITHOUT DRAGGING TWENTY-FIVE GIRLS OUT LIKE THEY WERE MARES AT AUCTION.

SHE KNEW HER THOUGHTS WERE HARSH, BUT IT WAS BETTER THIS WAY.

IF I DISTANCE MYSELF FROM THE MAN, AND REMIND MYSELF CONSTANTLY THAT I AM ONLY HERE FOR ONE THING, IT WILL MAKE MY JOB THAT MUCH EASIER.

He stood at the entrance to the ballroom, watching as the Prince danced with all his pretty little princesses . . .

His lips twisted into a smirk when he caught sight of the look on that stupid girl's face. She was jealous . . . .

The little twit.

This was what happened when they sent a little girl to do a man's job.

Leave it to her and the job will never get done.

Well, I'll show them.

I will get the job done — without her help — without anyone's help.

And no one will even realize what is going on until it is too late to do anything about it.

And I'll be gone . . .

Maybe I'll even take care of that silly twit — that ridiculous interloper — while I'm at it . . .

EIGHTEEN

KAYDEN CREPT THROUGH THE PALACE, KEEPING AS QUIET AS POSSIBLE. HER INTELLIGENCE HAD FINALLY ARRIVED WITH A REPLY TO HER LETTER.

IT HAD TAKEN ALL OF A MINUTE TO DECODE THE MISSIVE. WHEN SHE REALIZED WHAT WAS IN IT, SHE SIMPLY COULD NOT WAIT TO CHECK IT OUT FOR HERSELF.

SHE HAD TRIED FOR THE PAST WEEK TO FIND OUT WHERE THE PRINCE'S QUARTERS WERE, BUT THE FAMILY WING OF THE PALACE WAS FEROCIOUSLY GUARDED.

SHE CERTAINLY COULDN'T PRESS FOR THE INFORMATION WITHOUT GIVING HERSELF AWAY. THE PRINCE MIGHT NOT BE A FIT RULER, BUT HE INSPIRED LOYALTY IN HIS SERVANTS AND GUARDS — SOMETHING WHICH SAID A LOT ABOUT THE MAN HIMSELF, BUT SHE REMINDED HERSELF AGAIN

ABOUT HER MISSION AND PUSHED THE INFORMATION TO THE BACK OF HER MIND.

FORTUNATELY, THE MISSIVE ALSO INCLUDED DIRECTIONS TO A SECRET PASSAGEWAY SHE COULD USE TO GET PAST THE GUARDS OR THIS WOULD ALL BE FOR NAUGHT.

SHE MADE HER WAY TO THE IMMENSE LIBRARY ON THE THIRD FLOOR, TRYING NOT TO ATTRACT ANY ATTENTION . . . JUST IN CASE.

THEN SHE WALKED INTO THE ROOM AND WISHED SHE HAD WAITED JUST FIVE MINUTES MORE. ONE OF THE GIRLS WAS STANDING NOT TEN FEET FROM THE DOOR.

KAYDEN WASTED PRECIOUS SECONDS TRYING TO DECIDE WHAT TO DO.

ANY MOMENT, HER PRESENCE WOULD BE NOTICED — AND THEN IT WOULD BE TOO LATE.

JUST AS SHE STARTED TO TURN AND LEAVE, THE YOUNG WOMAN TURNED HER WAY. KAYDEN RECOGNIZED HER, NOT ONLY AS LADY CATARINE, BUT AS THE FIRST PARTNER THAT DETESTABLE ADVISOR PETERO HAD LED THE PRINCE TO ON THE NIGHT OF THE BALL, AFTER PULLING HIM AWAY FROM HER.

JUST KNOWING THE PRINCE HAD DANCED WITH HER, ENJOYED HER COMPANY. THAT HE HAD BEEN SPENDING TIME WITH HER — ROMANTIC TIME . . . ALONE — TRYING TO SEE IF THEY WOULD SUIT AS HUSBAND AND WIFE, MADE KAYDEN WANT TO HATE HER.

UNFORTUNATELY, THE SMILE THAT LIT UP LADY

Catarine's sweet face when she saw Kayden, made hate impossible.

Aw man . . . I can't hate her. I may as well go kick a puppy.

Resigning herself to idle chit-chat, Kayden moved further into the room.

I'll just pretend to be looking for something to read. Then, when she leaves, I'll find the passage and be off.

"You're Kayden, aren't you?"

The soft voice was as much a surprise as the fact that Lady Catarine knew who she was.

Of course, Kayden knew all about Catarine and her family, but then — she'd had the benefit of research provided by the Order.

How did she find out my name?

It was more than a little worrisome.

Idle chit-chat may not do it . . .

I have to find out how she knows me, and how she recognized me.

"I am indeed . . . and you are Lady Catarine."

Kayden watched for it, but there was no surprise on Catarine's face, nothing other than a pleasant smile.

"You're very brave."

Lady Catarine spoke the words as if she'd just told Kayden the sky was blue, and left her wondering what the point of the

STATEMENT WAS.

FORTUNATELY SHE DIDN'T HAVE LONG TO WAIT.

"I SAW YOU OUT RIDING THIS MORNING."

THE WORDS TOOK HER COMPLETELY BY SURPRISE.

OKAY . . . NOT WHAT I WAS EXPECTING.

KAYDEN WAITED PATIENTLY FOR LADY CATARINE TO SAY SOMETHING ELSE.

"YOU RIDE VERY WELL. I'VE NEVER EVEN BEEN ON A HORSE."

KAYDEN WAS SURPRISED TO SEE LONGING IN LADY CATARINE'S EXPRESSION.

"HAVE YOU NEVER HAD LESSONS?"

"OH NO, MY PARENTS WOULD NEVER APPROVE. I'M THEIR ONLY CHILD YOU SEE. THEY WOULD BE HEARTBROKEN IF SOMETHING WERE TO HAPPEN TO ME."

SHE SAID IT AS IF IT WERE THE MOST NATURAL THING IN THE WORLD, BUT KAYDEN COULD HEAR THE LONGING IN HER WORDS ALONG WITH A HINT OF WISTFULNESS.

CLEARLY, LADY CATARINE WANTED TO LEARN TO RIDE, BUT SHE WAS TERRIFIED TO DEFY HER PARENTS.

I SUPPOSE THAT COULD BE CONSIDERED ONE OF THE ADVANTAGES OF NOT HAVING PARENTS.

KAYDEN HAD TOLD HERSELF SIMILAR STORIES MANY TIMES OVER THE YEARS, BUT SHE'D NEVER REALLY BELIEVED IT. STILL, IN THIS PARTICULAR CASE, IT WAS AN ADVANTAGE FOR HER.

"I'M NOT BRAVE ENOUGH TO PUSH THE ISSUE. THEY WOULD LIKELY GIVE THEIR CONSENT IF THEY KNEW HOW IMPORTANT IT IS TO ME, BUT . . ." SHE THREW UP HER HANDS IN A CLEAR SIGN OF RESIGNATION.

HER WORDS WERE SAID WITH SUCH AN AIR OF SADNESS THAT KAYDEN COULD NOT HELP BUT FEEL A MOMENT OF REGRET FOR THE POOR GIRL.

SHE FOUND HERSELF WANTING TO TELL CATARINE THAT SHE SHOULD BE THANKFUL HER PARENTS CARED FOR HER . . .

BUT THE WORDS THAT CAME OUT OF HER MOUTH WERE NOT AT ALL THE ONES SHE'D INTENDED TO SAY.

"I COULD HELP YOU — IF YOU'D LIKE. WE CAN BE VERY CAUTIOUS. THEN YOU WON'T HAVE TO ASK PERMISSION — AND THINK HOW EXCITED THEY WILL BE WHEN YOU SHOW OFF YOUR NEW SKILLS."

DID I REALLY JUST SAY THAT? DID I JUST OFFER TO HELP HER?

WHY WOULD SHE OFFER TO HELP SOMEONE WHO WAS HER COMPETITION FOR THE PRINCE'S ATTENTION, MUCH LESS SOMEONE WHOM SHE WOULD NEVER SEE AGAIN ONCE THIS ASSIGNMENT WAS OVER?

IT MADE NO SENSE TO HER, BUT SHE LEFT THE OFFER DANGLING THERE ANYWAY — KNOWING THE CHANCES THAT LADY CATARINE WOULD TAKE HER UP ON IT WERE SLIM TO NONE.

AFTER SEVERAL MINUTES OF SILENCE, KAYDEN STARTED TO SPEAK AGAIN, THINKING SHE COULD RETRACT THE OFFER AND LET LADY CATARINE OFF

THE HOOK AT THE SAME TIME.

BUT THE MOMENT SHE OPENED HER MOUTH, LADY CATARINE DID, TOO.

"DO YOU REALLY THINK YOU COULD?"

KAYDEN LOOKED AT THE YOUNG WOMAN IN SURPRISE. THERE WAS A BRIGHT GLIMMER IN HER EYES AND KAYDEN KNEW SHE COULD NOT RETRACT ANYTHING NOW.

"WHEN I SAY I'VE NEVER BEEN ON A HORSE BEFORE, I SHOULD ADD THAT I'VE NEVER EVEN VENTURED NEAR ONE," CATARINE WENT ON AND KAYDEN WAS SURPRISED TO FEEL EXCITEMENT WELLING UP WITHIN HER.

I CAN DO THIS.

"AS LONG AS YOU CAN HANDLE BEING NEAR THEM WITHOUT SHOWING FEAR, YOU'LL BE JUST FINE."

AS SHE NODDED, LADY CATARINE LOOKED A BIT HESITANT, BUT THERE WAS ENOUGH EXCITEMENT IN HER EXPRESSION THAT KAYDEN FELT CERTAIN SHE WOULD DO JUST FINE.

"ALL RIGHT. WE'LL GET STARTED IN THE MORNING?"

KAYDEN LEFT HER WORDS IN A QUESTIONING TONE — GIVING CATARINE ONE MORE CHANCE TO BACK OUT.

BUT SHE WAS NODDING EXCITEDLY.

"WELL THEN, YOU'LL NEED A RIDING HABIT. I DON'T SUPPOSE YOU HAVE ONE."

WHEN CATARINE SHOOK HER HEAD, KAYDEN

STARTED FOR THE DOOR — HER EARLIER ERRAND COMPLETELY FORGOTTEN. CATARINE FELL INTO STEP BESIDE HER AND THEY CHATTED AS THEY WALKED TOWARD KAYDEN'S ROOMS.

"I'M SURE I HAVE SOMETHING THAT WILL WORK. YOU'RE A BIT TALLER THAN ME, BUT I THINK WE'RE ABOUT THE SAME SIZE."

LOOKING AT CATARINE'S TINY WAIST, SHE AMENDED HER WORDS. "CLOSE ENOUGH THAT YOU SHOULD FIT . . . ANYWAY."

CATARINE LAUGHED AT THAT AND KAYDEN WAS AMAZED TO REALIZE THAT SHE MIGHT HAVE ACTUALLY FOUND A FRIEND.

HERE, OF ALL PLACES . . .

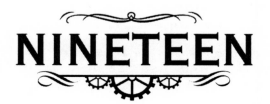

NINETEEN

DVARIUS STOPPED SHORT WHEN HE SAW KAYDEN AND LADY CATARINE LEAVING THE LIBRARY TOGETHER.

SHE WILL NEVER STOP SURPRISING ME.

WHENEVER HE'D CAUGHT SIGHT OF HER AT THE BALL, SHE HAD LOOKED READY TO STAB SOMEONE — MOST LIKELY EVERY WOMAN HE'D DANCED WITH OTHER THAN HER. AND NOW SHE HAD BEFRIENDED LADY CATARINE; THE ONE WOMAN WHO WAS HER MOST LIKELY COMPETITION.

A PUZZLE, INDEED.

"WELL, YOUR HIGHNESS . . . FANCY RUNNING INTO YOU HERE."

DVARIUS GROUND HIS TEETH TOGETHER, BUT FORCED A SMILE ONTO HIS FACE AT THE SOUND OF A VOICE HE WOULD BE PERFECTLY CONTENT TO NEVER HEAR AGAIN.

So much for going after Kayden . . . or Catarine.

He knew there would be no getting away from the woman behind him without a scene.

When he'd danced with her at the ball, he had known in two seconds that this woman was not the one for him.

He'd asked his advisors to send her home at once, but they had *insisted* he wait at least a week before sending anyone away.

They were certain it would look better that way.

Plans had been set into motion to have her sent home in the morning, but faced with having to speak to her, he needed to decide if he wanted a scene now — or tomorrow.

Turning to look at the woman, he realized he already knew the answer.

Better to have it done now — even if it means a scene.

"Lady Darotea, might I have a word with you?"

Her look of self-satisfaction revolted him.

"I have something I need to discuss with you about tomorrow."

He placed a hand on her back, careful to place it where the dress covered her skin and led her into the library, hoping it was empty.

As she moved into the room, Dvarius nodded

TO A GUARD, WHO STEPPED OVER TO THE DOORS AND WAITED.

"WE'RE NOT TO BE DISTURBED."

"UNDERSTOOD, YOUR MAJESTY."

THE GUARD BOWED AND THEN LOOKED AT THE PRINCE WITH A CURIOUS LOOK — ALMOST ONE OF PITY.

HMM, GOOD TO KNOW I'M NOT THE ONLY ONE WHO HAS SEEN RIGHT THROUGH HER.

HE WALKED INTO THE LIBRARY SHAKING HIS HEAD A LITTLE, CLOSING THE DOOR A BIT BEHIND THEM; WHILE STILL LEAVING PLENTY OF ROOM FOR THE SAKE OF DECORUM, AND TOOK A BRACING BREATH BEFORE WALKING OVER TO WHERE DAROTEA LOUNGED ON A LONG CHAISE.

SHE HAD MADE A POINT TO ARRANGE HERSELF SO THAT IT WOULD TAKE NOTHING AT ALL FOR HIM TO ENJOY HER . . . AH . . . WOMANLY CHARMS — BUT HE WAS NOT EVEN A LITTLE TEMPTED.

HE SAT ACROSS FROM HER IN A LARGE WING BACK CHAIR AND BRACED HIMSELF, LOOKING HER IN THE EYE AND SUPPRESSING A GRIN WHEN SHE GROUND HER TEETH TOGETHER.

"LADY DAROTEA, I APPRECIATE YOUR WILLINGNESS TO PARTICIPATE IN THIS . . ." HE SEARCHED FOR THE RIGHT WORD TO DESCRIBE WHAT HAD BEEN, IN REALITY, NOTHING MORE THAN AN EXPERIMENT. " . . . SPECIAL FUNCTION."

HE COULD ALREADY SEE THAT HIS WORDS HAD NOT FOOLED THE WOMAN ONE BIT.

She's quick; I'll give her that.

"I want to thank you for your time . . ."

But she didn't let him finish.

"It's okay, handsome. You don't have to go through the whole song and dance for me. I get it."

She said the words as she stood slowly and made her way across the room to him. There was a slight smile on her face, but no hint of it in those icy eyes of hers; and any thoughts of second guessing himself evaporated in that moment.

This woman was not someone he would choose to live with for another week, much less the rest of his life.

"I know my way out." And she sauntered past him, trailing a manicured finger across his shoulder as she went.

Any other time, he would have said something about protocol, but he was so relieved she was leaving with a minimum of fuss, he let it go.

As soon as Darotea left the library, letting the door shut a bit too hard behind her, Dvarius let out a breath of relief.

Well, that was not nearly as difficult as I expected it to be.

Now if I could only find a way to make it clear to Petero and the others that I will not accept someone such as her.

Kayden watched as Catarine turned this way and that in the riding habit.

It might be too fancy for the sort of riding Kayden typically did but the design, and even the coloring, was better suited to Catarine anyway.

"I am amazed at how well you fill that out."

"I think you fail to realize how slim you truly are, Kayden.

There was a teasing note in Lady Catarine's voice that took Kayden completely by surprise.

Slim . . . me? Who is she kidding? Muscular, well-toned maybe, but not slim.

"So what do you think? Tomorrow morning . . . join me for some introductory exercises?" she asked, as she shook her head a little at Lady Catarine's comment.

"Exercises?"

Kayden laughed heartily at the quizzical expression that had slipped onto Lady Catarine's features.

"Not at all what you are thinking, I promise."

"Oh, hmm . . ."

"You can't just walk into the stable and vault onto the first horse you come across,

YOU KNOW. YOU HAVE TO PREPARE YOURSELF."

"AND," KAYDEN ADDED AFTER A MOMENT, STRUGGLING TO SUPPRESS THE LAUGHTER THAT WAS DEMANDING TO BE LET OUT, "YOU HAVE TO MAKE CERTAIN YOU CAN ABIDE THE HORSES AS WELL."

"SO WE ARE GOING TO BEGIN WITH GETTING TO KNOW THE HORSES?"

KAYDEN GRINNED AT THE SOUND OF LADY CATARINE'S VOICE.

"SOMETHING LIKE THAT. YES."

THE YOUNG WOMAN WAS CLEARLY TERRIFIED BUT SHE WAS DOING EVERYTHING SHE COULD TO COVER IT UP AND EXUDE BRAVERY.

"I BELIEVE YOU MIGHT BE UNDERESTIMATING YOURSELF AS WELL."

"OH . . . I AM?"

"YES. YOU ARE MUCH MORE BRAVE THAN YOU REALIZE."

KAYDEN CHUCKLED AT THE STUNNED EXPRESSION THAT MET THAT STATEMENT.

"I'M NOT CONVINCED YOU'RE RIGHT, BUT I DO WANT TO TRY."

LADY CATARINE'S VOICE WAS STILL FULL OF UNCERTAINTY, BUT THERE WAS A BIT MORE STRENGTH TO HER PROCLAMATION AS WELL.

THE SOUND OF A KNOCK ON THE OUTER DOORS OF KAYDEN'S ROOMS, DISTRACTED THEM BOTH.

"EXCUSE ME A MOMENT." KAYDEN SAID AS SHE

WALKED INTO THE MAIN ROOM.

SHE WAS MET AT THE DOOR BY A YOUNG FOOTMAN WITH A NOTE FOLDED CAREFULLY ON A SILVER TRAY.

HE BOWED SHARPLY AS SHE LIFTED THE NOTE AND MUTTERED A DISTRACTED, "THANK YOU."

SHE SCANNED THE CONTENTS ABSENTLY. THE FEELING OF ICE CREEPING INTO HER VEINS AS SHE CAREFULLY DECODED THE WORDS IN HER HEAD, WORRIED HER.

"WHAT IS IT, KAYDEN?"

LADY CATARINE WALKED OUT OF THE DRESSING ROOM JUST AS KAYDEN READ THE LAST WORD OF THE NOTE.

"IS EVERYTHING ALRIGHT?"

"NO, NOT REALLY. I MUST RETURN HOME . . . IMMEDIATELY. I'M AFRAID OUR RIDING EXERCISES WILL HAVE TO WAIT."

"I DO HOPE IT'S NOTHING SERIOUS."

KAYDEN SHOOK HER HEAD AS SHE STRUGGLED TO CONTAIN HER DISAPPOINTMENT.

"I DON'T KNOW. IT . . . IT DOESN'T SAY."

THE ICE SPREAD QUICKLY THROUGH HER ENTIRE BODY AS SHE READ OVER THE CONTENTS AGAIN.

EITHER I AM NOT MOVING FAST ENOUGH TO SUIT DREY . . . OR HE'S FOUND OUT WHAT HAPPENED WITH THE ARROW AND HE'S PULLING ME OUT.

AND IF HE PULLS ME OUT . . .

SHE FORCED HER ATTENTION AWAY FROM THAT THOUGHT. SHE DID NOT EVEN WANT TO CONSIDER WHAT MIGHT AWAIT HER IF THAT WERE THE CASE.

TWENTY

NO MORE THAN TWO DAYS HAD PASSED SINCE HE'D SEEN KAYDEN, BUT IT FELT LIKE A LIFETIME TO DVARIUS.

HOW DID I EVER THINK I COULD CHOOSE SOMEONE ELSE?

HOW COULD I HAVE EVER CONVINCED MYSELF I COULD LIVE WITHOUT HER?

EVEN SPENDING TIME WITH CATARINE HADN'T HELPED. IT HAD ONLY SERVED TO REMIND HIM THAT HE WOULD RATHER BE WITH KAYDEN.

HE WAS HAVING A DIFFICULT TIME DEALING WITH THE FACT THAT SHE'D BEEN CALLED AWAY ON A FAMILY EMERGENCY.

HE MIGHT HAVE FELT AS IF HE HAD HAD NO CHOICE BUT TO LET HER GO . . . BUT NOW HE WAS STUCK HERE, WAITING FOR HER TO RETURN; HOPING DESPERATELY THAT SHE WOULD.

WHAT IF SHE DECIDED SHE DOESN'T ENJOY PALACE LIFE?

WHAT IF SHE DECIDED SHE WOULD NOT ENJOY LIFE HERE . . . WITH ME?

WHAT IF SHE IS UNABLE TO RETURN?

HE WAS TEMPTED TO SEND SOMEONE TO HER FAMILY HOME — JUST TO CHECK ON HER, BUT HE FEARED THAT WOULD MAKE HIM LOOK OBSESSIVE AND HE SHUDDERED TO THINK WHAT SHE WOULD MAKE OF THAT, KNOWING HER AS HE DID.

SO, EVEN THOUGH IT WAS MAKING HIM INSANE, HE WAS DETERMINED TO WAIT IT OUT.

HE WAITED . . . AND HE PRAYED, AS HE TRIED TO DECIDE IF HE COULD COME UP WITH SOME WAY TO MAKE HER COME BACK — OR IF HE COULD FIND AN EXCUSE TO GO TO HER.

NEITHER OPTION SEEMED LIKE THE BEST IDEA, SO HE DID HIS BEST TO GIVE CATARINE AND THE OTHER YOUNG LADIES MORE OF HIS ATTENTION.

AT LEAST THAT WOULD GIVE HIM A FULL SCHEDULE WHILE KAYDEN WAS AWAY.

HE ALSO COMFORTED HIMSELF WITH THE KNOWLEDGE THAT HE COULD SPEND AS MUCH TIME AS POSSIBLE TRYING TO ELIMINATE OTHER YOUNG WOMAN WHILE SHE WAS AWAY. IT WOULD MAKE THINGS THAT MUCH EASIER WHEN THE TIME CAME FOR HIM TO OFFICIALLY MAKE HIS DECISION.

IF HE WAS DOWN TO KAYDEN AND ONE OR TWO OTHERS BY THEN, THE ADVISORS WOULD AT LEAST HAVE LESS ARGUMENTS TO PUT FORTH AS TO WHY KAYDEN WAS NOT THE IDEAL CHOICE.

"You are a mess, man."

The sound of his best friend's voice did not bring the usual smile to Dvarius' face for once. He was much too intent on his brooding.

"Dvarius?" Marek's tone was curious now.

"I am in no mood for your banter today, Marek."

"I see that. Well then, I'll just go."

But, at the sound of Marek's boot heels on the marble floor behind him, Dvarius turned away from the window.

Guilt twisted inside him like a fist. No matter how he felt about the situation with Kayden, he had no right to take it out on his best friend; the man who had been there for him since they were children.

"Marek, please forgive me. You are absolutely correct; I'm a mess."

He held out a hand as his friend turned back to him, and was glad to see the look of anguish vanish and be replaced by Marek's usual self-assured smile.

"Hey, I always knew you were a mess. This thing just brought it out a bit more," and Marek laughed — lifting a bit of the strain from Dvarius' shoulders.

"This whole experiment has been one hassle after another. How did I ever let myself be talked into this?"

"Oh, come on, man."

"Come on . . . what?" Dvarius turned to look at his friend again. The look on his face was one of curiosity.

What is he talking about?

"You are not a mess over this experiment. You're upset because she's not here."

"Who?"

And how did Marek figure out about Kayden already?

Who else knows?

"Relax man. Your secret is safe with me . . . although I think your least favorite advisor has figured it out too. In fact, I'm sure he's thrilled that she's gone right now."

"How did you figure it out?" He didn't waste his breath trying to argue.

They had been friends for years — if anyone could see right through him, it would be Marek.

"We've been friends for years, Dvarius. I can read you like a book. Every time you're within sight of each other, it's obvious how you both feel."

"That can't be . . . wait, explain yourself."

He moved across the room and took hold of Marek's arm, pressing for an answer.

"Just what I said — when you two are together it's like a spontaneous combustion.

And don't worry, her feelings are just as obvious as yours."

The emotion that washed over Dvarius was confusing . . . He wanted to be excited, to shout with joy . . . but he knew he needed to be cautious.

Marek was his friend, and he probably knew Dvarius better than anyone.

But Kayden — she was a puzzle. There was nothing predictable or simple about her.

How can Marek be certain of anything where she's concerned?

I can't.

Or was it possible his best friend saw something in her — because of how Dvarius felt about her?

"Aren't you the one who is always telling me to have faith?"

Marek's voice was very quiet as he rested a hand on Dvarius' shoulder and squeezed gently.

"Where is your faith now? If she's the one for you, everything will work out fine . . . right?"

Dvarius looked back over his shoulder, nodding absently at his friend. He knew Marek was right. He knew he should have faith . . .

He also knew there was nothing he could think of that had ever felt this important to

HIM.

HIS FATHER'S DEATH HAD BEEN SO SUDDEN, SO UNEXPECTED — THERE WAS NOTHING HE COULD DO ABOUT IT. HE HAD GIVEN GOD HIS TRUST IN THAT SITUATION, BUT NO REAL FAITH WAS NEEDED.

BEFORE THAT, HIS LIFE HAD BEEN MUCH LESS COMPLICATED. HE'D KNOWN HE WOULD TAKE THE THRONE SOMEDAY, BUT IT ALSO WAS NOT SOMETHING THAT REQUIRED FAITH — IT WAS A GIVEN.

"HONESTLY MAREK, I'M NOT SURE I HAVE ENOUGH FAITH TO COVER THIS ONE. IT'S JUST SO BIG."

HIS FRIEND'S HAND SQUEEZED AGAIN, REASSURING HIM THAT — NO MATTER WHAT — MAREK WAS THERE FOR HIM.

IT WAS A GOOD FEELING.

"THEN TRUST ME . . . I CAN CERTAINLY RECOGNIZE A WOMAN IN LOVE. TRUST YOUR BEST FRIEND, AND LEAVE THE REST UP TO GOD."

DVARIUS NODDED AGAIN; MORE SOLEMNLY THIS TIME, BUT HE COULDN'T BRING HIMSELF TO SAY ANYTHING ABOUT IT. HE SHOULD TRUST GOD WITH THIS; HE KNEW THAT. IT WAS JUST PROVING TO BE MUCH MORE DIFFICULT THAN HE COULD HAVE EXPECTED.

"IT MAY BE EASY WHEN IT'S SOMETHING THAT'S UNIMPORTANT OR IF IT DOESN'T REALLY MATTER HOW IT TURNS OUT — BUT WHEN IT'S THIS BIG, THIS . . . LIFE-ALTERING, IT WOULD BE A WHOLE DIFFERENT PLAYING FIELD."

"THAT IS IT PRECISELY."

DVARIUS LET OUT HIS BREATH IN ONE LONG EXHALE. IT FELT GOOD TO KNOW THAT SOMEONE ELSE UNDERSTOOD.

NOT THAT IT SHOULD HAVE BEEN A SURPRISE TO HIM — IF ANYONE WAS GOING TO UNDERSTAND PRECISELY WHAT HE WAS GOING THROUGH, IT WOULD BE HIS BEST FRIEND.

TWENTY-ONE

KAYDEN STOOD BY THE WINDOW IN HER
"FAMILY" HOME, WISHING SHE WERE
ANYWHERE ELSE — BUT SHE HAD BEEN
SUMMONED AND THERE HAD BEEN NO OTHER
CHOICE. SHE HAD TO COME.

*WHAT COULD POSSIBLY BE SO IMPORTANT, THEY
HAD TO PULL ME OUT OF THE PALACE NOW?*

SHE HAD NO ANSWER OF COURSE, AND NOTHING
SHE'D COME UP WITH ON HER OWN MADE SENSE.

HER FIRST INSTINCT WAS TO TRUST THAT SOMEONE
WOULD BE ALONG TO TELL HER SOON, BUT THERE
WAS A TINY, NAGGING VOICE AT THE BACK OF HER
MIND THAT TOLD HER IT COULD BE SOMETHING
ELSE.

IT DIDN'T MAKE SENSE THAT THEY WOULD BRING
HER HERE IF SHE WERE IN TROUBLE . . . UNLESS
THAT WAS PART OF DREY'S PLANS.

Drey was notorious for having his own way of doing things — ways that only made sense to him. If he had wanted her brought here, no one would question it . . . and if she were in trouble, not one person in the organization would even hint at it.

She'd been wandering around the grounds for two days, waiting, bored, and surprisingly — missing the palace.

It was a shock to realize that, not only did she miss Catarine's company, she missed the Prince, too.

She wished there was some way to contact him, but her gut told her that would be a very bad idea, so . . . she waited.

And the waiting was making her more than a little nervous — and edgy. She'd snapped at Jace; the butler who'd been hired specifically for this assignment.

He was a good man, skilled at his job.

She had no idea whether he was with the Order or not because she hadn't asked . . . but he didn't blink when she'd practically taken his head off — just nodded and murmured "just so, Miss," — before backing slowly out of the room.

After that, she'd gone to the solarium — she'd been hiding out there ever since. Staying in the palace was getting to her.

Or staying away . . .

The restlessness was frustrating at best.

She'd never particularly enjoyed waiting, but she could not remember another time that had filled her with such distaste as this most recent experience.

She nodded her head absently at the young maid who set a gleaming tea service on the large table beside her.

Feeling no desire whatsoever to actually have tea, she asked the young woman for coffee instead and; clearly well-trained, she rushed off to do her mistress's bidding.

I'm getting soft — having servants all around; doing everything for me.

I need to get back to the palace and get this over, so I can go back to my life . . . my normal life.

The quicker she could get back to her normal pace, to remembering that she was pretty much on the same level as her maid and butler — maybe even a level or two below, considering her own humble beginnings — the better.

The sound of boot heels caught her attention and she turned to see Alfreid, her mentor — the only man she had truly ever trusted — walk into the solarium.

It was all she could do not to run to him . . . but Jace was standing just inside the door and she knew she was supposed to keep up pretenses so she waited for him to take his leave.

When he did, she raced across the room and threw herself into Alfreid's waiting arms.

"I fear we will never make a proper lady of you, Kay!" He was smiling as he said it, so she knew he wasn't upset with her at her lack of decorum.

She let out a delighted laugh and felt lighter than she had in weeks.

"What are you doing here? When did you get back into the country? How did it go? Do you have any idea when I can go back in and get this whole thing over with?"

The last was said with a bit of a whine, but Alfreid was the closest thing she had ever had to a father, and she felt comfortable being open with him.

"In a hurry, are we? Let an old man catch his breath for a minute."

"You are not old Al; never old."

"You are biased, young Miss," he grinned as he set her back on her feet, but he kept a companionable arm around her shoulders.

They walked slowly back to where she had been standing, and continued on around the spacious solarium, finally moving through the wide, glass doors to the garden.

She waited for him to continue; to answer her questions, but he just kept walking.

"Hmm . . . nice place you've got here. How could you ever be bored here?"

He glanced at her and let out a bark of a laugh before going on.

"Never mind; forget I said that. You would be bored anywhere you were required to sit . . . or wait — in other words — anywhere you can't be active."

He laughed again after she stuck her tongue out at him.

And just when she was ready to pounce on him for the answers to her earlier questions, he finally spoke again.

He is always doing that . . . He answers just when I can't take another moment of waiting.

"Actually, I am here to spring you. I got back last night. As soon as they debriefed me, they asked me to come and help you out. Apparently you're doing well and they think we're close to the end. That's fast work — even for you."

He looked at her as he said it; but there was something odd in his expression. It was a look she had never seen before, which was strange, as she had known Alfreid for seven years.

"As to when you can get on with it, you go back in this afternoon. And I will be going with you."

She thought about his words; decided not to push regarding the questions he didn't answer.

If she wasn't meant to know how his own op

HAD GONE, HE WOULDN'T TELL HER . . . BUT SHE STILL HAD ONE QUESTION HE HAD TO ANSWER.

"THEN WHY DID THEY PULL ME OUT? IF I'M GETTING CLOSE, WOULDN'T TAKING ME OUT FOR SEVERAL DAYS BE COUNTER-PRODUCTIVE?"

"NO. ACTUALLY, DREY THOUGHT IT WOULD HELP TIGHTEN YOUR HOLD, TO ALLOW THE PRINCE TO MISS YOUR PRESENCE FOR A FEW DAYS."

"THAT'S RIDICULOUS."

"ON THE CONTRARY, IT WORKS MORE OFTEN THAN YOU MIGHT THINK. THERE IS AN OLD EXPRESSION THAT DEALS WITH THIS VERY THING. 'ABSENCE MAKES THE HEART GROW FONDER' — IT'S A TRIED AND TRUE THEORY."

"THEN WHY HAVE I NEVER HEARD OF IT BEFORE NOW?"

"YOU'RE YOUNG."

"NOT THAT YOUNG. I HAVE DEALT WITH ROMANTIC ENTANGLEMENTS BEFORE, AL. YOU REMEMBER THE DICTATOR IN SALRI. THAT WAS ABOUT AS ROMANTIC AS YOU CAN GET."

"THAT WAS A VERY DIFFERENT SITUATION, KAY. YOU HAD NO COMPETITION THEN — AND HE PICKED YOU."

"I REMEMBER. HE WASN'T EVEN SUPPOSED TO BE THERE."

OH WHAT A DISASTER THAT OP WAS.

"YES, AND THAT WAS VERY WELL HANDLED, I MIGHT ADD."

His praise was a surprise. She had thought the whole situation was mostly a mess.

"Thank you." She shrugged off his praise. "I was just doing my job."

He waved a hand in dismissal.

"I don't need to tell you how skilled you are at your job. Drey would not have chosen you for this otherwise."

"Of course."

She laughed off his words, but the nerves in her stomach were turning into enormous knots of tension.

"So, how exactly does this theory of yours work?"

"It's quite simple actually. When someone has difficulty deciding whether or not they want you, go away for a few days."

He sent her a wink before he continued.

"They either miss you and anticipate your return so much that they never want to let you go again, or they don't miss you — and let you know when you come back . . . that you really could have stayed away."

She moved away from Alfreid a bit, thinking about what he had just said. Then she turned to look back at him.

Has he taken leave of his senses?

Had they really taken her from the palace just so the Prince could miss her . . .

ASIDE FROM THAT BEING THE MOST RIDICULOUS THING SHE'D EVER HEARD, IT WAS JUST SILLY. THE PRINCE WAS NOT GOING TO MISS HER — ESPECIALLY NOT WHEN HE HAD TWENTY-TWO OTHER GIRLS TO KEEP HIM COMPANY.

AFTER A MINUTE, SHE BEGAN TO WORRY. WHAT IF THE PRINCE HADN'T MISSED HER?

WHAT IF HE BARELY NOTICED I WAS GONE?

HE ONLY KNOWS I WAS GONE BECAUSE THE GUARD WAS REQUIRED TO HAVE HIS PERMISSION BEFORE THEY COULD LET ME GO.

WHAT IF HE LET HER KNOW THAT SHE COULD GO AWAY AGAIN — AS SOON AS SHE GOT BACK?

HE HAD ALREADY LET GO OF TWO OTHER GIRLS BECAUSE HE'D DECIDED THEY WOULD NOT SUIT HIM AS A WIFE.

WHAT IF SHE WAS NEXT, BECAUSE SHE HADN'T BEEN THERE TO CATCH HIS EYE?

PANIC CREPT IN, AND IT TOOK EVERY BIT OF TRAINING SHE HAD TO CONTROL HER BREATHING.

I HAVE TO BE VERY CAREFUL.

NO ONE KNOWS ME LIKE ALFREID.

I CAN'T AFFORD TO MAKE HIM SUSPICIOUS, OR TO LET HIM KNOW JUST HOW FRIGHTENED I'VE BEEN.

. . . OR SHE WOULD NOT BE RETURNING TO THE PALACE.

ALFREID WAS THE ONE PERSON WHO WOULD NOT HESITATE TO PULL HER OUT IF HE THOUGHT SHE WAS IN OVER HER HEAD.

She had to get back to the palace today. The quicker she returned to the palace, the better.

She took a slow, deep breath before turning to Alfreid again.

"So, when do we leave?"

TWENTY-TWO

DVARIUS WAS IN HIS SUITE, PACING BACK AND FORTH, WHEN THE DISCREET KNOCK SOUNDED ON HIS DOOR.

HAVING NO PATIENCE FOR PROTOCOL TODAY, HE WALKED OVER AND OPENED THE DOOR HIMSELF.

BREEN, ONE OF THE YOUNGER MESSENGERS, GAVE HIM AN ODD LOOK — BUT RECOVERED QUICKLY ENOUGH AND DELIVERED THE MESSAGE HE'D BROUGHT FOR THE PRINCE.

"YOUR MAJESTY, A CAR HAS JUST COME THROUGH THE MAIN GATES . . . WITH MISS ARGOS, SIR."

IF THERE WAS MORE TO THE MESSAGE, IT WAS LOST IN THE WAKE OF DVARIUS' EXIT.

HE CONTROLLED HIMSELF ENOUGH TO KEEP FROM RUNNING THROUGH THE MAIN HALL, BUT IT WAS CLOSE.

HE RUSHED PAST SERVANTS WHO LOOKED UP IN

SURPRISE AT HIS HASTY PASSAGE, BUT HE GAVE NO ONE TIME TO SPEAK TO HIM, AND IF THEY BOWED OR CURTSIED — HE DIDN'T NOTICE.

SHE'S BACK!

THAT WAS ALL THAT MATTERED AT THE MOMENT.

SHE WAS BACK AND IF HE HAD ANYTHING TO SAY ABOUT IT, SHE WOULD NEVER GO AWAY AGAIN.

HE REACHED THE GREAT HALL AS THE MAIN DOORS WERE OPENING . . .

JUST THEN, A THOUGHT OCCURRED TO HIM — THAT HE SHOULD BE CAREFUL ABOUT HOW MUCH HE LET ON IN FRONT OF THE STAFF.

HE HAD ALREADY MADE A SPECTACLE IN HIS RUSH TO REACH HER IN TIME. AN EMOTIONAL REUNION WOULD BE JUST THE BIT OF GOSSIP THEY NEEDED FOR THE RUMORS TO FLY.

WITH THAT IN MIND, HE WORKED HARD TO SCHOOL HIS FEATURES, JUST AS A SECOND THOUGHT OCCURRED TO HIM.

IT WOULD DO ME NO GOOD TO LET ON JUST HOW MUCH I HAVE MISSED HER — NOT THIS GIRL.

AND . . . AS PERVERSE AS SHE HAD BEEN ALREADY, SHE WOULD LIKELY TURN AND WALK RIGHT BACK THROUGH THE GATES.

SHOULD I EVEN GREET HER HERE? SHOULD I GO BACK TO MY ROOMS AND SIMPLY SEE HER AT DINNER? HE TURNED TO GO BUT STOPPED AS LADY CATARINE WALKED INTO THE HALL.

SHE DID NOT BOTHER TO SCHOOL HER FEATURES.

Excitement was evident on her delicate face and she even appeared to be bouncing a little as she moved across the wide hall.

She briefly acknowledged him, before turning her attention to the doors in front of them.

What is it about Kayden that inspires such strong emotions in people?

Here he was — anxious to welcome her back that he'd practically sprinted through the palace.

And Catarine, who was supposed to be her competition, looking positively thrilled to welcome Kayden back — as if she had not seen her in years, rather than days.

Of course Kayden walked through the door at that moment, sending every coherent thought tumbling from his mind.

He forgot that he was supposed to appear cool and calm.

He forgot that Catarine was standing nearby. Thoughts of Kayden pushed everything else from his mind and he moved forward to greet her.

Catarine was quicker though. She rushed forward and embraced Kayden. Immediately both women were talking and laughing. He thought he might have even seen a few tears.

They stood just like that for several minutes, until he was nearly ready to move forward and command them apart.

He must have made some sort of noise in his impatience, because Kayden looked over at him and that becoming blush bloomed across her smooth cheeks.

"Your Majesty."

She dropped into a curtsy, pulling Catarine along with her; since they were standing arm in arm.

He was surprised at how easily he was able to keep his cool, but it helped that he was more than a little annoyed with the two women in front of him. Didn't they know they were supposed to be competition?

"Your family is well?"

He might have imagined it, but he thought there was something in Kayden's eyes when he said it . . . something sad — almost as if his words hurt her.

"Thank you for asking, Your Majesty. They are well. I apologize for any inconvenience my absence might have caused," the last was said in that twisted way she had of making him feel as if she were scolding him.

Any other time he might have laughed and teased her about it — whether or not Catarine was present — but he was put out at the lack of reception. Especially after he had rushed all the way down here to greet her so his own answer was more terse than he might have meant it to be.

"Don't worry yourself. I'm sure no one even

NOTICED YOU WERE MISSING."

AND BEFORE HE COULD CHANGE HIS MIND, HE WENT ON.

"I HAVE SOME THINGS TO ATTEND TO. WELCOME BACK." WITH THAT, HE TURNED AND STRODE OUT OF THE HALL.

KAYDEN STIFLED THE GASP THAT THREATENED TO BREAK FREE WHEN THE PRINCE TURNED AND WALKED AWAY SO ABRUPTLY. SHE WAS RIGHT . . .

HE HASN'T MISSED ME AT ALL.

SHE TRIED TO IGNORE THE PAIN THAT HAD TAKEN UP RESIDENCE IN HER CHEST, BUT IT WAS UNLIKE ANYTHING SHE HAD EVER FELT BEFORE.

BESIDE HER, CATARINE LET OUT A QUIET GASP AND KAYDEN LOOKED OVER AT HER NEW FRIEND WITH CONCERN.

"I DON'T UNDERSTAND HIM AT ALL." SHE SAID, HER VOICE EVEN MORE QUIET THAN NORMAL.

"WHAT DO YOU MEAN?"

ONLY NOW, KAYDEN REALIZED THE PRINCE HAD BARELY EVEN ACKNOWLEDGED THE OTHER YOUNG WOMAN.

HAD HIS IRRITATION EXTENDED TO CATARINE BECAUSE OF HOW OBVIOUSLY EXCITED SHE'D BEEN TO SEE KAYDEN, OR HAD HE DECIDED SHE WOULD NOT SUIT HIM EITHER?

WOULD THEY BOTH BE LEAVING SOON?

"THE ENTIRE TIME YOU WERE GONE, HE LOOKED AS IF HE HAD LOST HIS BEST FRIEND."

THEY WATCHED THE PRINCE'S BACK UNTIL HE TURNED THE CORNER, AND THEN CATARINE TURNED BACK TO KAYDEN.

"WHEN YOU LEFT, HE STORMED AROUND THE PALACE FOR HOURS. AND ONCE HE STOPPED PACING, THE LISTLESSNESS SET IN." SHE SHOOK HER HEAD A BIT AS SHE SAID IT.

"WE HAD SEVERAL EVENTS PLANNED OVER THE LAST FEW DAYS, WHICH HE ATTENDED, BUT IT WAS CLEAR HE WAS NOT REALLY THERE WITH US."

SHE LOOKED OVER AT KAYDEN WITH ONE EYEBROW RAISED.

"I WAS CERTAIN HE WAS MISSING YOU THIS WHOLE TIME . . . BUT THAT . . ." SHE WAVED A HAND IN THE DIRECTION OF THE PRINCE'S RETREATING FOOTSTEPS — WHICH COULD STILL BE HEARD AS HIS BOOT HEELS HIT THE MARBLE FLOOR.

"THAT LITTLE SCENE DID NOT MAKE SENSE."

"I DON'T THINK HE MISSED ME AT ALL." KAYDEN SAID QUIETLY.

"NO. NO, I'M SURE HE DID." CATARINE SHOOK HER HEAD.

"I DON'T KNOW WHAT THAT WAS ALL ABOUT, BUT I CAN ASSURE YOU, HE HAS MISSED YOU."

SHE WAS NODDING HER HEAD AND SOMETHING ABOUT THE LOOK IN HER EYES MADE KAYDEN WONDER ABOUT IT.

CLEARLY CATARINE BELIEVED HER OWN WORDS —
BUT KAYDEN COULD NOT HELP THINKING OF THE
COLD LOOK IN THE PRINCE'S EYES, JUST BEFORE
HE HAD WALKED AWAY WITHOUT SO MUCH AS A
GLANCE BACK AT HER.

MAYBE HE HAD MISSED HER WHILE SHE WAS GONE,
BUT SOMETHING HAD HAPPENED BETWEEN THEN
AND NOW TO MAKE HIM CHANGE HIS MIND.

TWENTY-THREE

KAYDEN STEPPED INTO THE ENORMOUS ROOM — AS SHE MOVED FROM BEHIND THE LARGE BOOKCASE THAT CONCEALED THE ENTRANCE TO A SECRET PASSAGE.

METHODICALLY SHE LOOKED AROUND FOR THE PRINCE OR ANY OF HIS STAFF. SHE MOVED QUIETLY TO THE DOORWAY BETWEEN THE PRINCE'S BEDROOM AND HIS OFFICE.

A TOWERING STACK OF FILES SAT IN THE MIDDLE OF HIS DESK, WITH A SCATTERING OF PAPERS AMONG THE THICK FOLDERS, BUT THERE WAS NO SIGN OF ANYONE.

AFTER CHECKING THE ENTRYWAY AND THE SITTING ROOM, SHE FELT CONFIDENT THERE WAS NO ONE ELSE IN THE SUITE.

WOW! AND I THOUGHT MY SUITE WAS HUGE . . .

TAKING NOTE OF THE LAYOUT AND ENTRANCES, SHE SLOWLY MOVED BACK TO THE PRINCE'S BEDROOM.

Taking in the grand room was more intimidating than she'd expected . . . the rooms were not what she had thought she'd find.

The intricately-carved furniture was clearly hand-made. While the fabric hanging at his windows appeared to be silk and the floor was inlaid with gold — like she had observed on much of the palace floors — there was an almost-shocking absence of riches in an area she would have expected it most.

More and more about this man makes absolutely no sense.

As she made her way back to the bookcase, she turned and saw that she was at the foot of the Prince's bed.

Seriously . . . who needs a bed that large?

The image of him slipping between the sheets filled her thoughts and she felt heat crawling up her cheeks at the thought of the Prince — in his bed.

Where did that come from?

The memory of his hand holding hers; his arm holding her tightly against him while they danced, sent tingles dancing over her skin, and the heat in her cheeks burst into full flame.

Oh, why did I do this today?

Her decision to come here made no sense . . . even to her. The only reason she could come

UP WITH WAS A PERSONAL DESIRE TO SEE THE PRINCE'S ROOM BEFORE SHE LEFT.

AFTER HER LACK OF WELCOME YESTERDAY, SHE WAS CERTAIN THE PRINCE WOULD BE SENDING HER HOME AT ANY MOMENT. SOMETHING WITHIN HER HAD WANTED TO SEE WHERE HE SPENT MUCH OF HIS TIME . . . WHILE SHE STILL HAD THE OPPORTUNITY.

OH, WHAT AM I SUPPOSED TO DO WITH THESE RIDICULOUS FEELINGS? I HAVE A MISSION — AND THIS ISN'T PART OF IT.

NONE OF THIS MADE ANY SENSE TO HER. SHE WAS NOT HERE TO BE ATTRACTED TO THE PRINCE . . .

SHE WAS HERE TO KILL HIM.

WHAT AM I SUPPOSED TO DO NOW? IF I CAN'T COMPLETE MY MISSION — IF I FAIL — WHAT WILL I DO? THERE'S NO PLACE ON EARTH I CAN HIDE.

THROWING CAUTION TO THE WINDS, SHE WALKED OVER TO HIS ENORMOUS BED AND RAN A HAND OVER THE THICK COVERING.

SHE WAS SURPRISED TO FIND THAT, ALTHOUGH IT WAS SOFT, IT FELT MORE LIKE FLANNEL THAN SILK OR SATIN — WHICH WAS WHAT SHE'D EXPECTED.

THE ROOM HAD AN UNEXPECTED PERSONAL FEEL TO IT. AND THE LACK OF LUXURIES MADE HER WONDER IF THE PRINCE HAD CHOSEN EVERYTHING HIMSELF — OR LEFT IT TO OTHERS.

SHE RAN A HAND DOWN A GLOSSY WOOD PILLAR AT THE CORNER. IT WAS YET ANOTHER SURPRISE TO SEE WHIMSY IN THE DESIGN OF HIS FURNITURE.

EVERY PIECE WAS INTRICATELY CARVED — MASCULINE, BUT AT THE SAME TIME WHIMSICAL. IT WAS ALMOST AS IF HE WAS TRYING TO SURROUND HIMSELF WITH A FANTASY . . . OR A DREAM.

PERHAPS HIS LIFE HAS NOT BEEN AS . . . CAREFREE . . . AS I WAS LED TO BELIEVE.

THE THOUGHT DID NOT SIT WELL.

HOW COULD SHE JUSTIFY HER JOB WITH THIS NEW INFORMATION? HOW WAS SHE SUPPOSED TO ELIMINATE THE MAN WITH SO MANY QUESTION MARKS HANGING OVER THE ENTIRE SITUATION?

NOT THAT I COULD GET CLOSE ENOUGH TO DO THAT ANYWAY . . .

NOW THAT WAS A BITTER PILL TO SWALLOW — MUCH MORE THAN SHE WOULD HAVE LIKED.

IT WAS ONE THING TO HAVE AN ASSIGNMENT THAT PROVED CHALLENGING. IT WAS QUITE ANOTHER TO BE REBUFFED BEFORE SHE EVEN HAD A CHANCE TO REALLY BEGIN.

THE SOUND OF A DOOR CLOSING HAD HER RUSHING BACK TO THE BOOKCASE — AND THE HIDDEN PASSAGE.

NO SOONER HAD THE PANEL CLOSED BEHIND HER, THAN SHE COULD HEAR FOOTSTEPS ON THE OTHER SIDE.

HER FEET FLEW ALONG THE DARK PASSAGE AS SHE MADE HER WAY BACK TO THE LIBRARY QUICKLY AND SILENTLY.

Dvarius walked into his bedroom and immediately dropped onto his bed.

I do not understand why I let myself get so worked up over her absence. Clearly she only came back because she missed Lady Catarine.

He ground his teeth together as he lay there, thinking about the young woman who had somehow managed to tie him up into neat, little knots since returning to the palace.

And though it wasn't possible, he was certain he could smell the tantalizing scent that floated around her constantly.

I can't find her in the palace, but somehow her scent has found its way in here . . . taunting me.

The tightening of his stomach muscles sent a wave of frustration through him and a deep growl slipped between his lips at the thought of Kayden.

Even now she is most likely flitting about the palace, thinking of new ways to torture me.

He was ready to admit he'd overreacted yesterday when she'd arrived, but he could not find her anywhere in the palace.

How am I to apologize? Would a note suffice? Bah; too cowardly!

And Lady Catarine was no help whatsoever.

She had chattered away during their morning

WALK IN THE GARDENS ABOUT HOW THRILLED SHE WAS TO HAVE HER FRIEND BACK.

YOU WOULD THINK THE TWO OF THEM WERE RIPPED VIOLENTLY APART FOR YEARS.

WITH A GRUNT, DVARIUS ROLLED OFF THE BED AND WALKED TO HIS CLOSET TO PULL OUT HIS EXERCISE CLOTHES. A GOOD WORKOUT WAS PRECISELY WHAT HE NEEDED.

THERE WAS NO BETTER WAY HE COULD THINK OF TO SWEAT OUT HIS FRUSTRATIONS.

PERHAPS I CAN FIND A WAY TO SWEAT THAT RED-HAIRED VIXEN OUT OF MY SYSTEM AS WELL . . .

TWENTY-FOUR

KAYDEN WATCHED AS CATARINE TOOK HER FIRST SOLO WALK AROUND THE PADDOCK. IT HAD ONLY BEEN A WEEK AND SHE WAS ALREADY DOING SO WELL.

WHO WOULD HAVE THOUGHT THAT I COULD BE SUCH A GOOD TEACHER?

OF COURSE, SHE'D NEVER HAD THE OPPORTUNITY TO TEACH A SKILL TO ANYONE, SO SHE COULDN'T HAVE KNOWN WHAT TO EXPECT OF HERSELF.

WHAT SHE HAD DISCOVERED EXCITED HER. SHE FELT . . . USEFUL, PRODUCTIVE, HELPFUL — AND SHE LIKED IT. IT WAS CERTAINLY SOMETHING TO HOLD ONTO FOR THE FUTURE.

NOT THAT MANY PEOPLE VOLUNTARILY LEFT THE ORDER . . . BUT IF SHE EVER DID MANAGE TO FIND A WAY OUT, AT LEAST SHE HAD AN IDEA OF WHAT SHE COULD DO WITH HERSELF.

THINKING OF THE ORDER MADE HER THINK OF THE

PRINCE. SHE HAD SEEN HIM SINCE HER RETURN, BUT HE HAD NOT SOUGHT HER OUT TO SPEAK WITH HER AND SHE HAD NOT BEEN ALONE WITH HIM — EVEN ONCE.

CATARINE HAD JOKED WITH HER EARLIER THAT SHE SHOULD SADDLE UP AND HEAD OUT TO THE GROUNDS WITH HER BOW — WHICH HAD MADE KAYDEN WISH SHE HAD NEVER SHARED THAT PARTICULAR STORY.

OF COURSE, OTHERWISE, IT JUST MADE HER SAD.

WHILE SHE STOOD THERE, WATCHING CATARINE GO THROUGH HER PACES ON SPROUT — WHOM ANDRE HAD ASSURED HER WAS THE MOST GENTLE HORSE IN THE STABLES — MADE HER START THINKING OF THAT AFTERNOON, AND IT NEARLY BROUGHT TEARS TO HER EYES.

THE STRAIN WAS BEGINNING TO GET TO HER — WAITING FOR HIM TO SEND HER HOME, AS HE SURELY WOULD ANY DAY.

SINCE HER RETURN, THOSE DAYS FELT ALMOST LIKE ANOTHER LIFETIME. EVEN THOUGH SHE WAS GETTING ALONG FAMOUSLY WITH CATARINE, NOT ONE OF THE OTHER GIRLS SPOKE TO HER NOW.

IT WAS ALMOST LIKE THEY ALL KNEW SHE HAD DONE SOMETHING TO UPSET THE PRINCE AND THEY WERE WORRIED HE WOULD SNUB THEM BY ASSOCIATION.

BUT NOT CATARINE.

NO, SHE COULD NOT HAVE BEEN SWEETER TO KAYDEN. THEY HAD THEIR DAILY RIDING LESSONS AND THEY SPENT MOST OF THE REST OF THE DAY

SITTING IN KAYDEN'S OR CATARINE'S ROOMS, CHATTING.

IT WAS THE ONLY THING THAT MADE BEING HERE BEARABLE NOW.

DVARIUS PACED FROM HIS BED TO THE DRESSING ROOM DOOR, BEFORE MOVING BACK TO THE BED. THIS WAITING WAS MADDENING — HE HAD THOUGHT WAITING TO SEE HER FOR THREE WHOLE DAYS HAD BEEN DIFFICULT, BUT TO AVOID HER FOR AN ENTIRE WEEK WAS NEARLY MORE THAN HE COULD HANDLE.

THE WEEK MIGHT HAVE BEGUN WITH HER AVOIDING HIM BUT IT HAD QUICKLY BECOME CLEAR TO HIM THAT SHE HAD THE RIGHT IDEA.

I HAVE TO BE CERTAIN.

HE HAD TO KNOW THAT HE WAS MAKING THE RIGHT CHOICE. SHE HELD SO MUCH POWER OVER HIS EMOTIONS — HE COULD NOT AFFORD TO BE WRONG.

IF HIS ADVISORS WERE CORRECT AND HE ALLOWED HER TO HAVE INFLUENCE OVER HIM . . . AND HER MOTIVES WERE ANYTHING OTHER THAN IN THE INTEREST OF THE BEST FOR THE COUNTRY — WELL, IT WOULD BE DISASTROUS.

SO HE HAD AVOIDED HER ALL WEEK, WATCHING AS SHE INTERACTED WITH CATARINE EVERY MORNING — AND ONLY CATARINE — BECAUSE THE OTHER LADIES WOULD HAVE NOTHING TO DO WITH HER FOR SOME REASON, THEN SWEATING OUT HIS FRUSTRATION EVERY AFTERNOON WITH MAREK.

He had actually thought the isolation was Kayden's own doing until Catarine had set him straight.

He still remembered the shock he had felt at how Catarine had spoken to him.

Only yesterday, he had sought out the young woman's company, deliberately ignoring Kayden when he approached the two ladies — because they were rarely found apart anymore.

It was almost as if Catarine had appointed herself Kayden's protector, the way she stuck by her side and the way she had dressed him down as soon as the two of them were alone.

He had asked her to go for a walk, thinking that would be a good idea.

He had spent time with almost every one of the other ladies, but not one of them held his interest the way Kayden or Catarine did, so he'd finally relented and sought her out.

Once they were alone, she had torn into him in a way he never could have anticipated, and he had a feeling he might actually have been bleeding if words could cut a person.

Her sharp tongue had shown itself and her exceptional command of vocabulary was certainly a point in her favor.

She had spoken harshly, but not loudly — and she had gone on for a full five minutes before letting out a little huff, sending him

A RATHER NASTY SMILE AND TURNING ON HER HEEL TO RETURN TO THE PALACE AND, HE WAS CERTAIN, TO KAYDEN'S SIDE.

HE HAD WALKED THROUGH THE CASTLE AIMLESSLY FOR OVER AN HOUR AFTERWARD.

AND HE'D BEEN PACING MOST OF THE MORNING, TRYING TO PUZZLE IT OUT.

CLEARLY HE HAD SOME SERIOUS THINKING TO DO. HE HAD GIVEN HIMSELF A WEEK, BUT HE WAS NO CLOSER TO AN ANSWER THAN HE HAD BEEN WHEN THE WEEK STARTED.

WHAT ELSE COULD HE DO?

WHEN HE REACHED THE BED THIS TIME, HE DROPPED TO HIS KNEES BESIDE IT AND LAY DOWN, ALMOST PROSTRATE ON THE FLOOR, AND POURED IT ALL OUT TO GOD.

WHENEVER HE DIDN'T KNOW WHAT TO DO, DVARIUS KNEW HE COULD BRING IT TO HIS LORD AND THE ANSWER WOULD COME TO HIM.

ONLY GOD KNEW THE FUTURE — AND HE WOULD GUIDE DVARIUS TO MAKE THE RIGHT DECISION.

DVARIUS LET EVERYTHING OUT, INCLUDING THINGS HE HAD NOT REALIZED HE WAS BOTHERED BY OR UPSET ABOUT; THINGS HE HAD TRULY THOUGHT HE'D LET GO OF ALREADY.

HE VENTED HIS FEELINGS ABOUT HIS FATHER'S DEATH; ABOUT HIS MOTHER'S SELF-IMPOSED INCARCERATION; ABOUT THE FACT THAT HE MUST BE MARRIED BEFORE HE COULD TAKE THE CROWN; ABOUT THIS WHOLE DEBACLE WITH HIS ADVISORS — WHOM HE COULDN'T REPLACE UNTIL HE WAS

CROWNED, AND ABOUT THE CONFUSION WITH KAYDEN.

HE KNEW THAT GOD HAD A PERFECT PLAN FOR HIM . . . FOR HER . . . FOR ALL OF THEM. GOD WANTED THE BEST, NOT JUST FOR DVARIUS OR KAYDEN, BUT FOR THE ENTIRE COUNTRY.

DVARIUS WOULD SOON HAVE THE RESPONSIBILITY OF MAKING DECISIONS THAT WOULD AFFECT MILLIONS OF LIVES AND THIS TERRIFIED HIM MUCH MORE THAN HE WANTED TO ADMIT.

JUST HOW LONG HE LAY THERE, FACE AGAINST THE COOL MARBLE FLOOR, HE HAD NO IDEA. EVEN AFTER HE FELT COMPLETELY DRAINED, HE REMAINED THERE AND BEGAN GIVING THANKS TO GOD.

HE THANKED GOD THAT HIS MOTHER HAD SURVIVED THE ACCIDENT, THAT — EVEN THOUGH SHE REFUSED TO LEAVE HER ROOMS — SHE WOULD SPEAK TO HIM AND SHE WAS STILL FUNCTIONING . . . SOMEWHAT.

HE THANKED GOD FOR BRINGING KAYDEN AND CATARINE INTO HIS LIFE.

HE THANKED GOD FOR THE TIME HE HAD ALREADY HAD WITH BOTH OF THEM, AND FOR THE VERY REAL POSSIBILITY THAT HE WOULD BE ABLE TO CHOOSE ONE OF THEM FOR HIS WIFE SOON.

HE THANKED GOD FOR HIS OWN LIFE, AND THE OPPORTUNITY TO LEAD THIS COUNTRY.

HE LOOKED FORWARD TO A TIME WHEN HE HAD THE CHANCE TO CHANGE THINGS — TO MAKE LIFE BETTER FOR THE PEOPLE WHO HAD BEEN THROUGH

SO MUCH OVER THE PAST HUNDRED YEARS OF WAR AND STRIFE AND HUNGER.

AND HE THANKED GOD FOR SENDING HIS OWN SON TO SAVE THEM — ALL OF THEM — AND FOR THE HEALING HE FELT RIGHT AT THIS VERY MOMENT.

"YOU ARE NOT GOING TO BELIEVE WHAT IS GOING ON RIGHT NOW."

DVARIUS LET OUT A BREATH AT THE SOUND OF HIS BEST FRIEND'S VOICE. MAREK WAS THE ONLY PERSON WHO WOULD BARGE INTO HIS ROOM, WITHOUT SO MUCH AS THE COURTESY OF A KNOCK.

"IF I'M NOT GOING TO BELIEVE IT, WHY ARE YOU BOTHERING TO TELL ME ABOUT IT." HE GOT TO HIS FEET AS MAREK LET OUT A DARK CHUCKLE.

"HA HA, VAR. NO SERIOUSLY, YOU HAVE TO COME SEE THIS."

"COME SEE WHAT?"

"LIKE I SAID . . . YOU WON'T BELIEVE ME. YOU HAVE TO SEE IT FOR YOURSELF."

AS MUCH AS DVARIUS STILL FELT CONFLICTED ABOUT HIS DECISION, PERHAPS HE NEEDED A BREAK . . . AND A DISTRACTION.

"WELL, I BELIEVE YOU'RE NOT GOING TO LEAVE ME ALONE, UNTIL I DO WHAT YOU ASK."

"THEN COME ON." MAREK LAUGHED AS HE HEADED OUT INTO THE HALLWAY.

DVARIUS LET OUT A SHORT LAUGH AT HIS FRIEND'S ODD SENSE OF HUMOR BEFORE FOLLOWING HIM.

THE TWO OF THEM WALKED THROUGH THE PALACE

TOGETHER; THE ONLY SOUNDS HEARD WAS THEIR
BOOT HEELS HITTING THE MARBLE FLOOR . . .

UNTIL THEY APPROACHED THE MAIN GUEST FLOOR.

MAREK SUDDENLY STOPPED AT KAYDEN'S SUITE.
THE DOUBLE DOORS WERE OPEN WIDE, AND THE
SOUND OF LADY CATARINE'S VOICE WAS COMING
FROM THE ROOM. SHE SOUNDED ALMOST AS IF SHE
WERE PLEADING WITH SOMEONE

DVARIUS LOOKED AT MAREK, BUT ALL HIS FRIEND
GAVE HIM IN RESPONSE WAS A SLIGHT SHAKE OF
HIS HEAD. DVARIUS STEPPED UP TO THE OPEN
DOORS.

*MAREK WAS ABSOLUTELY RIGHT. I NEVER WOULD
HAVE BELIEVED THIS IF I HAD NOT SEEN IT FOR
MYSELF.*

BUT WHY?

TWENTY-FIVE

KAYDEN WALKED BACK AND FORTH FROM CLOSET TO BED, CARRYING DRESS AFTER DRESS TO THE ENORMOUS TRUNK THAT STOOD OPEN NEXT TO HER BED.

CATARINE SAT ON THE BED WATCHING HER. SHE HAD ARGUED WITH KAYDEN FOR NEARLY AN HOUR SINCE SHE'D COME IN AND FOUND HER PACKING, BUT KAYDEN HAD STEADILY IGNORED EVERY WORD AND CONTINUED WALKING BACK AND FORTH, HANGING ONE ITEM AFTER ANOTHER IN THE TALL TRUNK.

"HE HASN'T SENT YOU HOME, YOU KNOW."

KAYDEN WALKED BACK TO THE CLOSET WITHOUT ANSWERING.

"YOU PROBABLY WON'T BE ALLOWED TO LEAVE WITHOUT HIS PERMISSION. AND I DON'T THINK HE WILL GIVE IT," SHE SAID, IN A SING-SONG TYPE VOICE, AS KAYDEN HUNG THE NEXT DRESS IN THE

STANDING TRUNK.

KAYDEN HEARD HER FRIEND, BUT PAID LITTLE ATTENTION. SHE HAD MADE UP HER MIND — SHE WAS NOT GOING TO SIT HERE AND WAIT ANYMORE.

SHE WOULD FIND A WAY AROUND DREY. MAYBE ALFREID WOULD HAVE A SUGGESTION . . . OR SHE WOULD JUST DEAL WITH HIS ANGER.

IF SHE NEVER SAW THE PRINCE, SHE COULDN'T VERY WELL FULFILL THE MISSION THEY'D GIVEN HER — COULD SHE?

HE CERTAINLY COULDN'T FAULT HER FOR TRYING. HE HAD PLAYED HIS LITTLE GAME AND IT HAD BACKFIRED. CLEARLY, THE PRINCE HAD BEEN HAPPIER WITH HER GONE. SHE COULDN'T IMAGINE WHY HE HAD NOT SENT HER AWAY AGAIN YET, BUT SHE WAS DETERMINED TO LEAVE ON HER OWN TERMS.

SHE WALKED BACK TO THE CLOSET FOR ANOTHER DRESS.

SHE WAS TIRED OF LISTENING TO HER FRIEND'S ARGUMENTS, BUT SHE DIDN'T HAVE THE HEART TO SEND HER AWAY. AFTER ALL, SHE WOULD SURELY NEVER SEE CATARINE AGAIN AFTER TODAY.

THE LEAST SHE COULD DO WAS LISTEN AS CATARINE TRIED TO CONVINCE HER TO STAY — THOUGH SHE KNEW THE YOUNG WOMAN WAS WASTING HER BREATH.

"WHAT WILL I DO WITHOUT YOU HERE?" THOSE WORDS BROKE KAYDEN'S ALREADY BLEEDING HEART.

SHE SAT DOWN ON THE SMALL BENCH INSIDE THE

ENORMOUS CLOSET — CRUSHING THE DRESS IN HER HANDS.

WHAT WILL I DO WITHOUT CATARINE'S COMPANY?

HOW WOULD SHE GO BACK TO THE LONELY AND MONOTONOUS EXISTENCE SHE'D HAD BEFORE ALL OF THIS?

HOW HAD SHE NEVER SEEN HER LIFE FOR WHAT IT TRULY WAS; SAD AND LONELY — AND NOTHING MORE THAN JUST EXISTING?

WHY DID I THINK I DETESTED BEING HERE?

HOW WILL I EVER GO BACK TO WHAT I WAS BEFORE?

HOW COULD ANYTHING EVER MEASURE UP?

SHE SWIPED A HAND AT THE HOT TEARS THAT MADE THEIR WAY DOWN HER CHEEKS.

NOT ONLY HAD HER LIFE LOST ALL MEANING; SHE WAS BECOMING AN EMOTIONAL MESS, TOO.

"WHAT IS GOING ON HERE?"

THE PRINCE'S THUNDEROUS VOICE INTERRUPTED HER THOUGHTS AND SHE STRUGGLED TO CHOKE BACK THE SOBS THAT HAD QUIETLY BEGUN TO SLIP BETWEEN HER LIPS.

SHE HEARD NO NOISE FOR SEVERAL SECONDS; THEN CATARINE SPOKE AND HER WORDS SENT A FLOOD OF WARMTH THROUGH KAYDEN'S BATTERED HEART.

"KAYDEN IS PACKING, YOUR HIGHNESS. YOU HAVE GIVEN HER NO OTHER CHOICE. SHE WILL NO LONGER SIT HERE — WAITING FOR YOU . . . TO.

Grow. Up."

After another pause, Catarine added, "and neither will I."

A moment later, speaking louder and in the general direction of the closet, she added, "Kayden, if you need me, I'll be in my room . . . packing."

Kayden heard the door to her rooms shut — hard; all the more surprising when she thought of the heavy, solid, oak door.

For several seconds, all she could hear was the echo of Catarine's heels clicking on the marble floor as she walked away.

Kayden stayed where she was, clutching the dress like a lifeline, while she waited to hear something from the Prince; anything to help her gauge his mood.

But no sound came, not even the sound of footsteps.

She strained to hear anything.

What is he doing out there?

And what should I do?

He'd sounded so angry. Was he angry because she was leaving without permission?

Or had he gone after Catarine . . .

"Kayden?"

His voice was so near, it startled her.

She hadn't heard him move toward the door

OF THE CLOSET — AND SHE HAD NO IDEA WHAT TO DO ABOUT IT.

SHOULD I ANSWER?

SHOULD I TELL HIM TO GO AWAY?

OR SHOULD I JUST SIT HERE AND HOPE HE GOES AWAY?

"KAYDEN, COULD YOU PLEASE COME OUT? OR CAN I COME IN? ARE YOU . . . ARE YOU DECENT?"

THERE WAS SOMETHING ODD IN HIS VOICE — ALMOST AS IF HE WERE A YOUNG BOY WHO HAD BEEN CAUGHT SNEAKING SWEETS.

OH, WHY DOES HE HAVE TO BE SO CONFUSING?

AFTER WHAT FELT LIKE AN ETERNITY, AND HER STILL NOT CERTAIN WHAT TO DO ABOUT HIM, HE SOLVED THE PROBLEM FOR HER BY POKING HIS HEAD INTO THE CLOSET.

HE HAD A HAND HOVERING OVER HIS EYES, PREPARED TO COVER THEM IF SHE WAS NOT PROPERLY DRESSED — AND THE LOOK ON HIS FACE WAS SO COMICAL, SHE HAD TO LAUGH.

"OH GOOD. YOU ARE DRESSED. I WAS WORRIED."

HE WALKED ALL THE WAY IN AND LEANED AGAINST THE DOOR FRAME.

"SO . . . ARE YOU PLANNING TO GO SOMEWHERE; YOU AND CATARINE?"

HE WAVED HIS HAND IN THE GENERAL DIRECTION OF THE DOOR TO HER ROOMS AND LET OUT A SHORT LAUGH.

"BY NOW YOU'VE FIGURED OUT THAT SHE HAS

TAKEN YOUR SIDE IN ALL OF THIS. SHE IS NOT VERY HAPPY WITH ME AND SHE HAS LET ME KNOW IT. YOU HAVE A FIERCE PROTECTOR IN HER."

IT WAS KAYDEN'S TURN TO LAUGH THEN — AND THE LAUGH CAME OUT ALMOST LIKE AN EXPLOSION.

AFTER SHE LET IT GO, SHE REALIZED THAT QUITE A BIT OF THE STRESS SHE'D FELT, ONLY A MOMENT AGO, HAD DRAINED AWAY. BUT SHE WAS QUICK TO CLAMP DOWN ON IT.

SHE WAS NOT ABOUT TO LET HIM OFF THE HOOK SO EASILY.

"SO WHERE ARE YOU GOING, REALLY . . . ESPECIALLY CONSIDERING YOU JUST GOT BACK."

THE RESIGNATION IN HIS VOICE — MORE THAN ANYTHING ELSE — WAS WHAT GOT HER ATTENTION. HE WASN'T ANGRY, JUST SURPRISED.

"WELL, I THINK IT'S PERFECTLY CLEAR THAT YOU DON'T WANT ME HERE ANYMORE, SO I THOUGHT I WOULD JUST MAKE IT EASIER ON EVERYONE AND GO QUIETLY. I DON'T PARTICULARLY FANCY AN OVERDONE EXIT." SHE SAID, REMEMBERING THE SECOND GIRL HE HAD SENT HOME.

IT HAD HAPPENED RIGHT BEFORE SHE'D BEEN CALLED AWAY.

THEY HAD ALL BEEN AT DINNER AND THE GIRL HAD COME INTO THE ROOM SCREAMING AT A FRIGHTENING DECIBEL ABOUT THE INJUSTICE OF IT ALL.

SHE HAD KEPT SAYING; OVER AND OVER, "DO YOU KNOW WHO I AM . . . WHO MY FAMILY IS? YOU'LL BE SORRY!"

THE EXPERIENCE MIGHT HAVE BEEN HUMOROUS IF IT HAD NOT BEEN SO SAD.

KAYDEN DID NOT WANT TO GO OUT LIKE THAT.

SHE JUST WANTED A QUIET, DIGNIFIED EXIT . . . ON HER OWN TERMS.

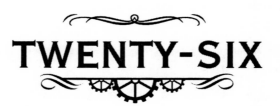

TWENTY-SIX

WHEN SHE LOOKED BACK AT THE PRINCE, KAYDEN WAS SHOCKED TO SEE HE WAS JUST STANDING THERE; SHOCK COLORING HIS FEATURES.

HE STOOD THERE FOR A FULL MINUTE BEFORE HE FINALLY SPOKE AGAIN.

"KAYDEN, THE LAST THING I WANT IS FOR YOU TO GO. I NEVER WANT YOU TO GO ANYWHERE."

HE SNAPPED HIS MOUTH SHUT; AS IF HE'D SAID SOMETHING HE HADN'T MEANT TO.

"THEN WHY . . . I'M SORRY, I DON'T UNDERSTAND."

SHE SHOOK HER HEAD AS SHE STOOD.

"WHY HAVE YOU BEEN AVOIDING ME ALL WEEK?"

THAT, MORE THAN ANYTHING ELSE . . . MADE NO SENSE, SO SHE WAITED FOR HIM TO REPLY — TO MAKE SENSE OF IT.

He turned away from her, gripping his hair in both hands and then he began pacing.

He went back and forth between the walls of the closet as she watched him.

There was only about four feet to walk back and forth and he had really long legs, so he made a lot of turns.

It was almost comical — the way he kept turning around.

"I've been trying to figure out the answers all week, but I didn't know what to say to you. There are so many things, Kayden. My advisors are all over me to pick anyone but you. This whole experiment is not going at all the way I expected it to."

He stopped to take a breath before going on.

"The only two ladies here whom I have any interest in are you — and Catarine. Can you understand how difficult that makes things for me?

I have to choose a wife, and I have to pick her from twenty-five women whom I've never met; women I know nothing about . . . who are complete strangers to me."

He stopped pacing and came to stand in front of her. Then he looked down at her with a look of pleading in his eyes.

"I have no idea what to do about all of this. I want to pick you. I want you to stay and be my Princess, but I'm unsure of so many things. I don't know how you feel about me. I don't

KNOW IF YOU ARE INTERESTED IN ME AT ALL — THAT WAY."

HE TOOK BOTH OF HER HANDS IN HIS, AS HE WHISPERED WORDS MEANT ONLY FOR HER.

"I DON'T KNOW IF I CAN LIVE WITHOUT YOU. I'VE TRIED. THAT IS WHAT I SPENT THIS WEEK TRYING TO FIGURE OUT. I HAVE STAYED AWAY FROM YOU ON PURPOSE. IT WAS EASIER WHEN YOU WERE GONE, BUT WHEN YOU CAME BACK . . ."

HE STOPPED, AS HER EYES FILLED WITH TEARS.

"I KNEW THEN THAT I DIDN'T WANT TO LIVE WITHOUT YOU . . . EVER."

HIS FINGERS GENTLY BRUSHED AWAY THE TEAR THAT ESCAPED.

"I HAD TO FIGURE OUT IF IT WAS WORTH TRYING TO LIVE WITHOUT YOU, TO MAKE EVERYONE ELSE HAPPY."

WHEN HE STOPPED AGAIN, SHE LOOKED UP AT HIM EXPECTANTLY.

"IT'S NOT," AND THEN HE PULLED HER INTO HIS ARMS.

AND THAT WAS WHEN SHE SAW IT — JUST THE HINT OF A SHADOW, BUT THERE WAS DEFINITELY SOMEONE ELSE IN HER ROOM.

IT DISTRACTED HER FROM WHAT THE PRINCE WAS WHISPERING INTO HER EAR.

SHE STRAINED TO SEE.

HAD CATARINE COME BACK OR WAS IT ONE OF THE SERVANTS?

EVERYTHING SEEMED TO HAPPEN VERY QUICKLY THEN.

A MAN RUSHED INTO THE CLOSET, SCREAMING AS HE CAME NEAR THEM.

SHE SAW A GLINT OF LIGHT AND ACTED INSTINCTIVELY, TURNING AND TWISTING SO THAT THE PRINCE WAS SAFE AND SHE COULD PROTECT HIM FROM THE MAN.

SHE FELT PAIN; SHARP, CLEAR, BURNING — AS THE KNIFE WAS RAMMED INTO HER BACK. AS IT SLID IN, SHE HEARD THE PRINCE SHOUT.

THE PAIN BROUGHT A MOMENT OF CLARITY WITH IT. THERE WERE OTHERS HERE, IN THE PALACE, WITH THE SAME MISSION AS HERS.

DREY PLANNED THIS.

WAS I JUST A DISTRACTION OR IS THIS EXACTLY WHAT HE THOUGHT WOULD HAPPEN?

SHE SHOOK HER HEAD SLIGHTLY, PUSHING EVERYTHING ASIDE; PAIN, SADNESS, ANGER, AND ALL THOUGHT OF HERSELF — AS SHE WHIRLED ON HER ATTACKER.

ACTING QUICKLY, SHE MANAGED TO TAKE HIM BY SURPRISE; SLIPPING PAST HIS OWN DEFENSES AND DELIVERING A SWIFT KICK TO HIS GROIN, FOLLOWED BY A SHORT CHOP TO HIS WINDPIPE; EFFECTIVELY CUTTING OFF HIS AIR SUPPLY.

HE DROPPED LIKE A STONE, BUT SHE KNEW SHE WOULD ALWAYS REMEMBER THE LOOK OF HATRED IN THOSE COLD EYES OF HIS; A LOOK THAT MADE NO SENSE — BEING THAT IT WAS DIRECTED AT HER . . . AND NOT THE PRINCE.

She had no more time to wonder about it, because the room filled with guards then, and she heard shouting from all around.

A moment later, she felt the room tilt as she was swept up into someone's arms. Everything seemed fuzzy around the edges and she was having trouble focusing on anything.

After several moments, Dvarius' face floated into her vision and she reached up a hand to him.

He hasn't shaved, was all she could think as she moved her hand over his rough cheek.

He was saying something to her, but his words sounded garbled. She tried to speak to him, but couldn't seem to understand the words coming out of her own mouth.

She felt tired, but she fought against the desire to sleep. She had something important to say and she wanted to make sure he heard her — before she slept.

He keeps looking around at other people . . .

The thoughts floated away from her as she waited; needing to tell him . . . something, yet unable to form the words.

Her eyes were getting heavy; she could barely keep them open.

When he looked back down at her, she concentrated on the words she was trying to say.

It took several tries to get the words out, but they finally came . . .

"I love you."

And then there was only black.

DISCUSSION QUESTIONS

WARNING : SPOILERS AHEAD!

If your book club is reading A Reluctant Assassin and would like to chat or skype with me, please contact me via my website:

HTTP://JCMORROWS.COM/CONTACT.

1) How strong is your faith? Would you stand firm in your beliefs, even if everyone around you has abandoned theirs?

2) How important is it to you, that the person you marry share the same faith?

3) Is it possible for someone to choose love over training, over fear of death, knowing that they may never fully experience it?

4) Do you think Dvarius should choose a Queen based on his feelings or something more tangible, such as lineage? Or faith?

5) Is there a person from the Bible that Kayden's character reminds you of?

6) Does Dvarius' faith make him stronger? Will it make him a better King?

7) In case you didn't notice, Auralius is what we know now as the U.S.A. — Can you imagine yourself and your life — living in Auralius?

TURN THE PAGE

FOR AN EARLY LOOK AT:

A TREACHEROUS DECISION

~THE MOONSTONE CHRONICLES ~
BOOK 2

PREFACE

DVARIUS SAT BESIDE THE LONG, WHITE BED IN THE FAMILY'S PART OF THE HOSPITAL WING; PRAYING WITH ALL HIS MIGHT FOR KAYDEN TO OPEN HER EYES.

THE DOCTORS HAD TOLD HIM SHE COULD WAKE ANYTIME, SO HE HAD WAITED BY HER BED THROUGHOUT THE NIGHT; WAITING, WATCHING, HOLDING HER HAND AND HOPING FOR ANOTHER CHANCE WITH HER.

DR. HAMA HAD TRIED TO CONVINCE HIM TO LEAVE THE HOSPITAL WING AND GET SOME SLEEP SEVERAL TIMES, BUT DVARIUS WAS DETERMINED HE WOULD NOT MOVE UNTIL KAYDEN OPENED HER EYES, UNTIL HE KNEW SHE WOULD BE ALL RIGHT.

THE EVENTS OF TWO DAYS AGO PLAYED OVER AND OVER IN HIS MIND AS HE SAT THERE.

HE THOUGHT ABOUT IT; WONDERING IF THERE WAS ANYTHING HE COULD HAVE DONE DIFFERENTLY. NO

MATTER HOW MANY TIMES HE THOUGHT ABOUT IT, HE REALIZED THERE WAS NO REAL WAY TO KNOW.

PERHAPS IF I HAD BEEN PAYING MORE ATTENTION . . .

NO. I'M NOT GOING TO DO THAT TO MYSELF. THERE WAS NOTHING I COULD HAVE DONE.

AT LEAST, THAT WAS WHAT HE TOLD HIMSELF.

HE HAD NOT MANAGED TO CONVINCE HIMSELF OF IT . . . YET.

THOSE LAST FEW MINUTES KEPT REPLAYING IN HIS HEAD. ONE MOMENT THEY HAD BEEN EMBRACING, AND THE NEXT . . . EVERYTHING HAD GONE CRAZY.

ONLY MOMENTS BEFORE HE HAD BEEN WORRIED SHE WAS LEAVING HIM — ESPECIALLY SINCE HE HAD WALKED IN TO FIND HER PACKING.

WHAT OTHER CONCLUSION COULD I HAVE DRAWN?

AND HOW I MANAGED TO CONVINCE HER TO STAY, I'LL NEVER UNDERSTAND . . .

THEN HE HAD BEEN HOLDING HER IN HIS ARMS AND THE WORLD COULD NOT HAVE BEEN A BETTER PLACE — UNTIL SHE HAD TWISTED HIM AROUND.

HE STILL WASN'T SURE HOW SHE HAD MANAGED THAT EITHER. HE ONLY REMEMBERED THE BLUR OF MOVEMENT.

HE HADN'T SEEN THE MAN BEHIND HER. ALL HE HAD NOTICED WAS HOW HER BODY JERKED IN HIS ARMS — AND THEN A SECOND LATER SHE HAD WHIRLED AROUND.

THE GUARDS HAD ALL ASSUMED HE'D TAKEN CARE

OF THE MAN.

HE HADN'T BOTHERED TO CORRECT ANYONE YET.

HE WANTED THE OPPORTUNITY TO SPEAK WITH KAYDEN FIRST.

I CAN ONLY HOPE SHE HAS AN EXPLANATION THAT MAKES SOME SORT OF SENSE . . .

BUT MOSTLY HE JUST HOPED SHE WOULD OPEN HER EYES SOON AND LOOK AT HIM, GIVE HIM A HARD TIME ABOUT SOMETHING, YELL AT HIM, GIVE HIM THAT SMILE OF HERS THAT TOOK HIS BREATH AWAY.

"YOUR MAJESTY," THERE WAS A DISCREET SOUND OF SOMEONE CLEARING OF THEIR THROAT FROM BEHIND HIM.

DVARIUS HEARD, BUT HE DIDN'T TURN AWAY FROM KAYDEN.

HE REPLIED TERSELY, HOPING IT WOULD GIVE THE SPEAKER SOME CLUE AS TO HOW UNWELCOME THEIR PRESENCE WAS RIGHT THIS MOMENT.

"YES?"

A MOMENT LATER, HE HEARD FOOTSTEPS BUT THEY WERE NOT MOVING TOWARD THE DOOR.

"I JUST WANTED TO COME AND INTRODUCE MYSELF, YOUR MAJESTY, AND CHECK ON KAYDEN, OF COURSE."

THE MAN STOPPED MOVING WHEN HE HAD REACHED THE FOOT OF THE HOSPITAL BED.

DVARIUS STILL DID NOT LOOK AWAY FROM KAYDEN.

"I AM SIR MALCOM, YOUR MAJESTY — AND I AM, FOR ALL INTENTS AND PURPOSES, KAYDEN'S

UNCLE."

"YOU'RE WELCOME TO JOIN ME BUT I'M NOT LEAVING HER SIDE."

DVARIUS WAS SURPRISED WHEN HE RECEIVED NO ARGUMENT — JUST THE SCRAPE OF CHAIR LEGS AND THEN SOUNDS OF STIFF CLOTH MOVING INTO A NEW POSITION AS ALFREID SETTLED IN TO WAIT WITH HIM.

DON'T MISS THE
BONUS SHORT
AVAILABLE IN E-BOOK ONLY

"*A PERILOUS ASSIGNMENT* IS A TENSION-FILLED GLIMPSE INTO THE EXCITING STORY WORLD OF THE ORDER OF THE MOONSTONE SERIES."

- MARISSA SHROCK — AUTHOR OF THE YA NOVEL, "THE FIRST PRINCIPLE"

ACKNOWLEDEMENTS

GIVEN WHERE THIS JOURNEY HAS TAKEN ME. . . CONSIDERING EVERYTHING THAT HAS HAPPENED IN MY LIFE OVER THE LAST YEAR, AND ESPECIALLY THE LAST MONTH, I FELT LIKE THIS SECTION NEEDED A BIT OF AN OVERHAUL.

I WROTE IT MONTHS AGO, JUST AFTER I HAD BEGUN THIS PROJECT; SHAPING AND RESHAPING THE WORDS I WROTE NEARLY THREE YEARS AGO FOR ANOTHER PROJECT.

BUT THIS ONE DESERVES A FRESH START.

I'M GOING TO DO THIS RIGHT. . . AND TO DO THIS RIGHT, I HAVE TO START WHERE IT ALL BEGAN.

MOM, THANK YOU FOR LISTENING TO THAT ANNOYING LITTLE GIRL WHO HAD THE MOST OVERACTIVE IMAGINATION POSSIBLE. I CAN'T REMEMBER HER, BUT I SEE THE LOVE BURNING IN YOUR EYES EVERY TIME YOU TALK ABOUT HER. AND THANK YOU FOR PUTTING UP WITH THE WOMAN WHO IS SUCH A DISASTER, SUCH A MESS, AND SUCH A NEEDY, PITIFUL WRECK SO MUCH OF THE TIME.

SAM, MY PRECIOUS GIFT, MY BEAUTIFUL MIRACLE — THANK YOU FOR ALWAYS ENCOURAGING ME. THANK YOU FOR ALL THE HARD HUGS, FOR ALL THE TIMES YOU REST YOUR CHIN ON MY SHOULDER AND WATCH ME AS I WORK. FAR TOO SOON, I WON'T HAVE TO BE SITTING FOR YOUR CHIN TO BE ON MY SHOULDER. . .

Gwendolyn, my sweet little princess, you have to know that so much of Kayden is you; my delicate little fluttery girl who wouldn't hesitate to knock some idiot who bothers you right in the teeth. I love that about you.

Rachel M, Nadine B, Amy C, Katie G, and Marissa S — My strength, my inspiration, my advisors. . . you are such a blessing to me!

And to the women who did not believe I could do this — you were right.

I didn't do this. God did this. I am His conduit. . . nothing more. I was the vessel He used to carry this story to the world and it is His will that will carry it out into the hands of the readers who need it, the readers who will find truth in it, the readers who need a seed planted within.

It's not me. . . it's HIM!

This is His story and I am only a willing participant, a truly blessed individual. I got to be there when this series was born. I was allowed to witness a miracle and it has forever changed me.

I pray that it changes you too.

GOD BLESS YOU!

ABOUT THE AUTHOR

JC MORROWS — WRITER OF CHRISTIAN YA SPECULATIVE FICTION. . . DRINKER OF COFFEE AND AVID READER — IS A STORYTELLER IN THE TRUEST SENSE OF THE WORD.

SHE FINISHED HER FIRST SPECULATIVE FICTION NOVEL PURELY FOR THE ENJOYMENT OF HER MOTHER — ALSO KNOWN AS HER BIGGEST FAN, BUT OF COURSE SHE COULDN'T STOP WITH JUST ONE.

JC HAS BEEN TELLING STORIES IN ONE FORM OR ANOTHER HER ENTIRE LIFE AND ONCE HER MOTHER CONVINCED HER TO WRITE THEM DOWN. . . WELL, SHE COULDN'T STOP.

BUT SHE GIVES GOD ALL OF THE GLORY FOR HER TALENT AND ABILITY!

"AND THE LORD ANSWERED ME, AND SAID, WRITE THE VISION, AND MAKE IT PLAIN UPON TABLES, THAT HE MAY RUN THAT READETH IT." HABAKKUK 2:2 KJV

Do Your Part . . .

If you have a personal blog, please consider featuring JC.

If you enjoyed reading *A Reluctant Assassin*, please consider rating this book and leaving a review on Amazon or GoodReads.

It only takes a sentence or two . . .

Of course, if you love it and you're inclined to write more, feel free — and THANK YOU!

ABOUT THE PUBLISHER

CHRISTIAN PUBLISHING FOR HIS GLORY

S&G PUBLISHING OFFERS BOOKS WITH MESSAGES THAT HONOR JESUS CHRIST TO THE WORLD! S&G WORKS WITH CHRISTIAN AUTHORS TO BRING YOU THE BEST IN "INSPIRATIONAL" FICTION AND NON-FICTION.

S&G IS PROUD TO PUBLISH A VARIETY OF CHRISTIAN FICTION GENRES:
INSPIRATIONAL ROMANCE
YOUNG READER
YOUNG ADULT
SPECULATIVE
HISTORICAL
SUSPENSE

CHECK OUT OUR WEBSITE AT

SGPUBLISH.COM

NON-FICTION FROM S&G PUBLISHING

JUNIOR AUTHOR SERIES

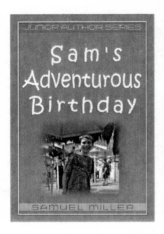

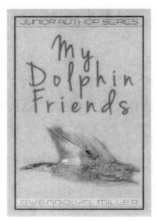

AUTHOR ENCOURAGEMENT SERIES

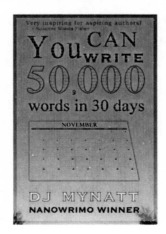

COMING SOON!

S&G'S COURTSHIP SERIES

TWO VERSIONS WILL BE AVAILABLE

BLUE FOR HIM...

PINK FOR HER...

CPSIA information can be obtained at www.ICGtesting.com
Printed in the USA
LVOW08s1830090516

487381LV00006B/700/P